lonely planet

Lonely Planet Publications
Melbourne | Oakland | London

D1487151

Sally O'Brien

Copenhagen

The Top Five

1 Strøget
Walk (about) a mile and raise a smile (p58)

2 The Little Mermaid
You can't keep a good woman down (p65)

3 Amalienborg Slot
The best royal balcony scenes in recent memory (p65)

4 Nyhavn
The gaily-painted canalside strip with many bars and eateries (p64)

5 Tivoli
Pretty lights, big smiles and innocent fun at every turn (p55)

Contents

Published by Lonely Planet Publications Pty Ltd
ABN 36 005 607 983

Australia Head Office, Locked Bag 1, Footscray,
Victoria 3011, ☎ 03 8379 8000, fax 03 8379 8111,
talk2us@lonelyplanet.com.au

USA 150 Linden St, Oakland, CA 94607,
☎ 510 893 8555, toll free 800 275 8555,
fax 510 893 8572, info@lonelyplanet.com

UK 72–82 Rosebery Ave, Clerkenwell, London,
EC1R 4RW, ☎ 020 7841 9000, fax 020 7841 9001,
go@lonelyplanet.co.uk

Printed through Colorcraft Ltd, Hong Kong.
Printed in China

The Author

SALLY O'BRIEN

Sally grew up surrounded by Danish furniture, jewellery and Danish pastries, making her a logical choice to spend time in Copenhagen on the trail of more bits and pieces to add to her various collections (the pastries keep getting eaten…). Prone to seasonal affective disorder, obsessed with stylish chairs, guilty about the way her home town of Sydney treated Jørn Utzon, a connoisseur of cod and herring, and ruddy enough to pass for a Dane before she opens her mouth and starts mangling the language, Sally absolutely loved her time in Copenhagen, attempting to really get into the spirit of all things Danish, except for the bicycles.

PHOTOGRAPHER

Martin Lladó, a freelance photographer and writer, lives in Copenhagen with his wife, Minna, and their son, Simon.

Martin, who has worked with Lonely Planet since 1998, often explores his hometown accompanied by his cameras – sometimes just for the fun of it. Thanks to a perfect Indian summer in Copenhagen, this photo shoot went like a breeze and was entirely enjoyable – except for the obligatory sore feet from all the walking.

Martin has spent a good deal of his 37 years visiting 35 different countries. His favourite areas are Southeast Asia and Europe.

Introducing Copenhagen

It's heart-warming to know that there's still a city where the term fairy tale can be used freely – from its most enduring literary legacy to its startlingly textbook castles and most recent royal romance. In a nutshell, Copenhagen (København) gets it right – old-fashioned charm embraces the most avowedly forward-looking design and social developments, and wins it a permanent spot on those 'world's most livable cities' lists. Scandinavia's coolest and most cosmopolitan capital will have you planning to make it your home as well – after all, this is style central, so you're guaranteed a nice place to live.

Copenhagen is an appealing and still largely low-rise city comprised of block after block of period six-storey buildings. Church steeples add a nice punctuation to the skyline, oxidised copper on roofs and spires catches the eye in the beautiful northern light and the neomodernist architecture of the city's new buildings only adds to the visual feast. Add the fact that all those great galleries, castles and canals are often within walking distance of each other (or a quick trip on efficient public transport), and you've got it easy.

Copenhageners of all persuasions tend to be fun-loving and you can get a sense of

Lowdown

- **Population** 1.7 million
- **Time zone** GMT +1hr
- **Price of a 3-star room** 1200kr
- **Price of a caffè latte** 24kr
- **Price of a 2-zone klippekort ticket** 105kr
- **Price of a hot dog** 24kr
- **Number of Australian-born queens-to-be** 1
- **Number of jaywalkers** 0
- **Number of Michelin-starred restaurants** 10
- **Number of smørrebrød toppings at Ida Davidsen** 250

Essential Copenhagen

- Statens Museum for Kunst (p84)
- Tivoli (p55)
- Hiring a boat in Christianshavn (p136)
- Det Kongelige Teater (p125)
- Smørrebrød at Ida Davidsen (p113)

this throughout the city. You'll find the pedestrianised street Strøget teeming with the music of street performers, the nearby Latin Quarter peppered with spirited clubs and the venerable Tivoli park offering family-oriented amusements – all within minutes of each other. You can hop on a canal boat and tour the waterfront, admire the world's finest collection of Viking relics, be dazzled by extraordinary collections of modern and impressionist art, lunch on *smørrebrød* (open-faced sandwiches) and Danish beer at outdoor cafés and dance till the sun rises at any number of stylish clubs.

Copenhagen is a city so safe and orderly that your greatest fear will be getting collected by a speeding bicycle because you've mistakenly wandered into the bike lane (which is wider than some of your hometown's highways). And if the words 'safe' and 'orderly' inspire panic, then relax, Copenhagen is not lacking in soul – after all, this bastion of Nordic order and discipline plays host to the Copenhagen Jazz Festival and is the birthplace of that most controversial cinematic movement, Dogme 95. Danes may seem like law-abiding, 'rules were meant to be kept' types (and nowhere will this be more evident than at traffic lights, when it seems that jaywalking is a crime beyond comprehension), but that's just a desire to make things work better – rule-making is in the blood (after all, even Dogme 95 required a manifesto, and although the movement doesn't really 'exist' any more, you can still submit your film to an expert here to determine whether your poorly lit, naturalistic, painful-to-watch efforts are 'Dogme' or not). And when it dawns on you that these rules are about making things better for *everyone,* then you'll appreciate this charming city even more.

Copenhagen's ability to bring so many wonderful things together makes its location seem perfectly logical – Denmark's capital serves as the bridge between mainland Europe and Scandinavia, and its dominance of the Øresund region reflects its historical and contemporary importance. Where other capital cities are noticeable for the ever-increasing gap between the 'haves' and the 'have nots', Copenhagen seems populated by the 'have enoughs', and the obviously rich and obviously poor are few and far between. This egalitarian spirit allows the best of the arts, architecture, eating and entertainment to be within easy reach of all, and the famed love of *hygge* – the pursuit of a sense of cosy wellbeing when the cares of the world have been set aside – is within reach of residents and visitors alike, whether solo or surrounded by friends and family.

If any gesture symbolises the city, it's the tradition of raising your glass, saying *skål* while meeting the eyes of your companion and downing something strong in one fluid, easy movement. It demonstrates a readiness to enjoy oneself, without guile – and if you can't do that in Copenhagen, you can't do it anywhere.

SALLY'S TOP COPENHAGEN DAY

With any luck, I look out the window and see the sun. If I've woken up in Nørrebro I head into town via a quick stop for a coffee in one of Sankt Hans Torv's cafés before crossing Dronning Louises Bro on foot and whistling as I watch devil-may-care bike riders whizz past. I meet up with friends to suss out one of the city's great museums – but if I really need an art fix, it's hard to beat Statens Museum for Kunst. After that, *smørrebrød* beckons, accompanied by fjord prawns at Ida Davidsen, which is a cliché, but I can't help but melt in front of the 250-strong selection of open-faced sandwiches. From here I cross my favourite bridge in the city, Knippels Bro and stroll around delightful Christianshavn before revelling in the afternoon sun and taking a dip at Islands Brygge Havnebadet. The sun's not going to set for ages, so I enjoy a glass of wine at an outdoor table at Bastionen & Løven and then make my way to Sushitarian for the best sushi in town before enjoying a night with friends at Det Kongelige Teater, where we catch the Danish Royal Ballet and marvel at the skill of principal dancers such as Mads Blangstrup. Afterwards we head to the city's best nightclub, Vega, to see whatever band's performing and sample the cocktail list at Ideal Bar, before heading home in the wee hours.

City Life

City Life

COPENHAGEN TODAY

At first glance it may strike you that everyone in Copenhagen is middle class, for as the Danes like to say: 'few have too much and even fewer have too little'. This is a city where fairness and consideration for others is ingrained in the communal psyche, so recent upheavals on the political scene, which have given a strong voice to certain ideas about immigration and the welfare system, have come as a somewhat disconcerting interruption to the famous welfare state's 'come one, come all' credo. Despite such hiccups in the city's carefully cultivated image, the dominant ethos is that things should not only work, they should be stylish too. Civic and communal spaces are frequently more attractive than their foreign counterparts, and when you get into the private sector you'll notice that the Nordic obsession with flattering lighting, beautiful furnishings and culture have reached some sort of apotheosis.

This need to ensure that everything is just so may seem to be the enemy of spontaneity. The combination with the Scandiavian tendency to stubbornly reject opposing opinion on the topic of 'how things are done' has seen tensions rise when it comes to such topics as the EU, the ageing population, the welfare state and the 'immigration question'. Protest about the level of personal taxation has become more vocal in recent years, especially from the right, as the welfare state is a hungry oven and requires a lot of tax to support it.

Nevertheless, at other times (particularly on a sunny day, when the gloom lifts and the people are transformed) it seems as though paradise has been regained. The wedding of Crown Prince Frederik to Mary Donaldson was an enormous boost to the city's morale. The golden couple have dazzled almost everyone and it seems as though the city has joined the happy pair on an extended honeymoon of sorts.

Get used to feeling cosy – because this city does it like no other.

Hot Conversation Topics

- **Mary and Frederik** Copenhagen's first couple and a national obsession for the women's mags
- **Is Mary too thin?** (See above)
- **Is Mary pregnant?** (See above)
- **Immigration** Scratch the surface and every local has a strong opinion on the matter
- **Christiania** Have the hippies had their day?

CITY CALENDAR

Scandinavia's coolest city has plenty to keep visitors and locals occupied year-round. Locals like to take advantage of the warmer months, when it seems that every other week or venue plays host to a festival of some sort, but they're even known to have a knees-up in the depths of winter – perhaps to stave off the worst of the winter glums. Following is a list of some of the larger Copenhagen-area annual events; see also Holidays (p201) in the Directory. Since the dates and venues can change a little from year to year, check with the tourist office for current schedule information. Summer holidays for schoolchildren begin around 20 June and end around 10 August. Schools also take a break for a week in mid-October and during the Christmas and New Year period. Many Danes take their main work holiday during the first three weeks of July.

Top Five Unusual Events

- **Copenhagen Distortion** (p10) Five days devoted to nightclubbing
- **Buster** (p11) The big film festival for small fry
- **Copenhagen Carnival** (p10) When the city goes Brazilian
- **Copenhagen Irish Festival** (p11) When Guinness takes over from Carlsberg as the tipple of choice
- **Copenhagen Jazz Festival** (p10) When the whole city becomes a stage, and everyone feels the need to tap their toes

Considering its northern latitude, Copenhagen has a relatively mild climate, although the winter months – cold and with short daylight hours – are certainly the least hospitable. Many tourist attractions have shorter opening hours in the winter, and a few are outright mothballed and don't come alive until April, when the weather begins to warm up and daylight hours start to increase.

July and August are the peak months and the time for open-air concerts and music festivals, lots of street activity and longer hours at sightseeing attractions. Of course you won't be the only tourist during summer, as many Europeans celebrate midsummer with gusto. The last half of August can be a particularly attractive time to visit.

Wide bike lanes in central Copenhagen

JANUARY
NEW YEAR CONCERTS
Popular concerts take place at various venues in the greater Copenhagen area to ring in the new year.

FEBRUARY & MARCH
NATFILM FESTIVAL
www.natfilm.dk
A Night Film Festival held at various Copenhagen cinemas. Features more than 100 films by Danish and international directors, shown in original languages, over a 10-day period from late March.

COPENHAGEN FASHION & DESIGN FESTIVAL
At the end of March or early April, it focuses on Danish design and the latest in fashion. There are special displays in many shops and exhibits at Nikolaj Kirke (Map pp239–41) near Strøget.

BAKKEN
This 400-year-old amusement park located in Klampenborg opens for the season at the end of March. The celebrations are kicked off by a parade of some 5000 very noisy motorcyclists.

APRIL
QUEEN MARGRETHE II'S BIRTHDAY
The queen's birthday is celebrated on 16 April at Amalienborg Slot with the royal guards in full ceremonial dress and the queen waving from the palace balcony at noon. Buses don the Danish flag as a tribute.

TIVOLI
www.tivoligardens.com
Copenhagen's venerable amusement park, situated in the heart of Copenhagen, opens for the season in April after its long winter slumber.

MAY
LABOUR DAY
Celebrated on 1 May, this is not officially a public holiday. Try telling that to thousands of people who take the day off, dust off the Che flag and end up in Fælledparken, where there's often a big celebration (read: big booze-up).

COPENHAGEN MARATHON
www.copenhagenmarathon.dk
This 42km race through the streets of Copenhagen is held on a Sunday in mid-May and is open to both amateur and professional runners.

JUNGE HUNDE
www.jungehunde.dk
An excellent festival devoted to international stage art (mostly dance) that takes place for a few weeks from mid-May in Kanonhallen. Tickets cost around adult/child 60/30kr for an evening performance.

COPENHAGEN CARNIVAL
www.karneval.dk

This three-day event in the heart of the capital takes place on Whitsunday weekend (usually late May or early June) and sees the Danes try to go Brazilian. Highlights include a parade and dancing in the streets. There are special events for children too.

JUNE

BOURNONVILLE FESTIVAL
www.bournonvillefestival.dk

Denmark's ballet master is saluted with his very own festival, which features performances of many of his works by, who else, the Royal Danish Ballet. The festival generally takes place (it's still quite new) in early June.

COPENHAGEN DISTORTION
www.cphdistortion.dk

A five-day clubbing marathon that celebrates all things nocturnal and noisy. Takes place from the Wednesday before the first Sunday in June, and events occur in a range of bars and clubs throughout the city centre.

FOOLS 25
www.kanonhallen.dk

This theatre festival is held in Kanonhallen and features local and international theatre practitioners, plus master classes. It takes place all summer long, from the end of May until the end of August.

MIDSUMMER'S EVE

Held on 23 June and also called Sankt Hans Aften, this is a time for evening bonfires at beaches all around Denmark. Copenhagen's Fælledparken is the site of a big bonfire, and there are special activities at Tivoli and Bakken.

DANISH DERBY

Denmark's most important horse race is held in late June at Klampenborg.

ROSKILDE FESTIVAL
www.roskilde-festival.dk

Northern Europe's largest rock music festival is held in the town of Roskilde on the last weekend in June. Some 150 bands, including big-name international performers, attract 80,000 concertgoers. See p126 for more details.

JULY

COPENHAGEN JAZZ FESTIVAL
www.jazzfestival.dk

Held over 10 days in early July, this is one of the world's major jazz festivals, with indoor and outdoor concerts all around the city, featuring local and big-name artists. See p20 for more details.

KLOKKESPILSKONCERTER I VOR FRELSERS KIRKE

Features free carillon recitals each Saturday during July at the atmospheric Vor Frelsers Kirke in Christianshavn.

COPENHAGEN GUITAR FESTIVAL
www.copenhagenguitarfestival.dk

Held over two weeks from late July at the Rundetårn in the Latin Quarter.

AUGUST

CULTURAL HARBOUR
www.kulturhavn.dk

During the first week of August, a range of free cultural events are held on and around Copenhagen's harbour, with most events taking place around the Islands Brygge neighbourhood.

SOMMERKONCERTER I VOR FRUE KIRKE

Features free classical music performances throughout the month at Vor Frue Kirke, the city's theatre-like cathedral.

MERMAID PRIDE PARADE
www.mermaidpride.dk

Held the first or second Saturday in August, this festive gay-pride parade marches with Carnival-like extravagance through the city to Slotsholmen. Expect a cast of thousands and lots of fun.

COPENHAGEN INTERNATIONAL BALLET FESTIVAL
www.copenhageninternationalballet.com

Held from the first to the third week in August. Features top solo dancers from the Royal Danish Ballet and visiting performers from international companies, with an emphasis on modern choreography.

COPENHAGEN SUMMERDANCE
www.copenhagensummerdance.dk
Local and international dance companies get together for five days from mid-August to stage open-air performances in the city centre.

DANISH TROTTING DERBY
Denmark's major trotting event is held in late August at the Charlottenlund Travbane.

SEPTEMBER
GOLDEN DAYS IN COPENHAGEN
www.goldendays.dk
Held over three weeks from early September, this festival features art exhibits, poetry readings, theatre, ballet and concerts that focus on Denmark's 'Golden Age' (1800–50) – a hugely influential period in the city's cultural life. A great combination of art and history.

BUSTER
www.busterfilm.dk
Buster – the Copenhagen International Children's Film Festival – is devoted to kids and has been running for more than five years. It takes place over one week in mid-September.

COPENHAGEN FILM FESTIVAL
www.copenhagenfilmfestival.com
Highlighting Danish and international film, the festival is held during the second half of September. A must for film buffs – with a solid international reputation and strong entries in the official competition section.

OCTOBER
CULTURAL NIGHT IN COPENHAGEN
www.kulturnatten.dk
Held on the first night of the autumn school holidays (typically the second Friday in October) when museums, theatres, galleries and Rosenborg Slot throw open their doors. Free buses transport visitors between the various sites.

COPENHAGEN GAY & LESBIAN FILM FESTIVAL
www.cglff.dk
Spread over a week from mid-October, this festival screens contemporary gay and lesbian

films from around the world and is Copenhagen's longest-running film festival.

NOVEMBER
CPH:DOX
www.cphdox.dk
A new festival, geared towards documentary making and screening. Excellent productions from around the world are screened from early to mid-November.

COPENHAGEN IRISH FESTIVAL
www.irishfestival.dk
Three days of traditional Irish folk music at various venues in the city; held in early November.

COPENHAGEN AUTUMN JAZZ
www.jazzfestival.dk
Produced by the Copenhagen Jazz Festival folks, it features top jazz musicians performing at clubs around the city for four days in early November.

GREAT CHRISTMAS PARADE
Held on the last Saturday in November. Father Christmas (*julemand*) parades through the city followed by jazz musicians, costumed fairytale characters and scores of children, lighting Christmas trees in public squares and ending in Rådhuspladsen to light the city's largest tree.

DECEMBER
TIVOLI
www.tivoligardens.com
Tivoli reopens its gates from mid-November until a few days before Christmas with a holiday market and fair. There's ice skating on the pond and some Tivoli restaurants offer menus with hot mulled wine and traditional holiday meals.

CHRISTMAS FAIRS
Held throughout December and featuring food booths, arts and crafts stalls, and sometimes parades. The most important time of the year as far as locals are concerned, so an excellent opportunity to see them at their happiest. Check the tourist office for the latest venues.

CULTURE

IDENTITY

Copenhagen is a mid-sized city with a population of over 1.7 million people, of whom about 500,000 live in the central districts that form the core of Copenhagen municipality. Slightly more than 25% of the country's population live within the greater Copenhagen area. Many of them, at first site, appear to come from the same gene pool, so close are they to the stereotype of the tall, ruddy-cheeked, flaxen-haired Viking.

The vast majority of Copenhageners are people of Teutonic ancestry common to Scandinavia. The total immigrant population in Denmark represents about 5% of the total population – and of this 5% of immigrants, more than half reside in the Copenhagen area, with the majority from Scandinavian and other European countries.

A relaxation of immigration policies during the economic expansion of the 1960s attracted 'guest workers', many of whom established a permanent niche, and there are now sizable Turkish and Pakistani communities in the city. More recent humanitarian policies, introduced in response to famine and war crises, have resulted in small Somali and Ethiopian immigrant communities and a sizable number of refugees from the former Yugoslavia.

The city's population is ageing – with increased life expectancies straining the welfare system. One interesting fact is that there are twice as many women over 80 years of age than there are men aged over 80.

Fewer than 5% of Danes are regular churchgoers. The majority of Copenhagen's churchgoing inhabitants belong to the Folkekirken (the Danish People's Church), the state-supported national church, an Evangelical Lutheran denomination. A visible Islamic community exists in the city – especially in the Nørrebro and Vesterbro areas.

Strolling inside Assistens Kirkegård (p80)

The city's population is well educated. Education is free and nine years of schooling, starting at the age of seven, is compulsory. Preschool and kindergarten are optional; about two-thirds of children aged five and six attend.

About half of all Danish students who graduate from secondary school continue on to higher education. Slightly more than half of these graduates enrol in vocational programs providing training in business, nursing, maritime studies and other career-specific fields. Most of the remainder attend one of Denmark's five state-supported universities. The most elite of these institutions is Copenhagen University, which was founded in 1479, and has campuses in the Latin Quarter of central Copenhagen and in Amager on the southern side of the city.

Naming Names

Of the five-million-plus Danes on the planet today, two-thirds have a surname ending in 'sen'. The three most common – Jensen, Nielsen and Hansen – account for 23% of all Danish surnames. Next, in order of frequency, are Pedersen, Andersen, Christensen, Larsen and Sørensen.

You may notice a trend here. The most common Danish surnames are derived from the most common given names with 'sen' added as a suffix. This is because up until the mid-19th century most folks did not have a permanent family name but simply added 'sen', meaning 'son', onto their father's first name. Thus, if your father was Peder Hansen and your name was Eric, you were known as Eric Pedersen.

LIFESTYLE

Visitors will find Copenhageners to be relaxed, casual and not given to extremes. The Danes like to think of themselves as a classless society and there are seldom any hints of chauvinism, sexism or any other 'ism'. Copenhageners are known for their love of irony and rather biting sense of humour – they prefer a clever retort to a slapstick spectacle any day, and are an easy-going bunch for the most part. To get a Dane really worked up, you'll have to bring up a fiery topic such as income tax, the Danes' relationship with the Swedes, and liquor licensing laws. Even though the language has two forms of address, most people will use the informal form, unless they are in the company of someone older or much more important.

This tendency to regard everyone as equal stems not only from an innate sense of fair play, but also from a strongly held fear of being regarded as arrogant or too big for one's boots. The author Aksel Sandemos (1899–1965) created a fictitious philosophy known as *Janteloven* to describe this phenomenon of the deeply ingrained sense of modesty that stops any local from bragging.

Social changes since the 1960s have had a dramatic effect on Copenhagen families. There are better career opportunities for women, easier access to abortions and a growth in childcare institutions.

About 20% of all couples living together these days aren't married and the average age for those who do opt to tie the knot has risen to 35 years. Family size has dropped dramatically, with Danish women bearing an average of 1.8 children. One in three marriages ends in divorce and many families are single-child/sole-parent constructs.

Danes in their 30s and 40s today were the first generation to be raised with a great deal of time spent outside the family. Perhaps as a result of being around many different people at an early age, they are notably tolerant and have a high degree of social responsibility. Danes also tend to be involved in club activities and organisations at a rate that surpasses most other societies.

More than 80% of all Danish women are in the workplace, nearly twice as many as in 1970. The law prevents job discrimination between the sexes but opportunities at the highest echelons have opened slowly. Many members of parliament are women, but a female prime minister has yet to be elected.

Copenhageners are very open-minded on lifestyle issues. In 1989 Denmark became the first European country to legalise same-sex marriages and to offer gay partners most of the same rights as heterosexual couples. In 1999 a further step in recognising a broader definition of the family was taken when the decade-old Registered Partnership Act was amended to allow married gays to legally adopt the children of their partners.

Copenhageners pride themselves on being utterly modern, and the wearing of folk costumes, the celebration of traditional festivals and the tendency to cling to old-fashioned customs are all much less prevalent here than in most other European countries. There are, of course, traditional aspects of the Danish lifestyle that aren't apparent at first glance.

Nothing Like a Dane

If you're looking to be taken for a local, here are five quick tips on behaviour best avoided...

- Never complain about the dangers of passive smoking in public places
- Never wander into the bicycle lane for a stroll
- Never avoid eye contact when toasting
- Never indulge in jaywalking, no matter how quiet the street
- Never big-note yourself, no matter how great your achievements

Queue Tips

Nothing out of the ordinary is expected of visitors to Copenhagen, but there are a couple of potential pitfalls to avoid. Copenhageners generally queue by a number system; when you go to the post office, a bakery, the tourist office – just about any place there can be a queue – there's invariably a machine dispensing numbered tickets. Grab one as you enter and always wait until your number is called. If you're picking up after-5pm discount tickets for the Royal Theatre, you'll get to experience the thrill of joining a queue to join a queue if you arrive at the box office before 5pm.

That said, getting on a bus, metro or S-train is an exercise in frustration – locals don't seem to have any interest in queuing for public transport or in allowing passengers to disembark before clambering aboard. Go figure...

Perhaps nothing captures the Danish perspective more than the concept of *hygge* which, roughly translated, means cosy and snug. It implies shutting out the turmoil and troubles of the outside world and striving instead for a warm, intimate mood. *Hygge* affects how Danes approach many aspects of their personal lives, from the design of their homes to their fondness for small cafés and pubs. There's no greater compliment that you can give your host than to thank them for a cosy evening.

The Danish obsession with good design is well known throughout the world, and one of the most noticeable truisms that will grab your attention when you visit the city is just how stylish everything is – homes (generally apartments) are clean, airy and filled with well-made furniture and always comfortable – again it's all part of the quest for *hygge*.

Then again, if you stumble into performance artist Peter Land's Copenhagen apartment, you're likely to find a portly naked guy dancing wildly to modern pop music after a week-long drinking binge, and filming the experience… all, of course, in the name of art.

FOOD

It's been said that the Danes live to eat, the Norwegians eat to live and the Swedes eat to drink, and one thing that will make an impression on you while you visit Copenhagen is that almost every corner that has not been occupied by a bank has been occupied by a restaurant, a café or a food store.

Nothing epitomises Danish food more than *smørrebrød*, an open-faced sandwich that ranges from very basic fare to elaborate sculpture-like creations. Typically it's a slice of rye bread topped with either roast beef, tiny shrimps, roast pork or fish fillet and finished off with a variety of garnishes. Although *smørrebrød* is served in most restaurants at lunch time, it's cheapest at bakeries or at specialised *smørrebrød* takeaway shops found near train stations and office buildings.

Also distinctively Danish is the *koldt bord* (literally 'cold table'), a buffet-style spread of cold foods, including salads, cold cuts, smoked fish, cheeses, vegetables, condiments, breads and crackers, and usually a few hot dishes such as meatballs and fried fish. The cornerstone of the cold table is herring *(sild)*, which comes in pickled, marinated and salted versions.

Generally the most prominent top-end restaurants feature what's dubbed 'Danish–French' cuisine, a creative fusion combining the flavourful sauces that characterise French fare with the addition of fresh Danish vegetables and seafood that aren't typical in traditional French recipes.

Danish cuisine relies heavily on fish, meat and potatoes, and between large portions of such fare the Danes love to snack on cakes, pastries, biscuits and from the ubiquitous *pølsemandens,* the wheeled carts that sell a variety of hot dogs and sausages.

In terms of beer, the locally brewed Carlsberg and Tuborg labels are the undisputed home-town favourites in Copenhagen. Beer *(øl)* can be ordered as draught beer *(fadøl),* lager *(pilsner),* light beer *(lyst øl),* dark lager *(lagerøl)* or stout *(porter).*

The most popular spirit in Denmark is the Aalborg-produced aquavit *(akvavit).* There are several dozen types, the most common of which is spiced with caraway seeds. In Denmark, aquavit is not sipped but is swallowed straight down as a shot and most commonly followed by a chaser of beer. A popular Danish liqueur, made of cherries, is Peter Heering, which generally sipped straight or served over vanilla ice cream.

Common wine terms are *hvidvin* (white wine), *rødvin* (red wine), *mousserende vin* (sparkling wine) and *husets vin* (house wine). *Gløgg* is a mulled wine that's a favourite speciality during the Christmas season.

A Treat by Any Name

Bakeries abound in Copenhagen, all selling those sinfully rich breakfast pastries – flaky, butter-laden pastry with a dollop of icing or jam – that are so synonymous with Denmark they're known around the world simply as 'Danish'.

As legend has it, the naming of the pastry can be traced to a Danish baker who moved to Austria in the 18th century, where he perfected a pastry in a style that has since been known to the Danes as *wienerbrød* (literally 'Vienna bread') and to the rest of the world as Danish pastry.

Top Five Cookbooks

- *Madjournal* (Paul Cunningham) Paul's restaurant, modestly named the Paul, is Michelin-starred and situated in Tivoli. His food journal will placate your tummy if you've been unsuccessful in procuring a table at his digs.
- *Hverdagsmad* (Nikolaj Kirk) Kirk used to work at Copenhagen's famous formel b (p120) restaurant, but with this cookbook he turns his hand to interesting twists on daily dining – and shows you how to do it too.
- *Dejligt* (Camilla Plum) Plum is as close to a Danish Martha Stewart as you can get, and this book concentrates on sweet treats.
- *Lyst* (Claus Meyer) Another local chef with an eye for fresh ingredients and inventive variations of Danish staples.
- *Frøken Jensens Kogebog* (Kristine Marie Jensen) A classic of Danish cooking, first published in 1901.

Beer, wine and spirits are served in most restaurants and cafés. They can be purchased at grocery stores during normal shopping hours and prices are quite reasonable.

FASHION

Citizens of Copenhagen are stylish for the most part, and while slavishly following fashion is deemed uncool, being aware of what's going on style-wise is important. The city's inclusive nature means that all budgets can generally be catered to, and retro-chic (ie vintage shopping) is enormously popular among the city's students and arty crowd. Locals are stern judges of shoddy workmanship, and tend to appreciate quality over quantity in all things, including clothing, hence the number of well-patronised expensive clothing stores throughout town.

Local fashion labels that have attracted a loyal following and that you'll want to save some room in the wardrobe for include Munthe plus Simonsen, Helle Mardahl, Punk Royal, Birger & Mikkelsen, Mads Nørgaard and Bruuns Bazaar.

Danes are not especially formal in their dress sense – smart casual attire is perfectly suitable for any number of occasions, except the most formal events.

SPORT

Football (soccer) is the dominant sport in Copenhagen, with many residents of the city following local teams and their beloved national team with enthusiasm. Danish footballers who have found success overseas include Michael and Brian Laudrup and tough-as-nails midfielder Claus Jensen.

Other popular sports include ice hockey, tennis, swimming and golf. Most locals consider themselves quite sporty, and a rather puritanical attitude to physical fitness (healthy mind in a healthy body and all that) prevails. Still, anyone who spends more than a minute here will realise that the locals' love of smoking, drinking and eating vast quantities of meat undoes some of the good work that's done on the field or in the gym. Many people belong to sporting clubs and associations (the Nordic desire to 'organise' is a strong one), thus transforming physical activity and 'body culture' into a social exercise. See p135 for details on watching sport or participating.

Denmark excels on the world stage in sports such as yachting, cycling and badminton, but the country's biggest champs in the last few years have been the members of the All-Denmark female handball team, who have collected gold medals at the 1996, 2000 and 2004 Olympic Games and also at the 1997 World Championships.

MEDIA

Denmark's media is fairly even-handed in terms of political analysis and/or bias, but most of the city's newspapers started out as mouthpieces for various political parties. Reporting of international news and foreign affairs is good, and detailed coverage of domestic politics is the norm for the broadsheets. The tabloid papers and magazines tend to focus on royal gossip and murkier stories, with a distinct right-wing leaning to issues such as immigration. Local papers to look out for include *Berlingske Tidende* (not unlike the *Guardian*), *Børsen* (financial news), *Information* (meaty current affairs investigation), *Jyllandsposten* (wide foreign coverage) and *Politiken* (a good source of local news and current affairs). International newspapers are freely available throughout the city.

TV is subtitled and cable is widely subscribed to, meaning that you should be able to watch news and other regular programs from home with no fuss.

LANGUAGE

The national language is Danish, which belongs to the northern branch of the Germanic language group. The local Copenhagen accent is generally regarded (by other Danes) as fast and flat – a true urban dialect that has no time for the rural drawl.

Most Danes speak at least basic English, and it is easy for English-language speakers to get around without a workable knowledge of Danish. In fact, you may sometimes feel that Danes speak better English than you do. German is also widely spoken.

Mind Your Manners

Note that there is no equivalent to the word 'please' in Danish. Politeness is most often expressed by tone of voice and/or by beginning the sentence with phrases such as 'May I...' *(Må jeg...)* or 'Could I...' *(Kunne jeg...)*.

For more information on Danish, including a guide to pronunciation and a list of useful words and phrases, see p208. The best advice we were ever given about trying to sound Danish when pronouncing local words is to pretend you're talking with a boiling hot potato in your mouth and that you love nothing more than swallowing your vowels and glottal stops.

ECONOMY & COSTS

Copenhagen's citizens enjoy a very high standard of living. Relative to other European countries the Danish economy remains strong, with low inflation, solid growth and high employment, despite the fact that the government impounds almost half of its GNP for social services and payments to the disadvantaged. About one-quarter of the country's GDP goes towards public expenditure.

Almost all government funding is derived from taxes: over 50% comes from taxes on personal income and about one-third comes from value-added tax (VAT) and taxes on petrol, alcohol and other dutiable items. This value-added tax (called MOMS) is a flat 25% on most goods and services.

Copenhagen's position as the country's centre of government and commerce is reflected in its employment market, with almost 30% of Copenhageners working in finance, IT and business services, 11% in public service and 15% in social and health services. Tourism is also an important sector in the local economy.

Copenhagen has one of the most gender-equitable workplaces in Europe, although there is still some wage disparity, with male workers earning about 20% more than their female counterparts.

Many of Denmark's leading industrial exports, which include beer, home electronics, furniture, silverware and porcelain, are produced in the Copenhagen area or elsewhere on the island of Zealand.

How Much?

A litre of petrol 9kr
A litre of bottled water 6kr–16kr
A litre of Carlsberg 20kr
A cup of coffee 18kr–25kr
A souvenir T-shirt 100kr
A short taxi ride 80kr
An hour of parking 7kr–20kr
A film ticket 75kr
A bag of tea-light candles 30kr
A Munthe plus Simonsen dress 1000kr–2000kr

GOVERNMENT & POLITICS

Copenhagen is the seat of both municipal and national government. Within walking distance of each other in the city centre are the rådhus (p54), where local government is administered; Folketinget (parliament, p62), where national legislation is enacted; and Amalienborg Slot (p65), home to the monarchy.

Denmark is a constitutional monarchy with a single-chamber parliamentary system. The parliament, called Folketing, is responsible for enacting legislation. The prime minister leads the government with the assistance of cabinet ministers who head the various government departments. Queen Margrethe II, who has been on the throne since 1972, has a largely ceremonial role but her signature is required on the enactment of new legislation.

The minimum voting age is 18; parliamentary elections are held at least once every four years. There are numerous parties represented in the 179-seat parliament. The two largest parties are Socialdemokratiet (Social Democrats) and Venstre (Liberals – a right-of-centre party), who currently hold power, following the 2001 general election. The country's prime minister is Anders Fogh Rasmussen, and his party's victory saw the marginalisation of the centre parties and the diminution in power of the Social Democrats. Concurrent with this trend was the increased popularity of the Dansk Folkeparti (the Danish People's Party), a right-wing body dedicated to reducing immigration and even repatriating many immigrants, plus anti-EU policies. It's now the third-most powerful party in the country.

Despite the domination of these two parties, any party that wins 2% of the vote gains representation in parliament.

Heated parliamentary debates are uncommon, and consultation and consensus across party lines are the norm, with most legislation passed by large majorities. Denmark belongs to the EU, the UN, NATO and the Nordic Council.

In 1998 the city of Copenhagen adopted a new system of government intended to provide greater accessibility to citizens. Copenhagen's municipal government now consists of a city council and a system of committees. The city council, which has 55 elected members, establishes overall policy but it's the committees that are now charged with enacting the details of these policies.

ENVIRONMENT

CLIMATE

Copenhagen is at a latitude of 55°41′, approximately the same as Moscow, central Scotland and southern Alaska. Considering its northerly location, the climate is relatively mild.

Expect to see rain and grey skies – for about 170 days of the year at least. The rainiest months are September, October and November, and the driest are February, April and June.

If you're a 'glass is half-full' type, then you can look forward to about 1670 hours of sunshine each year. While Danes will not strike you as prone to mood swings, it helps to remember that, like many of their Scandinavian counterparts, they can be described as 'mercurial' – that is, quite emotionally dependent on the weather. On overcast, wet and cold days you might find the general mood a little withdrawn and introspective. On a balmy, sunny day you'll come across a certain communal gaiety and gregariousness.

THE LAND

Copenhagen is on the eastern coast of Zealand (Sjælland), the largest of Denmark's 406 islands and the most heavily populated. A harbour city, Copenhagen borders the Baltic Sea and is separated from Sweden by the 16km-wide sound, Øresund. The close proximity to Sweden is perhaps the most obvious reason for the love–hate (but mostly hate) nature of the Danish–Swedish relationship. After all, the Danes lorded it over the Swedes when they could and filled their coffers with the Øresund tax (see Helsingør, p175), and when the tables were turned the Swedes revelled in their new-found superiority. The flow of traffic between the neighbours is still a topic for discussion – the Danes like to tut-tut about the booze-cruise boats that ply Øresund with drunken Swedes in search of cheap alcohol and the Swedes like to notice that many Copenhagen natives are settling in the Malmö region to avoid Denmark's higher tax rates.

Copenhagen municipality covers 88.3 sq km and consists of 15 small districts radiating in an arc shape about 7km from Copenhagen harbour. The greater Copenhagen urban area, also sometimes referred to as the Copenhagen Region or the Capital Region, covers a much broader swath that includes North Zealand and extends west to Roskilde and south to Køge. It encompasses many small cities and towns and covers an area of 2866 sq km.

GREEN COPENHAGEN

Overall, Copenhageners have a high degree of awareness of environmental issues and have made significant efforts to address environmental concerns on both personal and political levels. Far more people commute to work by public transport than by private vehicle, and thousands of commuters go one step further by hopping on a bicycle rather than a bus.

Relative to other cities of its size, Copenhagen's air quality is good and pollution levels have decreased dramatically in recent years. Since 1993, when Danish businesses were first required to pay a tax based on their pollution emissions, Copenhagen's levels of sulphur dioxide have decreased by 80%, carbon monoxide emissions have been halved and levels of nitrogen dioxide and soot have fallen by about a third.

Recycling is extensive, with more than 80% of all paper produced from used paper and

Rickshaw driver, Rådhuspladsen (p55)

nearly 60% of all of Copenhagen's waste recycled. All industries, including tourism, are expected to contribute to efforts to reduce unnecessary waste and energy expenditures.

In the late 1990s the Danes introduced a system called the 'Green Key' *(Den Grønne Nøgle)* in which hotels can display a special environmental-friendly logo if they enact a series of conservation efforts. These include using biodegradable cleaning products and energy-efficient light bulbs, refitting bathrooms with low-flow shower heads and low-flush toilets, and offering breakfast items grown without chemical pesticides and fertilisers.

In 1971 Denmark created a cabinet-level ministry to deal specifically with environmental matters, becoming the first industrialised country to do so. The EU has placed its European Environment Agency in Copenhagen and the Danes have taken an active role in promoting international efforts to reduce pollution.

If you're flying into the city, grab a window seat and try to spot the enormous windmills that are positioned at the harbour entrance – a good example of Danish common sense and ingenuity.

Copenhagen Jazz Festival

Copenhagen Jazz Festival

JAZZ IN COPENHAGEN

Jazz came to Denmark in the 1920s and developed a loyal following among Copenhageners that continues to this day. In 1923 the first Danish jazz combo was formed by Valdemar Eiberg (a saxophonist). Danish jazz experienced a sort of Golden Age during the hard years of the German occupation during WWII, when jazz was a means to express opposition and protest. Spurred on in the 1950s and '60s by new innovations and a major revival, jazz musicians came back on the scene in force. Curiously, at about the same time that jazz was making a strong resurgence in Copenhagen, it was facing dwindling audiences back in the USA, where the music has its roots.

From the 1950s on, a number of accomplished US jazz musicians began to tour Europe for their main gigs and some ended up settling in jazz-friendly cities like Copenhagen, Paris and Amsterdam. Among those who selected Copenhagen were saxophonist Ernie Wilkins, pianist Butch Lacy and Ella Fitzgerald's former drummer Ed Thigpen. Ella Fitzgerald herself lived in Copenhagen briefly. Tenor sax legend Stan Getz also called the city home, as from the late 1950s did Oscar Pettiford. Other jazz greats who made the move to this sympathetic and cultivated city were Dexter Gordon, Ben Webster and Keeny Drew.

Today, the Copenhagen Jazz House, in the city centre, is the venue for top Danish and international performers and a focal point for the summertime Copenhagen Jazz Festival (see below), one of Europe's (if not the world's) foremost jazz events. Copenhagen has been a high-profile centre of jazz for a considerable length of time, which means that many of the city's residents are jazz-literate and extremely keen on supporting the art form. Among the leading local jazz performers to look for are bass players Niels-Henning Ørsted Pedersen (often referred to as NHØP) and Mads Vinding, saxophonist Christina Nielsen, drummer Jonas Johansen, trumpeter Thomas Fryland and popular vocalist Cæcilie Norby.

Copenhagen remains one of the jazz capitals of the world, with an exceptionally high proportion of talented musicians and devoted fans for such a small population, plus a conscientious system of support from public authorities and public funding bodies, who see the fostering of talent and training as an important local issue.

THE FESTIVAL

You may have come to Copenhagen expecting a feast for the eyes – after all, isn't Denmark devoted to good design and little else? What may surprise you is that the city is also a feast for the ears. Listen up. Amid the hum of chatter, traffic and white noise, you'll be engulfed by the melodies, tonal experiments and hypnotic percussion of that magical musical art form: jazz. The Copenhagen Jazz Festival is the biggest entertainment event of the Copenhagen year, with 10 days of music beginning on the first Friday in July. It's a cornucopia of hundreds of indoor and outdoor concerts, with music wafting out of practically every public square, park, club and café throughout the city.

The city kicked off the first Copenhagen Jazz Festival in 1978, initiating a citywide event that featured Denmark's top jazz musicians and many international names. Since that time the Copenhagen Jazz Festival has mushroomed into one of Europe's leading jazz events. Over the years, performers have included such renowned names as Dizzy Gillespie, Miles Davis, Sonny Rollins, Oscar Peterson, Ray Charles and Wynton Marsalis. In 1998 the Woody Herman Orchestra and Tony Bennett highlighted; in 1999 Keith Jarrett and Gary Peacock were lead acts; and in 2000 there was a large international representation that included Canadian Diana Krall, the Australian Art Orchestra, Ian Bellamy from the UK, Cæcilie Norby from Denmark, and Americans Natalie Cole and David Sanborn. More recent guests of the festival have included Gilberto Gil, Keith Jarrett, John Mayall, Steve

Winwood, Herbie Hancock, Cassandra Wilson and Dee Dee Bridgewater – mixing things up and keeping punters guessing as to who's been chosen for next year's bill.

It's a fun, slightly haphazard scene that brings everyone in the city out to party. Most of the open-air events are free. Those held in the cafés are either free or have small cover charges and it's only the largest big-name events that have significant ticket prices.

Note that events and venues can change from year to year so what follows is intended as a general guide only. For the latest in schedules, contact **Copenhagen Jazz Festival** (Map pp22–3; ☎ 33 93 20 13; www.jazzfestival.dk; Nytorv 3, 1450 Copenhagen K). The festival program is usually published in May.

If you can't make it to Copenhagen in the summer for the main jazz festival, you can take heart that a smaller festival takes place in autumn. It's called, not surprisingly, Autumn Jazz. Some who have experienced both festivals say that Autumn Jazz has a mellower, less-harried atmosphere (the summer festival can seem a rather poorly organised affair at times – perhaps an example of Danes deciding to use jazz as a means to cut loose from their generally rigid and organised tendencies…).

VENUES

At last count the Copenhagen Jazz Festival had grown to nearly 800 events held at more than 50 venues throughout the city. The music is virtually nonstop, with events beginning in the morning and going throughout the day and night. Many of the biggest-name musicians perform at the Cirkus Bygningen concert hall and at Tivoli; both places are just minutes from Central Station, so easily accessible via public transport.

But literally the whole city is a venue. The rest of the musical performances occur in Copenhagen's numerous clubs and small cafés, in the city's public squares and alongside the canals. And there are also plenty of street parades and special events such as midnight concerts at Nationalmuseet and daily children's jazz programs at Kongens Have.

The music at the Copenhagen Jazz Festival is as varied as the venues. Traditional sounds range from old-fashioned Dixieland jazz and Satchmo-style solo improvisation to the WWII-era swing music that reigned in Duke Ellington and Benny Goodman's day – the Danish free jazz scene also gets a look-in. There's plenty of modern jazz along the lines of that inspired by legendary trumpeter Miles Davis and you can also find lots of contemporary hybrid sounds, free-jazz, acid jazz, soul jazz, nu-jazz, jazz vocals and rhythm and blues.

Among the top venues are the venerable **Copenhagen Jazz House** (Map pp22–3; ☎ 33 15 26 00; Niels Hemmingsensgade 10), the city's leading jazz spot, and Copenhagen's three other foremost jazz venues: **La Fontaine** (Map pp22–3; ☎ 33 11 60 98; Kompagnistræde 11), **JazzHuset Vognporten** (Map pp22–3; ☎ 33 15 20 02; Rådhusstræde 13) and **Mojo** (Map pp22–3; ☎ 33 11 64 53; Løngangstræde 21). All four venues are in the heart of the city. Dozens of other clubs and cafés turn themselves into temporary jazz venues during the festival – details can be found on the festival website.

Some Popular Venues

Café Blågårds Apotek (Map pp22–3; ☎ 35 37 24 42; Blågårdsgade 20)

Café Sommersko (Map pp22–3; ☎ 33 14 81 89; Kronprinsensgade 6)

Café Victor (Map pp22–3; ☎ 33 13 36 13; Ny Østergade 8)

Christianshavns Bådudlejning og Café (Map pp22–3; ☎ 32 96 53 53; Overgaden neden Vandet 29)

Cirkus Bygningen (Map pp22–3; ☎ 70 16 65 65; Jernbanegade 8)

Den Blå Hund (Map pp22–3; ☎ 38 87 46 88; Godthåbsvej 28)

Diamanten (Map pp22–3; ☎ 33 93 55 45; Gammel Strand 50)

Drop Inn (Map pp22–3; ☎ 33 11 24 04; Kompagnistræde 34)

Huset (Map pp22–3; ☎ 33 32 40 77; Rådhusstræde 13)

Kruts Karport Café (Map pp22–3; ☎ 35 26 86 38; Øster Farimagsgade 12)

Kul-Kaféen (Map pp22–3; ☎ 33 32 17 77; Teglgårdsstræde 5)

MG Petersens Familiehave (Map pp22–3; ☎ 36 16 11 33; Pile Allé 16)

JAZZ FESTIVAL

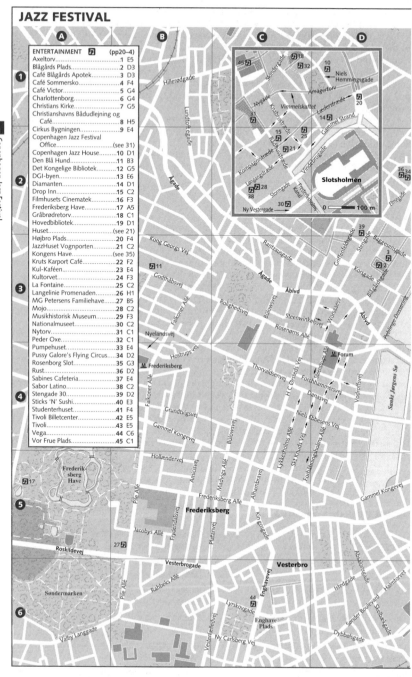

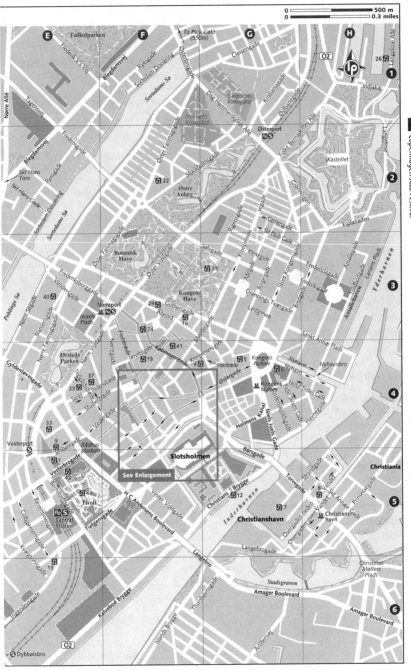

0   500 m
0   0.3 miles

E   Fælledparken   F   To Park Café (550m)   G   H

Frederik V's Vej   1

Bleğdamsvej   Ryesgade   Classengade   O2   26

Tagensvej   Sortedam Dossering   Østerbrogade   Kristianiagade   Langelinie Allé

Nørre Allé   Indiakaj

Sortedams Sø   Garnisons Kirkegård

Østbanegade

Dag Hammerskjölds Allé

Holmens Kirkegård

Fredensgade   Øster Farimagsgade   Østerport   P&S

Bleğdamsvej   Folke Bernadottes Allé

Skt Hans Torv   Ryesgade   Kastellet   2

Skt Hans Gade

Stockholmsgade

Langelinie

22   Østre Anlæg

Sortedam Dossering   Esplanaden

Ryesgade   Gernersgade

Kronprinsessegade   Skt Pauls Gade

Øster Farimagsgade   Fredericiagade   Yderhavnen   3

Peblinge Sø   Frederiksborggade   Øster Voldgade

Botanisk Have   Sølvgade   35

Vendersgade   Klerkegade   Frederiksgade

40   Nørre Søgade

Kongens Have   Store Kongensgade   Bredgade

Amaliegade   Larsens Plads

Nørre Farimagsgade   Nørre Voldgade   Gothersgade

Dronningens Tværgade

Nørreport   M P&S   29   Landgreven

Israels Plads   Abenrå   16

Gyldenløvesgade   Ørsteds Parken   24   Møntergade   Sankt Annæ Plads

Nørre Voldgade   41   Kronprinsensgade

Frederiksberggade   Krystalgade   Købmagergade   5   Kongens Nytorv   Nyhavn   Nyhavnbro

37   19   4   Pilestræde   6   Nyhavn   4

23   Studiestræde   Østergade   M Kongens Nytorv   Herluf Trolles Gade   Havnegade

33   Vestergade   Niels Juels Gade

Vesterport   S   9   Holmens Kanal

Jernbanegade   Rådhus-pladsen   Børsgade   Christiania

1   Vesterbrogade   Slotsholmen

42   Strandgade   Strandgade

43   Tivoli   See Enlargement   8   Skt Annæ Gade   5

Bernstorffsgade   H C Andersens Boulevard   Vester Voldgade   Christians Brygge   12   Torvegade

Reventlowsgade   Tietgensgade   Inderhavnen   7   M Christianshavn

Colbjørnsensgade   P&S S   Central Station   Christianshavn   Overgaden oven Vandet

Kvægtorvsgade   Langebrogade   Christmas Møllers Plads

13   Langebro   Stadsgraven   6

Ingerslevsgade   Amager Boulevard

Kalvebod Brygge   Islands Brygge   Thorshavnsgade   Artillerivej   Amager Boulevard

O2

S Dybbølsbro

23

Park Café (Map pp236–7; ☎ 35 42 62 48; Østerbrogade 79)

Peder Oxe (Map pp22–3; ☎ 33 11 00 77; Gråbrødretorv 11)

Pumpehuset (Map pp22–3; ☎ 33 93 14 32; Studie-stræde 52)

Pussy Galore's Flying Circus (Map pp22–3; ☎ 35 24 53 00; Sankt Hans Torv)

Rust (Map pp22–3; ☎ 35 24 52 00; Guldbergsgade 8)

Sabines Cafeteria (Map pp22–3; ☎ 33 14 09 44; Teglgårdsstræde 4)

Sabor Latino (Map pp22–3; ☎ 33 11 97 66; Vester Voldgade 85)

Stengade 30 (Map pp22–3; ☎ 35 36 09 38; Stengade 18)

Sticks 'N' Sushi (Map pp22–3; ☎ 33 11 14 07; Nansensgade 59)

Studenterhuset (Map pp22–3; ☎ 35 32 38 61; Købmagergade 52)

Vega (Map pp22–3; ☎ 33 25 70 11; Enghavevej 40)

Pussy Galore's Flying Circus (p132)

Public squares where events take place include Vor Frue Plads, at the side of Vor Frue Kirke in the Latin Quarter; Højbro Plads and Nytorv, Strøget's two main squares; Gråbrødretorv, a historic square north of Strøget; Kultorvet, in the Latin Quarter; Axeltorv, the square fronting the Cirkus Bygningen concert hall; Blågårds Plads, fronting Floras Kaffe Bar in the Nørrebro area; and Langelinie Promenaden, along the waterfront north of the Little Mermaid.

Gardens where events take place include Kongens Have at Rosenborg Slot and Frederiksberg Have in the Frederiksberg area.

There are a number of other nonconventional sites where music events also take place:

Nonconventional Venues

Charlottenborg (Map pp22–3; ☎ 33 93 20 13; Kongens Nytorv) A former palace, now an art museum.

Christians Kirke (Map pp22–3; ☎ 33 93 78 70; Strandgade 1) A Christianshavn church, with a theatrical atmosphere.

Det Kongelige Bibliotek (Map pp22–3; ☎ 33 93 20 13; Christians Brygge 9) The royal library, and an excellent venue, thanks partly to its startling architectural forms.

DGI-byen (Map pp22–3; ☎ 33 29 80 00; Tietgensgade 65) The redeveloped hotel and sports centre.

Filmhusets Cinematek (Map pp22–3; ☎ 33 74 34 12; Gothersgade 55) The national film institute.

Hovedbibliotek (Map pp22–3; ☎ 33 73 60 60; Krystalgade 15) The main public library, in the heart of the Latin Quarter.

Musikhistorisk Museum (Map pp22–3; ☎ 33 11 27 26; Åbenrå 30) The music history museum.

Nationalmuseet (Map pp22–3; ☎ 33 13 44 11; Ny Vestergade 10) Denmark's national museum.

Tivoli (Map pp22–3; ☎ 33 15 10 01; Vesterbrogade 3) The city's grand amusement park, and easily one of the best spots to take in a night-time gig, amidst the twinkling lights.

TICKETS

Tickets should be purchased in advance for big-name events, such as those held at the concert halls at Cirkus Bygningen and Tivoli.

If you're already in Denmark, tickets for main events can be purchased by calling **BilletNet** (☎ 38 48 11 22; www.billetnet.dk) or contacting the **Tivoli Billetcenter** (Map pp22–3; ☎ 70 10 20 14; Vesterbrogade 3).

Residents of foreign countries can purchase tickets from agents at home or you can order them from the aforementioned Tivoli Billetcenter using a credit card.

Arts & Architecture

Arts & Architecture

Aside from interior design, for which Denmark has long been regarded as a powerhouse and leading light, film has generally been acknowledged as Denmark's great cultural export and gift to the world of arts. This is generally a modern (ie postwar) phenomenon, and Denmark's reputation has been growing stronger and stronger, especially since the 1990s, with local cinema provoking debate and igniting inspiration in Denmark and abroad. The Danish Film Institute's powerful patronage of many films has allowed the cinematic scene to flourish, with international *enfant terrible* Lars von Trier starting his own style of cinema, known as Dogme 95.

In terms of music, the Danish love of jazz has seen Copenhagen frequently labelled as the European capital of the genre, and all types of jazz are appreciated in the city, with many US musicians (particularly in the past) finding Copenhagen a haven and source of inspiration. For information on Copenhagen's love of jazz and the Copenhagen Jazz Festival, see p20.

Wanna Play?

With all the fuss being made over the construction of the new Opera House, it's easy to overlook the fact that another successful marriage between art and architecture is being planned for Copenhagen. In 2008, Det Kongelige Teater's new playhouse at Kvæsthusbroen will open, designed by Danish architects Boje Lundgaard and Lene Tranberg. It will have seating for 750 at its main stage, and will take over theatrical duties from the Old Stage at Kongens Nytorv and TurbineHallerne.

Denmark, with its cold climate and love of indoor pursuits, has always allowed the arts to flourish – and so theatre, opera, ballet and classical music have a long and firm hold on many locals' hearts. Sell-out crowds to performances at Det Kongelige Teater (the Royal Theatre) are not unknown, and state subsidies mean that all manner of performances are featured on the cultural calendar.

Little Danish literature is translated into English, but there are a few literary powerhouses to be found in the city's Latin Quarter bookshops should you want a textual companion during your time in the city.

Denmark's art museums and galleries are well patronised and the visual arts scene is in a particularly strong position – with both established and emerging artists allowed the freedom to create in relative peace. The avant-garde – both in theatrical performance and in installation work – occupies a solid position in Copenhagen; any stroll around Bredgade's fine galleries or to one of the city's fringe theatres will confirm this.

MUSIC

Virtually all forms of music are alive and well in Copenhagen and locals are both erudite and ardent on the topic.

Danish music has come a long way since the days of the *lur*, a long, curved horn used in the Bronze Age (you can see examples in Nationalmuseet – p53). While the purpose of the *lur* has never been agreed upon, it's regarded as a musical instrument of some description by scholars of the period.

CLASSICAL

Denmark's best-known classical composer is Carl Nielsen (1865–1931). In 1888 he wrote his first orchestral work, *Suite for Strings,* for a performance at Copenhagen's Tivoli concert hall. It received critical acclaim and since then has become a regular feature of the Danish concert repertory. Nielsen's music includes six symphonies, several operas, and many hymn tunes and popular songs, often with patriotic themes.

The 20th-century experimental movement's best Danish exponent was the Copenhagen-born composer Rued Langgaard (1893–1952), who once proclaimed that 'Carl Nielsen is humbug' and led a life at odds with the classical music establishment of his time. Some of his compositions with a strikingly local titular flavour include *Ved Tordenskjold i Holmens Kirke* and *Memories at Amalienborg*.

The city's leading orchestra is the wonderful Danish National Radio Symphony Orchestra, which often performs at its home, Radiohusets Koncertsal in Frederiksberg. The orchestra's concerts are always broadcast on national radio, and it plays at festivals such as Golden Days in Copenhagen (p11).

Choral music is performed regularly in the city's churches and details of performances are often posted on church notice boards throughout the city centre.

FOLK, POP, ROCK & ELECTRONICA

Danish folk and rock music have been strongly influenced by American and British trends. One folk-music idol is Bob Dylan, who has performed in Denmark on numerous occasions, and whose influence in both music and lyrical style continues to resonate in contemporary Danish folk music. In the field of popular modern music, Copenhageners will give anything a go: hard rock, punk, pop, new wave, no wave, hip-hop, grunge, electronica and techno. Danish bands who have attracted attention outside Denmark in the recent past include DAD (formerly Disneyland After Dark), a heavy metal hair-band, and Aqua, whose cheesy synth pop infiltrated and infuriated ears the world over in the late 1990s and sold by the truckload (a mammoth 28 million copies of the album are somewhere in the world).

Dance music has been represented by the technologically minded Safri Duo, who blend beats with electronic sounds to widespread acclaim in Europe.

Newer rock/pop music to keep your ears primed for includes the most popular Danish band of the new millennium, Kashmir, whose recent work *Zitilites* (sung in English) has sparked comparisons to both Radiohead and Coldplay and produced the popular hit 'Surfing the Warm Industry', one of the catchiest songs to burst out of the bars and cafés of Copenhagen in a long time. If you want to hear a grotty garage-inspired sound, then look no further than the Raveonettes, the leather-clad team of Sune Rose Wagner and Sharin Foo. Their debut album *Chain Gang of Love* is great fun.

Pretty popsters Swan Lee burst onto the scene in 2001 with their debut album *Enter* and then kept their punters waiting another three years before releasing their enormously popular follow-up *Swan Lee*. Their sound recalls the influence of bands such as the Pretenders and Blondie, mainly due to the vocals of singer Pernille Rosendahl.

Other bands that are making a splash (albeit modest) in Denmark (and sometimes England – where many bands often settle in a bid to move beyond the Danish music industry) include the raucous Breakers, Mew and Nephew.

In 2004 the Danish Music Industry, at the urging of Culture Minister Brian Mikkelsen, launched a PR campaign to shine a spotlight on modern Danish music. The campaign, known as Music Export Denmark (MXD) is funded by both the government and private industry and aims to get Danish music heard outside Scandinavia.

Awards ceremonies for Danish artists include the Danish Music Awards, which take place around February each year and attract a large viewing audience of around one million people.

Top Five Copenhagen Soundtracks

- 'Wonderful Copenhagen' (Danny Kaye) Don't pretend you haven't been singing this to yourself since you got here...
- 'Zitilites' (Kashmir) Atmospheric pop that's the perfect accompaniment to a day in Vesterbro.
- 'Swan Lee' (Swan Lee) Breezy, toe-tapping pop loved by young Copenhagen spunks.
- 'That's the Way for Me' (Erann DD) This song was part of the 'People's Gift' to Mary and Frederik for their wedding and was mighty popular in 2004, despite what cynics may tell you.
- 'Barbie Girl' (Aqua) It's easy to get an inferiority complex when surrounded by Danish culture, beauty and sophistication. This song will get you back on top.

LITERATURE

The literary arts began to flourish in Copenhagen during the first half of the 19th century, which has been characterised as the 'Golden Age' of Danish literature. The foremost writers of that period included Adam Oehlenschläger (1779–1850), a romantic lyric poet who also wrote short stories and plays; Hans Christian Andersen (1805–75), whose fairy tales have been translated into more languages than any other book except the Bible; and philosopher Søren Kierkegaard (1813–55), who is considered the father of existentialism.

Around 1870 a trend towards realism emerged, focusing on contemporary issues of the day. A writer of this genre, novelist Henrik Pontoppidan, won the Nobel Prize for Literature in 1917 shortly after publishing the epic *The Realm of the Dead*, which attacked materialism. Another Dane who won the Nobel Prize for Literature was Johannes Vilhelm Jensen (1873–1950), who wrote the six-volume novel *The Long Journey* and *The Fall of the King*, a story about Danes in Renaissance times.

The most famous Danish writer of the 20th century, Karen Blixen (1885–1962), started her career with *Seven Gothic Tales,* which was published in New York under the pen name Isak Dinesen. She is best known for *Out of Africa,* the memoirs of her farm life in Kenya, which she wrote in 1937. Other works include *Winter's Tales* (1942), *The Angelic Avengers* (1944), *Last Tales* (1957), *Anecdotes of Destiny* (1958) and *Shadows on the Grass* (1960). Her family home in Rungsted, north of Copenhagen, has been turned into a museum (p93) detailing her life and works.

Dan Turèll was a hard-drinking, hard-living, hard-writing Danish author of immense popular appeal. Sadly, he died at the age of 47 and his works have not been translated into English, but if you want to get closer, you can (suitably enough) have a drink at a bar named after him in the city centre (p131).

Denmark's foremost contemporary novelist is the wonderful Peter Høeg, a former ballet dancer who burst onto the world literary stage in the 1990s with his deservedly popular work *Miss Smilla's Feeling for Snow* (written in 1992 and published in the USA as *Smilla's Sense of Snow*). Since then, three other Høeg novels have been published in English. All of Høeg's works focus on nonconformist characters on the margins of Danish society, and the way people establish or find themselves in civilisation is a prominent theme.

For details on more Danish writers, visit the website www.literaturenet.dk.

Sage Søren

Denmark's most famous philosopher, Søren Kierkegaard, was born into a prosperous Copenhagen family on 5 May 1813. When he was in his early 20s, his father died and left Søren with an inheritance that freed him from the need to work. He studied theology and philosophy at Copenhagen University and devoted his entire life to studying and writing.

Kierkegaard was vehemently opposed to the philosophy of Georg Wilhelm Friedrich Hegel, which was prevalent in 19th-century Europe and embraced by the Danish Lutheran Church. In contrast, Kierkegaard's writings challenged individuals to make choices entirely of their own among the alternatives that life offered. In his first great work, *Either/Or,* published in 1843, the alternative was between aesthetic pleasures or an ethical life. This work, like many that followed, was in part inspired by Kierkegaard's lifelong pain over breaking off an engagement to a young woman named Regine Olsen. He continued to wrestle with the implications of his broken engagement in subsequent writings, including *Fear and Trembling* (1843), which compares the biblical tale of Abraham's sacrifice of Isaac to Kierkegaard's own sacrifice.

Kierkegaard's greatest attack on Hegelianism, and his most philosophically important work, was *Concluding Unscientific Postscript to the Philosophical Fragments* (1846), which passionately expounded the tenets of existentialism.

Kierkegaard was considered by many members of the Copenhagen establishment to be a fanatic and his friends were few, even in the literary world. His works remained virtually unknown outside Denmark until the 20th century.

The last years of Kierkegaard's life were dominated by an acrimonious battle with the established Church. The toll was so great that it slowly drained his health and he died of exhaustion in a Copenhagen hospital in 1855 at the age of 42. His funeral was held in the city's cathedral, Vor Frue Kirke (p59). At the time of his death, Kierkegaard felt his works had largely fallen upon deaf ears, but his writings posthumously have become the vanguard for existentialist philosophers worldwide. If you fancy paying your respects at his gravesite, visit Assistens Kirkegård in Nørrebro (p80).

Once Upon a Time...

Born on 2 April 1805 in Odense, Hans Christian Andersen was the son of a poor cobbler. At the age of 14 he ran away to Copenhagen 'to become famous' and the following year entered Det Kongelige Teater (the Royal Theatre) as a student of dance and music. In 1822, on the recommendation of the theatre board, he was sent to a preparatory school in Helsingør, and in 1828 he passed his university entrance exams.

The following year Andersen self-published his first book, *A Walk from Holmen's Canal to the Eastern Tip of Amager*. In 1831, after being jilted in a love affair, Andersen travelled to Germany and wrote the first of a number of stories about his travels abroad.

In 1835 he finally made a name for himself with the successful novel *The Improvisators*. He followed that with his first volume of fairy tales, *Tales, Told for Children,* which included such classics as 'The Tinderbox' and 'The Princess and the Pea'. Over the next few decades, he continued writing novels and accounts of his travels, but it was his fairy tales that brought him worldwide fame.

Andersen had a superb talent for humanising animals, plants and innate objects without compromising their original character. In his stories the villains are not evil characters such as witches or trolls, but rather human weaknesses such as indifference and vanity, and his tales are imbued with moral realism instead of wishful fantasy. Some of his most famous fairy tales are 'The Little Mermaid', 'The Ugly Duckling', 'The Snow Queen', 'The Constant Tin Soldier', 'The Nightingale' and the satirical 'The Emperor's New Clothes'.

Besides his fairy tales and poems, Andersen wrote six novels, numerous travel books, many dramatic works and two autobiographies, of which the most highly regarded is *The Fairy Tale of My Life*. All in all, he published 156 stories and other works.

Andersen had a penchant for travel and over his lifetime made 29 journeys abroad, several of them lasting many months. On 4 August 1875, at the age of 70, he died of liver cancer at a villa outside Copenhagen. His funeral was held at Vor Frue Kirke (p59) and his grave is in the city's Assistens Kirkegård (p80). Other city sights that have a strong connection with this great writer include Nyhavn (numbers 20 and 67 – where he lived and worked), Tordenskjoldsgade 17 (where he lived), Bakkehuset (p87), which he often visited, and Tivoli Gardens. There is a statue of him at the southeastern edge of Rådhuspladsen (see p55). In 2005 the city of Copenhagen will stage numerous events dedicated to celebrating the 200th anniversary of his birth.

Statue of Hans Christian Andersen (p55)

Top Five Copenhagen Reads

- *The Complete Fairy Tales* (Hans Christian Andersen) A firm favourite the world over, and with many Copenhagen locales at centre stage. Deservedly popular with children and those who read to them.
- *Early Spring* (Tove Ditlevsen) This memoir recounts Ditlevsen's childhood in Vesterbro during the Depression. Her later preoccupation with childhood themes is evident in her works of fiction and poetry. Ditlevsen suicided in 1976 and is mourned by many of her devoted readers.
- *Miss Smilla's Feeling for Snow* (Peter Høeg) A wonderful, suspense-filled mystery set largely in Copenhagen's Christianshavn district, which touches upon Danish colonialism and the struggle for Greenlandic cultural identity, plus the search for meaning within oneself.
- *Music and Silence* (Rose Tremain) A delightful historical novel set in the time of Christian IV. Romantic and moving, with some wonderfully evocative descriptions of courtly life in Copenhagen.
- *Silence in October* (Jens Christian Grøndahl) An engaging meditation on the dissolution of a marriage, as a Copenhagen man pieces together his wife's disappearance and his own inner life. Features numerous Copenhagen locations, especially around the Three Lakes.

VISUAL ARTS

Prior to the 19th century, Danish art tended to revolve around formal portraits of the bourgeoisie, the aristocracy and the royal family. One of the most highly regarded portrait painters was Jens Juel (1745–1802), whose works can be found in Statens Museum for Kunst (p84).

Denmark's 'Golden Age' of the arts (1800–50) produced the Copenhagen artist Christoffer Wilhelm Eckersberg (1783–1853), who depicted more universal scenes of everyday Danish life, and Eckersberg's student Christen Købke (1810–48), who was little known in his time but is now regarded as one of the most important painters of the era. Exceptional collections of 'Golden Age' works can be found at the city's Statens Museum for Kunst (p84) and the nearby Den Hirschsprungske Samling (p83).

The leading Danish sculptor of the day was Bertel Thorvaldsen (1770–1844), who re-created classical sculptures during a long sojourn in Rome and returned to Copenhagen to establish his own museum. The works of Thorvaldsen can be seen at Copenhagen's cathedral Vor Frue Kirke (p59) and at Thorvaldsens Museum (p63) on Slotsholmen.

Another important art movement (although not Copenhagen-based) captured the uniquely beautiful qualities of the light at Denmark's northernmost town, Skagen. The Skagen Painters, as they were known, included Anna and Michale Ancher, PS Krøyer and Holger Drachmann. Examples of their work can be viewed at the Statens Museum for Kunst (p84).

The Cobra (COpenhagen–BRussels–Amsterdam) movement, partially centred in Copenhagen, was formed in 1948 with the aim of exploiting the free, spontaneous artistic expression of the unconscious in forceful depictions of imagined animal and human figures. One of its founders, Danish artist Asger Jorn (1914–73), achieved an international following for his abstract paintings, many of which evoke imagery from Nordic mythology. The Louisiana modern art museum (p175) north of Copenhagen has a fine collection of Cobra works, as does the Statens Museum for Kunst (p84).

The prolific Per Kirkeby (1938–) keeps modern times percolating with his dextrous excursions into performance art, painting, sculpture, architecture, film and graphic art. Pop art played a part in his work in the 1960s and '70s, although subsequent

Top Five Artists

Top Danish artists whose works you'll find easily in Copenhagen include the following:

- CW Eckersberg (at Statens Museum for Kunst, p84)
- Asger Jorn (at Louisiana, p175)
- Per Kirkeby (at Det Kongelige Bibliotek, p62, and Geologisk Museum, p83)
- Bjørn Nørgaard (at Folketinget, p62, and Statens Museum for Kunst, p84)
- Torben Christensen (at Arken, p94)

works have demonstrated a strong preference for structuralism. Another notable painter/sculptor of the late 20th century was Svend Wiig Hansen (1922–97), whose monumental bulbous bronzes can be seen at Louisiana and whose works were often concerned with the theme of mankind under threat of time.

One young local artist whose paintings were garnering praise when we last visited was Thomas Kluge (1969–), who represents the next generation of figurative painters. His realistic depictions are based on portraiture tradition but always feature a dark, subversive twist.

Since the 1990s, many young artists (particularly females) have concentrated on video and installation art that concentrates on autobiographical and personal narratives, rather than the traditional disciplines of sculpture and painting. A strong performance element has featured in modern Danish art since the 1970s.

Potent Patron of the Arts

The brewer Carl Jacobsen (1842–1914) was a great supporter of culture and the arts. After a fire swept the Frederiksborg castle, north of Copenhagen, Jacobsen took on the task of restoring the badly damaged building and converting it into a national museum. In 1876 he established the Carlsberg Foundation to provide the financial support to maintain that museum.

Despite his vast wealth, Jacobsen believed that great works of art were treasures that should be available to the general public rather than items to be held as private trophies by the rich. In the late 19th century he founded the Ny Carlsberg Glyptotek (p53) and donated his own exceptional collection of art to the museum.

In 1902 Jacobsen donated his brewery to the Carlsberg Foundation, making it the most richly endowed private foundation in Denmark. To this day, that foundation is still the majority shareholder in Carlsberg Brewery. So if you want to support the arts, you know which beer to order!

DESIGN

The cool, clean lines of industrial design are evident in Danish silver and porcelain, both of which merge aesthetics and function. Danish silverworks are highly regarded both in Denmark and abroad, with the company named after the late silversmith Georg Jensen the most renowned. You can view some of his works at the museum in the Georg Jensen shop (p144) on Strøget.

One of the world's most famous sets of porcelain is the Royal Porcelain Manufactory's Flora Danica dinner service. No two pieces of this 1800-plus-piece set are alike, each hand-painted with a different native Danish wildflower or other plant, and then rimmed with gold. Some of the pieces have *trompe l'oeil* applications, such as cup handles that appear as flower stems. Commissioned in 1790 by crown prince Frederik, the original set took 13 years to complete, and is still part of the Danish royal collection today. Pieces of the set are on display at Copenhagen's Rosenborg Slot.

Modern Danish furniture focuses on the functional refinement of style, and the principle that design should be tailored for the comfort of the user. In 1948, Hans Wegner designed the Round Chair, whose smooth, curving lines made it an instant classic and a model for many furniture designers to follow – so popular was the chair at the time that it appeared on the cover of many international interior design magazines. A decade later Arne Jacobsen

Top Five Chairs

You'll see fine examples of Danish chair design almost everywhere in the city, from your hotel to plenty of bars and restaurants. You can also visit websites such as www.furnitureindex.dk or pop into the lovely furniture stores along Bredgade.

- Arne Jacobsen's Egg (see it at Radisson SAS Royal hotel, p156)
- Hans J Wegner's Cow Horn (at Klassik Modern Møbelkunst, p147)
- Kaare Klint's Safari Chair (at Klassik Modern Møbelkunst, p147)
- Verner Panton's System 123 Chair (at Klassik Modern Møbelkunst, p147)
- Nanna Ditzel's Wicker Chair (at Kunstindustrimuseet, p75)

produced the Ant, a form chair designed to be mass produced, which became the model for the stacking chairs found in schools and cafeterias worldwide. You can see chairs by both designers in Copenhagen at the Dansk Design Center (p52) and at Kunstindustrimuseet (the Museum of Decorative Art, p75).

Danish architects place such great emphasis on 'form following function' that they typically design a room only after considering the styles of furniture that are most likely to be used in it. Not surprisingly, many of Denmark's architects (such as Arne Jacobsen – the undisputed master of functionalism) have crossed over into furniture design.

Denmark's best-known lamp designer is Poul Henningsen, who has emphasised the need for lighting to be soft, for the shade to cast a pleasant shadow, and for the light bulb to be blocked from direct view. His PH-5 lamp is one of the most popular hanging lamps sold in Denmark today. Check out how good you can look while eating at Langelinie Pavillonen (p113), which features his stunning shades.

CINEMA & TV

The best-known Danish director of the early 20th century was Carl Theodor Dreyer (1889–1968), who directed numerous films including the 1928 French masterpiece *La Passion de Jeanne d'Arc*, which was acclaimed for its rich visual textures and innovative use of close-ups. In the midst of WWII, Dreyer boldly filmed *Vredens Dag* (Day of Wrath), which made so many allusions to the tyranny of Nazi occupation that he was forced to flee to Sweden.

Since 1972 most Danish films have been produced with the support of government-funded subsidies. These days the funding comes via the Danish Film Institute, which generally covers at least 40% of a film's production costs. Despite the fact that only about 20 feature-length Danish films are made annually, Danish film makers have managed to attract an international audience and win some notable awards.

In 1988 *Babette's Feast,* directed by Gabriel Axel, won the Academy Award for Best Foreign Film. *Babette's Feast* was an adaptation of a story written by Karen Blixen, whose novel *Out of Africa* had been turned into an Oscar-winning Hollywood movie just three years earlier.

In 1989 Danish director Bille August won the Academy Award for Best Foreign Film as well as the Cannes Film Festival's Palme d'Or award for *Pelle the Conqueror,* a film adapted from Martin Andersen Nexø's book about the harsh reality of life as an immigrant in 19th-century Denmark. August also directed *Smilla's Sense of Snow* (1997), based on the bestseller by Peter Høeg, starring Julia Ormond and Gabriel Byrne, and *Les Misérables* (1998), an accessible adaptation of Victor Hugo's classic tale of good and evil, starring Liam Neeson and Geoffrey Rush.

The leading director of the new millennium is Lars von Trier, whose better-known films include the melodrama *Breaking the Waves* (1996), which featured Emily Watson and took the Cannes Film Festival's Grand Prix award, and *Dancer in the Dark* (2000), a musical starring Icelandic pop singer Björk and Catherine Deneuve. *Dancer in the Dark* won the Cannes Film Festival's Palme d'Or in 2000. In 2003 von Trier released the frequently difficult and experimental *Dogville,* starring Nicole Kidman. Set in a small town in the US during the 1930s, the film examines themes such as cruelty and US aggression, and has proved as controversial as his other works. Von Trier, who has never set foot in the US, is planning a trilogy on the topic of the country, but generally films in Sweden.

Another Danish director to keep an eye on is Thomas Vinterberg, whose film *Festen* (The Celebration) won the jury prize at the 1998 Cannes Film Festival. Vinterberg was the youngest person ever to be admitted to the National Film School. He has subsequently directed *It's All about Love* and *Dear Wendy.* The actor Thomas Bo Larsen is a regular cast member in his work.

Both Vinterberg and von Trier were instrumental in developing Dogme 95, sometimes dubbed the 'vow of chastity'. This artistic manifesto pledged the use of a minimalist approach, which involves using only hand-held cameras, shooting on location with natural light and rejecting the use of special effects and pre-recorded music. It attracted both ardent

Top Five Copenhagen Films

- *I Kina spiser de hunde* (Lasse Spang Olsen, 1999) A love it-or-hate it heist flick set in Copenhagen that has also been filmed in English.
- *The Prince & Me* (Martha Coolidge, 2004) A big-budget US film about a commoner who marries a Danish prince. Partly filmed in Copenhagen.
- *Reconstruction* (Christoffer Boe, 2003) An elegant mystery/romance with a few twists and turns and some attractive local settings.
- *Smilla's Sense of Snow* (Bille August, 1997) The big-screen adaptation of one of Denmark's most popular books. It's actually pretty damn good, with some beautiful skyline shots.
- *Open Hearts* (Susanne Bier, 2003) Gritty Dogme drama filmed in Copenhagen and bound to start a few debates between viewers.

fans and widespread dismissal, but its impact and influence cannot be underestimated in modern cinema.

Lars von Trier's production company, Zentropa, along with most other Danish film companies, maintains studios at the site of a converted military base at Hvidovre, 20 minutes south of central Copenhagen. In 2004 von Trier was filming the follow-up to *Dogville*, *Mandalay*, in Trollhatten, Sweden.

Two Danish actresses who have jumped into the international film scene are Connie Nielsen, who co-starred in the Roman Empire epic *Gladiator* (2000) with Russell Crowe, and Copenhagen native Iben Hjejle, who made her Hollywood debut as the lead actress in the quirky romantic comedy *High Fidelity* (2000) and features in plenty of local work – including the odd Carlsberg commercial.

THEATRE, DANCE & OPERA

Det Kongelige Teater at Kongens Nytorv first opened in 1748 as a court theatre, performing the plays of Denmark's most famous playwright, Ludvig Holberg (1684–1754). Today its repertoire encompasses international works, including Shakespearian plays, as well as classical and contemporary Danish plays.

Smaller local theatre companies pepper the local scene, their repertoires moving away from the 'issues-based' drama of the 1980s to increasingly focus on aesthetic innovation and experimentation. Copenhagen has a boldly experimental theatre scene, which fairly hums with good-natured rivalry as to who can push the fourth wall the most. One local company whose performances are well worth frequenting is Hotel Pro Forma (www .hotelproforma.dk).

In the mid-19th century, Den Kongelige Ballet (the Royal Danish Ballet), which also performs at Det Kongelige Teater, took its present form under the leadership of the choreographer and ballet master August Bournonville (1805–79). Today, Den Kongelige Ballet, which has a troupe of nearly 100 dancers, still performs a number of Bournonville's romantic ballets, such as *La Sylphide* and *Napoli*, along with more contemporary works. Bournonville, who was born in Copenhagen, was announced the artistic director of Det Kongelige Teater in 1830, and held the position for the next 47 years. His influence over Danish classical ballet technique is considerable, and is still in evidence today.

Also based in Det Kongelige Teater is Den Kongelige Opera (the Royal Danish Opera), which has an ensemble of 32 singers and a renowned 60-member opera chorus. It performs about 16 operas each season.

Det Kongelige Kapel (the Royal Danish Orchestra) was founded in 1448, giving rise to the claim that it's the oldest orchestra in the world. It accompanies the ballet and opera performances at Det Kongelige Teater.

For those after a less traditional opera performance, Den Anden Opera (the Other Opera; www.denandenopera.dk), based on Kronprinsensgade in the Latin Quarter, stages innovative performances on a regular basis. Staging often relies on video and digital projection, both of which feature heavily in edgy, often humorous productions such as *Viktors Golgotha*.

In terms of modern dance, Copenhagen was a bit of a late starter. In the 1960s, after visits to Copenhagen by the American modern dance luminary Martha Graham, local dance initiatives began to emerge. Today, the leading modern dance group is Nyt Dansk Danseteater (the New Danish Dance Theatre), which was formed in 1980. The company's current artistic director is Tim Rushton, who is committed to keeping the company as innovative as possible. Other dance companies based in the city include Åben Dans Production (www.aabendans.dk) and Corona Danseteater.

The best place to see performances of modern dance works is at Dansescenen (p128) in the Østerbro neighbourhood.

ARCHITECTURE

'AS AN ARCHITECT I BELIEVE IT IS VERY IMPORTANT TO FALL IN LOVE WITH THE NATURE OF THINGS INSTEAD OF FIGHTING FOR FORM AND STYLE.'

Jørn Utzon

Copenhagen has a low skyline with only a few high-rise buildings. The city centre is predominantly historic, but it does have blocks of mundane office buildings as well as some sleek modern structures.

If you want to start at the very beginning of Copenhagen's architectural story, then head to Slotsholmen, where the construction of Bishop Absalon's 12th-century fortress took place. Today, you can still see the ruins of this structure under Christiansborg Slot (p60). On Strøget, Helligåndskirken (Map pp239–41) still has a wing which dates from medieval times, although most of the building was rebuilt after a fire in 1732.

If any one person can claim to have radically altered the city in terms of architecture it's Christian IV, whose extraordinary building program saw the construction of the elaborately embellished Børsen (the Stock Exchange, p60), Rundetårn (p58) and Rosenborg Slot (p84) – although at a great cost.

Christian V ruled over the completion of Kastellet, in the city's north, and the construction of Kongens Nytorv (p66).

The ornate baroque style was a popular design for public building in the 17th century, and two splendid buildings representative of the style are the church Vor Frelsers Kirke (p79), in Christianshavn, and Charlottenborg (p66) at Kongens Nytorv, a former palace that now houses an art gallery.

Pre-eminent among the city's rococo structures are Amalienborg Slot's (p65) four nearly identical mansions, which were designed by architect Nicolai Eigtved at the end of the 18th century. The buildings are the residence of the royal family, but one of them is accessible to the public as a museum.

The city's leading architect of the late 19th century was Vilhelm Dahlerup, who borrowed from a broad spectrum of European Renaissance influences. His most spectacular works include Ny Carlsberg Glyptotek (p53), the nearby Peacock Theatre at Tivoli and the richly ornate Det Kongelige Teater (p125).

Over the years, Copenhagen has been struck by a number of fires, and architectural styles are often the consequence of whatever was fashionable at the time of rebuilding. Around Strøget and the Latin Quarter, for example, there are numerous neoclassical buildings that were erected following devastating 18th-century blazes. Some of the

Top Five Eye-Catching Buildings

- Arne Jacobsen's **Radisson SAS Royal Hotel** (p156)
- Henning Larsen's **Opera House** (p78)
- Schmidt, Hammer & Lassen's **Det Kongelige Bibliotek (the Black Diamond)** (p62)
- Anna Maria Indrio's modern extension of **Statens Museum for Kunst** (p84)
- Søren Robert Lund's **Arken** (p94)

Spire of Børsen (p60)

grander neoclassical buildings of the period are the cathedral Vor Frue Kirke (p59) in the Latin Quarter and the city courthouse Domhuset (p57) on Nytorv.

One of the greatest examples of Art Deco architecture that can be found in the city is the yellow-brick Grundtvigs Church (designed in 1922), designed by Peder Vilhelm Jensen-Klint. Expressionist influences can also be found in the building, as can influences from the Middle Ages. The church is in the northwestern suburb of Bispebjerg, at På Bjerget 14B, and has a great pipe organ (designed by Kaare Klint, the architect's son).

The two great modern-day architects whose influence dominates all others are Arne Jacobsen and Jørn Utzon. Jacobsen (1902–71) was a Copenhagen native and spent most of his life in his beloved city. His best-known architectural effort is the Radisson SAS Royal Hotel (p156), but he also turned his hand to designing the Dansk National Bank Building at Holmens Canal and to a petrol station on Kystvejen in Charlottenlund, which still pumps petrol today. You can learn more about Jacobsen's life and works at www.arne-jacobsen.com.

Utzon's most famous work is the Sydney Opera House. Completed in 1974, it remains one of the best-recognised buildings in the world. To see an example of Utzon's stunning talent while in Copenhagen, visit the Bagsværd Kirke (1973–6) at Taxsvej 14 in the city's north. With an aluminium roof and stark, simple external features, the airy interior of this building is breathtaking and highlights Utzon's command of spatial relationships. In 2003 Utzon was awarded the Pritzker Prize for architecture.

Probably the leading architect from the present day is Henning Larsen. His five-storey Dansk Design Center (p52) incorporates a double-glass wall of windows that was originally intended to hold a layer of liquid crystal, thus allowing the building's streetside exterior to act as a huge video screen, but to his chagrin the concept was axed as too costly. Another of his recent achievements is the impressionists wing of the Ny Carlsberg Glyptotek, which was built in 1996.

In January 2005 Copenhagen's new Opera House opened. Designed by, you guessed it, Henning Larsen and occupying a specially made island north of Christianshavn, this dazzling space features a 32m-long cantilever and six theatres. The inaugural opera performed here was Verdi's *Aïda,* a fitting production given the epic qualities of this building.

In terms of ground-breaking modern design, the pride of the city is the new Royal Library, which incorporates a slanting cube shape so that no two exterior walls are parallel. Canalside, on the edge of historic Slotsholmen, the multistorey building dubbed the 'Black Diamond' (Den Sorte Diamant) has a striking façade of black granite and smoked glass and a brilliant use of internal space. It was designed by the respected firm of Schmidt, Hammer & Lassen.

If you'd like to get more information about local architecture, visit the Dansk Arkitektur Center at Gammel Dok (p78).

History

History

THE RECENT PAST

Postwar Denmark saw the establishment of a comprehensive social-welfare system under the leadership and guidance of the Social Democrats.

During WWII and in the economic depression that had preceded it, many Copenhagen neighbourhoods had deteriorated into slums. In 1948 an ambitious urban renewal policy called the 'Finger Plan' was adopted and redeveloped much of the city, creating new housing projects interspaced with green areas of parks and recreational facilities that spread out like fingers from the city centre.

On a national level the cradle-to-grave securities that guarantee medical care, education and public assistance were expanded. As the economy grew and the labour market increased, women entered the workforce in unprecedented numbers and household incomes

A Thoroughly Modern Monarchy

Denmark's current monarch, Queen Margrethe II, was born on 16 April 1940, the eldest daughter of Frederik IX (1899–1972), who had no sons. As a result of a 1953 referendum that amended the sex-bias of the Danish constitution to allow women to succeed to the throne, Margrethe was proclaimed queen on 15 January 1972, the first female monarch of Denmark since the 14th century.

Margrethe II is a popular queen who has been credited with giving a fresh perspective to the Danish monarchy and minimising the privilege that has traditionally separated royalty from commoners.

In addition to performing her ceremonial roles as head of state, the queen is an accomplished artist. She has illustrated a number of books, including Tolkien's *Lord of the Rings,* and has also designed Christmas seals for Unicef and stamps for the Danish postal service. The queen has been active in the theatre as well, designing costumes for a production of Hans Christian Andersen's *The Shepherdess and the Chimney Sweep* and creating both the settings and costumes for the Royal Theatre's ballet *Et Folkesagn* (The Legend). Together with her French-born husband, Prince Henrik, the queen translated Simone de Beauvoir's novel *Tous les hommes sont mortels* (All Men Are Mortal) from its original French into Danish.

Queen Margrethe and Prince Henrik have two sons. Crown Prince Frederik was born in 1968 and, like his mother, is a graduate of Århus University, where he studied politics and law. Prince Joachim was born in 1969 and attended a smaller Danish college. Both princes did stints in the armed services following their graduation and have also undertaken work internships overseas, Joachim on a farm in Australia and Frederik at a California winery.

Frederik, who spent his 20s and early 30s as the undisputed title-holder in the country's 'most eligible bachelor' comp, is a world traveller whose journeys have taken him far and wide. In 2000, the crown prince, along with five companions, completed a 110-day Arctic journey by dogsled across the frozen tundra of northern Greenland. In May 2004, he married the smart, capable and sincere Mary Donaldson, a Tasmanian law graduate-turned-real estate agent. Their obvious love for each other and marital happiness has won many hearts throughout Denmark, and Frederik's ease with his own displays of emotion have seen him praised for his open, sensitive and genuine nature – no stiff upper lip here.

In September 2004, the Danish royals again demonstrated their 'everyman' qualities by facing the same difficulties as many of their fellow Danes with the announcement that Prince Joachim and Princess Alexandra were breaking up – making them the first Danish royals to divorce since 1846. In true Danish fashion, they have kept things civilised.

TIMELINE	1043	1167	1238
	First written mention of the city, as 'Havn'.	There's a new sheriff in town – Bishop Absalon takes over.	Copenhagen's first monastery is established on Gråbrødretorv.

reached lofty new heights. It was this urban and social change that saw Denmark and its liberal capital Copenhagen become symbols of Nordic tolerance and the Scandinavian welfare model.

In the 1960s a rebellion by young people, who were disillusioned with growing materialism, the nuclear arms race and an authoritarian educational system, took hold in Copenhagen. Student protests broke out on the university campus and squatters began to occupy vacant buildings around the city. The movement came to a head in 1971 when protesters tore down the fence of an abandoned military camp at the eastern side of Christianshavn and began an occupation of the 41-hectare site.

The squatters declared the area the 'free state of Christiania', based on the concept of communal living, and outside the realm of Danish laws. As word of the new community spread, all sorts of people – hippies, the homeless, back-to-the-earth folks who wanted to live off the land, and idealists attracted by the idea of turning a military base into a peaceful utopian community – began to flock to Christiania.

Because of the size of the movement, police attempts to remove people from the site were largely futile, and Christiania became a controversial issue in the Danish parliament, which after much debate reluctantly allowed the community to continue as a 'social experiment'.

The occupants of Christiania quickly grew to around 1000 people who set up their own system of rule, organised social activities and started progressive businesses. Most controversial was the establishment of Pusherstreet, a market where vendors could sell hashish and marijuana openly, although not legally.

In the late 1970s heroin became a problem in Copenhagen and some users and dealers saw Christiania as a safe haven from which to ply their trade. This made the community a target for police raids and in 1980 Christiania itself outlawed hard drugs and demanded that junkies either go into rehabilitation programs or face banishment from the community.

After three decades, self-governing Christiania continues to serve as a bastion for alternative lifestyles. Its population has settled somewhat and between 800 and 1000 people continue to call Christiania home. In 1996 opinion polls showed that about two-thirds of Danes thought that the 'Free State' should be preserved, while about one-fifth of respondents believed that the area should be vacated and put to better use. The future of the area is uncertain and the issue is being debated in parliament – when we visited, a very heavy police presence meant that Christiania seemed anything but 'free'. Watch this space.

One of the most controversial issues of recent times has been Denmark's role in the European Union (EU). Denmark joined the European Community, the predecessor of the EU, in 1973, but Danes have been hesitant to support expansion of the EU's powers. Indeed, when the Maastricht Treaty, which established the terms of a European economic and political union, came up for ratification in 1992, Danish voters rejected it by a ratio of 51% to 49%. After being granted exemptions from the Maastricht Treaty's common defence and monetary provisions, the Danes, by a narrow majority, voted to accept the treaty in a second referendum held in 1993.

In September 2000 the Danes signalled a deeper discontent with European integration when they rejected adopting the euro, the EU's common currency. Denmark, the first EU country to place that decision in the hands of the people, saw a remarkable 87% voter turnout. Despite a passionate campaign to win support for the euro by Danish prime minister Poul Nyrup Rasmussen and the business community, the euro was rejected by a 6% margin. Protesters in Copenhagen and other cities had been effective in convincing Danes they had more to lose than gain, arguing that local control over Danish issues would be ceded to a European bureaucracy dominated by stronger nations, and that Denmark's generous welfare-state securities would also be endangered by the provision.

1443	1479	1534	1536
Copenhagen takes over from Roskilde as the country's capital.	University of Copenhagen is established.	Civil War begins.	Copenhagen's population reduced to eating rats, cats and grass during the siege of Copenhagen.

In 2003 over 2500 Danes moved to Sweden, at least on paper, many to escape high car registration fees, car purchase costs (a new car in Sweden is half as expensive as in Denmark) and Denmark's strict immigration laws (which apply to many Danes' non-Danish spouses). 'Fictitious relocation' is widespread in the Øresund region, especially since the completion of the bridge between Copenhagen and Malmö.

The hottest topic in the city is immigration, with the Danish People's Party advocating that repatriation must be made a top priority. Many immigrants and refugees remain fearful of enforced repatriation; at the time of writing, some 4000 refugees had gone missing within Denmark, presumably to avoid detection by the state. So hot is this potato that the 2001 general election was fought mostly on this issue, with Anders Fogh Rasmussen's Liberal Party forming a coalition with the Conservative People's Party, and the Danish People's Party wielding considerable power and influence in modern-day political affairs.

Denmark's monarchy continues to move with the times while providing a stable sense of tradition. Queen Margrethe gave permission for Crown Prince Frederik to marry his girlfriend Mary Donaldson and they became engaged in October 2003. Mary had to relinquish her Australian citizenship and become a Dane in order to marry, but she had far less trouble with the immigration authorities than many other foreigners. In May 2004 Crown Prince Frederik and Mary Donaldson married, turning the entire city of Copenhagen into a giant party as over 200,000 locals flocked to the streets to celebrate the nuptials with flag-waving, concerts and lots of toasts.

FROM THE BEGINNING

Founding of Copenhagen

Until the mid-12th century Copenhagen was a lightly settled trading hamlet surrounded by salt marsh. King Valdemar I, wanting to put an end to the free movement of marauding Wends who were staging frequent raids along the East Zealand coast, turned the area over to his close friend and 'blood brother', Bishop Absalon of Roskilde (Valdemar was raised by Absalon's father, Asser Rig, after Valdemar's own father was killed a week after he was born). Absalon, who was from one of Zealand's most prominent families, was not only a religious leader but also a successful military commander. He had spent time studying in Paris (a popular custom for the sons of powerful families of the time), although he did not have a reputation as a great scholar.

The city of Copenhagen dates its founding to 1167, when Absalon constructed a fortress on Slotsholmen Island, fortifying the previously unprotected harbourside village with ramparts and a moat. At the time, the town was known as *Havn,* meaning 'haven' or 'harbour'. Under the guidance of Absalon, a series of successful crusades into eastern Germany were launched against the Wends, and the town developed as a trading station.

In the years that followed, the harbourside village expanded and took on the name Købmandshavn (Merchant's Port), which over time was condensed to København. The port did much of its trade in salted herring, which was in high demand, in part due to the religious restrictions against eating meat during Catholic holy days, such as Lent. The supply of herring in Øresund was bountiful, and it's not far-fetched to say the city owed much of its prosperity to this oily fish.

Perched on the edge of the Baltic Sea and just across the sound from Sweden, Copenhagen grew in importance as a regional trading centre. Its success made it a target of the powerful Hanseatic League, the northern German traders who dominated Baltic commerce. The league attacked Copenhagen several times, and Absalon's fortress was destroyed during a particularly fierce battle in 1369. To stop the raids, the Danish Crown agreed to pay an annual ransom and give the league a voice in Danish affairs.

1596	1650	1711	1728
Christian IV is crowned.	Copenhagen's population reaches 30,000.	Plague strikes – over 20,000 perish.	Fire ravages the city.

In 1376 construction began on a new Slotsholmen fortification, Copenhagen Castle. In the years that followed, the Crown wrested control of the city from the Church. In 1416 King Erik of Pomerania (who enjoyed a reputation as an extremely handsome, flaxen-haired, ruddy-cheeked chap) took up residence at the castle, marking the beginning of Copenhagen's role as the capital of Denmark. He also moved the headquarters of his navy and army to Copenhagen.

During this era the Danish Crown convinced Norway and Sweden to join Denmark in an alliance known as the Kalmar Union. A primary objective of the union was to counter the influence of the powerful Hanseatic League. The Danish monarchy, which by marriage had intertwined royal ties with the other two countries, headed the union. In essence the union made Copenhagen not only capital of Denmark but of the tricountry Kalmar Union as well.

One unpopular move by Eric was the imposition of the 'Sound Dues' – a toll on all who entered Øresund, one of Europe's busiest shipping channels. Since southern

Statue of Bishop Absalon (p63)

Sweden (Scania) was essentially under Danish control at the time, this meant that a great deal of money came into Denmark, and that a great deal of Swedish resentment was banked by the residents of Scania. The toll stayed in place for over 400 years, and one of the collecting depots was the famous Kronborg Slot (p176), although the present edifice is the result of 16th-century work.

Erik of Pomerania also had a penchant for appointing Danes to public offices in Sweden and Norway, which soured native aristocrats in those countries. In 1438 the Swedish council withdrew from the union, whereupon the Danish nobility deposed Erik.

Erik's successor, the Danish king Christopher III, made amends and was accepted as king by both Norway and Sweden. The union continued to be a rocky one, however, marred by Swedish rebellions and a few fully fledged wars between Denmark and Sweden. In 1523 the Swedes elected their own king, Gustav Vasa, and the Kalmar Union was permanently dissolved. Norway, however, remained under Danish rule for another three centuries.

Reformation & Civil War

A pivotal power struggle involving the monarchy and the Catholic Church was played out during the Danish Reformation. Frederik I ascended the throne in 1523, promising to fight heresy against Catholicism, but in an attempt to weaken the influence of Danish bishops he switched course and instead invited Lutheran preachers to Denmark. Their fiery messages against the corrupt power of the Catholic Church, which over the centuries had accumulated an ungodly amount of property and wealth, found a ready ear among the disenchanted.

1775	1795	1801	1805
Royal Copenhagen Porcelain Manufactory is founded.	Fire ravages the city again!	British attack.	August Bournonville born in Copenhagen.

The king governed in consultation with the Rigsråd, a powerful national council comprised of nobles and bishops. After Frederik I died in 1533, the Catholic majority in the Rigsråd postponed the election of a new king, afraid that heir-apparent Prince Christian, Frederik's eldest son and a declared Lutheran, would favour the further spread of Lutheranism. Instead, they attempted to position Christian's younger brother Hans as a candidate for the throne.

The country, already strained by social unrest, erupted into civil war in 1534. Mercenaries from the Hanseatic city of Lübeck, which hoped to gain control of Baltic trade by allying with Danish merchants against the Danish nobility, took advantage of the situation and invaded Denmark. By and large the Lübeckers were welcomed as liberators by peasants and members of the middle class.

Alarmed by the revolt against the nobility, the Rigsråd now threw its support behind Prince Christian and his skilful general, Johan Rantzau. Even the Catholic bishops, who realised the coronation of Christian would signal the end of the Catholic Church in Denmark, felt compelled to add their support rather than face the consequences of a peasant uprising. In 1534 the prince was crowned King Christian III.

The rebellion raged strongest in the countryside, where manor houses were set ablaze and the peasants made advances against the armies of the aristocracy. Rantzau took control and quickly secured Denmark's southern border by cutting Lübeck off from the sea. He then swept north through the countryside, smashing the peasant bands in brutal fighting.

Copenhagen, whose merchants supported the uprising and the idea of becoming a Hanseatic stronghold, was besieged by Rantzau's troops for more than a year. Totally cut off from the outside world, Copenhagen's citizens suffered widespread starvation and epidemics before finally surrendering in the summer of 1536, marking the end of the civil war.

With the war's end, Christian III took advantage of the opportunity to consolidate his power. He took a surprisingly lenient approach to the Copenhagen merchants and burghers who had revolted, and in turn they now pledged their allegiance to the Crown, seeing opportunities for themselves in a stabilised Denmark. The Catholic bishops, however, were arrested, and monasteries, churches and other ecclesiastical estates became the property of the Crown.

The Danish Lutheran Church was established as the only state-sanctioned denomination and was placed under the direct control of the king. For all practical purposes the church officials, appointed at the whim of the king, now became civil servants – reliant upon the government for approval of their actions and for financial support.

Sharing power only with the nobility, the monarchy emerged from the civil war stronger than ever, buoyed by a treasury that was greatly enriched by the confiscated church properties.

Copenhagen Comes of Age

It was during the reign of Christian IV (1588–1648) that Copenhagen was endowed with much of its splendour – so much so that the king is sometimes referred to as the second founder of the city.

Christian IV ascended the throne at the age of 10 and ruled for more than 50 years. When he took power, Denmark held a firm grip on Baltic trade, providing strong export markets for Danish agricultural products and reaping handsome profits for landowners and merchants. With a robust economy and a seemingly boundless treasury at hand, the ambitious king established trading companies and a stock exchange, using this wealth to build new Renaissance cities, castles and fortresses throughout his kingdom.

1807	1819	1843	1853
British attack again!	Hans Christian Andersen arrives in the city as a stowaway from Odense.	Tivoli opens.	Cholera epidemic – 5000 perish.

Rundetårn (p58)

Many of Copenhagen's most lavish buildings were erected during Christian IV's reign. The king also extended the city significantly, developing the district of Christianshavn, which he skilfully modelled on Amsterdam. Among the many grand buildings that have survived through the centuries are Børsen, the ornately embellished stock-exchange building; Rosenborg Slot (p84), the king's Dutch Renaissance summer home; and the Rundetårn (p58), Europe's oldest astronomical observatory.

Unfortunately, the king's foreign policies weren't nearly as brilliant as his domestic undertakings. When the Swedes began to vie for greater influence in the Baltic, Christian IV, hoping to neutralise Swedish expansion, dragged Denmark into a protracted struggle that came to be known as the Thirty Years' War.

The war drained Danish resources and resulted in substantial territorial losses for Denmark. The king himself, always anxious to be in the midst of the action, lost an eye to shrapnel when his flagship was attacked in battle. In a treaty in 1645, signed after a Swedish invasion of Denmark, the Baltic island of Gotland and two Norwegian provinces were handed over to the Swedes, while a second treaty signed in 1648 relinquished Denmark's southern territories.

In 1655 the Swedish king invaded Poland and, although the victory was swift, the Swedes found themselves bogged down trying to secure that vast country. Word of the Swedish troubles ignited nationalistic fervour throughout a Denmark that was seething for revenge.

In 1657, Christian IV's successor, Frederik III, hoping to take advantage of the Polish situation, once again declared war on the Swedes. For the Danish government, itself ill-prepared for battle, it was a tremendous miscalculation.

Sweden's King Karl X Gustav, looking for an honourable way out of war-ravaged Poland, which had already been pillaged to the limit, gladly withdrew and readied his forces for an invasion of Denmark. He led his troops through Germany and into Denmark's Jutland peninsula, plundering his way north.

In the winter of 1657–58 – the most severe winter in Danish history – King Karl X Gustav marched his soldiers across the frozen seas of the Lille Bælt between Jutland and the island of Funen. His uncanny success unnerved the Danes and he proceeded without serious resistance across the similarly frozen Store Bælt to the islands of Lolland and Falster.

The Swedish king had barely made it across the frozen waters of Storstrømmen to Zealand when the thawing ice broke behind him, separating Gustav and his advance detachment from the main body of his forces.

However, the Danes, who had amassed most of their troops in Zealand to protect Copenhagen, were in such a state of panic that they failed to recognise their sudden military advantage. Instead of capturing the Swedish king, they sued for peace and agreed to yet another disastrous treaty.

On 26 February 1658 the Treaty of Roskilde, the most lamented treaty in Denmark's history, was signed. The territorial losses were staggering, with Denmark's borders shrinking by one-third.

1892	1904	1908	1924
Electricity comes to Copenhagen.	George Jensen opens his first shop on Bredgade.	Women allowed to vote in local elections.	Architect Kaare Klint becomes lecturer in Furniture Design at Copenhagen's Royal Academy of Fine Arts.

Rampant Ramparts

In the early 1600s, Christian IV, intent on protecting his growing capital from outside siege, started work on a ring fortress consisting of earthen ramparts, moats and bastions. This ring fortress, also referred to as the city wall, extended some 10km in circumference and defined Copenhagen's boundaries. For two centuries it proved effective in warding off sieges, but with the devastating British naval attack of 1807, launched with cannon volleys from the harbour, it was clear that the ramparts offered little protection against the powerful new weapons of the day.

In addition to losing their military value, the ramparts restricted the growth of the city, resulting in crowded, unsanitary conditions. During the 1850s work began on demolishing the ramparts and the city quickly expanded its boundaries beyond the old fortifications.

Today the ramparts remain intact only at Kastellet (Map pp236–7), the citadel at the northern side of the city centre, and along the outer canal of Christianshavn (Map pp232–4).

Remnants of the western portion of the ramparts have been incorporated into a curving arc of public parks: Østre Anlæg, Botanisk Have and Ørstedsparken. The lakes found in these parks were once part of the moat system.

No Smoke Without Fire

In spite of all the military setbacks, international trade continued to flourish and Copenhagen became the home port to one of the largest merchant fleets in Europe. The ships, which travelled far and wide, not only returned with great wealth for Copenhagen's trading companies, but unavoidably served as carriers for pestilence as well. In 1711 an outbreak of the bubonic plague hit the city, reducing Copenhagen's population by a third.

In 1728 a sweeping fire razed most of Copenhagen's medieval buildings, levelling one-third of the city, including the centre of government, Copenhagen Castle. A new and grander edifice, Christiansborg Slot, was built to replace it, and the city began to rebuild. Then in 1795 a second fire ravaged the city's remaining timber buildings, destroying the final remnants of Absalon's medieval town and the new Christianborg Slot as well.

Copenhagen recovered from this fire only to find itself getting caught up in international strife. Britain, which dominated the seas, was not altogether keen on the growth of Denmark's foreign trade. In 1800, trying to counter potential threats posed by the British, Denmark signed a pact of armed neutrality with Sweden, Prussia and Russia. Britain regarded the act as hostile and in 1801 sent a naval expedition to attack Copenhagen, inflicting heavy damage on the Danish fleet and forcing Denmark to withdraw from the pact.

Denmark managed to avoid further conflicts and Copenhagen merchants actually profited from war trade until 1807, when a new treaty between France and Russia once again drew the Danes closer to the conflict. The British, weary of Napoleon's growing influence in the Baltic, feared, without solid grounds, that the Danes might soon be convinced to place their fleet at the disposal of the French.

In September 1807, without attempting diplomacy, a British fleet unleashed a brutal bombardment upon neutral Copenhagen. The attack targeted the city's heart, inflicting many civilian casualties and setting hundreds of homes, churches and public buildings ablaze.

The British then proceeded to confiscate the entire Danish fleet, sailing away with nearly 170 gunboats, frigates, transports and sloops. Ironically, the only ship left afloat in Copenhagen harbour was a private yacht that the king of England had bestowed upon his nephew, Denmark's Crown Prince Frederik, two decades earlier.

In October 1807 the Danes, incensed by the assault, joined the continental alliance against Britain. In turn, Britain blockaded Danish waters, crippling its economy. When Napoleon fell in 1814 the Swedes, by then allied with Britain, successfully demanded that Denmark cede Norway to them.

1940	1945	1960	1967
Germany invades; Queen Margrethe II born.	The city is liberated by Field Marshall Montgomery on 4 May.	Copenhagen's first skyscraper, designed by Arne Jacobsen, is constructed.	Pornography is legalised.

The Golden Age

Although the 19th century started out dismal and lean, by the 1830s Copenhagen had awakened to a cultural revolution in the arts, philosophy and literature. The times gave rise to such prominent figures as philosopher Søren Kierkegaard, theologian Nikolaj Frederik Severin Grundtvig and writer Hans Christian Andersen. It was the 'Golden Age' of the arts, with sculptor Bertel Thorvaldsen bestowing his grand neoclassical statues on Copenhagen while painter Christoffer Wilhelm Eckersberg introduced a new art movement to the city.

Spurred on by new ideas and the rising expectations of a growing middle class, the absolute rule of the Crown was challenged by an unprecedented interest in democratic principles. The powers of the monarchy were already on the wane when revolution swept across the continent from Paris to Germany in the spring of 1848. In its wake Denmark adopted its first democratic constitution. Enacted on 5 June 1849, it established a parliament with two chambers, Folketing and Landsting, whose members were elected by popular vote.

Although the king retained a limited voice, legislative powers shifted to the parliament. An independent judiciary was established and citizens were guaranteed the rights of free speech, religion and assembly. Denmark changed overnight from a virtual dictatorship to one of the most democratic countries in Europe.

At the same time Copenhagen, which had previously been under royal administration, was granted the right to form a municipal council. Industry flourished in the last half of the 19th century, bringing a wave of new workers from the countryside into the capital. A labour movement developed and by the 1870s many of the city's workplaces had begun to unionise. Copenhagen's boundaries were extended into the districts of Østerbro, Vesterbro and Nørrebro to accommodate the city's growth and the new working class.

20th-Century Advances

The growth of industrialisation had a major impact on national politics, with old power bases losing ground to new urban movements. In 1901 Denmark's conservative landowners, who had long held a stranglehold on national government, were ousted by the Left Reform Party.

The party completed a number of broad-minded reforms, most notably applying the progressive principles of NFS Grundtvig to the educational system and amending the constitution in 1915 to extend national voting rights to women.

With universal suffrage, the political landscape changed dramatically. The union movement and the growing mass of industrial workers organised themselves politically and formed the Social Democratic Party, which quickly became Denmark's largest party and leading political force.

Denmark remained neutral during WWI and in the period between the two world wars, under the leadership of the Social Democratic Party, the government passed landmark legislation that not only softened the effects of the Great Depression but also laid the foundations for a welfare state.

WWII

Denmark again declared its neutrality at the outbreak of WWII but, with the growing Allied presence in Norway, Germany became intent on acquiring advance coastal bases in northern Jutland.

In the early hours of 9 April 1940 the Germans crossed the frontier in southern Jutland and simultaneously landed troops at strategic points throughout Denmark. A military airfield in

1971	1992	1995	1996
The Free State of Christiania is established.	Denmark wins the European Championship – Copenhagen gives the football team a heroes' welcome.	Dogme '95 is unleashed.	Copenhagen is named European Cultural Capital.

A Right Royal Scandal

One of the more curious political players of the 18th century was not a Danish king but a German doctor named Johan Struensee. In 1768 Struensee was appointed court physician to King Christian VII, who suffered from bouts of insanity. The doctor managed to win favour both with the ailing king, who granted Struensee broad powers of state, and with the 18-year-old queen, Caroline Matilda, who became Struensee's lover.

Emboldened by his assumed powers, the 34-year-old physician dismissed the prime minister and, over the next 16 months, succeeded in proclaiming some 2000 decrees in the name of the monarch. Contemptuous of the aristocracy, Struensee applied the same laws for all citizens across class lines. The exploitation of peasants for the benefit of landlords was restricted and ill treatment in prisons, orphanages and poorhouses was outlawed. Trade barriers were lifted and money from the king's treasury was transferred to public sources for the support of new social endeavours.

Unfortunately for Struensee he was ahead of his time – the French Revolution that would stir similar passions was still some 20 years away. Instead of broad support, Struensee elicited widespread resentment that was inflamed by unfounded rumours of his ill treatment of the ailing king. In actuality, however, it seems that the mad king had taken some comfort in being relieved of both his stately and marital duties.

In January 1772 a coup d'état was instigated at a palace ball and the conspirators, led by the queen mother, forced the king to sign a statement against Struensee, who was being arrested elsewhere in the palace. Unable to prove that Struensee had forcibly taken control of the government, or even that he had been corrupt, the court instead condemned him to death for his illicit relations with the young queen, which it ruled to be lese-majesty.

The queen, incidentally, had her marriage dissolved by a special court and was subsequently taken by a British frigate to England to live on the estate of her brother, King George III. Forbidden to take her young daughter (who was deemed Christian VII's heir although fathered by Struensee) with her to England, Caroline Matilda died a broken woman at the age of 24.

Copenhagen was attacked and commandos landed in the city, promptly taking Kastellet, the citadel that served as a headquarters for the Danish military.

The German troops proceeded to the royal family's residence, Amalienborg Slot, where they met resistance from the royal guards. In the meantime the German envoy delivered an ultimatum, warning that if the Danes resisted Copenhagen would be bombed.

With German warplanes flying overhead, Christian X and parliamentary heads hastily met at Amalienborg and decided to yield, under protest, to the Germans. The Danish government gained assurances from the Nazis that Denmark would be allowed to retain a degree of internal autonomy.

The Danes, with only nominal military forces, had no capacity to ward off a German attack and little alternative but to submit. In all, the lightning blow lasted only a matter of hours, and before nightfall Denmark was an occupied country.

For three years the Danes managed to tread a thin line, basically running their own domestic affairs but doing so under Nazi supervision, until August 1943 when the Germans took outright control. The Danish Resistance movement quickly mushroomed. In October 1943, as the Nazis were preparing to round up Jewish Danes, the Resistance used night-running fishing boats to quickly smuggle 7000 Jews (some 95% of those remaining in Denmark) from Zealand into neutral Sweden.

During the occupation, King Christian X became an important and much-loved symbol of stability, stoicism and continuity to the city, as he continued to take his daily constitutional walk or ride through the city centre. His presence boosted morale and the naming of his granddaughter Margrethe recalled the strength of Queen Margrethe and her victory over the Germans in the 14th century.

Despite the occupation, Copenhagen and the rest of Denmark emerged from WWII relatively unscathed.

2000	2002	2004	2005
The Øresund bridge is opened.	Denmark assumes presidency of EU; the city's new Metro system opens.	Crown Prince Frederik marries Australian-born Mary Donaldson.	200th anniversary of Hans Christian Andersen's birth; 150th anniversary of Søren Kierkegaard's death; 120th anniversary of Karen Blixen's birth.

Neighbourhoods

Neighbourhoods

Compact in size, flat as a tack and organised by Danes, Copenhagen is a very good place to find yourself (in the enjoyable sense, not the spiritual sense) as a visitor. Everything is within easy reach, thanks to the city's manageable layout and the excellent transport network that helps you gain access to the city's wealth of palaces, galleries, museums, parks, waterways, beaches and beautiful streets. And thanks to sensible policies on preservation, Copenhagen retains many of its historical buildings (despite bad luck with fire), meaning that even the exteriors of many attractions are sights in themselves. You'll find any number of ways to fill your timetable – from frantic dashes to all the city has to offer to lounging outdoors and admiring the passing traffic (generally bicycle-powered). Another bonus is that you'll get to mix with Danes – who love taking advantage of all that their capital has to offer.

ITINERARIES

One Day

You'll be wanting the stars of the show for this one, so in the morning head straight to the Statens Museum for Kunst (p84) for a massive dose of fine art, before catching the swanky new metro from Nørreport to Kongens Nytorv (p66), from where you can proceed on foot to Nyhavn (p64) and enjoy a drink and the easy-going waterside atmosphere of this vibrantly painted canal street. For lunch, a trip to Ida Davidsen (p113) is a must – yes, it's a little touristy, but the *smørrebrød* is mouth-watering and the menu is longer than your arm. Re-enter the impressively grand Kongens Nytorv before heading down pedestrianised Strøget (p58), where a spot of shopping might beckon. At the end of the mall, cross massive Rådhuspladsen (p55) and head down Vesterbrogade to Tivoli (p55), where you can take in the rides, the lights and, hopefully, the fireworks.

Three Days

On your second day in the city, marvel at the Gauguins and other French masterpieces at the Ny Carlsberg Glyptotek (p53) before strolling to that modern architectural masterpiece Det Kongelige Bibliotek (p62), where you may want to enjoy lunch at Søren K (p112), which has some great water views of the harbour and of other exciting modern buildings on Christianshavn. From there, head over the eye-catching, copper-clad Knippelsbro (p78) to Christianshavn (p76), where you may want to visit Christiania (p77) or just spend time admiring this charming island suburb. At 5pm, head to the box office of Det Kongelige Teater (p125) and pick up half-price tickets to whatever's on that night before dining at Sushitarian (p110) – the best sushi in town.

On your third day you can give in and head to Copenhagen's cheesiest attraction, the Little Mermaid (p65) before taking a stroll around Kastellet (p64). From there, head down Bredgade (p147) for a quick tour of Copenhagen's most fabulous design and decorative-art shops. In the afternoon, catch a train to Louisiana (p175), one of the world's premier modern-art museums.

One Week

Take in all of the above, but be sure to add churches such as Marmorkirken (p75), Vor Frue Kirke (p59) and Vor Frelsers Kirke (p79). Also visit Nationalmuseet (p53) and attractions on Slotsholmen (p60) such as the Christiansborg Slot (p61). Other royal attractions that warrant a look include Amalienborg Slot (p65) and Rosenborg Slot (p84). Wander into charming Frederiksberg (p87) to visit the zoo (p88) and the Carlsberg Visitors Centre (p88), and head out of town to see Arken (p94) at Ishøj and Dragør (p94). If you're visiting during summer and the weather's sunny, you'll find a dip at **Islands Brygge Havnebadet** (p89) is a novel experience. Shopping sprees around the **Latin Quarter** (p142) or along **Istedgade** (p149) or **Ravnsborggade** (p101) are also worth squeezing in.

Copenhagen for Kids Top Five

Hey – a city with one of the world's most-loved amusement parks at its centre has got to be child-friendly...

- **Tivoli** (p55) For kids big and small, and a rite of passage for all Danish youngsters
- **Experimentarium** (p90) Educational and exciting, with plenty of hands-on exhibits
- **Guinness World of Records Museum** (p57) Teeming with youthful record-spotters
- **Ripley's Believe it or Not! Museum** (p54) Kinda cheesy, but also appealing to the freak-show fan in all of us
- **Louis Tussaud's Wax Museum** (p53) Kids seem to love this sort of thing, and many of the depictions are so bad that adults will be laughing in no time

---

ORGANISED TOURS

Copenhagen is so easy to get around that there's little need to consider a sightseeing tour, although they can be a good way to cram in the sights easily, and save yourself the odd blister due to too many wrong turns or a bad bike seat.

Bus Tours

COPENHAGEN CITY SIGHTSEEING

☎ 32 66 00 00; www.citysightseeing.dk; departures from Rådhuspladsen; from adult/child 120/60kr; departures btwn 9.45am & 4.15pm

Many cities have a hop-on/hop-off red double-decker bus tour operator, and Copenhagen is no different. Options manage to include the most popular sites and sights in the city. If you buy a 140kr 'all-line' ticket, you can take part in every tour on offer over two days, which is handy if you're short on time. Multilingual recordings make sure everyone gets the picture.

COPENHAGEN EXCURSIONS

☎ 32 54 06 06; www.cex.dk; departures from Rådhuspladsen; from adult/child 130/65kr; ☉ year-round

This reputable firm offers guided tours (1½ to 2½ hours) of the city. The well-maintained modern buses cruise by some of the main sights, such as Amalienborg Slot, Slotsholmen, the Little Mermaid and Nyhavn. Excursions out of the city are also available (to Hamlet's castle etc) – check the website for more details.

COPENHAGEN VINTAGE EXPERIENCE

☎ 38 10 20 48; www.vico.dk; Rentemestervej 25A; 1hr tour max 15 people 2800kr, private tour max 4 people per hr 680kr; ☉ departures 9.30am, 11.30am & 1.30pm May-Sep

A pricey way to explore the city even if you're part of a group, but lovers of vintage vehicles will get a kick out of cruising Copenhagen in style. Sights include the Little Mermaid, Nyhavn, and Amalienborg and Christiansborg palaces. English is spoken.

Boat & Kayak Tours

For a different angle on the city, hop aboard one of the boat tours that wind through Copenhagen's canals. Although most of the passengers are usually Danes, multilingual guides give a lively commentary in English as well.

All the boat tours follow a similar route, passing by Slotsholmen, Christianshavn and the Little Mermaid.

COPENHAGEN ADVENTURE TOURS

Map p231

☎ 40 50 40 06; www.kajakole.dk; Gammel Strand 50; tickets 165-210kr; ☉ 1 May-1 Oct

Multilingual sightseeing tours with a (shoulder) twist are available from this energetic company. You'll need to be reasonably fit to tackle this, but they are fun and offer some fabulous views.

DFDS CANAL TOURS Map pp239-41

☎ 33 42 33 20; www.canaltours.com; 50-min tours from adult/child 50/20kr; ☉ 10am-5pm late Mar–mid-Dec

DFDS, the biggest company of this kind, operates boats that leave approximately twice an hour from two locations – one at the head of Nyhavn and the other on Gammel Strand, north of Slotsholmen (see the Slotsholmen map, p231). The tours are both enjoyable and informative.

Copenhagen for Free

In egalitarian Denmark some of the finest things in life are free – at least one day a week – so you might want to plan your museum browsing accordingly.

Every Wednesday, Statens Museum of Kunst (p84), Nationalmuseet (p53), Den Hirschsprungske Samling (p83), Post & Tele Museum (p58), Geologisk Museum (p83), Thorvaldsens Museum (p63), Frilandsmuseet (p93) Frihedsmuseet (p66) and Ny Carlsberg Glyptotek (p53) turn off their cash registers and open their doors gratis to all. Ny Carlsberg Glyptotek is also free on Sunday.

Københavns Bymuseum (p87) is free on Friday. In addition, there are a handful of Copenhagen museums that never charge for admission: Davids Samling (p83), Georg Jensen (p144), B & W Museum (p77), WØ Larsen Tobacco Museum (p59) and the Botanisk Museum (p82).

Of course, the city's lovely parks and gardens, including the botanical garden with its tropical Palmehus (p82), are free for strolling every day. Copenhagen churches are also free of entrance charges and some, such as the city's cathedral, Vor Frue Kirke (p59), are virtual museums unto themselves. Also free, all the time, are Assistens Kirkegård (p80), Christiania (p77), Folketinget (p62) and Kastellet (p64). If free beer gets you going, then a visit to the Carlsberg Visitors Centre (p88) is a must.

DFDS WATERBUS Map pp232-4

☎ 33 42 33 20; www.canaltours.com; ticket adult/child 30/20kr, day pass adult/child 45/20kr; ⏱ 10.15am-4.45pm 7 May-5 Sep, to 5.45pm 18 Jun-22 Aug

DFDS Canal Tours operates a summertime 'waterbus' that runs along a route similar to its guided tours but has no commentary. These boats leave Nyhavn every 30 minutes and make 10 stops, including Slotsholmen, Christianshavn and the Little Mermaid. A day pass allows you to get on and off as often as you like.

NETTO-BÅDENE Map p231

☎ 32 54 41 02; www.havnerundfart.dk; Holmens Kirke jetty; 1hr tour adult/child 25/10kr; ⏱ 10am-5pm mid-Apr–mid-Oct

A better deal than many organised tours of this kind is this local operator, whose cruises, which last an hour, leave from Holmens Kirke, east of Slotsholmen (see the Slotsholmen map, p231), as well as from Nyhavn, between two and five times an hour, with the greatest frequency in the summer high season.

Walking Tours

COPENHAGEN EXCURSIONS

☎ 32 54 06 06; www.cex.dk; departures from Rådhuspladsen; adult/child 70/35kr; ⏱ 11.15am Tue, Thu, Sat & Sun 1 Jul-31 Aug

This reliable company offers chatty 1½-hour strolls through Copenhagen's medieval quarter, with time to sit down and watch the world go by in various squares.

COPENHAGEN HISTORY TOURS

☎ 28 49 44 35; www.copenhagenhistorytours.dk; departures from Højbro Plads; 70kr; ⏱ 10am Sat & Sun; metro Kongens Nytorv, bus Nos 1A, 2A, 650S

These informative English-language tours depart from under the statue of Bishop Absalon at the top of Strøget. The Saturday tour covers Copenhagen in the 17th and 18th centuries, while the Sunday tour covers the city from the 19th century to the present day. Tours last between one hour and 1½ hours.

COPENHAGEN WALKING TOURS

☎ 40 81 12 17; www.copenhagen-walkingtours.dk; Vesterbroggade 4A; 100kr; ⏱ 11am Sat & Sun; S-train Vesterport or Central Station, bus No 6A

This tour follows the footsteps of Hans Christian Andersen, allowing tourists to learn more about his life and times, and also gain a real feel for Copenhagen life, past and present. There's no need to book – simply show up at the tourist office and look for a red-suited guide.

THE OLD NIGHT WATCHMAN

☎ 39 64 48 94; www.viseknud.dk; Gråbrødretorv; 40kr; ⏱ 9pm Thu-Sat 29 May-30 Aug; metro Kongens Nytorv, bus Nos 1A, 6A, 350S

Dressed in period clothing (from the early 19th century – the time of Frederik VI's reign), the old night watchman takes tourists (no booking needed) through the historic streets of the city, with commentary and song in both Danish and English. Tours last about 1½ hours. Meet at 9pm at Gråbrødretorv, the small square fronting Peder Oxe restaurant.

ROSENBORG SLOT TOUR

☎ 40 81 12 17; www.copenhagen-walkingtours.dk; departures from castle ticket office; 50kr; ⊙ 1pm Sat-Mon 15 May-15 Sep; metro & S-train Nørreport, bus Nos 5A, 6A, 150S, 350S

If you would like to learn a little more about this fascinating and beautiful Dutch Renaissance–style castle, built as a summer home by Christian IV, give these hour-long English-language tours a try. Not only are the tours convenient (there is no need to book, you can simply show up and hand your money over to the red-jacketed guide), but they are also educational. Admission to the castle is not included in the tour price. The tours need a minimum of five people in order to run.

Museum Tours

HANS CHRISTIAN ANDERSEN NATIONALMUSEET TOUR

☎ 32 84 74 35; www.copenhagenwalks.dk; departures from Nationalmuseet; 50kr; ⊙ 1.30pm Wed & Sat 10 May-18 Sep; bus Nos 1A, 2A, 5A, 650S

An excellent way to make a trip to National-museet come alive is to show up for this guided tour (why it's hosted by Mr Andersen, we're not entirely sure). He'll explain history, culture and geography over the course of an hour. Museum entry is not included in the price. A similar tour is offered at Thorvaldsens Museum (p63) at 1.30pm Tuesday and Friday from 10 May to 18 September.

RÅDHUSPLADSEN & TIVOLI

Eating p105; Shopping p141; Sleeping p155

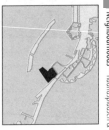

Neighbourhoods – Rådhuspladsen & Tivoli

A first glance at Rådhuspladsen (especially on an overcast day) will not bring to mind the idea that this area contains some appealing family-friendly attractions, but this area marks the start of the bustling shopping street Strøget at the northeast side of the square and the famed amusement park Tivoli glitters in the southwest. The sort of place that seems eerily deserted early in the morning and late at night, Rådhuspladsen picks up speed when peak-hour traffic starts whizzing past and its role as a transport hub shows you just how many people use public transport in this car-unfriendly city.

It may not pack the political punch of Slotsholmen either, but it does mark the site of Rådhuset (the City Hall), where local politicians keep the wheels in motion to run this most efficient and well-organised of cities. The square itself is surrounded by large-scale, imposing edifices dedicated to business, culture and tourism, with a blend of 19th-century flourishes and 20th-century solidity. At night when the neon advertisements flicker into life around the square you could almost be forgiven for thinking that there's a competition taking place between here and the illuminated extravaganza at Tivoli. It's Piccadilly Circus with elbow room, Times Square without the cheap sleaze.

The area is an appealing mix of cheesy tourist tack (Guinness World of Records, Louis Tussaud's) and highbrow pleasures (Ny Carlsberg Glyptotek, Nationalmuseet), plus a few quintessentially iconic statues thrown in to remind you that you're in Copenhagen.

Orientation

This busy area holds the large public space of Rådhuspladsen, which is contained between the parallel thoroughfares of Vester Voldgade and HC Andersens Blvd. Important central streets that radiate from the square include traffic-clogged Vesterbrogade, which heads to Vesterbro, and pedestrian-clogged Frederiksberggade, which doesn't head to Frederiksberg at all – it marks the start of pedestrian-clogged Strøget and the Latin Quarter (p56).

Glittering Tivoli is bordered by Vesterbrogade to the north, Tietgensgade to the south and HC Andersens Blvd and Bernstorffsgade on either side. Across Bernstorffsgade lies Hovedbanegården (Central Station), which marks the end of this area and the start of southern Vesterbro. Sydhavn, the harbour running to Blvd Langebro, marks a natural boundary to the area, as does the canal that separates this particular area from the island of Slotsholmen (p60).

Rådhuspladsen (p55)

The streets southwest of Stormgade (containing Nationalmuseet) are also included in our breakdown for this guide, while to the north of Tivoli, we've included the busy station of Vesterport and its surrounding streets to the man-made lake called Sankt Jørgens Sø, which flows to Kampmannsgade.

DANSK DESIGN CENTER Map pp232-4

☎ 33 69 33 69; www.ddc.dk; HC Andersens Blvd 27; adult/pensioner/student 40/20/25kr; ⏰ 10am-5pm Mon, Tue, Thu & Fri, 10am-9pm Wed, 11am-4pm Sat & Sun; train Central Station, bus Nos 2A, 5A, 6A, 250S, among others

The Dansk Design Center opened in 2000 as a place to display Danish industrial design alongside international design trends. And you may as well face it – spaces like this are only going to highlight how unbearably cluttered and poorly designed your own living space is.

The five-storey building was designed by senior Danish architect Henning Larsen (see p35) and incorporates a double-glass wall of windows. Larsen originally intended for the windows to hold a layer of liquid crystal that would allow the building's streetside exterior to act as a huge video screen, but to his chagrin that concept was axed as too costly.

The centre has a dual function, providing a meeting place for people in the field of design, as well as display space for exhibitions. The ground floor holds an exhibit of classic Danish chairs (chairs are one of the Danes' great obsessions), while upstairs are changing exhibits on topics such as the development of fashion trends and the history of the avant-garde audiovisual company Bang & Olufsen. There's a handy **café** (p107) on site and a natty little gift shop, with the focus on items that marry form and function for the traveller.

JENS OLSENS CLOCK Map pp239-41

☎ 33 66 25 82; www.copenhagencity.dk; Rådhus, Rådhuspladsen; adult/child 10/5kr; ⏰ 8.30am-4.30pm Mon-Fri, 10am-1pm Sat; train Central Station, bus Nos 2A, 5A, 6A, 250S, among others

This elaborate clock, designed by Danish astro-mechanic Jens Olsen (1872–1945) and built at a cost of one million kroner, is of special note to chronometer buffs. The clock, which lays bare its extraordinarily complicated machinations, is unlike any other timepiece you'll ever see – and worth making time for (ahem). It displays not only the local time, but also solar time, sidereal time, sunrises and sunsets, firmament and celestial pole migration, planet revolutions, the Gregorian calendar and even changing holidays, such as Easter. Of its numerous wheels, the fastest turns once every 10 seconds, while the slowest will finish its first revolution after 25,753 years. It may sound time-consuming, but it's actually rather hypnotic. The clock was first put into motion in 1955 and its weights are wound weekly. It can be viewed in a side room off the foyer of Rådhuset (the City Hall).

LOUIS TUSSAUD'S WAX MUSEUM
Map pp232-4

☎ 33 11 89 00; www.tussaud.dk; HC Andersens Blvd 22; adult/child 79/34kr; ☀ 10am-11pm mid-Apr–mid-Sep, 10am-6pm mid-Sep–mid-Apr; train Central Station, bus Nos 2A, 5A, 6A, 250S, among others

What can we possibly tell you about this place that the name hasn't already given away? At this wax museum, celebrities such as Elvis, Clint Eastwood and Frankenstein can be found in the company of Danish notables, including the royal family, Søren Kierkegaard and Karen Blixen. Young kids will enjoy the scenes from Hans Christian Andersen's Snow Queen, but then they'll have to make their way through the creepy house of horrors that wraps up the show. And adults will have to deal with the enormous sense of disappointment at forking out good cash for this least-imaginative form of tourist attraction.

NATIONALMUSEET Map pp232-4

☎ 33 13 44 11; www.natmus.dk; Ny Vestergade 10; adult/child 50kr/free, Wed free; ☀ 10am-5pm Tue-Sun; bus Nos 1A, 2A 5A, 650S

If you want to learn more about Danish history and culture, you couldn't do better than spending an afternoon at Nationalmuseet (the National Museum), opposite the western entrance to Slotsholmen.

Nationalmuseet has first claims on virtually every antiquity found on Danish soil, whether it be unearthed by a farmer ploughing his field or excavated in a government-sponsored archaeological dig. Consequently, this quality museum boasts the most extensive collection of Danish historical artefacts in the world. These relics range from the Upper Palaeolithic period to the 1840s and include Stone Age tools, Viking weaponry and impressive Bronze Age, Iron Age and rune-stone collections.

Don't miss the exhibit of bronze luren (horns), some of which date back 3000 years and are still capable of blowing a tune, and the finely crafted 3500-year-old Sun Chariot, unearthed in a Zealand field a century ago.

There are also sections on the Norsemen and the Inuit of Greenland, collections of solid

18th-century Danish furniture and a 'Please Touch' exhibit for sight-impaired visitors. And naturally, considering the Danes' fascination for playthings, the museum has a noteworthy collection of historic toys, which along with other fun items comprise a special children's wing, thus making this an excellent place to satisfy all age groups within a family.

The museum also includes a noteworthy numismatic collection, containing Greek, Roman and medieval coins, and a Classical Antiquities section complete with Egyptian mummies.

The museum has a café and gift shop, and ramps and lifts provide access for disabled visitors. Interpretive signs are in English as well as Danish.

The newest addition to Nationalmuseet is the Victorian Home, a c 1850 house just east of the main museum building. A flat in the home that was owned by a successful merchant has been preserved with its original furnishings and décor, encapsulating a slice of late-19th-century life. The kitchen has a peat-fired stove, the stairways are adorned with marble dadoes, and the woodwork and upholstery are classic patterns of their day. The Victorian Home can only be visited on a guided tour; there's no additional charge beyond Nationalmuseet's regular admission fee, but you must book ahead as the number of visitors is limited. Call the museum for more details.

Transport

Bus 1A, 2A, 5A, 6A, 10, 12, 14, 26, 29, 33, 48, 67, 68, 69, 173E, 250S, 650S
S-train Central Station or Vesterport
Parking Street parking costs 12kr per hour from 8am to 6pm Monday to Friday and 8am to 2pm Saturday

NY CARLSBERG GLYPTOTEK Map pp232-4

☎ 33 41 81 41; www.glyptoteket.dk; Tietgensgade 25; adult/child 20kr/free, Wed & Sun free; ☀ 10am-4pm Tue-Sun; train Central Station, bus Nos 2A, 5A, 6A, 250S, among others

This exceptional museum on HC Andersens Blvd, southeast of Tivoli, has a superb collection of Greek, Egyptian, Etruscan and Roman sculpture and art. It was built a century ago by beer baron Carl Jacobsen, an ardent collector of classical art. The museum's century-old main building, designed by Danish architect

Vilhelm Dahlerup, is built around a beautiful glass-domed conservatory replete with palm trees and Mediterranean greenery, creating an atmospheric complement to the antiquities collections it exhibits.

The museum's extensive sculpture displays are arranged to depict the history of Western sculpture from 3000 BC to the end of the Roman Empire. Particularly notable is the Greek collection – in terms of its breadth and calibre it's the finest in northern Europe.

Although Ny Carlsberg Glyptotek was originally, and primarily remains, dedicated to classical art, a later gift of more than 20 paintings by Paul Gauguin led to the formation of an impressive 19th-century French and Danish art collection. The Danish collection includes numerous works by JC Dahl, CW Eckersberg, Jens Juel and Christian Købke.

The French collection is centred on the Gauguin works, which now number 45. These are displayed alongside pieces by Cézanne, Van Gogh, Pissarro, Monet and Renoir in a wonderful new wing of the museum that opened in 1996. This 'French Wing' also boasts one of only three complete series of Degas bronzes – including his famous ballerina sculpture. There's also a rooftop area on the modern wing that offers some attractive views of the city.

A treat for off-season visitors are the chamber concerts given on Sundays from October to March in the museum's concert hall, which is lined by life-size statues of Roman patricians. And you won't have to pay a penny for this high-brow experience since the concerts, like Sunday admission itself, are gratis. At the time of research, the museum was undergoing extensive remodelling, with certain areas closed to the public until 28 June 2006.

RIPLEY'S BELIEVE IT OR NOT! MUSEUM Map pp239-41

☎ 33 91 89 91; Rådhuspladsen 57; adult/child 80/40kr; ☺ 10am-8pm 10-31 May, 9.30am-10pm 1 Jun-31 Aug, 10am-8pm 1-12 Sep, 10am-6pm Sun-Thu & 10am-8pm Fri & Sat 13 Sep-9 May, closed 1 Jan; train Central Station, bus Nos 2A, 5A, 6A, 250S, among others
This whacky (or just plain whack, depending on your age) museum displays the expected collection of unexpected oddities from all over the world (such as a six-legged calf) replicated in wax figures and tableaux. Revelling in its own outlandish clichés, this place gets packed with young folk, but is eminently missable once you've passed puberty.

Rådhuspladsen & Tivoli Top Five

- Getting the twinkle back in your eye as you watch the twinkling lights at **Tivoli** (opposite)
- Revelling in masterpieces by Gauguin, Monet and Pissarro at **Ny Carlsberg Glyptoteket** (p53)
- Watching the cogs turn at **Jens Olsens Clock** (p52)
- Ringing in the New Year with the whole city on **Rådhuspladsen** (opposite)
- Travelling back through time at **Nationalmuseet** (p53)

RÅDHUS Map pp232-4

admission free; ☺ 7.45am-5pm Mon-Fri; train Central Station, bus Nos 2A, 5A, 6A, 250S, among others
Copenhagen's grand red-brick city hall had its groundwork laid in 1892 and was completed in 1905. Designed by the Danish architect Martin Nyrop, it reflects many of the trends of its period, displaying elements of 19th-century national Romanticism, medieval Danish design and northern Italian architecture, the last-mentioned most notable in its central courtyard.

Adorning the façade above the main entrance is a golden statue of Bishop Absalon, who founded the city in 1167. The entrance leads to the main hall, a grand room that serves as a polling station during municipal elections. With a capacity to seat up to 1200 people, the theatre-like hall is also sometimes used for official receptions and concerts. Near the hall's main portal you'll find a bust of Nyrop, along with busts of three of the city's leading citizens: writer Hans Christian Andersen, sculptor Bertel Thorvaldsen and nuclear physicist Niels Bohr.

You can poke into the main hall on your own but to tour the rest of the building, which includes the city council meeting hall, a formal banquet hall and committee rooms, you'll need to join a tour. Rådhus tours cost 30kr and take place year-round at 3pm Monday to Friday and at 10am and 11am Saturday.

Another sightseeing option is to make the climb up the 105m clock tower that tops city hall, but expect a decent workout as there are some 300 steps along the way. Guided tours of the tower cost 20kr and are given at noon Monday to Saturday from October to May. During summer, tower tours are at 10am, noon and 2pm weekdays and at noon only on Saturday.

RÅDHUSPLADSEN Map pp232-4

train Central Station, bus Nos 2A, 5A, 6A, 250S, among others

This large central square, flanked on one side by city hall (Rådhus) and on another by Copenhagen's municipal bus terminus, marks the heart of Copenhagen.

Rådhuspladsen sees more foot traffic than anywhere else in Copenhagen and thus the square is laid out in an open format without barriers, which tends to give it a rather barren appearance in autumn and winter, when it exudes a certain Soviet-era bleakness. The unobstructed openness of the square, however, makes it a great place to stop and observe the classic buildings that surround it, and when spring has sprung and giant boxes of colourful blooms are placed throughout the open space it becomes much more fetching.

On New Year's Eve, many locals flock to Rådhuspladsen to ring in the New Year with as many other Danes as possible in a good-natured, tipsy free-for-all.

STATUE OF HANS CHRISTIAN ANDERSEN Map pp239-41

Rådhuspladsen; train Central Station, bus Nos 2A, 5A, 6A, 250S, among others

At the southwestern end of Rådhuspladsen sits this popular statue of the city's most famous writer, Hans Christian Andersen, no doubt silently chuffed with his position on the boulevard that bears his name. It's a good spot to nab a photo, and a far better likeness than you'll find inside the wax museum (p53).

Fair-Weather Friend

From Rådhuspladsen, be sure to look over at the Unibank building on the northwestern corner of Vesterbrogade and HC Andersens Blvd. The building is topped with a unique barometer that displays a girl on her bicycle when the weather is fair, or with an umbrella when rain is predicted. This charming bronze sculpture was created in 1936 by the Danish artist E Utzon-Frank.

STATUE OF TWO VIKINGS Map pp239-41

Rådhuspladsen; train Central Station, bus Nos 2A, 5A, 6A, 250S, among others

As you face the Palace Hotel (p156), look up and you'll spy the noteworthy and imposing column that's capped with a bronze statue of two Viking men blowing *luren* (curved bronze horns – there's a great collection in Nationalmuseet, p53). The sculpture (which is from the early 20th century) is by Siegfried Wagner.

TIVOLI Map p231

☎ 33 15 10 01; www.tivoligardens.com; Vesterbrogade 3; adult/child 65/40kr; ⏰ 11am-11pm Sun-Wed, 11am-midnight Thu & Sat, 11am-1am Fri 16 Apr-17 Jun & 16 Aug-19 Sep, 11am-midnight Sun-Thu, 11am-1am Fri & Sat 18 Jun-15 Aug; train Central Station, bus Nos 1A, 2A, 5A, 6A, among others

Situated right in the heart of the city and firmly entrenched in the heart of every Dane, Tivoli is a tantalising combination of flower gardens, food pavilions, amusement rides, carnival games, open-air stage shows, fairy lights, fireworks and a warm, fuzzy nostalgia for a carefree childhood. This genteel entertainment park, which dates from 1843, is delightfully varied and arguably Denmark's most famous and popular tourist attraction. Visitors can ride the new 'Demon' roller coaster, take aim at the shooting gallery, enjoy the pantomime of Commedia dell'Arte or simply sit and watch the crowds stroll by.

During the day children flock to Tivoli's Ferris wheel, carousel, bumper cars and other rides. In the evening Tivoli takes on a more romantic aura as the lights come on and the cultural activities unfold, with one stage hosting traditional folk dancing as another prepares a theatrical performance.

Each of Tivoli's numerous entertainment venues has a different character. Perhaps best known is Commedia dell'Arte, the open-air pantomime theatre, which features mime and ballet and was built in 1874 by Vilhelm Dahlerup, the Copenhagen architect who also designed the royal theatre. Tivoli also has an indoor cabaret theatre and a large concert hall (Koncertsal) featuring performances by international symphony orchestras and ballet troupes such as Alvin Ailey.

Between all the neon, twinkling lights and action, Tivoli is a fun place to stroll around, and if you start to feel peckish and fancy something a little more substantial than a hot dog, then there are some very good restaurants that make for a memorable dining experience (see p105). Bear in mind, Tivoli also features a fair number of clip joints, with ordinary, over-priced food and some of the sloppiest service in Copenhagen.

Neighbourhoods – Rådhuspladsen & Tivoli

55

Cracker of a Job

Tivoli has its own fireworks factory – with a crack team of 10 pyrotechnicians working hard to ensure that the dazzling fireworks that Tivoli is so famous for continue to uphold a proud tradition.

Saturday is the best night to visit as there are fireworks at 11.45pm. There's also a nightly sound and light display on Tivoli Lake, 30 min-utes before closing. Amusement ride tickets cost 15kr (some rides require up to four tickets); there are also multiticket schemes and passes.

The numerous open-air performances are free of charge; however, there's usually an admission fee for the indoor performances. For more detailed information, see p125.

Tivoli opens for a few weeks prior to Christmas for holiday festivities, a Christmas market and ice-skating on the lake. Some of Tivoli's restaurants also reopen for that period, serving traditional Danish Christmas fare.

STRØGET & THE LATIN QUARTER

Eating p107; Shopping p142; Sleeping p157

This is picture-postcard Copenhagen at its best. A delightful blend of all the things that make you want to hum Danny Kaye's 'Wonderful Copenhagen' without the slightest twinge of embarrassment, this area hums with Danes enjoying the good things in life – walking with friends and family, a little shopping, cosy cafés and restaurants, attractive architecture, old-fashioned streets and squares filled with charm, not to mention pretty blooms and even more decorative cyclists.

Snaking its way through central Copenhagen is the city's most famous street, Strøget (pronounced '*stroy*-eth'), which is often referred to as 'the walking street' and the backbone of the city. It's just over a kilometre long and is actually made up of five continuous streets: Frederiksberggade, Nygade, Vimmelskaftet, Amagertorv and Østergade. It's crammed with hundreds of shops, cafés and arcades, and takes on some quite distinct flavours, depending on which section you happen to be strolling along: the boutique-filled Kongens Nytorv end is noticeably more salubrious and high-class than the Rådhuspladsen end, where US junk-food multinationals have set up shop among the kebab outlets. Even with its international flavour and chain-store demographics, there remains an avowedly local, old-fashioned feel to the strip, largely due to some well-preserved architecture, some sensitive urban planning and the fact that many locals don't just shoot through after buying what they need – they linger, on benches, on the ground, in beautiful cafés with outdoor seating (and cosy blankets for when the sun's out but the mercury isn't rising) and in just one more shop with edible-looking trinkets.

Strøget & the Latin Quarter Top Five

- Strolling along lovely **Strøget** (p58) and taking the city's pulse
- Spiralling upwards to the wonderful panorama from **Rundetårn** (p58)
- Shopping for second-hand clothes, books and music in the shops of the cobblestone-lined **Latin Quarter** (p140)
- Letting time slip away from you as you relax at an outdoor table on **Gråbrødretorv** (opposite)
- Admiring Thorvaldsen's sculptures in **Vor Frue Kirke** (p59)

With its cafés and second-hand bookshops, the area north of Strøget surrounding the old campus of Københavns Universitet (Copenhagen University) is good for ambling around. The university, which was founded in 1479, has largely outgrown its original quarters and moved to a new campus on Amager, but parts of the old campus, including the law department, remain here.

On the north side of the Latin Quarter is Kultorvet, a lively pedestrian plaza and summertime gathering place with beer gardens, flower stalls and produce (generally fruit and veg) stands, plus the odd hot-dog vendor. On sunny days you'll almost always find impromptu entertainment here, which can range from near-ubiquitous Andean flute playing to local street theatre (consider yourself warned) and dancing.

Another square you'll stumble upon and may want to explore further is Grå-brødretorv (Grey Friars' Square) – a low-key, pretty open space with a smattering of good places to eat (see p107). Between Nygade and Frederiksberggade you'll find the wide-open adjoining spaces of Gammeltorv and Nytorv, which hold the gilded Caritas Springvandet (the Charity Fountain) and

Transport

Bus 1A, 5A, 6A, 150S, 350S
Metro Kongens Nytorv and Nørreport
S-train Nørreport
Parking Much of the area is pedestrianised. Street parking costs 20kr per hour between 8am and 8pm Monday to Friday and 8am and 2pm Saturday

Domhuset (the Courthouse) respectively. Both squares are pleasant spots to rest during a tour of Strøget. The Caritas Fountain was erected in 1608 by Christian IV and marks what was once the city's central market – pedlars still sell fruit, flowers and jewellery here.

The following streets and squares are pedestrianised in this area: Strøget, Købmagergade, Kompagnistræde, Læderstræde, Mikkel Bryggers Gade, Fiolstræde, Store Kannikestræde, Rosengården, Frederiksberggade, Gammeltorv, Nytorv, Gråbrødretorv, Kultorvet and Frue Plads. Parts of Ny Østergade, Kristen Bernikows Gade, Pilestræde and Højbro Plads are also pedestrianised.

Orientation

This area is bounded by the busy thoroughfares of Vester Voldgade and Nørre Voldgade to the southwest and northwest respectively, Gothersgade to the northeast and the streets approaching the large square of Kongens Nytorv, from which Strøget cuts a swathe down to Vester Voldgade and the start of Rådhuspladsen. The area is bordered to its south by the canal that separates Slotsholmen from the city centre, and we have included the waterfront streets Gammel Strand and Ved Stranden in our breakdown of the Slotsholmen section.

DOMHUSET Map pp239-41
Nytorv; ☺ 8.30am-3pm Mon-Fri; bus No 6A
If you think Copenhagen's courthouse shares something in common with its grand cathedral, Vor Frue Kirke, you're correct. They were both designed by architect CF Hansen, and the courthouse has a strong neoclassical flavour, with Ionic columns and an imposing presence on Nytorv. The building has served as a courthouse since 1815, and even has its own 'Bridge of Sighs', which prisoners would cross as they entered the prison on Slutterigade. Inscribed above the entrance to Domhuset are the words *Med Lov Skal Man Land Bygge* (With law shall a land be built), which are taken from the Jutland Code that codified laws in Denmark in 1241.

GUINNESS WORLD OF RECORDS MUSEUM Map pp239-41
☎ 33 32 31 31; www.guinness.dk; Østergade 16; adult/child 80/40kr; ☺ 10am-6pm Sun-Thu, 10am-2pm Fri & Sat 1 Jan-9 May & 13 Sep-31 Dec, 10am-8pm 10 May-31 May & 1 Sep-12 Sep, 9.30am-10.30pm 1 Jun-31 Aug; metro Kongens Nytorv, bus Nos 1A, 350S

This touristy museum uses displays, photos and videos to depict the world's superlatives: the tallest, fastest, oddest and so on. It's a raucous, popular attraction for kids, but not exactly friendly to a family budget.

JARMERS TÅRN Map pp232-4
Jarmers Plads; bus No 5A
You'll find what looks like a pile of rocks on this small square where Nørre Voldgade and Vester Voldgade meet. It's the remains of the city's medieval fortifications from the 13th century, when Copenhagen was encircled by ramparts and a moat.

MUSEUM EROTICA Map pp239-41
☎ 33 12 03 46; www.museumerotica.dk; Købmagergade 24; single/double ticket 99/178kr; ☺ 10am-11pm May-Sep, 11am-8pm Oct-Apr; metro Kongens Nytorv or Nørreport, bus Nos 5A, 6A, 350S

Like most museums of its ilk, this is probably the least erotic place in town. It's a cross between a peepshow and a museum, and tame (often lame) in parts. Things get interesting when you get to read about the sex lives of famous historical figures (Hitler, Marx, Freud, Monroe and the surprisingly well-hung Toulouse Lautrec et al) and see some of the artworks and displays concentrating on other cultures. The 'shock room' at the end of the tour had the desired effect on us, which was so far removed from arousal as to be a cause of mild nausea. Highly missable and overpriced to boot – expect to be accompanied throughout by sad-looking couples, and don't be surprised if you don't feel more than a little depressed by the aftereffects of the porn films containing acts best described as degrading to both women and animals. Thank God there's not a cafeteria on site.

MUSIKHISTORISK MUSEUM Map pp232-4

☎ 33 11 27 26; www.musikhistoriskmuseum.dk; Åbenrå 30; adult/child 40/10kr; 🕒 1-3.50pm 2 May-30 Sep, 1-3.50pm Mon, Wed, Sat & Sun 1 Oct-30 Apr; metro & S-train Nørreport, bus No 350S

The Music History Museum, housed in a couple of 18th-century buildings just north of Kultorvet, contains a quality collection of antique musical instruments dating from AD 1000 to 1900.

There's a particularly large collection of beautiful stringed instruments. The exhibits are grouped according to themes, such as folk music of the Middle Ages, Renaissance instruments, 19th-century military music etc, some accompanied by musical recordings that you can listen to on headphones. There are occasional concerts and special presentations.

POST & TELE MUSEUM Map pp239-41

☎ 33 41 09 00; www.ptt-museum.dk; Købmagergade 37; adult/child 30kr/free, Wed free; 🕒 10am-5pm Tue & Thu-Sun, 10am-8pm Wed, noon-4pm Sun; metro & S-train Nørreport, bus Nos 5A, 6A, 350S

Get out your train-spotter's cardigan for the Post & Tele Museum, a few minutes' walk north of Strøget. It depicts the history of the Danish postal and telecommunications system with displays of historic postal vehicles, uniforms, letterboxes, radio equipment etc. And of course, it also boasts a fine stamp collection. The building also has a very pleasant rooftop **café** (see p107), with a great city view, which can be visited without paying museum admission.

RUNDETÅRN Map pp239-41

☎ 33 73 03 73; www.rundetaarn.dk; Købmagergade 52A; adult/child 20/5kr; 🕒 10am-5pm Mon-Sat, noon-5pm Sun; metro & S-train Nørreport, bus Nos 5A, 6A, 150S, 350S

The Rundetårn (Round Tower) is a great vantage point from which to admire the old city's red-tiled rooftops and abundant church spires. Helpful signs point out major landmarks – a great way to get your bearings from on high. This vaulted brick tower, 35m high, was built by Christian IV in 1642 and used as an astronomical observatory in conjunction with the nearby university. Although the university erected a newer structure in 1861, amateur astronomers have continued to use the Rundetårn each winter, which gives credence to its claim to be the oldest functioning observatory in Europe.

A 209m spiral walkway winds up the tower around a hollow core; about halfway up is a small exhibition hall housing changing displays of art and culture. It's an easy uphill corkscrew of a walk, and should present no problems.

Winter visitors who'd like to view the night sky from the 3m-long telescope that's mounted within the rooftop dome should make inquiries at the ticket booth; the observatory is generally open Tuesday and Wednesday nights. In September the observatory opens between 1pm and 4pm on Sunday.

SANKT PETRI KIRKE Map pp239-41

☎ 33 13 38 33; www.sankt-petri.dk; cnr Nørregade & Sankt Pedersstræde; admission free; 🕒 10am-1pm Tue-Thu; bus No 6A

In addition to Vor Frue Kirke, this is another noteworthy place of worship in the Latin Quarter. Sankt Petri Kirke (St Peter's Church) dates from the 15th century and is the oldest church building in Copenhagen. Since 1585 it has served the city's German Lutheran congregation and services are still held in German today. Recently renovated, the church is open to the public again. Note how much lower it sits than the land surrounding it.

STRØGET Map pp239-41

metro Kongens Nytorv, bus Nos 1A, 6A, 350S

Billed as 'the world's longest pedestrian street', Strøget runs through the city centre between Rådhuspladsen and Kongens Nytorv, the square at the head of the Nyhavn canal.

Strøget, which abounds with shops, eateries and entertainment venues, is actually made up of five continuous streets: Frederiksberggade, Nygade, Vimmelskaftet, Amagertorv and Østergade. Strøget is a fun place to stroll, its broad squares bustling with street musicians, tourists and urbanites who play off each other's energies. It's a particularly vibrant scene on sunny days, when people seem to pour out of the woodwork.

SYNAGOGEN Map pp239-41
Krystalgade 12; ✪ closed to public; bus No 6A
Synagogen (the main synagogue for the Jewish community) was built in 1831 in neoclassical style and restored in 1958. It can be viewed from the exterior, but the ornate interior with its Doric columns and carved woodwork is not open to the general public.

TRINITATISKIRKE Map pp239-41
☎ 33 12 91 00; Landemærket 2; admission free; ✪ 9.30am-4.30pm Mon-Sat; metro & S-train Nørreport, bus Nos 5A, 6A, 150S, 350S
Situated at the base of the Rundetårn, it's easy to miss this baroque church, which was constructed in 1637 and features an interesting baroque altar, as well as a fine vaulted ceiling with gold details. The handsome pews feature shell motifs, and there's a small yard at the church's front that may tempt you if Købmagergade is just too noisome.

UNIVERSITY LIBRARY Map pp239-41
☎ 33 47 47 47; Fiolstræde 1; admission free; ✪ 10am-7pm Mon-Fri; metro & S-train Nørreport, bus Nos 5A, 6A, 350S
Ascend the stairs of the university library (enter from Fiolstræde) to see one quirky remnant of the 1807 British bombardment of Copenhagen: a glass case containing a British cannonball in five fragments and the target it ironically hit, a book titled *Defensor Pacis* (Defender of Peace).

VOR FRUE KIRKE Map pp239-41
☎ 33 37 65 40; www.koebenhavnsdomkirke.dk; Nørregade 8; admission free; ✪ 8am-5pm Mon-Sat, noon-5pm Sun; bus No 6A
Opposite the university is Vor Frue Kirke (Our Lady's Church), Copenhagen's cathedral, which was founded in 1191 and rebuilt on three occasions after devastating fires. The current structure dates from 1829 and was designed in neoclassical style by architect CF Hansen, who also designed Domhuset, the city's law courts.

With its high vaulted ceilings and columns, Vor Frue Kirke seems as much museum as church – quite apropos because it also displays sculptor Bertel Thorvaldsen's statues of Christ and the 12 apostles, his most acclaimed works, which were completed in 1839. Thor-

valdsen's depiction of Christ, with comforting open arms, became the most popular worldwide model for statues of Christ and remains so today. In May 2004 the cathedral was given a thorough Spring cleaning for the Danish wedding of the year – that of Crown Prince Frederik to Mary Donaldson.

There are occasional organ recitals throughout the year, including at noon on Saturday in July and August.

WØ LARSEN TOBACCO MUSEUM
Map pp239-41
☎ 33 12 20 50; Amagertorv 9; admission free; ✪ 10am-6pm Mon-Thu, 10am-7pm Fri, 10am-5pm Sat; metro Kongens Nytorv, bus Nos 1A, 350S
At the fashionable end of Strøget is this lavish-looking smoke shop (p146), where it's said the Queen buys her lungbusters. The smoking museum in the basement details all sorts of interesting facts about tobacco and its hold on humanity (remember – one-third of Danes are smokers, in case you hadn't noticed). Interesting tidbits and objects abound, and they probably won't mind if you light up.

WØ Larsen Tobacco Museum, Strøget (above)

SLOTSHOLMEN

Eating p111

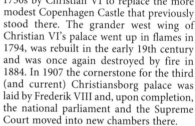

Slotsholmen is the seat of Denmark's national government and a repository of historical sites. Located on a small island separated from the city centre by a moat-like canal, Slotsholmen's centre-piece is Christiansborg Slot, a rambling neobaroque palace that now contains four of the state's major institutions under one powerful roof – the Supreme Courts, the Royal Reception Rooms, the parliament and the prime minister's office.

If you walk into Slotsholmen from Ny Vestergade, you'll cross the western part of the canal and enter Christiansborg's large main courtyard, which was once used as a royal riding ground. The courtyard still maintains a distinctively equestrian character, overseen by a **statue of Christian IX** (1863–1906) on horseback and flanked to the north by stables and to the south by carriage buildings.

The stables and buildings surrounding the main courtyard date back to the original Christiansborg palace, which was built in the 1730s by Christian VI to replace the more

Transport

Bus 1A, 2A, 48, 650S
Boat 901, 902
Parking Street parking costs 12kr per hour between 8am and 6pm Monday to Friday and 8am and 2pm Saturday

modest Copenhagen Castle that previously stood there. The grander west wing of Christian VI's palace went up in flames in 1794, was rebuilt in the early 19th century and was once again destroyed by fire in 1884. In 1907 the cornerstone for the third (and current) Christiansborg palace was laid by Frederik VIII and, upon completion, the national parliament and the Supreme Court moved into new chambers there.

It's a fascinating area to walk around, not only for its grand architecture and beautiful setting, but also because of its palpable sense of the past still having an impact on the present. This isn't some fusty historical area that's long past its use-by date – decisions of national importance are made here and this is where the queen regularly conducts official functions. New additions to the list of things to see are always being made – check out the new Dansk Jødisk Museum and Det Kongelige Bibliotek for unbeatable examples of how to marry history, architecture, education, innovation and style.

Orientation

Being an island (albeit one barely differentiated from the rest of the city thanks to a narrow moat), Slotsholmen's natural boundaries are very straightforward. It lies east of Strøget and west of Christianshavn (p76) and is connected to the centre of town via eight short bridges. It is connected to Christianshavn by the attractive Knippelsbro.

BØRSEN Map p231

Børsgade; ⊙ closed to public; bus No 2A

A striking Renaissance building, Børsen (the stock exchange) is at the eastern corner of Slotsholmen on Børsgade. Constructed in the 1620s, it's particularly noted for its ornate spire (over 50m tall), formed from the en-twined tails of four dragons, and for its richly embellished gables.

This still-functioning chamber of commerce, which first opened during the bustling reign of Christian IV, is the oldest in Europe. One of its doors is adorned with the following

words from Christian himself: 'The House that you see here has not been built for Mercury's secret arts, but first and foremost for the glory of God and secondly for the profitable use of Buyer and Seller'.

CHRISTIANSBORG RUINS Map p231

☎ 33 92 64 92; www.ses.dk; adult/child 25/10kr;
⊙ 10am-4pm May-Sep, 10am-4pm Tue-Sun Oct-Apr;
bus Nos 1A, 2A, 48, 650S

A subterranean walk through the crypt-like bowels of Slotsholmen offers a unique perspective on Copenhagen's lengthy history. In

Slotsholmen Top Five

- Getting floored by the architecture at **Det Kongelige Bibliotek** (p62)
- Getting plastered (kinda) at **Thorvaldsens Museum** (p63)
- Seeing the tapestries at **De Kongelige Repræsentationslokaler** (right)
- Admiring the exhibitions and the architecture at the **Dansk Jødisk Museum** (below)
- Getting nautical-but-nice at **Holmens Kirke** (p62)

the basement of the current palace, beneath the tower, are the remains of two earlier castles. The most notable are the ruins of Absalon's fortress, Slotsholmen's original castle, built by Bishop Absalon in 1167. The excavated foundations, which consist largely of low limestone sections of wall, date back to the founding of the city.

Absalon's fortress was demolished by Hanseatic invaders in 1369. Its foundations, as well as those of the Copenhagen Castle that replaced it and stood for more than three centuries, were excavated when the current tower was built in the early 20th century.

CHRISTIANSBORG SLOTSKIRKE

Map p231

admission free; noon-4pm Jul, noon-4pm Sun Aug-Jun; bus Nos 1A, 2A, 48, 650S

Christiansborg Slotskirke, Slotsholmen's domed church, was built in 1826 in the neoclassic style by architect CF Hansen. It was in the final stages of restoration in 1992 when stray fireworks set fire to the construction scaffolding encompassing the dome and set the roof ablaze – Copenhagen has been a rather unlucky city in terms of fire. The entire dome collapsed, but much of the church interior, including a frieze of angels by Bertel Thorvaldsen that rings the ceiling just below the dome, miraculously survived. The restorers went back to work and the church was reopened to the public in January 1997 with a service commemorating the 25th anniversary of Queen Margrethe II's reign.

DANSK JØDISK MUSEUM Map p231

☎ 33 11 22 18; www.jewmus.dk; Købmagergade 5; adult/concession/child 40/30kr/free; 1-4pm Tue-Fri, 10am-5pm Sat & Sun; bus Nos 1A, 2A, 48, 650S

The Danish Jewish Museum takes pains to emphasise the concept of *mitzvah*, or the

'good deed' in its presentation of Jewish life in Denmark through its collection of artefacts, art and audiovisual recordings. It's a concept that has extended to the building's design, with architect Daniel Libeskind imbuing the space with unusual lighting shapes and an intriguing use of geometry that highlight the textual and textural representations of the Danish Jewish experience. Housed in what was originally the Royal Boat House (early 17th century), the museum is a wonderful new addition to the city's roster of fine museums. Special themed exhibitions are held here, and there's a reading room and shop on the premises. And, in a nice touch, it closes for both Jewish and Christian holidays. Enter through the Royal Library Garden, via Proviantpassagen.

DE KONGELIGE REPRÆSENTATIONSLOKALER Map p231

☎ 33 92 64 92; www.ses.dk; adult/concession/child 50/40/20kr; English guided tours 11am, 1pm & 3pm Tue-Sun May-Sep, 3pm Tue, Thu, Sat & Sun Oct-Apr; bus Nos 1A, 2A, 48, 650S

The grandest part of Christiansborg is De Kongelige Repræsentationslokaler (the Royal Reception Chambers), an ornate Renaissance hall where the queen holds royal banquets and entertains heads of state.

Of particular note are the very colourful (almost cartoonish) but grand wall tapestries depicting the history of Denmark from Viking times to the present day. Created by tapestry designer Bjørn Nørgaard to celebrate the queen's 50th birthday in 1990, the tapestries took a full 10 years to complete, finally arriving in time for the queen's 60th birthday. Tapestries to pay particular attention to include the representation of the queen and her husband as Adam and Eve (albeit clothed) in a Danish Garden of Eden. The queen's admirable qualities of creativity, intelligence and compassion are embodied by the symbolic enlargement of her hands, forehead and arms respectively. Her less admirable quality of heavy smoking is best represented by the small reception room she ducks into for a quick fag – you'll see it at the start of your tour.

Another interesting section of the reception rooms is the queen's private library, with beautiful gold and peacock-blue accents throughout and a delightfully cute private elevator (easily confused with the more prosaic matching broom closet). It's also worth looking downward to the fabulous wooden parquetry floors throughout the rooms – a blend of oak, mahogany and walnut – and the reason you'll be asked to don elasticised slippers over your own footwear.

The chambers are closed to the public when in official use. Disabled parking is available in the courtyard, but the building itself is not wheelchair accessible.

DE KONGELIGE STALDE & KARETER

Map p231

☎ 33 40 10 10; www.kongehuset.dk; Christiansborg Ridebane 12; adult/child 20/10kr; ☽ 2-4pm Fri-Sun May-Sep, 2-4pm Sat & Sun Oct-Apr; bus Nos 1A, 2A, 48, 650S

At De Kongelige Stalde og Kareter (the Royal Stables and Coaches), visitors can view a collection of antique coaches, uniforms and riding paraphernalia, some of which are still used for royal receptions. You can also see the royal family's carriage and saddle horses, which are trained on the grounds here. And who knows? You may spy Crown Princess Mary, a keen and accomplished horsewoman.

DET KONGELIGE BIBLIOTEK Map p231

☎ 33 47 47 47; www.kb.dk; Søren Kierkegaards Plads; admission free, exhibition adult/child 30/10kr; ☽ 10am-7pm Mon-Sat; bus No 48, Harbour bus Nos 901, 902

If only we'd had such a library in our student days we may have been tempted to actually hit the books! This is a fabulously effective merger of the classic Royal Library building near parliament and a new ultramodern extension on the waterfront. The seven-storey extension, dubbed the 'Black Diamond', sports a shiny black granite façade, smoked black windows and a leaning 'parallelogramatic' design. Opened in late 1999, on the eve of the new millennium, this sleek canalside addition gives the once solidly historic waterfront a futuristic juxtaposition.

The Royal Library, which dates from the 17th century, is the largest library in Scandinavia. It not only serves as a research centre for scholars and university students, but also doubles as a repository for rare books, manuscripts, prints and maps. As Denmark's national library it contains a complete collection of all Danish printed works produced since 1482 and houses some 21 million items in all.

There's a spacious lobby with canal views, a 210-sq-metre ceiling mural by renowned Danish artist Per Kirkeby (look up as you're crossing the walkway that connects the new with the old) and exhibition areas. Everything is ultra-modern – researchers now do their reference searches on computers, which line the library's corridors, and place all of their requests to the librarian online. The lobby contains a good branch of GAD bookshop, a cheap **café** (p112) and one of the city's flashest-looking restaurants, **Søren K** (p112).

The enclosed overhead walkway straddles the motorway on Christians Brygge and connects the Black Diamond with the library's historic building. The old wing preserves its period character with arched doorways, chandeliers and high-ceilinged reading rooms. Det Kongelige Bibliotek is also home to the **Photography Museum**.

The Royal Library has to be entered from the waterfront on Christians Brygge.

An Author Applies Himself…

In 1834, Hans Christian Andersen applied for work at the Royal Library in Copenhagen 'to be freed from the heavy burden of having to write in order to live'. Apparently the library administrators weren't too impressed with his résumé, as he was turned down. Ironically, Andersen's unsuccessful application is now preserved as part of the library's valued archives, along with many of his original manuscripts. They can be viewed with advance notice.

FOLKETINGET Map p231

☎ 33 37 55 00; www.folketinget.dk; Rigsdagsgården; admission free; ☽ guided tours 2pm Jul & Aug, 2pm Sun Sep-Jun; bus Nos 1A, 2A, 48, 650S

The parliamentary chamber, called Folketinget, is where the 179 members of parliament meet to debate national legislation. In July and August, free tours in English are given daily. The rest of the year the tours are given on Sunday, but are in Danish only. In addition to the parliamentary chamber, the tour also takes in Wanderer's Hall, which contains the original copy of the Constitution of the Kingdom of Denmark, enacted in 1849.

HOLMENS KIRKE Map p231

☎ 33 13 61 78; www.holmenskirke.dk; Holmens Kanal 9; admission free; ☽ 9am-2pm Mon-Fri, 9am-noon Sat; bus Nos 1A, 15, 19, 26, 29, DFDS & Netto-Bådene tours

Just across the canal to the northeast of Slotsholmen is Holmens Kirke (Church of the

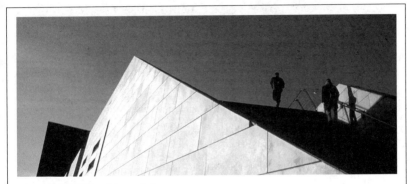
Det Kongelige Bibliotek (opposite)

Neighbourhoods – Slotsholmen

Royal Navy). This historic brick structure, with a nave that was originally built in 1562 to be used as an anchor forge, was converted into a church for the Royal Navy in 1619. Most of the present structure, which is predominantly in Dutch Renaissance style, dates from 1641. The church's burial chapel contains the remains of some important naval figures, including Admiral Niels Juel, who beat back the Swedes in the crucial 1677 Battle of Køge Bay.

It was at Holmens Kirke that Queen Margrethe II took her marriage vows in 1967. She chose this church as a tribute to her sea-loving father, the king, who was also the head of the navy. The interior of the church has an intricately carved 17th-century oak altarpiece and pulpit.

ROYAL LIBRARY GARDENS Map p231
bus Nos 1A, 2A, 48, 650S
These lovely flower gardens back onto the historic section of Det Kongelige Bibliotek and can be entered from Rigsdagsgården (Parliament Yard), just west of Tøjhusmuseet. It's a nice spot for a summer's picnic, and there's a statue of Copenhagen's most famous philosopher, Søren Kierkegaard.

STATUE OF BISHOP ABSALON Map p231
Ved Stranden 1; bus Nos 1A, 2A, 650S
Marking the point where you cross the bridge from 'the mainland' to Slotsholmen is this large statue of Archbishop Absalon astride a horse. Absalon, who was from one of Zealand's most prominent families, was not only a religious leader but also a successful military commander. The city of Copenhagen dates its

founding to 1167, when Absalon constructed a fortress on the island of Slotsholmen, fortifying the previously unprotected harbourside village with ramparts and a moat. Under the guidance of Absalon, a series of successful crusades into eastern Germany were launched against the Wends.

TEATERMUSEET Map p231
☎ 33 11 51 76; www.teatermuseet.dk; Christiansborg Ridebane 18; adult/concession/child 30/20/free; 11am-3pm Tue-Thu, 1-4pm Sat & Sun; bus Nos 1A, 2A, 48, 650S
This museum occupies the Hofteater (Old Court Theatre), which dates from 1767 and fairly drips with historic (albeit a little faded) character. Performances over the years have ranged from Italian opera and pantomime to shows by local ballet troupes, one of which included fledgling ballet student Hans Christian Andersen. The theatre, which took on its current appearance in 1842, drew its final curtain in 1881 but was later reopened as a museum in 1922.

The stage, boxes and dressing rooms can be examined, along with displays of set models, drawings, costumes and period posters tracing the history of Danish theatre. Royal-watchers will enjoy peeking into the royal boxes – Christian VIII's entertainment area is even equipped with its own commode!

THORVALDSENS MUSEUM Map p231
☎ 33 32 15 32; www.thorvaldsensmuseum.dk; Bertel Thorvaldsens Plads 2; adult/concession/child 30/20kr/free, Wed free; 10am-5pm Tue-Sun; bus Nos 1A, 2A, 48, 650S

This eye-catching museum (its painted exterior is worth a closer inspection even if you don't intend to enter) exhibits the works of famed Danish sculptor Bertel Thorvaldsen (1770–1844), who was heavily influenced by Greek and Roman mythology. After four decades in Rome, Thorvaldsen returned to his native Copenhagen and donated his private collection to the Danish public. In return, the royal family provided this site for the construction of a museum to house Thorvaldsen's drawings, plaster moulds and statues. The museum also contains Thorvaldsen's collection of antique art from the Mediterranean region. In July and August the museum offers English-language guided tours at 3pm on Sunday. The entrance is on Vindebrogade.

TØJHUSMUSEET Map p231

☎ 33 11 60 37; www.thm.dk; Tøjhusgade 3; adult/concession/child 40/20kr/free; ☽ 11am-4pm Tue-Sun 14 May-31 Aug; bus Nos 1A, 2A, 48, 650S

Tøjhusmuseet (the Royal Arsenal Museum) contains an impressive collection of historic cannons, hand weapons and armour that will satisfy every last gun nut. The 163m-long building which houses the arsenal was constructed by King Christian IV in 1600 and boasts Europe's longest vaulted Renaissance hall – enough to satisfy the architecture nuts. Interesting temporary exhibitions take a variety of military themes – a recent display was devoted to Soviet Special Forces in Afghanistan. Access to the museum is from Tøjhusgade.

NYHAVN TO KASTELLET

Eating p112; Shopping p147; Sleeping p159

The picturesque Nyhavn canal was dug in the 17th century to allow traders to bring their wares into the heart of the city. Long a haunt for sailors and writers (including Hans Christian Andersen, who lived in the house at No 67 for nearly 20 years), Nyhavn today is a half-salty and half-gentrified tourist magnet of bright colours, herring buffets and foaming beers. The canal is lined with restored gabled townhouses and trendy pavement cafés that pack in a crowd whenever the weather is warm and sunny, and do decent business even when it's not. The area is filled with smartly restored granaries, warehouses and dockside structures that have been expertly restored, allowing the whole 'village' to retain its original maritime vibe.

At the head of the Nyhavn canal is a huge frigate anchor that commemorates the Danish seamen who died in WWII serving with the Allied merchant marines. Further north, you'll find the Frihedsmuseet, a moving tribute to the men and women of the Danish Resistance, who gamely sabotaged and stirred the Nazi pot during WWII.

The Amalienborg area, also known as Frederiksstaden for Frederik V, who laid out the neighbourhood in a sensible grid in the mid-18th century, has upmarket residences (including that of the royal family), a grand marble church and other historic sites. It's a lovely area for a quiet, well-mannered experience – although there are a few edgy galleries and design stores along Bredgade, and there are some fabulous views to be had from Amaliehaven over to the city's brand spanking-new Opera House over the water. The northern Kastellet area includes a 17th-century citadel and the city's best-known statue, the Little Mermaid, making this a popular spot on the tour-bus circuit. Even so, the discreet good taste of the area's inhabitants and superb baroque and neoclassical architecture never allow any tack to overtake the experience.

Orientation

This area starts with impressive Kongens Nytorv, which punctuates the end of Strøget and the start of busy Nyhavn, the canal-side street (of sorts) that opens out onto Inderhavnen. The western edge of

Nyhavn to Kastellet Top Five

- Seeing the best in Decorative Arts from around the world at **Kunstindustrimuseet** (p75)
- Immersing yourself in the modern art scene at **Charlottenborg** (p66)
- Timing your visit with the **Changing of the Guard** (p66)
- Peeking inside **Amalienborg Slot** (opposite)
- Scaling the heights of **Marmorkirken** (p75)

this area is bordered by this part of the harbour. From Nyhavn, sophisticated Bredgade stretches for about 1km and bisects the upper-class suburb known as Frederiksstaden. At the end of this street starts Churchillparken, and beyond that you'll find the star-shaped and moated fortress known as Kastellet, with the Little Mermaid to its northwest. East of Kastellet is Østerport station, and south from this runs a straightforward grid of streets to the intersection of Sølvgade and Kron-prinsessegade, which marks the beginning of the area referred to as Nørreport & Around (p81) in this guide. West of Kronprinsessegade are various other handsome streets with some shops, homes and restaurants, heading south to Gothersgade.

Transport

Bus 1A, 15, 19, 29, 650S
Metro Kongens Nytorv
Boat 901, 902
Parking Street parking costs between 7kr and 12kr per hour between 8am and 6pm Monday to Friday and 8am and 2pm Saturday (no fee on Saturday in 7kr zones)

ALEXANDER NEWSKY KIRKE Map pp232-4

☎ 33 13 60 46; Bredgade 53; admission free; ☪ only for services

Built in the Russian Byzantine style in 1883 by Tsar Alexander III, who was married to a Danish princess. Its ornate exterior is topped by three gold onion-shaped domes. Today the church continues to serve Copenhagen's Russian Orthodox community.

AMALIENBORG SLOT Map pp232-4

☎ 33 12 21 86; www.rosenborg-slot.dk; Amalienborg Plads; adult/child 45/10kr; ☪ 10am-4pm 1 May-31 Oct, 11am-4pm Tue-Sun 2 Jan-30 Apr & 1 Nov-30 Dec; bus No 1A

Most of this palace, which is the residence of Queen Margrethe II, is not open to the public,

but visitors can enter one wing that features exhibits of the royal apartments used by three generations of the monarchy from 1863 to 1947.

The rooms, faithfully reconstructed in the styles of the period, are decorated with heavy oak furnishings, gilt-leather tapestries, family photographs and old knick-knacks. They include the study and drawing room of Christian IX (1863–1906) and Queen Louise, whose six children married into nearly as many royal families – one eventually ascending the throne in Greece and another marrying Russian tsar Alexander III. Also displayed is the study of Frederik VIII (1906–12), who decorated it in a lavish neo-Renaissance style, and the study of Christian X (1912–47), the grandfather of Queen Margrethe II. It's

Den Lille Havfrue – Headless Statue of Topless Lady

In 1909 the Danish beer baron Carl Jacobsen was so moved after attending a ballet performance of *The Little Mermaid* that he commissioned sculptor Edvard Eriksen to create a statue of the fairy-tale character to grace Copenhagen's harbourfront.

The face of the famous statue was modelled after the ballerina Ellen Price, while Eline Eriksen, the sculptor's wife, modelled for the body.

The Little Mermaid (Den Lille Havfrue) survived the Great Depression and the WWII occupation unscathed, but modern times haven't been so kind to Denmark's leading lady.

In January 1998, in the middle of the night, someone took a saw and decapitated the bronze statue. The next day, international news services spread the gory scene around the world, as divers searched the waters around the statue for clues, to no avail. Three days later the severed head turned up in a box outside a Copenhagen TV station – and it was speedily reattached.

That wasn't the first time the gentle lady had been the subject of undesired attention. In 1964 the original head was lopped off and in 1983 an arm was sawn off – neither were ever found again and both appendages had to be recast and welded back on. Various paint-splashing episodes have also taken place over the years, and in 2003 the Little Mermaid was 'loosened' from her mooring and shoved into the harbour. Pundits have made the supposition that frustration with the sheer 'so bloody what?' reaction that the statue inspires (it's top of our list for over-rated tourist sights) could be the reason for such savagery. Maybe the next time someone will manage to kidnap the whole thing, sparing thousands of tourists each year the disappointment of the inevitable deflation that comes from a date with the Little Mermaid...

a fascinating glimpse into the daily lives of past royals, and the unique character of each member of the family shines through in their respective rooms.

CHARLOTTENBORG Map pp239-41

☎ 33 13 40 22; www.charlottenborg-art.dk; Nyhavn 2; adult/concession 30/15kr; ☺ 10am-5pm Thu-Tue, 10am-7pm Wed; metro Kongens Nytorv, bus Nos 1A, 350S, boat Nos 901, 902

Fronting Kongens Nytorv, southwest along Nyhavn, is Charlottenborg, which was built in 1683 as a palace for the royal family. Since 1754 Charlottenborg has housed Det Kongelige Kunstakademi (the Royal Academy of Fine Arts). Its exhibition hall on the eastern side of the central courtyard features changing exhibitions of modern art by Danish and international artists. When we popped in we were impressed by the exhibition of modern Scandinavian art from emerging artists. There's good wheelchair access and a very decent **café** (p114) on the premises.

DEN KONGELIGE
AFSTØBNINGSSAMLING Map pp232-4

☎ 33 74 85 75; www.smk.dk; Toldbodgade 40; admission free; ☺ 10am-8pm Wed; bus Nos 1A, 15, 19 or 29

Den Kongelige Afstøbningssamling (the Royal Cast Collection) is housed in an old waterfront warehouse and exhibits plaster casts of some of the world's greatest sculptures.

The casts, about 2000 in all, depict roughly four millennia of sculptural history and were originally used as models for teaching Danish art students. They include the *Venus de Milo*, reliefs from medieval churches and statues from the Acropolis. Art students still make up the lion's share of visitors here.

FRIHEDSMUSEET Map pp232-4

☎ 33 13 77 14; www.natmus.dk; Churchillparken; adult/child 25kr/free; ☺ 10am-4pm Tue-Sat, 10am-5pm Sun, 1 May-15 Sep, 11am-3pm Tue-Sat, 11am-4pm Sun 16 Sep-30 Apr; S-train Østerport, bus No 1A

The Museum of the Danish Resistance in Churchillparken, south of Kastellet, features exhibits from the time of the German occupation in 1940 to liberation in 1945. There are displays on the Danish underground press, the clandestine radio operations that maintained links with England, and the smuggling operations that saved approximately 7000 Danish Jews from capture by the Nazis by smuggling them under cover of darkness across Øresund and into Sweden. It's a mov-

The More Things Change…

When the queen is in residence at Amalienborg Slot (p65), mainly from December to April, a colourful changing of the guard takes place in the palace square at noon. The ceremony begins with a procession from Rosenborg Slot (p84) by the Royal Guard, bedecked in full regalia and marching to the tune of fifes and drums.

The guard contingent leaves the Rosenborg Slot gardens at 11.30am and marches to Amalienborg Slot on a curving route that takes them to Kultorvet in the Latin Quarter, south on Købmagergade and then east along Østergade to Kongens Nytorv. From there they continue to Amalienborg Slot along Bredgade, Sankt Annæ Plads and Amaliegade.

Upon reaching the square, the old guards are ceremoniously relieved of their duties by their fresh replacements, who take up sentry posts in front of the palace. The relieved guards then join the marching band and return to their barracks at Rosenborg Slot, via a route that takes them along Frederiksgade, Store Kongensgade and Gothersgade.

In spring and early summer, when the queen takes up residence at her summer palace in Fredensborg, a version of the changing of the guard occurs there instead.

ing, low-key museum, and well worth a visit – Copenhagen's pristine appearance and lack of visible damage from WWII make it easy to forget that the city was occupied by the Nazis for five long years.

HOUSE OF AMBER Map pp232-4

☎ 33 11 04 44; Kongens Nytorv 2; adult/child 25/10kr; ☺ 10am-6pm Mon-Sat; metro Kongens Nytorv

The House of Amber is an amber jewellery shop (p147) at the head of Nyhavn canal that maintains a small museum on the upper floor of its 17th-century quarters.

It gives the lowdown on various types of amber, with examples of clear drops, white amber and curious specimens that encapsulate different insects. There's also an 8.8kg piece of Baltic amber that's one of the largest of its type and various pieces of amber carved into jewellery, chess sets and the like.

KONGENS NYTORV Map pp239-41
metro Kongens Nytorv

This overbearing public square has been having a tough time of late, with disease striking

(Continued on page 75)

1 *Boats at Christianshavn Bådudlejning og Café (p136)* 2 *Poster of Tivoli amusement park (p55)* 3 *Copenhagen in a nutshell: café culture and Copenhagen bike* 4 *Kongens Have (p83)*

1 *Sculpture outside Ny Carlsberg Glyptotek (p53)* 2 *Statues outside Marmorkirken (p75)* 3 *Bridgehouse on Knippelsbro (p78)* 4 *Christiania (p77)*

1 *Flower stall, Israels Plads produce market (p146)* 2 *Statue, Statens Museum for Kunst (p84)* 3 *Tower of Vor Frue Kirke (p59)* 4 *View from Vor Frelsers Kirke (p79)*

1 Canalside cafe, Overgaden Oven Vandet, Christianshavn (p114)
2 Ida Davidsen (p113) **3** Konrad (p109) **4** Busker on Strøget (p58)

1 *Hotel Opera (p159)* 2 *Hot dog cart outside Radisson SAS Royal Hotel (p156)* 3 *Hotel Alexandra (p155)* 4 *Copenhagen Admiral Hotel (p159)*

1 *Fisk (p144)* **2** *Window decoration of Illums Bolighus (p144)* **3** *Munthe Plus Simonsen (p145)* **4** *Arne Jacobsen chair (p31)*

TILBUD
Arne Jacobsen
DKK 1.000

1 *Dansk Design Center (p52)* **2** *Jørgen L Dalgaard (p147)* **3** *Bang & Jensen (p129)* **4** *Susanne Juul (p146)*

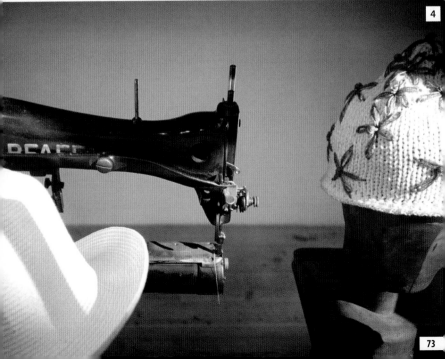

1 Øresund Bridge, seen from Malmö (p188) 2 Frederiksborg Slot (p172) 3 Pier, Roskilde (p180) 4 Louisiana (p175)

(Continued from page 66)

down its lovely beech trees a few years ago (they have been replaced), the construction of the metro station requiring lots of barricades in the late 1990s and the new millennium, and further redevelopment making it a veritable minefield to get through, past or around in 2004. That said, it should be back to its best by the time you read this. The square is ringed by many handsome (and important) buildings, such as the Royal Theatre and fancy Hotel d'Angleterre. It's a good spot to start a tour of the city, as it's close to many of the attractions listed in this chapter. When students graduate from high school they don white clothing and dance around the square's central statue of Christian V – in winter part of the square is given over to ice skating, so get your skates on if you're in town at this time.

Marmorkirken (right)

KUNSTINDUSTRIMUSEET Map pp232-4

☎ 33 18 56 56; www.kunstindustrimuseet.dk;
Bredgade 68; adult/concession/child 40/25kr/free;
🕐 10am-4pm Tue-Fri, noon-4pm Sat & Sun; bus No 1A

Kunstindustrimuseet (Museum of Decorative Art) is housed in the former Frederiks Hospital, which was built in 1752. This large, rambling place feels much like an oversized antiques shop, or at times an undersized V&A, with an eclectic collection of nearly 300,000 items from Asia and Europe, dating from the Middle Ages. It's a wonderful spot to spend a rainy afternoon – some of the rooms contain fine English furniture, which provided much of the inspiration for Danish designs that followed, and others hold theme exhibits.

The displays include a fairly extensive collection of Danish silver and porcelain, and good coverage of innovations in contemporary Danish design, making its location on Bredgade (one of the shopping strips for Danish design collectibles) particularly apt. Pop in here and suss out the basics before making a purchase at one of the stores down the road! One exhibit, for example, shows Denmark's contribution to chair design, displaying chairs by influential 20th-century designers Kaare Klint, Hans Wegner and Arne Jacobsen. By the end of your visit, you will wonder what people were sitting on before the Danes came along.

There's a **café** (p114) on site and wheelchair access is reasonable.

MARMORKIRKEN Map pp232-4

☎ 33 15 01 44; www.marmorkirken.dk; Frederiksgade 4; admission free, dome adult/child 20/10kr;
🕐 10am-5pm Mon-Thu, noon-5pm Fri-Sun, dome 1pm & 3pm Sat & Sun; bus No 1A

The Marble Church, also known as Frederikskirken, is a stately neobaroque church on Frederiksgade, a block west of Amalienborg Slot. The church's massive dome, which was inspired by St Peter's in Rome and measures more than 30m in diameter, is one of Copenhagen's most dominant skyline features.

The original plans for the church were ordered by Frederik V and drawn up by Nicolai Eigtved as part of a grand design that included the Amalienborg mansions. Although church construction began in 1749, it encountered problems as costs spiralled, due in part to the prohibitively high price of Norwegian marble, and the project was soon shelved.

It wasn't until Denmark's wealthiest 19th-century financier, CF Tietgen, bankrolled the project's revival that it was eventually completed. It was consecrated as a church in 1894.

Marmorkirken's exterior, scrubbed clean of a century's worth of soot in the new millennium, is ringed by statues of Danish theologians and saints and surrounded by some of urban Copenhagen's most attractive buildings.

The church interior, with its immense circular nave, can be viewed free – access to the wonderful dome will cost though, and opening hours are limited. Views from the dome are quite stunning – you'll get a broad vista of the city. Note that the church closes for events such as weddings, however, so it's best not to plan your visit for a Saturday in spring!

MEDICINSK-HISTORISK MUSEUM Map pp232-4

☎ 35 32 38 00; www.mhm.ku.dk; Bredgade 62; adult/concession 30/20kr; 🕙 guided tours 11am & 1pm Wed-Fri, 1pm Sun Nov-Jan, 7pm Wed & Thu Feb-Apr & 18 Aug-Oct, 11am Wed & Thu, 2pm Sun 16 Jun-17 Aug; bus No 1A

Housed in a former surgical academy dating from 1786, this museum deals with the history of medicine, pharmacy and dentistry over the past three centuries. Guided tours are conducted in English.

ODD FELLOW PALÆET Map pp232-4

☎ 33 14 82 24; Bredgade 28; 🕙 closed to public; bus No 1A

The beguiling façade of this Danish baroque palace will make you wish it was yours. Constructed in 1755, it's not open to the general public, but it is visible from Bredgade. If you simply must look inside, you can book a table at the Odd Fellow Restaurant – visit its website at www.oddfellow-restaurant.dk for more details.

SANKT ANSGARS KIRKE Map pp232-4

☎ 33 13 37 62; Bredgade 64; admission free; 🕙 10am-4pm Tue-Fri; bus No 1A

If all those dour Lutherans have got you down, the Roman Catholic cathedral, built in 1841 in the neo-Romanesque style., has a colourfully painted apse, some graven images and a small museum on the history of Danish Catholicism.

CHRISTIANSHAVN

Eating p114; Shopping p148

Christianshavn, on the eastern flank of Copenhagen, was established by Christian IV in the early 17th century as a commercial centre and a military buffer for the expanding city. It's cut with a network of canals, modelled after those in Holland, which leads Christianshavn to occasionally (and not unfairly) be dubbed 'Little Amsterdam'. After all, with a laid-back café culture and a past reputation for a relaxed attitude to cannabis consumption, it could be easy for some visitors to forget where they are.

Still surrounded by its old ramparts, Christianshavn today is a hotchpotch of newer apartment complexes and renovated period warehouses that have found second lives as upmarket housing and restored government offices. The neighbourhood attracts an interesting mix of not-really-struggling artists, yuppies doing their best to look like 'boho' creative types and booze-and-pot-addled dropouts. Christianshavn is also home to a sizeable Greenlandic community and was the setting of the public housing complex in the popular novel *Miss Smilla's Feeling for Snow* and movie *Smilla's Sense of Snow*.

One of the main reasons that visitors will find themselves in this part of town is the 'free state' of Christiania. In 1971 an abandoned 41-hectare military camp on the eastern side of Christianshavn was taken over by squatters who proclaimed it the 'free state' of Christiania, subject to their own laws. Police tried to clear the area but it was the height of the 'hippie revolution' and an increasing number of alternative folk from throughout Denmark arrived, attracted by communal living and the prospect of reclaiming military land for peaceful purposes.

The momentum became too much for the government to hold back and, bowing to public pressure, the community was allowed to continue as a 'social experiment'. About 1000 people settled into Christiania, turning the old barracks into schools and housing, and starting their own collective businesses, workshops and recycling programs.

Transport

Bus 2A, 19, 48, 350S
Metro Christianshavn
Boat 901, 902
Parking Street parking costs 7kr per hour from 8am to 6pm Monday to Friday

Further northeast of Christiania and Christianshavn is the rediscovered area of Holmen, which is undergoing a rapid and exciting redevelopment, as art schools take over and the area brims with creative young types making great art that will fill the galleries of the future. And even more exciting for the average visitor to Copenhagen is the brand-new Opera House that has been built on a specially constructed island.

Orientation

Christianshavn is a long, crescent-shaped island studded with battlements along its western flank and intersected by canals. Torvegade runs through it from the city centre before connecting it to Amager. The middle and eastern section of the island is home to Christiania, while the northern area includes rejuvenated education facilities utilising existing structures and the city's new Opera House on the part known as Holmen. The southernmost tip of Christiania is connected to Amager and an area known as Islands Brygge.

B & W MUSEUM Map pp232-4

☎ 32 54 02 27; www.bw-museum.dk; Strandgade 4; admission free; ⏰ 10am-1pm Mon-Fri & 1st Sun of month; metro Christianshavn

The friendly B & W Museum displays the history of Burmeister & Wein, the shipbuilding company that was founded in 1843 and in 1912 pioneered the use of diesel engines (named after Rudolf Diesel) in ocean-going ships. In January 1943 Burmeister & Wein became the target of the first Allied air raid on Copenhagen, when British bombers levelled the company's Christianshavn factory to put an end to its production of German U-boat engines. Displays (mostly in Danish) will appeal mainly to sea-dogs, but historians with a maritime predilection will also be intrigued, as will machine nuts (some of the engine displays can actually be cranked up).

CHRISTIANIA Map pp232-4

☎ 32 95 65 07; www.christiania.org; Prinsessegade; metro Christianshavn

In 1971 the 'free state' of Christiania was proclaimed. The police tried to halt proceedings but people power held sway. When the government eventually agreed to let the social experiment continue, somewhere between 700 and 1000 people went about the task of rejuvenating the area and nurturing it as a semi-Utopian community with its own businesses, social services and environmental programs. As well as hosting progressive happenings, Christiania also became a magnet for runaways and junkies. Although Christiania residents felt that the conventional press played up an image of decadence and criminality – as opposed to portraying Christiania as a self-governing, ecology-oriented and tolerant community – they did, in time, find it necessary to modify their free-law approach. A new policy was established that outlawed hard drugs in Christiania, and the heroin and cocaine pushers were expelled.

Still, Christiania remains controversial. Some Danes resent the community's rent-free, tax-free situation and many neighbours want sections of Christiania turned into public parks and school grounds. But the Christiania community has managed to hold its own over the years. The sheer size and incredible location of the land means that chances are Christiania won't last much longer – the government has put the wheels in motion to take back what it's been 'lending' to the Christiania locals for the last 30-odd years.

Although the police didn't always regularly patrol Christiania, they did stage numerous organised raids on the community and it's not unknown for police training to include a tactical sweep along Pusherstreet. When we visited, the police presence could best be described as 'heavy', with officers kitted out in riot gear rounding up dealers and the like, and some ugly scenes between locals and the authorities ensuing – and all as if for the benefit of rowdy young rubberneckers up for a bit of aggro while trying to score hash (that's no longer freely available).

Visitors are welcome to stroll or cycle through car-free Christiania, though large dogs may intimidate some free spirits. Photography is frowned upon, and outright forbidden on Pusherstreet, where marijuana joints and hashish were openly (though not legally) sold and smoked before the 2004 police crackdown on such activities.

Christiania has a small outdoor market where pipes and T-shirts are sold, a few fairly crap craft shops, a bakery and several excellent eateries. It also has a large, deservedly popular nightclub called Loppen (p135), where many live acts perform throughout the week.

The **main entrance** (Map pp232–4) of Christiania is located on Prinsessegade, 200m northeast of its intersection with Bådsmandsstræde. Pusherstreet and most shops are within a few minutes' walk of the entrance. You can take a **guided tour** (☎ 32 57 96 70; per person 30kr; 3pm 20 Jun-31 Aug, Sat & Sun 1 May-19 Jun & 1 Sep-31 Oct) of Christiania. Meet just inside the main entrance. There's also a Pusher St **information office** (☎ 32 95 65 07; nytforum@christiania.org; ⏰ noon-6pm

Mon-Thu, noon-4pm Fri) of sorts – it's just next to Oasen café.

Away from the main 'action', Christiania is a sweet place for a stroll – at it northern end you'll find many happy families going about their business, with horse rides, veggie patches and some of the coolest housing you'll see in a large city (teepees, crazy little barns and cute shacks). It's this side of Christiania that seems most worth keeping, rather than the dropout-centre atmosphere that predominates a little to the south.

CHRISTIANS KIRKE Map pp232-4
☎ 32 54 15 76; Strandgade 1; admission free; ⏰ 8am-6pm Sun-Thu, 8am-5pm Fri & Sat; metro Christianshavn

Christians Kirke was designed by Danish architect Nicolai Eigtved and completed in 1759. This church once served the local German congregation. It has an expansive, theatre-like rococo interior with tiered galleries painted a delicate shade of dove grey. During the day it's a serene escape from the outside world, although it's also the venue for numerous music recitals throughout the year (leaflets at the entrance to the church will advise on details).

GAMMEL DOK Map pp232-4
☎ 32 57 19 30; www.dac.dk; Strandgade 27B; exhibition adult/child 40kr/free; ⏰ 10am-5pm; metro Christianshavn

Gammel Dok houses the Dansk Arkitektur Center, a foundation devoted to the advancement of architecture. The site features changing exhibitions of Danish and international architecture, design and industrial art. Generally, descriptions of what you're seeing are in Danish, which makes things a little tricky, but it's still a worthwhile stop on a tour of this architecture-obsessed capital.

The building itself is suitably atmospheric – a renovated early-18th-century warehouse on the site of Copenhagen's first dock (Gammel Dok means Old Dock). See p115 for a review of the building's café and p148 for details on the great bookshop on the premises.

KNIPPELSBRO Map pp232-4
bus No 2A

This wonderful Funkis-style bridge was constructed in 1935 and connects the island of Christianshavn with Slotsholmen. Its distinctive copper cladding and lookout boxes make it a favourite landmark with many locals and

it's worth walking across at least once during your time in the city.

LILLE MØLLE Map pp232-4
☎ 33 47 38 38; www.natmus.dk; Christianshavns Voldgade 54; adult/concession/child 50/40kr/free; ⏰ guided tours 1pm, 2pm & 3pm Tue-Sun May-Sep; metro Christianshavn

This 17th-century windmill was turned over to Nationalmuseet in the 1970s and has been preserved as its last owners left it – and they left it in a very interesting state (ie filled with all manner of knick-knacks and dust-gathering goodies). It's situated on the ramparts that are southeast of Christiania, and if you time your visit just right, it's perfect for a guided tour preceded or followed by an excellent meal at the attached **restaurant/café** (p114).

OPERA HOUSE Map pp232-4
www.kgl-teater.dk; Dock Island

The finishing touches were being added to the stupendous new Henning Larsen-designed Opera House when we visited. Construction commenced in November 2001, lasting until January 2005, and the state-of-the-art structure features six stages (with 1400 seats in the main auditorium) and a 'floating' roof with a 32m-long cantilever. A gift to the people of Denmark from the super-firm AP Møller-Maersk, the building cost a tidy 2.4 billion kroner. Even if you don't like what's being performed you can marvel at the stunning views across the water to Amalienborg Slot and Marmorkirken. The Opera House, which takes up its own specially constructed 'island' (a former shipyard) north of Christianshavn, can be seen from many waterside vantage points in the city.

ORLOGSMUSEET Map pp232-4
☎ 32 54 63 63; www.orlogsmuseet.dk; Overgaden oven Vandet 58; adult/child 40/25kr; ⏰ noon-4pm Tue-Sun; metro Christianshavn

Orlogsmuseet (the Royal Danish Naval Museum) occupies an appealing custard-yellow former naval hospital on Christianshavn Kanal. This museum houses more than 300 model ships, many dating from the 16th to the 19th century – if you like tooling around with hobby glue, then you have stumbled upon the motherlode.

Some of the models were built by naval engineers to serve as design prototypes for the construction of new ships. They range from cross-sectional examples detailing frame proportions to full-dressed models with working

Lille Mølle (opposite

Neighbourhoods – Christianshavn

We have five favourite places for enjoying views of Copenhagen, each one quite unlike the others.

- **Vor Frelsers Kirke** (left) In terms of overall experience, top honour goes to this Christianshavn church where some 400 stairs lead to the crest of the 95m tower. The thrill is in the last 150 steps, which spiral up the tower's outside rim, narrowing to disappear at the top. Assuming you're not prone to vertigo, it's lots of fun and the tower tip offers an unbeatable view of Christianhavn's canals and the city's harbourfront buildings.

- **Rundetårn** (p58) For those who prefer to do their climbing on the tamer inside of a building, a ramped walkway gently winds up the tower's hollow core to a rooftop observatory. Because it sits in the heart of the old city, it makes a splendid vantage point for observing the historic buildings that comprise the city centre.

- **Post & Tele Museum** (p58) The rooftop café above this museum on Købmagergade isn't imbued with the centuries-old historic charm of the other two buildings, and access is via an ordinary elevator, but the view is similar to that from the top of the Rundetårn and you can admire the cityscape while lingering over afternoon tea or a cold beer.

- **Marmorkirken** (p75) The baroque-style dome of this church is a lovely spot to escape to on a sunny day and spy on the swanky streets below and into the distance.

- **Demon roller coaster** (p55) Perhaps not a traditional candidate for a panoramic experience, Tivoli's new roller coaster p120certainly puts things in a blindingly fast, topsy-turvy perspective that brings new meaning to the phrase 'my heart was in my stomach'.

sails. The detail involved in these extraordinary creations is well worth admiring.

The museum also displays a collection of figureheads, navigational instruments, ship lanterns, a Fresnel lens from a lighthouse and the propeller from the German U-boat that sank the *Lusitania*. Temporary exhibitions with a maritime theme are held here throughout the year, and there's a cafeteria on the premises in case you get peckish.

VOR FRELSERS KIRKE Map pp232-4

☎ 32 57 27 98; Sankt Annæ Gade 29; admission free, tower adult/child 20/10kr; ☺ 11am-4.30pm Mon-Sat, noon-4.30pm Sun; metro Christianshavn

A few minutes southwest of Christiania is the 17th-century Vor Frelsers Kirke (Our Saviour's Church), which once benefited from close ties with the Danish monarchy and has a suitably grand (albeit slightly faded) interior.

Take a good look at the immense pipe organ, built in 1698, which contains some 4000 pipes and is decorated with flabbergastingly elaborate wood carvings, seemingly supported by two large elephants bedecked in blue and gold. Also noteworthy is the ornate baroque altar adorned with marble cherubs and angels, designed by the Swede Nicodemus Tessin in 1695.

For a soul-stirring panoramic city view (many of the attractions listed in this chapter will be visible from these dizzy heights), make the head-spinning 400-step ascent up the church's 95m-high spiral tower – the last 150 steps run along the outside rim of the tower, narrowing to the point where they literally disappear at the top. If heights or confined spaces make you panic, then you should probably avoid this particular hike. The colourful spire was added to the church in 1752 by Lauritz de Thurah, who took his inspiration from Boromini's tower of St Ivo in Rome. It was climbed in 1752 by King Frederik V on inauguration day.

If you'd like to hear the organ, it's used in church services, including an English-language one that's held at noon on Sunday. Piped music is often played in the church anyway, making it a rather nice spot to collect your thoughts before resuming a tour of the area.

NØRREBRO

Eating p116; Shopping p148; Sleeping p160

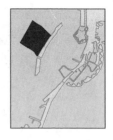

The Nørrebro quarter of the city developed in the mid-19th century as a working-class neighbourhood. More recently it has attracted a large immigrant community and has become a haunt for students, musicians, artists and a fair few upwardly mobile types. In the 1980s and '90s, Nørrebro was the scene for civil unrest and protest on a number of issues, not least of which was the attempted deportation of second-generation immigrants in the late 1990s. Although parts of the suburb seem as bustling and commerce-obsessed as, for example, Vesterbro, there are a few social problems in Nørrebro, and as Copenhagen goes, some of the streets have a down-at-heel, depressed feel that might seem a little intimidating late at night.

The suburb boasts lots of interesting Middle Eastern and Asian restaurants and some of Copenhagen's hippest nightspots. There are a number of second-hand clothing shops in the streets radiating out from Sankt Hans Torv, antique/retro shops along Ravnsborggade, and a Saturday-morning flea market a few blocks to the west on Nørrebrogade along the wall of the Assistens Kirkegård. Blågårdsgade is a pedestrianised street with a number of cool little cafés and a counterculture-meets-proletarian aesthetic.

Orientation

Nørrebro itself is a very large suburb, but for the purposes of this guide, it's easiest to consider it as the area bounded by the Three Lakes (Sankt Jørgens Sø, Peblinge Sø and Sortedams Sø), Tagensvej (running from Fredensbro in a northwest direction), Åboulevard (running northwest from the

road that divides Sankt Jørgens Sø and Peblinge Sø) and Jagtvej (running between the two at the northern boundary of Assistens Kirkegård). Despite its name, Nørrebro station is all but useless as a transport option for sightseeing – it's best to stick with buses or walking.

ASSISTENS KIRKEGÅRD Map pp236-7

☎ 35 37 19 17; Kapelvej 4; admission free; ☼ 8am-5pm 1 Jan-28 Feb, 8am-6pm 1 Mar-30 Apr & 1 Sep-31 Oct, 8am-8pm 1 May-31 Aug, 8am-4pm 1 Nov-31 Dec; bus Nos 5A, 350S

This cemetery in the heart of Nørrebro is the burial place of some of Denmark's most celebrated citizens, including philosopher Søren Kierkegaard, physicist Niels Bohr, authors Hans Christian Andersen and Martin Andersen Nexø, and artists Jens Juel, Christen Købke and CW Eckersberg. It's an interesting place to wander around – as much a park and garden as it is a graveyard, with people walking pets, picnicking and enjoying the sunshine. There are tall trees, green lawns and quiet spaces where people come on summer days to sunbathe.

The cemetery is divided into sectors, which helps in locating specific sites. A good place to start is at the main entrance on Kapelvej, which has an office, the **Assistens Kirkegårds**

Formidlingscenter (☎ 35 37 19 17; ☼ 9am-2pm Mon-Fri), where you can pick up a brochure mapping famous gravesites.

Even without the brochure you should be able to meander your way along the paths to some of the big-name graves. From the office, turn southwest (left) just before the chapel and continue for a couple of minutes in that direction to reach Hans Christian Andersen's grave at P1; you'll pass Martin Andersen Nexø's en route at H2. To get to Søren Kierkegaard's grave, turn right instead of left at the chapel and walk a few minutes to the northeast until you reach A17; Jens Juel (A21) and Christen Købke (A9) are nearby.

If you want to dig deeper into cemetery lore, the Assistens Kirkegårds Formidlingscenter, a cultural group based inside the main entrance at Kapelvej 4 (and whose motto is 'Meet the Danes – both the living and the dead!'), arranges guided tours.

Dying to Get In

Assistens Kirkegård, which translates as 'assistant or auxiliary cemetery', was established in 1760 to provide an overflow for the more prestigious burial places in central Copenhagen. In those days Nørrebro was considered well beyond the city limits and the new cemetery was so shunned by Copenhagen's elite that during its first few decades it was little more than a pauper's burial ground.

By 1800 churches in crowded Copenhagen were restricting new burials and city folk began to warm to the Nørrebro cemetery's garden-like setting. The widely held image of the place changed so dramatically that Assistens Kirkegård suddenly became a fashionable resting place for the well-heeled.

Although people from all walks of life are buried here, there's simply no other place in Denmark that can claim the bones of so many famous 19th- and 20th-century Danes.

POLITIHISTORISK MUSEUM Map pp236-7
☎ 35 36 88 88; Fælledvej 20; adult/child 25kr/free;
⏰ 11am-4pm Tue, Thu & Sun; bus Nos 3A, 5A, 350S
Given the city's well-deserved reputation as a law-abiding haven of safety, perhaps you'll feel the need to come here and see that yes, Danes do break the law sometimes. And they get punished for it. We'd gone so long without seeing a cop we were beginning to wonder if there were any in the city, but this museum (not much information in English) set us straight. Even though children are admitted free, some of the photos on display are pretty unsavoury and quite graphic.

NØRREPORT & AROUND
Eating p118; Sleeping p161

Nørreport takes its name from the fact that it was once the site of the northern gate to the city. The gate, which was situated near the intersection of Nørre Voldgade and Nørregade, is long gone but the area still plays a significant role in providing access to the city as it is home to a bustling transport station and some natty restaurants, bars and cafés. The area between the station and the Three Lakes, especially the charming street of Nansensgade, is often compared to Greenwich Village in New York. If you've ever been to Greenwich Village, the connection will seem a little tenuous overall, but there are a few traces in the area's funky little restaurants and cafés, art boutiques and savvy locals.

This neighbourhood has a posh side though, as it's also home to a magnificent royal castle, three worthwhile art museums and a couple of the city's finest public gardens crammed with trees and flowers. Not surprisingly, it draws lots of visitors from both Copenhagen's citizens and visitors alike. As many of the sights, including the gardens, are adjacent to each other, this is a great area to explore on foot. Transport, via metro, S-train or bus, is a breeze. Accommodation here is also very good, including some gay-friendly options (p161). There's also a gay-friendly park.

Nørreport is home to the city's main outdoor produce market, Israels Plads, and a museum dedicated to the working class, who were once the dominant demographic in most of this region. Nowadays

Keys to the City

From the 1600s to the 1850s, Copenhagen was enclosed by a ring-shaped fortification of earthen ramparts. These fortifications made it necessary to pass through a guarded gate in order to enter or leave the city. There were four such gates – Amagerport, Vesterport, Nørreport and Østerport – the last three on the sites of present-day S-train stations.

Until 1821, each gate was locked at night with a big iron key, and the keys were taken to the king's castle where they were kept until dawn. Over the next few decades the policy was relaxed a bit, although residents still had to present a special pass to the night watchman to be able to leave the city after 10pm.

The gates served more than just a security purpose. The Nørreport gate, which provided a beeline along Nørregade to the city market at Gammeltorv, doubled as a busy toll station where farmers had to pay duty to bring their produce to market.

Nørreport is one of the most desirable and sought-after residential areas in the city – especially if you can nab a room with a view over the lakes.

Orientation

For the purposes of this guide, this area is comprised of the eastern edge of the Three Lakes starting at the top of Sortedams Sø and continuing down to the bottom of Peblinge Sø and Gyldenløvesgade. East of this the area extends to Nørre Voldgade, past Nørreport station to Gothersgade and further east to Kronprinsessegade, where it heads north to Dag Hammarskjölds Allé.

ARBEJDERMUSEET Map pp232-4

☎ 33 93 25 75; www.arbejdermuseet.dk; Rømersgade 22; adult/child 50/30kr; 10am-4pm; metro & S-train Nørreport

Arbejdermuseet (the Workers' Museum) occupies the site of an old union hall and pays homage to the working class with exhibits portraying the lives of Danish labourers in the 19th and 20th centuries. There's a traditional café and ølhalle (beer hall) on the premises, which are fun additional attractions. The museum was closed for refurbishment in the first half of 2004, but reopened, looking better than ever, in the second half of the year.

BOTANISK HAVE Map pp232-4

☎ 35 32 22 40; www.botanic-garden.ku.dk; Gothersgade 128; admission free; 8.30am-6pm May-Sep, 8.30am-4pm Tue-Sun Oct-Apr; metro & S-train Nørreport, bus Nos 5A, 6A, 150S, 350S

In the 10-hectare Botanisk Have (Botanical Gardens) to the west of Rosenborg Slot you can wander along fragrant paths amid arbours, terraces and rock gardens.

The garden encompasses part of the now-defunct city ramparts, creatively including some of the old walls to hold rock-garden plants and giving the old moat a second life as a garden pond, replete with water lilies and marsh plants.

Originally developed in 1874 for Copenhagen University's botanical studies, the garden now holds some 20,000 species of plants from around the world.

Within the botanical garden is the **Palmehus** (Map pp232–4; Palm House; 10am-3pm Tue-Sun), a large walk-through glasshouse containing a lush collection of tropical plants.

The plants are divided into different groupings, including tropical rainforest plants such as banana trees and palms, tropical savannah plants with ferns and pepper vines, and subtropical plants such as coffee trees and citrus.

There's also an opportunity to admire the miracles of modern botany by visiting the enchanting **orchid greenhouse** (2-3pm Wed, Sat & Sun), with some 500 different species of this most beautiful warm-weather flower, and the **cactus house** (1-2pm Wed, Sat & Sun), with more than 1000 species of another type of plant that really has no business being in this part of the world.

The gardens are encircled by a fence and there are only two entrances, one at the intersection of Gothersgade and Øster Voldgade and the other off Øster Farimagsgade.

BOTANISK MUSEUM Map pp232-4

☎ 35 32 22 00; www.botaniskmuseum.dk; Gothersgade 130; admission free; noon-4pm 19 Jun-31 Aug; metro & S-train Nørreport, bus Nos 5A, 6A, 150S, 350S

The modest Botanical Museum at the southern corner of the Botanisk Have features exhibits of plants from Denmark, Greenland and the rest of the world, and also stages various exhibitions related to botanical subjects.

Transport

Bus 5A, 6A, 150S, 350S, among others
Metro Nørreport
S-train Nørreport
Parking Street parking costs between 7kr and 12kr per hour between 8am and 6pm Monday to Friday and 8am and 2pm Saturday (for 12kr zones)
Bicycle Bike racks at Nørreport station

Nørreport & Around Top Five

- Getting arty at the magnificent **Statens Museum for Kunst** (p84)
- Being bedazzled by the crown jewels at **Rosenborg Slot** (p84)
- Wishing that the delightful art-filled **Davids Samling** (opposite) was your home.
- Taking time out in **Kongens Have** (opposite)
- Filling your lungs with fresh air around the **Three Lakes** (p85)

DAVIDS SAMLING Map pp232-4

☎ 33 73 49 49; www.davidmus.dk; Kronprinsesse-gade 30; admission free; ☻ 1-4pm Tue & Thu-Sun, 10am-4pm Wed; bus Nos 1A, 26, 350S

Davids Samling is a private collection that once belonged to Christian Ludvig David, a successful barrister who died in 1960, and is now maintained by a foundation he established. It occupies David's former home, a neo-classical mansion dating from 1806 just east of Kongens Have on pretty Kronprinsessegade. The scale is intimate and the displays are tastefully presented, creating an atmosphere that's more like visiting a well-to-do private home than rambling through a museum.

Davids Samling is best known for housing Scandinavia's largest collection of Islamic art, which occupies its entire 4th floor. It includes ceramics, silks, tapestries, jewellery and such exquisite works as an Egyptian rock crystal jug from AD 1000 and a 500-year-old Indian dagger inlaid with rubies.

The 1st floor of the museum is given over to Danish fine and applied arts, including 18th-century furniture, porcelain, silverware and paintings by such notable artists of the day as Jens Juel and CW Eckersberg.

The 2nd floor is largely dedicated to French furniture and porcelain of the same period, while the 3rd floor contains English Chippendale, lacquer ware and Chinoiserie.

DEN HIRSCHSPRUNGSKE SAMLING

Map pp236-7

☎ 35 42 03 36; www.hirschsprung.dk; Stockhol-msgade 20; adult/child 35kr/free, Wed free; ☻ 11am-4pm Thu-Mon, 11am-9pm Wed; bus Nos 6A, 150S

This seemingly hidden gem of a museum, dedicated to Danish art of the 19th and early 20th centuries, can be found in Østre Anlæg, the same park that holds the mighty Statens Museum for Kunst.

Den Hirschsprungske Samling is a cosy place with a delightfully personal scale, which makes it a fun spot to visit after the commodious Statens Museum for Kunst – although it may be better to wait a day or two before attempting to sample any other art after a visit to the latter.

Originally the private collection of tobacco magnate Heinrich Hirschsprung, the museum includes works by 'Golden Age' artists such as Christen Købke and CW Eckersberg, as well as pieces by the Danish symbolists and the Funen painters.

Hirschsprung was a sponsor for some of the Skagen painters and hence there's also a notable collection of works by PS Krøyer and Anna and Michael Ancher.

Hirschsprung turned his collection over to the city with the stipulation that Copenhagen build a suitable site in which to house it. The museum opened in 1911, three years after Hirschsprung's death.

Pause in the entrance room, which is itself a work of art, with a mosaic floor depicting a tobacco plant encircled by smoke, and a portrait of Hirschsprung by PS Krøyer.

GEOLOGISK MUSEUM Map pp232-4

☎ 35 32 23 45; www.geological-museum.dk; Øster Voldgade 5; adult/child 25/10kr, Wed free; ☻ 1-4pm Tue-Sun; metro & S-train Nørreport

Denmark's foremost geological museum is on the eastern corner of the Botanisk Have. It covers the geology of both Denmark and Greenland.

An affiliate of Copenhagen University, the museum has all the usual exhibits of fossils, minerals, crystals and rocks. In addition, it houses some interesting Danish displays, such as a 4.5kg chunk of amber, and some quite notable finds from Greenland; a highlight is the world's sixth-largest iron meteorite, which weighs in at 20 tonnes. Another highlight is the recently discovered collection of dinosaur footprints from the island of Bornholm. In 2004 Danish artist Per Kirkeby took on the task of 'decorating' the museum, to stunning effect, with walls, ceilings and arches given the Kirkeby treatment.

KONGENS HAVE Map pp232-4
metro & S-train Nørreport

The expansive green space behind Rosenborg Slot is the city's oldest public park and is known both as Kongens Have (the King's Gardens) and Rosenborg Slotshave (Rosenborg Castle Gardens).

Created to complement the castle, the gardens were designed by Christian IV incorporating Renaissance features, including a rectangular grid of walking paths that still provides the main pattern today. Many other features of the gardens, which once doubled as the king's private vegetable patch, have evolved over the centuries. In the early 18th century, the royal family opened the gardens to the public.

These pleasant gardens have manicured box hedges, lovely rose beds, the requisite statues,

Statens Museum for Kunst (below)

a fun children's playground and many shaded areas. The Grønnebro (Green Bridge), which leads over the moat to the castle, is flanked by copper lions. The gardens are a popular picnic spot with Copenhageners and the site of a free marionette theatre that performs on summer afternoons.

ROSENBORG SLOT Map pp232-4

☎ 33 15 32 86; www.rosenborg-slot.dk; Øster Voldgade 4A; adult/child 60/10kr; ☾ 10am-4pm May & Sep, 10am-5pm Jun-Aug, 11am-3pm Oct, 11am-2pm Tue-Sun Nov-Apr; metro & S-train Nørreport, bus No5A, 6A, 150S, 350S

This early-17th-century castle, with its fairy-tale moat and garden setting, was built in Dutch Renaissance style by Christian IV to serve as his summer home. A century later Frederik IV, who felt cramped at Rosenborg, built a roomier palace north of the city in the town of Fredensborg. In the years that followed, Rosenborg was used mainly for official functions and as a place in which to safeguard the monarchy's heirlooms.

In the 1830s the royal family decided to open the castle to visitors as a museum, while still using it as a treasury for royal regalia and jewels. It continues to serve both functions today.

The 24 rooms in the castle's upper levels are chronologically arranged, housing the furnishings and portraits of each monarch from Christian IV to Frederik VII. However, the main attraction lies on the lower level – the dazzling collection of crown jewels. These include Christian IV's ornately designed crown; the jewel-studded sword of Christian III; and Queen Margrethe II's emeralds and pearls, which are kept here when the queen is not wearing them at official functions. These items are considered such national treasures that the queen is not permitted to take the royal jewels with her when she travels outside Denmark. You'll want to wear your sunglasses for some displays – the glittering, winking diamonds and precious stones are quite dazzling.

The main entrance to the castle is off Øster Voldgade. There is also entry from the adjacent gardens via a moat footbridge when the castle is open. A good **café** (p118) is on the premises. Wheelchair access is not good.

STATENS MUSEUM FOR KUNST
Map pp232-4

☎ 33 74 84 94; www.smk.dk; Sølvgade 48; adult/child 50kr/free, Wed free; ☾ 10am-5pm Tue & Thu-Sun, Wed 10am-8pm; metro & S-train Nørreport, bus No 6A

Denmark's fabulous national gallery, Statens Museum for Kunst (the Royal Museum of Fine Arts), was founded in 1824 to house art collections belonging to the royal family. Originally sited at Christiansborg Slot, the museum opened in its current location in 1896. Statens Museum for Kunst, which has recently been renovated and has doubled in size, now lays claim to being the largest art museum in Denmark. Its facilities are first-class, and there's a wonderful and wide-ranging program of complementary activities attached to the museum, including music performances and a great children's wing. If your time is limited in Copenhagen and you need an art fix, then make this the museum you visit.

The museum's collection covers seven centuries of European art, ranging from medieval works with stylised religious themes to free-form modern art. There's an interesting collection of old masters by Dutch and Flemish artists, including Rubens, Breughel, Dürer and Frans Hals, as well as more contemporary European paintings by Matisse, Picasso and Munch. Look out for famous older works such as Cranach's portrait of Martin Luther (1532) and Rembrandt's *Supper at Emmaus* (1648). The museum also has an extensive collection of drawings, engravings and lithographs representing the works of such prominent artists as Piranesi, Degas and Toulouse-Lautrec.

As might be expected, Statens Museum also contains one of the world's best collections of Danish art. Classic works by Jens Juel, including a self-portrait, highlight the 18th century.

There's a whole room of works, nearly 60 in all, by the leading 19th-century 'Golden Age' artist CW Eckersberg, and his best-known student, Christen Købke. The early 20th century is represented in the paintings of the Skagen artists PS Krøyer and Michael Ancher, whose seaside images are among the most recognised artworks in Denmark, with their dominant use of the colour blue. In the 1830s, a number of Danish painters (Fritz Petzholdt, Christen Købke, August Wilhelm Boesen and Thorald Læssøe) visited and painted the Italian isle of Capri in the Bay of Naples, and these works are well represented in the museum.

The splendid new modern art wing has numerous works by Danish artists Richard Mortensen, Per Kirkeby and Palle Nielsen, as well as pieces by such international heavyhitters as Picasso, Braque and Gris, and contemporaries like Sam Taylor Wood and Donald Judd. One of the more spectacular pieces from the modern Danish collection is Svend Wiig Hansen's (1922–97) *The Earth Weeps* (1981), which he painted in one extraordinary hour, obviously as a man possessed.

The museum is free on Wednesdays. Wheelchair access is excellent throughout the building. For details of the museum's **café**, see p118.

THE THREE LAKES Map pp232-4
metro & S-train Nørreport, bus Nos 2A, 5A, 6A, 150S, 250S, 350S

Forming an elemental boundary between Copenhagen's city centre (Indre By) are these three man-made lakes. The first, which starts at Gammel Kongvej and borders Vesterbro, runs north, and is known as Sankt Jørgens Sø. It's crossed by Gyldenløvesgade and met by Peblinge Sø, which in turn is crossed by Dronning Louises Bro (Queen Louise's Bridge), taking you into Nørrebro and its busy main drag of Nørrebrogade. The next lake is Sortedams Sø, which is bisected by Fredensbro. The apartment buildings that surround the lakes are some of the most sought-after in Copenhagen, as they offer abundant light and some delightful greenery-and-water views. Still, egalitarian Copenhagen won't just settle for the elite having access to such a nice area – there are walking tracks (Sortedam Dossering) surrounding the lakes, and they make for incredibly popular spots for people to get some fresh air and unwind, with tables and chairs placed under the trees and plenty of prams, bikes, Frisbees and smooching on display when the sun comes out.

ØRSTEDS PARKEN Map pp232-4
metro & S-train Nørreport, bus No 5A

This lovely mid-size park is an easily found oasis off busy Nørre Voldgade. It's named after the famous Danish physicist Hans Christian Ørsteds (he discovered electromagnetism) and features a nice pond to relax next to by day. At night, things hot up and it's a popular cruising spot for gay men practising magnetism of a different sort, and close to the gay bars of the Latin Quarter.

> ## Top Five Museums
>
> - **Statens Museum for Kunst** A wonderful collection of Danish and European art from the 13th century to today (opposite)
> - **Ny Carlsberg Glyptotek** Gauguin paintings galore and sculptural marvels from Ancient Greece and Rome (p53)
> - **Arken** Where the art competes with the building for your attention (p94)
> - **Nationalmuseet** The best place to get the lowdown on Denmark (p53)
> - **Kunstindustrimuseet** A treasure-trove of decorative art (p75)

VESTERBRO

Eating p119; Shopping p149; Sleeping p161

Despite the fact that the Vesterbro district boasts few conventional sightseeing attractions, for many visitors to Copenhagen it's the first place they'll see, as it's home to both Central Station and the city's main hotel district – not to mention the red-light district. The rosy-hued promise of this once-fabled area still draws a few nostalgic types who have their hearts (not to mention other parts of their anatomy) set on believing the corny old myth that Copenhagen is the city of easy-going sexcapades taking place round the clock in warm Nordic beds staffed solely by randy natural blondes.

When Denmark became the first country to legalise pornography in the boon year of 1967, Vesterbro's porn shops and seedy nightclubs became a magnet for tourists and voyeurs and the consumption of porn boomed. Although it's not necessarily any tamer these days, liberalisation in other countries has made the area less of a novelty and the locals seem quite unfazed and unfussed by the whole business.

Vesterbro in the new millennium has a varied character that's readily observed by walking along its best-known street, Istedgade, or jam-packed Vesterbrogade, which hums with commercial activity emanating from a range of business hotels, ethnic restaurants, cheap-and-cheerful shops and unpretentious, fun bars.

If you're heading down Istedgade, about halfway down you'll notice the red-light district receding and the neighbourhood becoming increasingly multiethnic, with a mix of Pakistani, Turkish and Asian businesses. Vesterbro, together with the adjacent Nørrebro, is home to much of the city's immigrant community and abounds with a thriving mix of the new and the old.

> ## Transport
>
> **Bus** 1A, 2A, 3A, 5A, 6A, 10, 250S, 650S
> **S-train** Central Station, Dybbølsbro
> **Parking** Street parking is free for two hours between 9am and 7pm Monday to Friday

Move further westward and another shift occurs as coolly designed cafés with smart light fittings, classic chairs and arty-looking patrons make their presence felt among the fashion shops, gift shops and snug little bars. Vesterbro is also home to the lovely open space of Halmtorvet, which hosts a number of great outdoor cafés away from the traffic fumes and bright lights.

Orientation

Vesterbro is a relatively large area that starts at Central Station on Bernstorffsgade. Heading west through streets such as Vesterbrogade, Istedgade and Sønder Blvd, it eventually connects with Frederiksberg (opposite). It also contains Dybbølsbro train station at its southeastern flank before it meets the water.

IMAX TYCHO BRAHE PLANETARIUM

Map pp232-4

☎ 33 12 12 24; www.tycho.dk; Gammel Kongevej 10; adult/child 85/65kr; 🕑 10.30am-8.30pm Fri-Tue, 9.45am-8.30pm Wed & Thu; S-train Vesterport or Central Station

This planetarium, about 750m northwest of Central Station, has a domed space theatre that offers shows of the night sky using state-of-the-art equipment capable of projecting more than 7500 stars, planets and galaxies.

The planetarium's 1000-sq-metre screen also hosts Imax natural science films on subjects ranging from astronauts in the space shuttle to divers exploring tropical reefs in flavour-of-the-moment Australia.

The planetarium was named after the famed Danish astronomer Tycho Brahe (1546–1601), whose creation of precision astronomical instruments allowed him to make more exact observations of planets and stars and paved the way for the discoveries made by later astronomers.

These days the most popular shows are IMAX films, which last about 50 minutes and are usually followed by a 10-minute show featuring the night sky. In addition there's a planetarium-only show a couple of times a week; call ahead for the schedule.

There are also some general astronomy exhibits that include a small moon rock and photos of planets, satellites and astronauts.

KØBENHAVNS BYMUSEUM Map pp232-4

☎ 33 21 07 72; www.bymuseum.dk: Vesterbrogade 59; adult/child 20kr/free, Fri free; ☯ 10am-4pm Wed-Mon May-Sep, 1-4pm Wed-Mon Oct-Apr; bus No 6A

The Copenhagen City Museum features displays about the history and development of Copenhagen, mainly in the form of paintings and scale models. The exhibits begin with the city's origins from a seaside trading post in the 11th century, detail its blossoming as a Renaissance capital under Christian IV and wrap up with the industrial revolution and founding of the welfare state.

One curiosity is the small exhibit dedicated to the religious philosopher Søren Kierkegaard, who was born in Copenhagen in 1813 and maintained an often-turbulent relationship with local authorities before dying in a city hospital at the age of 42 (he is buried in Assistens Kirkegård; see p80). The collection includes a handful of the philosopher's personal possessions and some unflattering caricatures exaggerating Kierkegaard's spinal deformity that appeared in the local media of the day.

OUTLYING DISTRICTS

Copenhagen stretches north, south and west (Sweden lies east), with a number of interesting suburbs encouraging visitors to escape the city centre and explore new terrain. We've included the following suburbs and areas in this section: Frederiksberg, Østerbro, Islands Brygge, Hellerup, Charlottenlund, Klampenborg, Rungsted, Lyngby, Ishøj and Dragør.

Orientation

Frederiksberg lies west of Vesterbro and southwest of Nørrebro, and is easy to reach from the city centre by bus or metro or even on foot. Østerbro is on the other side of Nørrebro and west of the area called Kastellet and Østerport station. Islands Brygge lies in the area called Amager, just southeast of Christianshavn.

The other areas mentioned in this chapter have been organised in an anticlockwise direction starting north of central Copenhagen: Hellerup, Charlottenlund, Klampenborg and Rungsted are all found on the coast to the city's north, while Lyngby is inland and northwest. To the southwest you'll find Ishøj, and Dragør is southeast of the main central area.

Outlying Districts Top Five

- Swimming in **Islands Brygge Havnebadet** (p89)
- Flooding your senses with modern art at **Arken** (p94)
- Being inspired by the **Karen Blixen Museet** (p93)
- Going Dutch in **Dragør** (p94)
- Scoring a free beer or two at the **Carlsberg Visitors Centre** (p88)

FREDERIKSBERG

Eating p120; Sleeping p165

Frederiksberg is a pleasant, upmarket area with an abundance of green space, the most notable of which is Frederiksberg Have (Frederiksberg Garden). It is actually a separate city to Copenhagen (a bit like Christiania, only legit and wealthy), with its own administrative system that even includes slightly lower taxes to the rest of the city, making this area, with its handsome streets and houses, an even more desirable address to many aspiring locals.

BAKKEHUSMUSEET Map p238

☎ 33 31 43 62; www.bakkehusmuseet.dk; Rahbeks Allé 23; adult/child 10/1kr; ☯ 11am-3pm Wed, Thu, Sat & Sun; S-train Valby

This handsome building, the oldest in Frederiksberg, was once the house of Knut and Kamma Rahbek. The Rahbeks were a prominent couple of Danish literature's 'Golden Age', and their former home (they lived here 1802–30) now serves as a sort of museum for that period, with artistic artefacts and mementoes throughout the building and interesting period details. There's also a sweet garden. A regular guest at the Rahbeks' home was none other than Hans Christian Andersen (among other writers from the period).

CARLSBERG VISITORS CENTRE Map p238

☎ 33 27 13 14; www.carlsberg.com; Gamle Carlsberg Vej 11; admission free; ⏲ 10am-4pm Tue-Sun; S-train Enghave, bus No 3A

The Carlsberg Visitors Centre, adjacent to Carlsberg brewery, has an exhibition area on the history of Danish beer from 1370 BC (yes, they carbon-dated a bog girl who was found in a peat bog caressing a jug of well-aged brew!). Dioramas, in English as well as Danish, give the lowdown on the brewing process and en route to your final destination you'll pass antique copper vats and see the stables that still keep a team of one dozen beautiful Jutland drayhorses.

The self-guided tour ends, apropos, at a little pub where you get your choice of two free beers – make one of them the Carls Special, a deliciously smooth, dark malt that's a local favourite.

Worthy of note as you enter the brewery grounds is the **Elephant Gate** (Map p238), two stone elephant pillars that span Ny Carlsberg Vej, the main road through the complex.

ROYAL COPENHAGEN Map p238

☎ 38 14 92 97; Smallegade 45; 40kr; ⏲ 9am-3pm Mon-Fri; metro Frederiksberg

Founded in 1775, Royal Copenhagen, Denmark's leading porcelain company, moved its operations to this Frederiksberg site in 1884. The factory complex was so large that the company referred to it as a community. In 2004, the site was sold and the buildings are being converted into luxury apartments. If you're curious to see how the porcelain is produced, the finer pieces of which are still hand-painted, you can visit the Royal Copenhagen visitor centre, which retains a small office on the site of its former factory. You'll watch a video about the history of the company, concentrating on world-famous designs such as Flora Danica and Blue Fluted, see some historic pieces (including a few designed by the Queen herself) and turn your hand to painting some porcelain, which is a surprisingly enjoyable (albeit painstaking) experience.

The adjacent **factory shop** (☎ 38 34 10 04; ⏲ 9am-5.30pm Mon-Fri, 9am-2pm Sat) sells seconds at prices that are up to 50% off what you'd pay in stores.

STORM P MUSEET Map p238

☎ 38 86 05 23; www.stormp-museet.dk; Frederiksberg Runddel; adult/child 30/5kr; ⏲ 10am-4pm Tue-Sun 1 May-30 Sep, 10am-4pm Wed, Sat & Sun 1 Oct-30 Apr; metro Frederiksberg

Storm P (Robert Storm Petersen; 1882–1949) was a renowned Frederiksberg-born cartoonist, whose social commentaries and satirical illustrations made him an enormously popular figure in the 1920s with newspaper readers. You won't necessarily need to understand Danish to get the gist of the items on display, but you might feel as though you're stuck in a bit of a time warp. The museum itself is housed in a handsome red-brick building at one of the entrances to Frederiksberg Have.

ZOOLOGISK HAVE Map p238

☎ 70 20 02 80; www.zoo.dk; Roskildevej 32; adult/child 95/55kr; ⏲ 9am-6pm Jun-Aug, 9am-5pm Apr-May & Sep-Oct, 9am-4pm Nov-Mar; bus Nos 6A, 28

This national zoo, which dates from 1859, has a large (and well-looked-after) collection of 2500 caged creatures, including elephants, lions, zebras, hippos, gorillas and polar bears. Special sections include the Tropical Zoo, the Children's Zoo, the Ape Jungle, the African Savannah and the South American Pampas.

ØSTERBRO

Eating p120; Sleeping p166

The Østerbro section of the city, which extends north from Nørrebro, is largely residential and a bit upmarket. Nonetheless, it has the distinction of being home to Copenhagen's largest and oldest summer hostel, the national sports stadium Parken (p135), the inviting public park Fælledparken and a number of theatres.

Fælledparken circles the zoo and is crisscrossed with walking trails. It has large shade trees, a meandering canal and sunny lawns popular with sunbathers and picnickers.

BRUMBLEBY Map pp236-7
S-train Østerport, bus Nos 1A, 3A
This is a gaily painted example of public housing gone right. Constructed in the 1850s, the 500-or-so houses were built by the Danish Medical Association in order to provide housing for the city's poor. Today you can walk around the area and soak up the quiet, friendly atmosphere.

ZOOLOGISK MUSEUM Map pp236-7
☎ 35 32 10 01; Universitetsparken 15; adult/child 40/10kr; ⏰ 11am-5pm Tue-Sun; bus Nos 18, 42 43, 185, 150S, 173E
This modern zoological museum, on the corner of Jagtvej and Universitetsparken, is where magnificent creatures such as North Zealand deer and Greenlandic polar bears come to get well and truly stuffed. It also has interesting dioramas, recorded animal sounds, a 14m-long bowhead whale skeleton and insect displays.

ISLANDS BRYGGE
Eating p121; Shopping p150; Sleeping p167
Islands Brygge is a nifty area south of Christianshavn that has an arty feel and seems to have remained something of a secret, even amongst locals. It's not loaded with obvious tourist attractions but definitely rewards a wander, with the odd cool little café, shop or gallery and our favourite spot to swim in the whole city.

It's a largely residential area that also holds a number of converted warehouse and factory spaces that house edgy galleries and design firms and apartment developments. This influx of a bohemian population has brought a few businesses (cafés, retro shops and funky young designers) into the area, reflecting the changing mood of the neighbourhood.

There are some handy eating options scattered about (p121) and a few groovy shops (p150), and the area is easily reached by the metro.

ISLANDS BRYGGE HAVNEBADET
Map pp232-4
☎ 23 71 31 89; Islands Brygge; admission free; ⏰ 7am-7pm 1 Jun-31 Aug; metro Islands Brygge
Our favourite development in Islands Brygge, this is the funkiest public pool we've ever seen. With red-and-white striped barriers and clean canal water, this is a great spot to come on a summer's day and catch up with the world and his wife. For more information about the pool, see p138.

Islands Brygge Havnebadet (above)

HELLERUP

Eating p121

Hellerup is largely a suburb of the city, but it does have one site that's noteworthy for those travelling with children. It's a quiet, solidly respectable residential area on the coast, and therefore it has its fair share of wealthy (but avowedly modest) residents.

Transport

Bus 1A
S-train Hellerup

EXPERIMENTARIUM Map p235

☎ 39 27 33 33; www.experimentarium.dk; Tuborg Havnevej 7; adult/child 105/70kr; ☺ 9.30am-5pm Mon, Wed-Fri, 9.30am-9pm Tue, 11am-5pm Sat & Sun; S-train Hellerup, bus No 1A

This extensive hands-on technology and natural science centre is housed in a former bottling hall of Tuborg Breweries. The centre contains some 300 hands-on exhibits, making it a fun place for kids to play and learn at the same time. It features time-honoured standards such as the hall of mirrors, and computer-enhanced activities that make it possible to compose water music, stand on the moon or take a ride on an inverted bicycle. All the exhibits have instructions in both English and Danish.

CHARLOTTENLUND

Charlottenlund is a well-to-do coastal area on Copenhagen's northern outskirts. Despite being so close to the city, it has a decent sandy beach, although the smokestacks of Hellerup to the south are part of the backdrop. Just inland from the beach is the moat-encircled Charlottenlund Fort, which now harbours a camping ground. There's not much left of the old fort other than some cannons, but it's a pleasant place with swans, ducks and lots of birdsong.

Transport

S-Train Charlottenlund

CHARLOTTENLUND SLOTSPARK

Map p235
S-train Charlottenlund

From the Danmarks Akvarium (below) car park a path leads directly into Charlottenlund Slotspark (Charlottenlund Castle Park), where there are gardens and an attractive three-storey manor house called **Charlottenlund Slot** (Map p235) that once belonged to the royal family. The last royal resident was Princess Louise, the wife of Frederik VIII, who lived here until her death in 1926. An obelisk monument at the rear of the manor house commemorates the couple.

Since the 1930s the building has been the headquarters of the Danish Institute for Fisheries Research. Walkways lead around the park-like grounds, making for an enjoyable stroll.

DANMARKS AKVARIUM Map p235

☎ 39 62 32 83; www.akvarium.dk; Kavalergården 1; adult/child 70/35kr; ☺ 10am-6pm mid-Feb–mid-Oct, 10am-4pm mid-Oct–mid-Feb; S-train Charlottenlund

Danmarks Akvarium is 500m north of Charlottenlund Fort. By Scandinavian standards it's a fairly large aquarium and the well-presented collection includes cold-water fish, tropical fish, live corals, nurse sharks, sea turtles, electric eels, crocodiles and piranhas. There's also a 'touch pool' section for children that's open at weekends and school holidays.

KLAMPENBORG

Eating p121

Klampenborg, which is situated only 20 minutes from Central Station on the S-train's line C, is a favourite spot for Copenhageners on family outings, and with good reason. Its main attractions are a large amusement park, a wooded deer park crisscrossed with trails and Bellevue Beach, a sandy stretch that gets packed with sunbathers in summer; all are within walking distance of one another.

BAKKEN Map p230

☎ 39 63 55 44; www.bakken.dk; Dyrehavevej 62; admission free, rides adult/child from 50/25kr; ☺ 2-10pm Mon-Wed, 2pm-midnight Thu & Fri, 1pm-midnight Sat & noon-10pm Sun 1 Apr-23 May, 2pm-midnight Mon-Fri, 1pm-midnight Sat, noon-midnight Sun 24 May-20 Jun, noon-midnight 21 Jun-1 Aug, 2pm-midnight Mon-Fri, 1pm-midnight Sat & noon-midnight Sun 2 Aug-30 Aug; S-train Klampenborg, then 800m walk

Transport

Bus For Ordrupgaard, bus No 388 from Klampenborg, fifth stop from Klampenborg station
S-train For Bakken and Dyrehaven, get off at Klampenborg

The 400-year-old Bakken on the southern edge of Dyrehaven lays claim to being the world's oldest amusement park. A sort of blue-collar version of Tivoli, it's a honky-tonk carnival of bumper cars, roller coasters, slot machines and foaming beer halls filled with cheery kids and red-faced parents. All in all, there are more than 100 different amusements, with rides taking the shape of Viking ships, swans and the like. It also has all the requisite fast-food stalls and carnival games, plus a fun atmosphere at weekends, when it gets pretty crowded.

There are discounted multiuse passes. Bakken is an easy 10-minute walk west from Klampenborg station. If you come by car, parking is available for 50kr.

DYREHAVEN Map p230
S-train Klampenborg

Dyrehaven (Deer Park), more formally called Jægersborg Dyrehave, is an expansive 1000-hectare area of beech trees and meadows crisscrossed by an alluring network of walking and cycling trails. Dyrehaven was established as a royal hunting ground in 1669 and has evolved into the capital's most popular picnicking area.

At the centre of Dyrehaven is the manor house **Eremitagen** (Map p230), which was built as a hunting lodge by Christian VI in 1736; a relief of the king adorns the western façade. Located on a grassy knoll, it's a great vantage point from which to spot herds of grazing deer.

In all, there are about 2000 deer in the park, mostly fallow deer, but also red deer and Japanese sika deer. Among the red deer are a few rare white specimens, descendants of deer imported in 1737 from Germany, where they are now extinct. Eremitagen can be reached by walking 2km north of Bakken along the main route, Kristiansholmsvej, although it can also be reached from numerous other points

Bellevue Beach, Klampenborg (opposite)

in the park as most of the largest trails radiate like spokes from Eremitagen.

Hackney carriages provide horse-drawn rides into the park from the Dyrehaven entrance just north of Klampenborg S-train station. Rides cost 60kr per person for 30 minutes; the coaches carry up to five passengers, but it's most romantic with two…

ORDRUPGAARD Map p230

☎ 39 64 11 83; www.ordrupgaard.dk; Vilvordevej 110; ⏰ closed until 2005, 1-4pm Tue-Sun

Ordrupgaard is a small art museum specialising in French art, primarily from the impressionist period, and includes works by Gauguin, Degas, Monet, Renoir and Cézanne. It also has a collection of Danish contemporary art. The museum occupies the former home of its wealthy founder, Wilhelm Hansen, who bequeathed both his house and his private art collection to the people of Denmark. When this book was going to press, the museum was undergoing the construction of a new wing (designed by architect Zaha Hadid); the museum should be open by the time you read this. During construction, the extensive **grounds** (⏰ 8.30am-5.30pm Mon-Fri, 11.30am-5.30pm Sat & Sun) will remain open to the public.

RUNGSTED

Eating p121

Rungsted, on the super-exclusive (but non-glitzy, in typical Danish fashion) Øresund coast, is lined with the seaside homes of some of Copenhagen's wealthiest residents. It's also the site of Rungstedlund, the estate that houses the Karen Blixen museum. Rungstedlund was originally built as an inn around 1500. King Karl XII of Sweden stayed there in 1700 and the Danish lyric poet Johannes Ewald, who wrote Denmark's national anthem, was a boarder from 1773 to 1776. The property was later turned into a private residence and in 1879 was purchased by Karen Blixen's father, Wilhelm Dinesen. Blixen was born at Rungstedlund in 1885 and lived there off and on until her death in 1962.

Transport

S-train Rungsted
Parking Available at the museum

Out of Rungsted

Karen Blixen was born Karen Christenze Dinesen on 17 April 1885 in Rungsted, a well-to-do community north of Copenhagen. She studied art in Copenhagen, Rome and Paris. In 1914, when she was 28 and eager to escape the confines of her bourgeois family, she married her second cousin Baron Bror von Blixen-Finecke, after having a failed love affair with his twin brother Hans. It was a marriage of convenience – she wanted his title and he needed her money.

The couple then moved to Kenya and started a coffee plantation, which Karen was left to manage. The baron had several extramarital affairs and eventually infected Karen with syphilis. She came home to Denmark for medical treatment, but subsequently returned to Africa and divorced the baron in 1925. In 1932, after her plantation had failed and the great love of her life, Englishman Denys Finch-Hatton, had died in a tragic plane crash, Karen Blixen left Africa and returned to the family estate in Rungsted, where she began to write. Danes were slow to take to Blixen's writings, in part because she consistently wrote about the aristocracy in approving terms and used an old-fashioned idiomatic style that some thought arrogant. Her insistence on being called 'Baroness' also took its toll on her popularity in a Denmark bent on minimising class disparity.

Following rejection by publishers in Denmark and England, her first book, *Seven Gothic Tales*, a compilation of short stories set in the 19th century, was published in New York in 1934 (under the pseudonym Isak Dinesen) and was so well received that it was chosen as a Book-of-the-Month selection. It was only after her success in the USA that Danish publishers took a serious interest in her works.

In 1937, Blixen's landmark *Out of Africa*, the memoirs of her life in Kenya, was published in both Danish and English. This was followed by *Winter's Tales* in 1942, *The Angelic Avengers* in 1944, *Last Tales* in 1957, *Anecdotes of Destiny* in 1958 and *Shadows on the Grass* in 1960. Blixen died in 1962, and three of her books were published after her death: *Daguerreotypes and Other Essays, Carnival: Entertainments and Posthumous Tales* and *Letters from Africa 1914–1931*. Two of Blixen's works were turned into the Oscar-winning films *Out of Africa* and *Babette's Feast*. Despite being in the running for such an honour, she was never awarded the Nobel Prize for Literature.

A few years before her death, Blixen arranged for her estate to be turned over to the private Rungstedlund Foundation. For years the foundation had only enough money to maintain the grounds as a bird sanctuary, but the posthumous book sales that were spurred by the success of the films made it possible to turn her former home into a museum (opposite) in 1991.

Rungsted has a tourist information kiosk at the intersection of Rungstedvej and Rungsted Strandvej, opposite Rungsted's large yacht harbour.

KAREN BLIXEN MUSEET

☎ 45 57 10 57; www.karen-blixen.dk; Rungsted Strandvej 111; adult/child 40kr/free; ☯ 10am-5pm Tue-Sun 1 May-30 Sep, 1-4pm Wed-Fri & 11am-4pm Sat & Sun 1 Oct-30 Apr; S-train Rungsted

Karen Blixen's former home, now a small, but fascinating museum, is furnished in much the way she left it and has photographs, paintings, Masai spears and shields and other mementoes of her time in Africa. In the exhibition room is the old Corona typewriter that Blixen used to write her novels.

One wing of the museum, a converted carriage house and stables, houses a library of Blixen's books in many languages, a smart-looking **café** (mains 60kr) and a bookshop; there's also a very moving presentation on Blixen's life, detailing various familial, physical and personal tragedies, plus a host of artistic triumphs. You'll come away with a great deal of admiration for Blixen's sheer spunk and fortitude.

The grounds contain gardens and a wood, part of which has been set aside as a bird sanctuary. Blixen lies buried in a little clearing shaded by a sprawling beech tree, her grave marked by a simple stone slab inscribed with her name.

To get there, walk north from the train station up Stationvej, turn right at the lights onto Rungstedvej and then at its intersection with Rungsted Strandvej walk south about 300m and you'll come to the museum; the whole walk takes about 15 minutes. There's no disabled access at the museum.

LYNGBY

Sleeping p167

The main sight of interest in Lyngby is Frilandsmuseet, a sprawling open-air museum of old countryside dwellings, workshops and barns that have been gathered from sites around Denmark.

FRILANDSMUSEET Map p230

☎ 33 13 44 11; www.natmus.dk; Kongevejen 100; adult/child 25kr/free, Wed free; ☯ 10am-5pm Tue-Sun 3 Apr-30 Sep, 10am-4pm Tue-Sun 1-24 Oct; S-train Sorgenfri

Frilandsmuseet consists of 110 historic buildings arranged in 40 different groupings to provide a sense of Danish rural life as it was in various regions and across different social strata. The houses range from rather grand affairs to meagre, sod-roofed cottages. Many of the buildings are furnished from the period. For example, the smithy is equipped with irons and a hearth, and the post mill still has functioning sails. Grazing farm animals, selected from old Danish breeds, and costumed field workers add an element of authenticity to the setting.

There's a light schedule of demonstrations such as folk dancing, weaving and pottery making, mostly at weekends.

Visitors will need to set aside several hours to explore; in keeping with its rural nature, the sites are widely spread across the grounds. To avoid distracting from the period feel, buildings are not labelled or posted with descriptive signs. The main brochure maps out the sights and gives brief descriptions, but it is only in Danish; be sure to ask for the English translation that corresponds to the map key.

There's a kiosk selling ice cream and hot dogs and a cafeteria with more substantial food.

LYNGBY LAKES Map p230

The Lyngby area has a number of lakes, including Furesø, which is the deepest lake in Denmark. It's possible to hire rowing boats or canoes at the lakeside kiosk, **Holte Havn** (Map p230; ☎ 45 42 04 49; 22 Vejlesøvej; per hr 80kr; ☯ 10am-9pm), and row around either Furesø or the smaller Vejlesø, which are connected by a channel. **Frederiksdal Kano og Bådudlejning** (Map p230; ☎ 45 85 67 70; Nybrovej 520; boat hire from 100kr; ☯ 10am-8pm Tue-Sun), by the locks, hires out canoes and rowing boats for use on the river Mølleåen and the lakes Lyngby Sø, Bagsværd Sø and Furesø, which are interconnected.

Transport

Bus For Frilandsmusset, take bus No 184 from Nørreport, which stops at the entrance
S-train Holte Havn is near Holte S-train station, two stops north of Sorgenfri. For Frederiksdal Kano og Bådudlejning, get off at Sorgenfri S-train station and take bus No 191. Frilandsmuseet is a 10-minute, signposted walk from Sorgenfri station.

Neighbourhoods – Outlying Districts

ISHØJ

Eating p122; Sleeping p168

In contrast to the upmarket coastal suburbs on the northern side of Copenhagen, the southerly suburbs are more diverse, with a sizable concentration of Middle Eastern immigrants. The entire Ishøj community, not only its housing and commercial centre but even its beach, which is built upon reclaimed land dredged from the bay, has been developed over the past few decades, so you won't find architecture of any historical significance.

Most of what Ishøj has to offer visitors is along the coast where there's a vast sandy beach with good windsurfing, a great modern art museum and a very good hostel.

Transport

Bus Bus No 128 from Ishøj station
S-train Ishøj
Parking Available at Arken

ARKEN

☎ 43 54 02 22; www.arken.dk; Skovvej 100; adult/child 70/30kr; ☺ 10am-5pm Tue &Thu-Sun, 10am-9pm Wed; S-train Ishøj

Arken (the Ark) is a large contemporary art museum 17km south of central Copenhagen that opened in 1996 on the coast at Ishøj. The stark, modernistic building rises above Ishøj beach and is as much a work of art as the exhibits inside, inspiring passionate debate even today about whether it's an icon or an eyesore.

The Arken collection features the works of leading Danish and Nordic artists since 1945, with an emphasis on photo-based art, sculpture and installations. There are also changing exhibits of works by artists from the regional Cobra (COpenhagen-BRussels-Amsterdam) movement and by the Norwegian artist Edvard Munch, or blockbuster shows with works by Picasso.

Arken has good facilities for the disabled and great opportunities for keeping children inspired by the world of art. Free guided tours are at 7.30pm Wednesday and 1.30pm Sunday. A very decent café (that resembles a large lifeboat suspended from the side of the gallery) will assuage any hunger pains.

DRAGØR

Eating p121

If Copenhagen begins to feel crowded, consider an afternoon excursion to Dragør, an old maritime village on the island of Amager, a few kilometres south of the airport. In the early 1550s Christian II allowed Dutch farmers to settle in Amager to provide his court with flowers and produce. Today the town of Dragør retains a bit of Dutch flavour with its pretty painted cottages, flat topography and seaside location.

A fun pastime is to wander along the narrow, winding cobblestone streets leading up from the harbour, which are lined with the thatch-roofed, mustard-coloured houses comprising the old town.

One interesting little ramble is to take **Strandgade**, a pedestrian alley that begins opposite the museum, and continue up to **Badstuevælen**, an old cobbled square lined with some attractive houses dating from the 1790s.

Of particular interest on Strandgade, at its intersection with Magstræde, is **Dragør Kro**, built by JH Blichmann, who designed many of Dragør's finest homes. Of note on Badstuevælen square are houses at Nos 8 and 12, also built by Blichmann. Take a look, too, at the square's stone obelisk erected in Christian VII's day to mark the distance to central Copenhagen – 1.5 Danish miles or, in more contemporary measurement, 10.5km.

Returning to the waterfront via **Kongevejen**, note building No 11, now a pharmacy and bookshop. It originally belonged to the customs inspector and still sports the relief of Denmark's national arms.

Transport

Bus 30, 32, 73, 75E, 350S

DRAGØR MUSEUM Map p230

☎ 32 53 41 06; Havnepladsen Strandlinien 2; adult/child 20/10kr; ☺ noon-4pm Tue-Sun 1 May-30 Sep

The Dragør Museum is in a half-timbered house adjacent to the harbourfront tourist office. This quaint little museum displays model ships, antique ship paraphernalia and period furnishings from sea captain's homes.

Neighbourhoods – Outlying Districts

Walking Tours

Walking Tours

Setting out on foot is a good way to explore this grand city and its numerous historic sights. Copenhagen's polite (ie flat) topography, accessible attractions and compact layout mean that sightseeing on foot generally makes more sense than any other mode of transport (although in bike-crazy Denmark you'll find touring on two wheels an easy proposition). The city centre is filled with beautifully preserved buildings from the city's past, and most sites and sights are well signposted and within easy reach of each other.

One of the most delightful aspects of touring the city by foot is that you don't have to walk far to catch a dazzling glimpse of sea, nature or that beautiful light that takes so many people's breath away. Copenhagen's low-rise tendencies mean that you're not straining to see the sky or anything appealing in the distance, and finally, the Danes' love of eating, drinking and getting cosy means that there are a thousand and one charming ways to break up a stroll with a quick café, bar or restaurant stop.

We've chosen four detailed yet easy walks that cover a number of Copenhagen's most prominent themes: royalty, greenery, the water and the city's love of vintage attractions.

TRADITIONAL ROYAL RAMBLE

The Danes are a forward-thinking lot, but they still have a great regard for tradition and for their royal family. This walk takes you past some significant regal sights and quintessential Copenhagen locations that have almost become a part of the local psyche. It's a walk packed with gracious buildings and a real sense of history.

From **Rådhuspladsen 1** (p55), the large central square fronting city hall, walk down the famous Strøget (p58), which, after a couple of blocks, cuts between two spirited pedestrian squares, **Gammeltorv 2** and **Nytorv 3**. A popular summertime gathering spot in Gammeltorv is the gilded **Caritas Fountain 4**, erected in 1608 by Christian IV and marking what was once the old city's central market. As in days past, peddlers still sell jewellery, flowers and fruit on the square. At the southwestern corner of Nytorv is **Domhuset 5** (p57), an imposing neoclassical building that once served as the city hall and now houses the city's law courts.

Continuing along Strøget, eventually you'll reach **Højbro Plads 6**. At the southern end of this elongated square is a **statue of Bishop Absalon 7** (the city's founder) on horseback; behind it, the fitting backdrop is **Slotsholmen 8** (p60), which is where the bishop erected Copenhagen's first fortress and is the home of Christiansborg Slot – a royal palace used mostly for reception duties today.

At the end of Strøget you'll reach **Kongens Nytorv 9** (p66), a square boasting an equestrian statue of its royal designer, Christian V, and circled by gracious old buildings. Notable from Christian V's era are **Charlottenborg 10** (p66), a 17th-century Dutch baroque palace that houses the Royal Academy of Fine Arts, and **Det Kongelige Teater 11** (the Royal Theatre; p125), fronted by statues of the playwrights Adam Oehlenschläger and Ludvig Holberg.

To the east of Kongens Nytorv is the picturesque **Nyhavn 12** (p64) canal. Long a haunt for sailors and writers (including Hans Christian Andersen, who lived in the house at No 67 for nearly two decades), Nyhavn today is half salty and half gentrified, with a line of pavement cafés and restored gabled town-houses. It makes an invitingly atmospheric place to take a break for lunch or an afternoon beer.

From the northern side of Nyhavn, head north along Toldbodgade. When you reach the fountain that graces **Amaliehaven 13** (Amalie Gardens), turn inland to get to **Amalienborg Slot 14** (p65), the stately home of

---

Walk Facts

Start Rådhuspladsen
End Rosenborg Slot
Distance 4.3km
Duration 3 hours
Transport bus Rådhuspladsen, train Central Station (start); metro or S-train Nørreport (end)

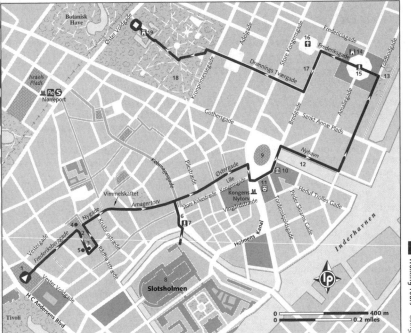

the royal family since 1794. The palace's four nearly identical rococo mansions, designed by architect Nicolai Eigtved, surround a central cobblestone square and an immense **statue of Frederik V 15** (1746–66) on horseback sculpted by JFJ Saly. Looking west from the square you'll get a head-on view of the imposing **Marmorkirken 16** (the Marble Church; p75), which was designed in conjunction with the Amalienborg complex as part of an ambitious plan by King Frederik to extend the city northward by creating a new district geared to the affluent.

From this point make a short detour along **Bredgade 17**, where there are a couple of churches and small museums, plus some very good furniture stores, before turning right at Dronnings Tværgade. You're now approaching the beautiful landscaped gardens of **Kongens Have 18** (p83), an ideal spot to sit in the sunshine with a picnic lunch or for a catnap. To the west you'll find **Rosenborg Slot 19** (p84), the home of the royal treasury.

GOING, GOING GREEN

As Scandinavia's biggest, coolest city, Copenhagen hums with an industrious energy and a seemingly city-wide desire to make everything more efficient, more ergonomic, more… Danish. That said, locals appreciate time spent relaxing and revel in the great outdoors (you would too after a long dark winter). If you want nature to surround you and wide skies overhead, you're in luck – Copenhagen is not geared towards the dominance of sky-scraper or the car. This walking tour takes in quiet green spaces, gardens and less hurried neighbourhoods.

Start your stroll at **Churchillparken 1**, a quiet green space located on the north side of the city centre.

On Esplanaden, at the southern end of Churchillparken, you'll find **Frihedsmuseet 2** (p66), a museum dedicated to the Danish Resistance movement of WWII. Nearby is the attractive Gothic-style **St Alban's Church 3**, which serves the city's English-speaking Anglican community.

Walk Facts

Start Churchillparken
End Statens Museum for Kunst
Distance 5.5km
Duration 2.5 hours – add 2 hours for a visit to Statens Museum for Kunst
Transport S-train Østerport (start); metro or S-train Nørreport (end)

The church's location, in the midst of a public park, may seem a bit curious – the site was provided by Christian IX following the marriage of his daughter to the Prince of Wales, who later ascended the British throne as King Edward VII.

Beside the church sits the immense **Gefionspringvandet 4** (Gefion Fountain), a monument to yet another overseas relationship. According to Scandinavian mythology, when the Swedish king offered the goddess Gefion as much land as she could plough in one night, Gefion turned her four sons into powerful oxen and ploughed the entire area that now comprises the island of Zealand. The bronze statue in the fountain depicts the goddess and her oxen at work.

A 10-minute walk through the park past the fountain and along the waterfront will lead you to the statue of the **Little Mermaid 5** (Den Lille Havfrue; p65), which was designed by Edvard Eriksen in 1913. Inspired by Hans Christian Andersen's fairy tale, the statue depicts a mermaid who fell in love with a prince but had to wait 300 years to become human.

From the Little Mermaid continue on the road inland. After just a few minutes you'll reach steps leading down to a wooden bridge that crosses a moat into **Kastellet 6**, a citadel built by Frederik III in the 1660s. Stepping across the moat is like walking back in history – the grounds and buildings have been preserved in their original character and the fortress is still surrounded by centuries-old ramparts. Although the fortress barracks remain in use by the Danish military, the park-like grounds are open to the public from 6am to sunset daily. Walk south through Kastellet and you'll pass its main row of historic buildings before reaching a second bridge that spans the moat and leads back into Churchillparken.

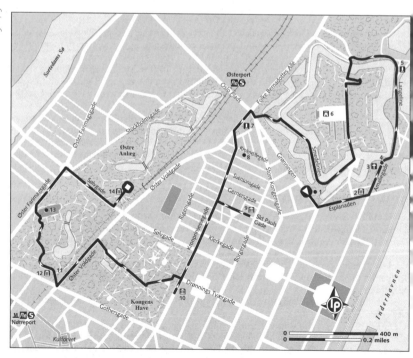

Nyboder terrace houses (below)

Walking Tours – Going, Going Green

Once you cross the moat, take the path to the right and you can walk along the outer moat ramparts northwest until you reach a side path leading to the intersection of Grønningen and Folke Bernadottes Allé. Cross Grønningen and walk southwest along Øster Voldgade and you'll soon come to a streetside **statue of Christian IV 7**. In the 1630s the king, who was expanding his military in response to threats from Sweden, developed this area to provide housing for his naval staff.

If you proceed south on Kronprinsessegade you'll pass the area known as **Nyboder 8**, which is comprised of row after row of long mustard-coloured houses with tiled roofs that once housed some 2200 naval personnel. Most of these buildings have been converted to public housing but if you turn left onto Sankt Paulsgade, the building at No 20 has been preserved as a museum called **Nyboders Mindestuer 9**.

Return to Kronprinsessegade and you can continue south to **Davids Samling 10** (p83), a splendid little museum with an eclectic art collection.

If you walk through Kongens Have and then proceed south on Øster Voldgade, passing Rosenborg Slot on your left, you'll reach the entrance to the **Botanisk Have 11** (p82), which has peaceful paths, a resplendent selection of native and exotic plants, and the **Botanisk Museum 12**, which has some exhibits on plants but is only open in summer. There's also a walk-through tropical glasshouse called the **Palmehus 13** (p82).

If you're up for more sightseeing there are a number of museums in the area you could visit, including the national gallery **Statens Museum for Kunst 14** (p84), which is opposite the northeast end of the gardens.

WATERSIDE WANDER

Copenhagen's manifold attractions include her stunning harbourside location, which begs visitors to explore canals, take in sea views and visit a magnificently positioned island or two. The fine mix of man-made gems and natural beauty will have you keen to fill your lungs with the clean sea air, and you can even end your walk with a harbourside swim – weather permitting!

Walk Facts

Start Kongens Nytorv
End Islands Brygge Havnebadet
Distance 3.9km
Duration 4 hours
Transport metro Kongens Nytorv (start); metro Islands Brygge (end)

From **Kongens Nytorv 1** (p66), head east along carnivalesque **Nyhavn 2** (p64), where five- and six-storey waterfront inns and taverns attract the lion's share of the city's guests and sun-lovers on sunny days. The canal was dug 300 years ago to allow traders to bring their wares into the heart of the city – nowadays the busiest trade is beer drinking or taking a waterside organised tour. Cross the canal at the bridge from Toldbodgade and then double back (on the other side), passing **Nyhavn 20 3**, where Hans Christian Andersen began to write his famous stories.

You'll arrive back at Kongens Nytorv, where you can veer left and stroll down Tordenskjoldsgade, pausing to look up and admire the mosaic work that covers the **footbridge 4** that connects the two famous stages of **Det Kongelige Teater 5** (the Royal Theatre; p125). The archway's mosaic depicts Danish poets and artists. Continue down the street until you reach Havnegade, which skirts the harbour and affords some pleasant water views (any time of the day). Cross Christian IV's Bro, which takes you to **Slotsholmen's 6** (p60) northeastern tip, then cross the eye-catching, copper-clad **Knippelsbro 7** (p78) to arrive on the charming island of **Christianshavn 8** – the home of hippies, Greenlanders, yuppies and the discreetly wealthy (such as supermodel-turned photographer Helena Christensen).

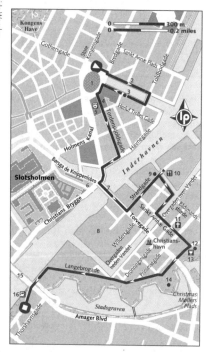

Turn left at Strandgade and walk past the appealingly renovated warehouses known as **Gammel Dok 9** (p78), which have been spruced up with typical Danish good taste. Continue to **Restaurant Kanalen 10** (p115), where one of the city's best-positioned lunches awaits. Afterwards, head down Overgaden neden Vandet to Sankt Annæ Gade, crossing over the narrow canal and continuing to the easy-to-spot **Vor Frelsers Kirke 11** (p79), where you can work off lunch by climbing the 400 steps to the top of the 95m-high spire and enjoy your reward of one of the city's most breathtaking views.

After your descent, head to the end of the street and revel in the verdant oasis that surrounds **Lille Mølle 12** (p78) – it's like a rural escape on quiet weekdays, and wonderfully restorative. We'd recommend a coffee or a glass of wine in the garden at **Bastionen & Løven 13** (p114) – one of the city's most delightful haunts. From here, trace your way along the **island's battlements 14**, until you cross under **Langebro 15** and arrive at Islands Brygge, an up-and-coming area populated by regular folk and a new generation of the city's not-quite-starving

Lifeguard at Islands Brygge Havnebadet (p89)

artists. If it's a warm summer's day you will have earned a swim, and there's no better place to take the plunge than **Islands Brygge Havnebadet 16** (p89), the immensely popular canalside baths designed by hip architecture firm Plot.

VINTAGE VANGUARD

This walk isn't so much packed with traditional sightseeing options, but it's got soul – vintage soul – and takes you through some of the city's most interesting rejuvenated quarters, where former working-class bastions are given new life and a dash of culture. There are also some great cafés and bars, and urban versions of the great outdoors.

Start your day with brunch at **Pussy Galore's Flying Circus 1** (p116) on **Sankt Hans Torv 2**, Nørrebro's hippest square, before heading along **Ravnsborggade 3** to source fabulous retro homewares and second-hand Danish design classics at stores such as **10A Modern 4** at No 10A or **Modern dk 5** at No 6.

Cross over bustling Nørrebrogade and enter Blågårdsgade, a pedestrianised haunt given over to smoky bars, retro-kitsch clothes shops, lively cafés, kids on bicycles and boisterous locals (both working-class stalwarts and newer arrivals who have injected a good dose of vigour into the area). If it's winter you can enjoy ice skating at the rink at **Blågårds Plads 6**.

Turn left at Korsgade and again at Peblinge Dossering. Follow the street until you get to Dronning Louises Bro. Cross the bridge and take a turn alongside man-made **Peblinge Sø 7** (p85), the lake that locals flock to in order to get a glimpse of water and some fresh air. It's surrounded by tracks and paths for walkers, roller-bladers and cyclists. From Gyldenløvsgade, head to so-cool-it's hot **Nansensgade 8**, the city's very own 'Greenwich Village', with great bars (such as **Bankeråt 9**, p129), Asian restaurants and some funky little galleries and boutiques. If you're hungry, don't miss the chance to jockey with your chopsticks at **Sticks 'n' Sushi 10** (p118)

Walk Facts

Start Pussy Galore's Flying Circus
End Filmhusets Cinematek
Distance 4km
Duration 2.5 hours (allow an extra two hours for a film)
Transport bus No 3A or 5A Sankt Hans Torv (start); bus No 350S Gothersgade (end)

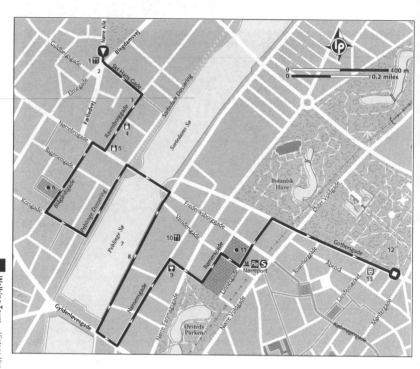

before you wander through the city's main market **Israel Plads 11**, which sells fruit, vegetables and flowers and also hosts a flea market.

The vintage mood continues as you walk along Gothersgade, skirting the delightful, old-fashioned gardens of **Kongens Have 12** (p83), to the swanky **Filmhusets Cinematek 13** (p128), where you can catch a classic film revival (Scandinavian if you're really playing the part) in stylish surrounds.

Eating

Eating

Eating in Copenhagen is a fundamental pleasure – and you should make every effort to sample as many of the city's dining options as time, budget and belt-loops allow. Various pockets of the city house many restaurants, and the inclusive nature of Copenhagen society means that eating out is available to everyone, despite what you may have heard about restaurant prices (from people who probably haven't eaten here).

The restaurant scene is an intriguing blend of stoutly traditional favourites that fall into the 'part of the family or furniture' category, and resolutely with-it havens of modern flavours, textures and culinary excellence, with stunning interior design to match. Immigration has broadened the city's palate too (for many older Danes, eating out means eating French-influenced cuisine), with Thai, Indian and Middle Eastern eateries adding spice to the mix (particularly in Nørrebro and Vesterbro). Good Japanese options appealing to the in-crowd (some things are universal, it would seem) can be found in Nørreport and the surrounding area. Well-known areas for dining of all types include Strøget and the Latin Quarter, the area around Nyhavn and the amusement park Tivoli. It won't take you long to find plenty of new places to add to your 'favourites' list, and it's not hard to combine your meal with a pleasant outlook, whether it be of greenery, water or attractive cityscapes.

Café culture is incredibly vital in Copenhagen, with many Danes popping into these bastions of *hygge* (cosiness) at all times of the day and night for a snack, a drink, a coffee and a chat. We've included a number of cafés in the following listings – mostly because the food is very good but sometimes because the atmosphere is unbeatable.

Opening Hours

The Danes are not Mediterranean, meaning that if you like to eat late, you'll have trouble finding a place to accommodate you after about 10pm at night, when many restaurants close their kitchens. Restaurants that open during the day will often commence business at 11am or noon, and keep the kitchen serving lunch until about 3pm, before opening again at about 6pm.

How Much?

Eating in Copenhagen can be as cheap as a cart-bought hot dog (about 24kr) or a splash-out five-course gastronomic odyssey for about 500kr, with another 500kr for the accompanying wines. On more everyday terms, you're looking at main courses in mid-range establishments setting you back between 100kr and 180kr, so a full meal (first course, main course, dessert and a glass of wine) will cost about 300kr per head. Cheap Eats listings in this chapter are for places where you'll pay under 85kr for a main course.

Booking Tables

It goes without saying that turning up to one of Copenhagen's 10 Michelin-starred restaurants without a reservation is going to see you going home empty-stomached. For many other restaurants it should be fine to simply show up and score a table if there's only you or one other person in your party. Large groups should make reservations, and anyone wanting to dine at a 'flavour of the month' sensation or firm local favourite should think about booking a table or getting there before 7.30pm.

Tipping

Restaurant bills include service charges in the quoted prices. Further tipping is unnecessary, although rounding up the bill is not uncommon when the service has been particularly good (and it almost always is at top-end places).

Self-Catering

Supermarket chains with dozens of branches throughout the city centre include Irma and Netto, which generally open at 8am and remain open until about 8pm. Many supermarkets close on Sunday though. Illum (Map p143; ☎ 33 14 40 02; Østergade 52; ⓨ 10am-7pm Mon-Thu, 10am-8pm Fri, 9am-5pm Sat) has a basement supermarket with gourmet food items, including Danish cheeses. There's a bakery and grocery shop on the ground floor of Magasin du Nord (Map p143; ☎ 33 11 44 33; Kongens Nytorv 13; ⓨ 10am-7pm Mon-Thu, 10am-8pm Fri, 10am-5pm Sat), a block south of Østergade at the eastern end of Strøget. In Central Station there's a handy supermarket (ⓨ 8am-midnight).

RÅDHUSPLADSEN & TIVOLI

Rådhuspladsen, the large square that fronts city hall and serves as the city's main bus terminal, has limited eating options compared with other neighbourhoods in the city, and it's most likely that if you dine out in these parts you'll be doing so in Tivoli, which boasts more than 30 places to eat. And now for the awful truth: most of them are awful, and awfully expensive. Eateries range from simple stalls offering eminently vomit-worthy amusement-park fare such as luridly coloured ice cream and hot dogs, to (thankfully) some of the city's most respected and hard-to-get-into eating establishments (which we've featured). You'll need to pay Tivoli admission to eat at these places – and they only operate during the Tivoli season. Most of the restaurants close about half an hour before Tivoli's closing time. Outside Tivoli, there's a smattering of places that will assuage hunger in fine style and one particular spot that stands head and shoulders above the others, thanks in part to its skyscraping location.

ALBERTO K Map pp232-4   *Italian-Danish*
☎ 33 42 61 61; Radisson SAS Royal, Level 20, Hammerischgade 1; menu from 345kr; ⓨ noon-3pm Mon-Fri, 6pm-midnight Mon-Sat; S-train Vesterport or Central Station

One of the top (literally – check out the 20th-floor views from this landmark skyscraper) dining experiences in Copenhagen, this place is a must on any design-loving gourmand's tour of the city. The menu takes Italian and Danish influences and presents dishes with new and inventive twists – for example, the venison fillet, accompanied by corn with sage and pearl barley and complimented with fresh nectarine

with salted almonds – not to mention an excellent wine selection. If the food leaves you unmoved (and your stomach must be made of stone for that to happen), then you can admire the Arne Jacobsen-designed trappings, right down to the cutlery, and that view – again.

Rådhuspladsen & Tivoli Top Five

- The Paul (p106)
- TyvenKokkenHansKoneOgHendesElsker (p106)
- Alberto K (left)
- Taj Indian Restaurant (p106)
- Oscar (p107)

CAFÉ BJØRG Map pp239-41   *Café*
☎ 33 14 53 20; Vester Voldgade 19; mains 98-132kr; ☽ kitchen 10am-10pm; bus Nos 2A, 5A, 6A, 250S
Occupying a corner of Vester Voldgade and Studiestræde, this good people-watching spot doubles as a popular after-work drinks haunt, and has tasty, inexpensive meals to accompany the large beers on offer. The excellent burgers get the thumbs up from many patrons, but we went posh and opted for the tiger prawns in curry with sweet chilli and vegetables (114kr).

CAFÉ ULTIMO Map p231   *Italian*
☎ 33 75 07 51; Tivoli; mains 205-215kr; ☽ noon-10.30pm; train Central Station, bus Nos 2A, 5A, 6A, 250S
All white napery, rotunda location and polished everything, Café Ultimo prides itself on creating delightful Italian dishes that break out of the pizza/pasta prison (although such things are available too, and always good). When we visited, the grilled guinea fowl was the stand-out dish of the night, but the menu changes with the seasons and according to ingredient availability.

DIVAN 2 Map p231   *French*
☎ 33 12 51 51; Tivoli; mains 195-365kr; ☽ noon-10.30pm; train Central Station, bus Nos 2A, 5A, 6A, 250S
Long considered to be one of Tivoli's finest restaurants for both food and service, Divan 2 has been in operation since Tivoli opened in 1843, and serves gourmet French food (a wonderful fillet of sole is on the menu) with a vintage wine collection. A very decent tasting menu will set you back 465kr for three courses. The tacky practice of adding a 5% surcharge for credit-card payment is alive and well here, so you may want to bring some cash. Vegetarians should get their fill of greens elsewhere.

GRØFTEN Map p231   *Danish*
☎ 33 75 06 75; Tivoli; mains 150-225kr; ☽ noon-11.30pm; train Central Station, bus Nos 2A, 5A, 6A, 250S
The speciality here (since 1874) is a type of *smørrebrød* with lip-smacking tiny fjord shrimps spiced with lime and fresh pepper; *smørrebrød* are priced from 40kr apiece. When we popped in, this place was doing a roaring trade, but we got the feeling that we'd stumbled into the 'early bird special'.

THE PAUL Map p231   *Modern Danish*
☎ 33 75 07 75; www.thepaul.dk; Tivoli; 5-course menu 600kr, 5-wine menu 600kr; ☽ 6-10pm; train Central Station, bus Nos 2A, 5A, 6A, 250S

White-hot inside and out, the Michelin-starred restaurant with the terrible name is a must for anyone who wants a memorable meal in relaxed yet beautiful surrounds. Chef Paul Conningham is one of the region's hottest chefs, and a look at the menu shows why. The pavilion itself is reminiscent of a wealthy friend's beach-house. Dishes such as warm quail salad with truffle butter vinaigrette are downright sublime. Reservations essential.

TAJ INDIAN RESTAURANT
Map pp232-4   *Indian*
☎ 33 13 10 10; Jernbanegade 5; mains 85-185kr; ☽ noon-midnight; train Central Station or Vesterport
Widely regarded as the best Indian restaurant in Copenhagen, the Taj is a fabulously central spot in which to fill up on beautifully fragrant dishes. It's best to come here with a few friends, so you can experience more dishes, but lone diners will also be in for a treat.

TYVENKOKKENHANSKONEOG-HENDESELSKER
Map pp239-41   *Modern Danish*
☎ 33 16 12 92; www.tyvenkokkenhanskoneoghendes-elsker.dk; Magstræde 16; menu 565kr; ☽ 6pm-2am Mon-Sat; bus No 6A
The name itself is a mouthful (it means The Cook The Thief His Wife and Her Lover – an homage to Peter Greenaway's 1989 masterpiece), but so is the ferociously inventive cuisine of this stand-out restaurant. We're willing to bet that bouillon of stinging nettle with baked sea trout doesn't feature on any other restaurant's menu – and if it does, it won't be as incredible. Flavours, artistry and even intellect all combine to make this a memorable experience. The restaurant closes for summer vacation between about mid-July and mid-August.

CHEAP EATS
CAFÉ GLYPTOTEK Map pp232-4   *Café*
☎ 33 41 81 41; Ny Carlsberg Glyptotek; snacks from 20kr; ☽ 10am-4pm Tue-Sun; train Central Station, bus Nos 2A, 5A, 6A, 250S
This delightful atrium café, overlooking the museum's palm garden, serves pastries, sandwiches, coffee and wine. Expect a crowd at weekends and revel in the civility of it all, as hushed conversation, greenery and all that beautiful art combine to create a great escape from the world outside.

DANSK DESIGN CENTER CAFÉ

Map pp232-4 *Café*

☎ 33 69 33 50; HC Andersens Blvd 27; salads 65kr, sandwiches 59kr; ☺ 10am-5pm Mon, Tue, Thu & Fri, 10am-9pm Wed, 11am-4pm Sat & Sun; train Central Station, bus Nos 2A, 5A, 6A, 250S

Every bit as stylish as the rest of the DDC, this is a handy spot to fill up on light café fare that's always fresh and nicely presented (of course). Try the fish cakes with pickles for a new take on a Danish classic. A good pile of magazines and design books are provided at each table.

NATIONALMUSEET CAFÉ

Map pp232-4 *Café*

☎ 33 13 44 11; Ny Vestergade 10; mains 65-89kr; ☺ 10am-5pm Tue-Sun; bus Nos 1A, 2A, 5A, 650S

Denmark's richest repository of Viking relics has a stylishly kitted-out (blond wood, grey paint, nice lights and a cool stainless-steel bar) 2nd-floor café offering creative sandwiches, salads, light meals and desserts – or you can just relax over a glass of wine. The prices are reasonable, the opening hours mirror those of the museum, and if you just want to dine you won't need to pay museum admission. Grab a bacon and turkey sandwich (48kr) as fuel before you hit the halls, or come on Sunday, when a terrific brunch is served between 11am and 3pm, and costs adult/concession/child 135/75/40kr.

OSCAR Map pp239-41 *Café*

☎ 33 12 09 99; Rådhuspladsen 77; mains 49-89kr; ☺ noon-2am; train Central Station, bus Nos 2A, 5A, 6A, 250S

Oscar is a stylish, easy-going lunch spot where you'll find gay men and their female friends having a bite to eat. It's an airy space, with room to breathe and good meals of the day (generally pasta and soup dishes) in substantial quantities. Oscar can seem so low-key in daylight hours that you may not realise it's a 'gay' place till you spy the wall of fame, with portraits of Oscar Wilde (of course), and other friends of Dorothy.

STRØGET & THE LATIN QUARTER

This popular area is populated with plenty of dining options – from simple lunch-time pit stops crammed with office workers to temples of gastronomy that feed all five senses. There are some charming places scattered about, with plenty of outdoor seating available in the warmer months and some lovely Scandinavian design touches indoors if it's simply too cold to sit outside.

ATLAS BAR Map pp239-41 *Café*

☎ 33 15 03 52; Larsbjørnstræde 18; mains 95-175kr; ☺ noon-10pm Mon-Sat; bus No 6A

This casual basement café, festooned with maps from around the world and situated in the heart of the gay district, has a changing blackboard menu that includes salads, vegetarian fare and a good range of organic meat dishes, mostly with some sort of international influence. Service is brisk and friendly, and the place can get very busy in the evening, so you may want to reserve a table.

AURA Map pp239-41 *Modern Danish*

☎ 33 36 50 60; Rådhusstræde 4; 8 courses from 325kr; ☺ 6-11pm Tue-Thu, 6pm-3am Fri & Sat; bus No 6A

This scorching-hot addition to the city's modern dining scene attracts an affluent, attractive crowd hellbent on being seen at this very popular restaurant. The eight-course menu (there's also an 11- and a 14-course option) hit the spot though – from the scrumptious mini-pizza that won us over when we were at our most cynical to some of the creamiest foie gras we've ever had. The wine list is pretty good too – with wines from as far away as Lebanon adding to the internationalist mix. On Friday and Saturday nights this place gets packed with the beautiful set, and very noisy.

CAFÉ HOVEDTELEGRAFEN

Map pp239-41 *Café*

☎ 33 41 09 86; Købmagergade 37; mains 55-155kr; ☺ 11am-5pm Tue-Fri, noon-4pm Sat, 11am-4pm & 5.30-8pm Sun; bus No 350S

On the upper level of the Post & Tele Museum, this handy café has a splendid rooftop view of the city and a decent local menu as well. We enjoyed munching on *karrysild* (curried herring) and lingering over a beer or cappuccino. It's an airy, pleasant space to get away from the shopping hordes too.

CAFÉ KETCHUP Map pp239-41 *Café*

☎ 33 32 30 30; Pilestræde 19; mains 99-155kr; ☺ 11am-midnight Mon-Wed, 11am-1am Thu, 11am-3am Fri & Sat; metro Kongens Nytorv, bus No 350S

Taking a leaf straight out of the Parisian bistro book, this bustling spot offers excellent hunger-assuaging sandwiches and scrummy lunch/dinner options. We plumped for the grilled salmon with lime and sesame marinade on a bed of celery-parsnip purée, topped with a Noilly Prat sauce – and we sat in utter contentment for hours nursing our wine (available by the glass) and watching the well-dressed locals come and go. On Friday and Saturday nights you can start the party with the house DJ.

DEN GRØNNE KÆLDER

Map pp239-41   Vegetarian
☎ 33 93 01 40; Pilestræde 48; mains 89-149kr;
⏰ 11am-10pm Mon-Sat; metro Kongens Nytorv, bus No 350S

Den Grønne Kælder is a strictly vegetarian restaurant. At lunch, served until 5pm, you can select two salads and a simple hot dish or quiche for around 65kr. For dinner there's a wider selection of hot dishes, and a nice cosy atmosphere. Organic wines are also available, making this a firm favourite with healthy types who also like to enjoy the finer things in life.

DET LILLE APOTEK

Map pp239-41   Traditional Danish
☎ 33 12 56 06; Store Kannikestræde 15; mains 98-188kr; ⏰ 11am-midnight Mon-Sat, noon-midnight Sun; bus No 6A

The Little Pharmacy is well known for its moderately priced traditional Danish food, served in an old-fashioned environment. Multi-item meals that include pickled herring, fish fillet, smørrebrød and other solid fare are available for lunch and dinner. By some claims, Det Lille Apotek, which traces its history to 1720 (it was a pharmacy, or apotek, before that), is the oldest restaurant in Copenhagen. Good deals are available at lunch, where two-course or three-course meals cost 168kr or 195kr respectively.

ENSEMBLE Map pp239-41   Modern Danish
☎ 33 11 33 52; www.restaurantensemble.dk; Tordenskjoldsgade 11; menu 500kr; ⏰ 6-11pm Tue-Sat, closed Jul; metro Kongens Nytorv

Perfectly named, Ensemble is the best choice you can make for a 'dinner and a show' experience. After all, Ensemble's proximity to Det Kongelige Teater makes it practically backstage, and the superbly timed efforts from everyone in the kitchen and dining room approach artistic heights. Sadly, though, you'll

want to linger over your meal, which means you'll probably miss the opera. Then again, the six-course menu starts with sevruga caviar, so let the fat lady sing.

GODT Map pp239-41   French-Danish
☎ 33 15 21 22; Gothersgade 38; menu from 480kr;
⏰ 6-11pm Tue-Sat; bus No 350S

With a simple blue façade and sparsely elegant décor (although it can seem a little chilly at times), Godt is a small-but-perfectly formed fine-dining experience with a handful of tables on two floors. We think they're being a little too modest with the name ('good' in Danish), but then again, modesty is a very Danish quality. Book ahead.

JENSEN'S BØFHUS

Map pp239-41   Steakhouse
☎ 33 32 78 00; Gråbrødretorv 15; mains 89-180kr;
⏰ 11am-10.30pm Mon-Thu & Sun, 11am-11.30pm Fri & Sat; metro & S-train Nørreport

This Danish steak restaurant, part of a popular nationwide chain, is in a period house fronting the pleasant cobblestone square of Gråbrødretorv. The food is pretty average, but prices are cheap and on warm summer days you can sit out on the square with plenty of Danes wolfing down large hunks of tasty steak. Don't knock it till you've felt the urge to order a chop for dessert.

KOMMANDANTEN

Map pp239-41   French-Danish
☎ 33 12 09 90; www.kommandanten.dk; Ny Adelgade 7; mains 320-340kr; ⏰ 5.30-10pm Mon-Sat; metro Kongens Nytorv

Just west of Kongens Nytorv, Kommandanten has received numerous accolades, including the highest rating among Copenhagen's restaurants – two fat shining Michelin stars – and that means that if you're in Copenhagen for a few days, haven't made a reservation and fancy eating here, you're in fantasy land. The food –

Strøget & The Latin Quarter Top Five

- Pierre André (opposite)
- Restaurationen (p110)
- Kong Hans Kælder (opposite)
- Sushitarian (p110)
- Ensemble (left)

beautifully prepared and presented according to the seasons and what's available locally – is superb, and easily matched by a wonderful wine list (mostly French). Chef Kaspar Rune Sørensen has every reason to be proud.

KONG HANS KÆLDER

Map pp239-41   *Modern Danish*
☎ 33 11 68 68; www.konghans.dk; Vingårdsstræde 6; mains 195-360kr; ☽ 6pm-midnight Mon-Sat; metro Kongens Nytorv

Located on a street where there were once vineyards (hence the name) and in Copenhagen's oldest building, this is a great place to savour a sense of history (Hans Christian Andersen wrote *Love in Nicolai Tower* here) and one of the most fabulous meals of your life under the Gothic vaulted ceiling. Start with tuna and oyster ravioli (195kr) or the warm lobster salad with pickled Asian-style vegetables and mushrooms (225kr), and let the wonderful staff look after you. Reservations essential.

KONRAD Map pp239-41   *International*
☎ 33 93 29 29; Pilestræde 12; mains 85-225kr; ☽ noon-midnight Tue-Thu, noon-3am Fri & Sat; metro Kongens Nytorv

This is one of those achingly hip restaurant/bar scenes with good, contemporary Danish cuisine, attentive service, modern décor and its own CD. The menu varies, as it incorporates items that are seasonally fresh, but generally adopts a traditional-meets-innovative approach. Acoustics are shocking – if you find yourself seated next to a large group of ad execs, prepare to learn sign language.

L'EDUCATION NATIONALE

Map pp239-41   *French*
☎ 33 91 53 60; Larsbjørnstræde 12; mains 129-159kr; ☽ noon-4pm & 6pm-midnight Mon-Sat; bus No 6A

Oozing a certain *je ne sais* what, this French-right-down-to-its-tennis-shoes (actually, they belonged to Arthur Ashe…) bistro offers good French fare, such as warm goat cheese salad and other Gallic staples. Service is just like in France (ie indifferent).

PASTA BASTA Map pp239-41   *Italian*
☎ 33 11 21 31; Valkendorfsgade 22; mains 79-169kr; ☽ 11.30am-3am Sun-Tue, 11.30am-5am Fri & Sat; bus No 6A

No surprises that the mainstay of this restaurant is a self-service buffet of various cold pasta and salad dishes. You can also order from the main menu, which includes hot pasta dishes served with the likes of red snapper and Argentine beef. Late opening hours make it a popular spot with cheery, party-loving night owls looking for a late meal to soak up all the booze.

PEDER OXE Map pp239-41   *Danish*
☎ 33 11 00 77; Gråbrødretorv 11; mains 79-199kr; ☽ 11.30am-11pm; metro & S-train Nørreport

Fronting the square, this stalwart of rustic dining offers wonderful Danish country grub with a particularly local ambience. It has great fish and organic meat dishes, served with a good salad buffet for dinner, and the *smørrebrød* (three for 128kr) is a popular option for lunch. It also has a house wine deal – you pay for only as much of the bottle as you end up drinking (apparently some people don't drink the whole thing!). We fell in love with the solid wood floors, Portuguese tiles and groovy little system whereby you let the staff know you're ready to order by flicking on a light above your table. Copenhagen's oldest monastery was built on this site in 1238 and the restaurant's wine cellar retains part of the old stone foundations.

PIERRE ANDRÉ

Map pp239-41   *French-Danish*
☎ 33 16 17 19; Ny Østergade 21; menu from 425kr; ☽ noon-midnight Tue-Fri, 6pm-midnight Sat; bus No 350S

This magnificent restaurant, run by a hard-working husband-and-wife team (and named after their sons), produces sublime French- and Mediterranean-influenced dishes that reflect seasonal variations (they will accommodate

Peder Oxe (above)

those fond of the hunting season with great meat-loving aplomb). The décor is subdued and smart, but the big empty space across the road wasn't much of a view. Here's hoping it's been filled by the time you hit town.

Hitting the Culinary Heights

For a city of its size and an undeserved reputation for providing little more than pork, meatballs, dark bread and other stodge for its citizens' and visitors' tables, Copenhagen has a very strong list of Michelin-starred restaurants. In fact, you can count them on two hands...

- **Ensemble** (p108)
- **Era Ora** (p114)
- **formel b** (p120)
- **Godt** (p108)
- **Kommandanten** (p108)
- **Kong Hans Kælder** (p109)
- **Pierre André** (p109)
- **Restaurationen** (below)
- **The Paul** (p106)
- **TyvenKokkenHansKoneOgHendesElsker** (p106)

Most of these restaurants have websites, so you can try to make a reservation (and you will need one) before you hit the city.

RESTAURANT GRÅBRØDRETORV 21

Map pp239-41 *Traditional Danish*
☎ 33 11 47 07; Gråbrødretorv 21; mains 130-225kr;
🕑 noon-midnight Mon-Sat, 6pm-midnight Sun; metro & S-train Nørreport
This traditional Danish restaurant has excellent service and a welcoming ambience – with bare wooden floors, clean white walls and rustic furniture. The menu features equally heart-warming attractions, such as roast chicken with rhubarb, pickled cucumber and parsley.

RESTAURATIONEN

Map pp239-41 *French-Danish*
☎ 33 14 94 95; www.restaurationen.dk; Møntergade 19; menu 620kr; 🕑 6pm-midnight Tue-Sat, closed Jul & Aug; bus No 6A
This highly regarded restaurant is a bastion of Copenhagen's fine-dining scene – the food is perfect, the service flawless, the wine list comprehensive and the atmosphere all grown up. Not as flashy as some of its equally Michelin-starred rivals, but every

bit as great. Food has a Mediterranean twist and the menu changes weekly, meaning that whatever you order, it's because the chef has judged it the best thing to eat at that time. Don't argue, just dig in.

RIZRAZ Map pp239-41 *Vegetarian*
☎ 33 15 05 75; Kompagnistræde 20; mains 99-169kr;
🕑 11.30am-midnight; bus No 6A
Conveniently located just south of Strøget, this pleasant basement café will have you feasting on a Mediterranean-style vegetarian lunch buffet that groans under the weight of felafel, pasta, hummus and salads, served daily to 5pm (to 4pm at weekends). You can also order from the menu, which includes lamb kebabs, grilled fish or fried calamari for the meat-lovers among us. A frequent winner of 'best and cheapest' awards.

SANKT GERTRUDS KLOSTER

Map pp239-41 *French-Danish*
☎ 33 14 66 30; Hauser Plads 32; mains 248-298kr;
🕑 4pm-midnight; metro & S-train Kongens Nytorv
Just off Kultorvet, this elegant restaurant is housed in a former medieval monastery, sections of which date from the 14th century. The most popular of the four dining rooms is the one occupying the cellar, which has arched brick walls and is lit by some 1500 candles. The restaurant specialises in French-Danish cuisine. On Sunday, there's also a fixed-price, three-course dinner served with wine for 349kr. Reservations advised.

SULT Map pp239-41 *Modern Danish*
☎ 33 74 34 17; Vognmagergade 8B; mains 55-175kr;
🕑 noon-midnight Tue-Sat, 11am-10pm Sun; bus No 350S
You'll find this modern, beautifully designed place inside the DFI (Dansk Filminstitut) and there's a great range of salad, bruschetta and pasta dishes if you're after a quick bite before the next round of classic cinema. More substantial dishes, such as braised lamb shank with a tagine of prunes, apricots, chickpeas and root vegetables (175kr), don't need to be accompanied by any films. *Sult* (Hunger), by the way, is a novel (and film) by Knut Hamson.

SUSHITARIAN Map pp239-41 *Japanese*
☎ 33 93 30 54; Gothersgade 3; menu 275kr;
🕑 noon-10pm Mon-Wed, noon-11pm Thu-Sat, 5.30-10pm Sun; metro Kongens Nytorv

This slick, split-level shrine to the charms of sushi is widely regarded as Copenhagen's best spot to indulge in Japanese fare and it also exudes a hip, right-now appeal. Service is utterly charming, and the food is from heaven (nigiri 30kr to 890kr – so every budget is catered to…). For those of you who want to learn more about the history and etiquette of sushi, handy instructions are on the menu. There's a nonsmoking area too.

CHEAP EATS

ANKARA Map pp239-41   Turkish
☎ 33 15 19 15; Krystalgade 8; mains 69-99kr; ⏰ noon-11pm; bus No 6A

This Turkish restaurant offers surprisingly good food for the money, as well as a pleasant setting with candle-lit tables and somewhat authentic décor in attractively dark surrounds. There's a generous bargain-priced buffet of salads, rice and numerous hot and cold dishes available all day for those on a strict budget. Other branches of this restaurant are located at Vesterbrogade 35 and 96.

CAFÉ SORGENFRI
Map pp239-41   Traditional Danish
☎ 33 11 58 80; Brolæggerstræde 8; smørrebrød from 45kr; ⏰ 10am-11pm; bus No 6A

This traditional-style corner pub has abundant local character and serves good, honest, cockle-warming Danish food. Traditional cold dishes such as smørrebrød and pickled herring cost little but pack a punch. Hot dishes, including tasty roast pork, are always reliable – or you can jump in and sample it all with a variety plate that includes herring, roast pork and meatballs with beets, cheese and other items.

Top Five Eat Strips

- **The Latin Quarter** Not just the haunt of students, it also attracts plenty of gourmands
- **Værnedamsvej in Vesterbro** A well-known strip of providores and food shops, perfect for picnic provisions
- **Christianshavn** For its beauty and its wealth of choices
- **Tivoli** Dozens of options for all tastes and all budgets
- **Gammel Strand** Views to Slotsholmen, outdoor seating and plenty of people-watching

---

HUSET MED DET GRØNNE TRÆ
Map pp239-41   Danish
☎ 33 12 87 86; Gammeltorv 20; smørrebrød from 40kr; ⏰ noon-4pm Mon-Fri year-round, noon-3pm Sat Sep-Mar; bus No 6A

This excellent lunch-time café is at the northwestern corner of Gammeltorv and beside the linden tree from which it takes its name (the House with the Green Tree). Housed in a period building dating from 1796, it offers quintessential Danish fare, with smørrebrød sandwiches, draught beer and a dozen brands of schnapps.

LA GLACE Map pp239-41   Patisserie
☎ 33 14 46 46; Skoubogade 3; pastries from 40kr; ⏰ 8.30am-5.30pm Mon-Thu, 8.30am-6pm Fri, 9am-5pm Sat; bus No 6A

This is the classic konditori (bakery-café) in town, and it has been serving tea and fancy cakes to socialites for more than a century. A rite of passage if you have a sweet tooth, or are looking to develop one.

SUPPE INSTITUTTET Map pp239-41   Soup
☎ 33 11 77 00; Grønnegade 41; mains 41-85kr; ⏰ 11am-8pm Mon-Fri, 11am-5pm Sat; bus No 350S

Small as a shoebox but filled to capacity with slurping Danes who've followed their noses and hip pockets to this delightful gourmet soup kitchen, this is an excellent spot to grab a takeaway soup or broth (the black-bean soup gets rave reviews) and head to Kongens Have.

SLOTSHOLMEN

Although there's no place to eat within the historic quarters of Slotsholmen, there are some interesting options just beyond, allowing you to fill your tummy not too far from some of the big sights.

KROGS FISKERESTAURANT
Map p231   Seafood
☎ 33 15 89 15; Gammel Strand 38; mains 340-490kr; ⏰ 5.30-10.30pm Mon-Sat; bus Nos 1A, 2A, 650S

A smidgen north of Slotsholmen Kanal, the famous Krogs specialises in fresh seafood served with organic produce in smart, subdued surroundings, where relaxed good taste rules the roost. You can also choose from a selection of menus, with matching wines for about 730kr. Imaginative fishy fare includes cod braised in Burgundy with pork jaw and scallops.

SØREN K Map p231 *Modern Danish*

☎ 33 47 49 49; Det Kongelige Bibliotek, Søren Kierke-gaards Plads 1; menu from 345kr; ☷ noon-midnight Mon-Sat; bus No 48, boat Nos 901, 902

In the lobby of the sleek new Royal Library, this gorgeous restaurant has become a fashion-able place for an upmarket meal, offering a fine canal view, beautiful design flourishes and a well-travelled wine list (including selections from the US, France and Australia). Fish dishes predominate, and with good reason – they really show off the inventive qualities of those at the stove.

Søren K (above)

THORVALDSENS HUS

Map p231 *Danish*

☎ 33 32 04 00; Gammel Strand 34; mains 99-185kr; ☷ 10am-midnight Mon-Thu, 10am-2am Fri & Sat; bus Nos 1A, 2A, 650S

Opposite the canal and affording a lovely vantage point on a sunny day. The interior is elegant and welcoming if the weather proves inclement – in which case we'd recommend the quail stuffed with cabbage, accompanied by couscous, chickpeas, tomatoes and eggplant. If you're only after a snack, there are also good salads, sandwiches and Mediterranean fare.

CHEAP EATS

SLOTSKÆLDEREN HOS GITTE KIK

Map p231 *Smørrebrød*

☎ 33 11 15 37; Fortunstræde 4; smørrebrød from 38kr; ☷ 11am-3pm Mon-Fri; metro Kongens Nytorv, bus No 1A

This snug little lunch spot is a few minutes' walk from Folketinget, so you can literally rub shoulders with members of parliament. Quint-essentially Danish, its menu features fantas-tic *smørrebrød* and an energetic atmosphere, thanks to all that sensibly wielded power.

ØIEBLIKKET Map p231 *Café*

no phone; Det Kongelige Bibliotek, Søren Kierkegaards Plads 1; snacks 20-32kr; ☷ 9.30am-6pm Mon-Sat; bus No 48, boat Nos 901, 902

In the lobby of the Royal Library, this is a good place for sandwiches and muffins that won't hurt the pocket. It's also the place to come to suss out studious young Danes puffing wildly on their cigarettes before going back upstairs to hit the books. Coffee, as you'd expect for a place frequented by the studious, is pretty ordinary. The water views, however, are every bit as good as those at Søren K, but for a fraction of the price – another example of those democratic Danes ensuring that everyone gets a fair go.

NYHAVN TO KASTELLET

Nyhavn is the area that many visitors to the city will choose for lunch or dinner, and with good reason – it's a lively, colour-ful waterside strip with plenty to choose from in the eating and drinking stakes. The streets radiating from Kongens Nytorv have more subdued, often formal places, with excellent cuisine of the French-Danish persuasion.

Nyhavn to Kastellet Top Five

- Le Sommelier (opposite)
- Ida Davidsen (opposite)
- Langelinie Pavillonen (opposite)
- Den Sorte Ravn (opposite)
- Els (opposite)

AMADEUS Map pp232-4 *Modern Danish*
☎ 33 32 35 11; Store Kongensgade 62; smørrebrød lunch 149kr, 4-course menu 265kr; 🕑 11am-11.30pm; metro Kongens Nytorv

This smart, comfortable restaurant-cum-café specialises in fresh, wholesome food and maintains a low-key, 'no sudden moves' demeanour, even during lunch hour. This is one of those low-profile gems that tourist brochures tend to ignore, even though the champagne sorbet is sublime. There's dining both indoors and in a rear courtyard.

CAP HORN Map pp232-4 *Danish*
☎ 33 12 85 04; Nyhavn 21; mains 160kr; 🕑 9am-1am; metro Kongens Nytorv

Another canal favourite, this deservedly popular spot specialises in Danish fare and uses mainly organic ingredients. Grab a lunch plate of three open-faced sandwiches, a two-course meal of herring, steak and potatoes, wash it all down with a beer and revel in your 'localness'. Open until the crowds die down, usually late.

DEN SORTE RAVN
Map pp232-4 *Modern Danish*
☎ 33 13 12 33; Nyhavn 14; mains 245kr; 🕑 11.30am-10.30pm; metro Kongens Nytorv

The Black Crow is an elegantly attired creature that keeps things smart but subtle in this sometimes touristy strip. The menu reflects a French influence in many of the traditional Danish dishes (which include *smørrebrød*) – try the fillet of turbot in puff pastry with lobster salmon mousse and parsley if you need proof.

ELS Map pp232-4 *French-Danish*
☎ 33 14 13 41; Store Strandstræde 3; mains 198-258kr; 🕑 noon-1am Mon-Sat, 5.30pm-1am Sun; metro Kongens Nytorv

Els dishes out formal food in a classic, upmarket, mind-your-manners, Danish-meets-French setting. Although the décor is solidly (and in some ways, stolidly) 19th century, the menu blends contemporary Danish and French influences to good effect where it counts – the food. Oh, and there's a good wine list, although the 4.75% surcharge on foreign credit cards is a bit rich.

IDA DAVIDSEN
Map pp232-4 *Smørrebrød*
☎ 33 91 36 55; www.idadavidsen.dk; Store Kongensgade 70; smørrebrød 50-150kr; 🕑 10am-5pm Mon-Fri (last order at 4pm); metro Kongens Nytorv

Ida's is widely (and rightly) considered the top *smørrebrød* purveyor in not just Copenhagen,

but all Denmark, and therefore the world. It has a nearly limitless variety of open-faced sandwiches – the only limit is Ida's imagination and the actual dimensions of the piece of (homemade) rye bread that you're dealing with. A rite of passage – skip a museum to get here if time is tight, and never say no to anything with fjord prawns in the list of ingredients.

LANGELINIE PAVILLONEN
Map pp236-7 *French-Danish*
☎ 33 12 12 14; Langelinie; mains 70-200kr; 🕑 noon-midnight; S-train Østerport

This is generally the sort of place we'd walk a mile to avoid – the only place to eat within spitting distance of a wildly over-rated tourist attraction with an industrial backdrop? No thanks – but actually, this place (designed by architects Eva and Niels Koppel) is a fabulously upmarket-looking 2nd-floor restaurant with some great flourishes (flash light fittings and swish chairs, orchids on the tables) and Philippe Privat at the stove. At dinner there's a changing menu of French-Danish fare. Because of its water views it's sometimes booked out by private parties.

LE SOMMELIER Map pp232-4 *French*
☎ 33 11 45 45; Bredgade 63; mains 180-195kr; 🕑 noon-2pm & 6-10pm Mon-Thu, noon-2pm & 6-11pm Fri, 4-11pm Sat & Sun; bus No 1A

Dishes here are routinely praised as amongst the best in the city, and the service is impeccable. Put your fork up for any of the exquisite lamb dishes. Needless to say, with a name like Le Sommelier, you won't be stuck for anything to drink with your meal – it may well have one of the best wine lists in the city.

RESTAURANT OLSEN
Map pp232-4 *Modern Danish*
☎ 33 93 91 95; Store Kongensgade 66; mains 79-179kr; 🕑 noon-1am Mon-Sat; metro Kongens Nytorv

This pleasant, formerly too-trendy-for-words restaurant has a mixed menu of classic Danish dishes with a twist and well-executed European and Asian dishes, such as a tangy mango salad (89kr) and other daily specials. Look for the big 'O' on the street.

TAPAS BAREN Map pp232-4 *Spanish*
☎ 33 36 07 70; Dronningens Tværgade 22; tapas 20-155kr; 🕑 noon-11pm Mon-Wed, noon-midnight Thu-Sat; metro Kongens Nytorv

As close as you'll get to thinking you're in Barcelona – good morsels of tapas can be washed down with plenty of Spanish wine, sherry and cava, and all in easy-on-the-eye surrounds. Our fave snack was the *albóndigas* – or meatballs to you and me.

CHEAP EATS

CHARLOTTENBORG CAFÉ

Map pp239-41   *Café*
☎ 33 13 11 58; Charlottenborg; mains 58-88kr;
🕑 11am-4pm; metro Kongens Nytorv

This elegant-looking café in the former palace that now houses Det Kongelige Kunstakademi (the Royal Academy of Art) has a changing chalkboard menu of reasonably priced light eats that satisfy some surprisingly fussy patrons (at least when we visited). *Smørrebrød* sandwiches are pretty damn good, a herring plate is 68kr and the café also serves cakes, coffee and beer. The café is wheelchair accessible.

KUNSTINDUSTRIMUSEET CAFÉ

Map pp232-4   *Café*
☎ 33 18 56 86; Bredgade 68; 🕑 10am-3.30pm Tue-Fri, noon-3.30pm Sat & Sun; bus No 1A

With putty-coloured walls, views out to a lovely walled garden (there's outdoor seating in summer) and easy-going chatter between all ages, this is a great spot to unwind whilst browsing the museum's extensive collection of decorative arts. Kick back with a salad of red beet, rocket and ricotta-parmesan 'cakes' – a wildly successful marriage of flavours and textures in a light, yet energy-boosting serve. Service is friendly too.

NYHAVNS FÆRGEKRO

Map pp232-4   *Danish*
☎ 33 15 15 88; Nyhavn 5; herring buffet 89kr;
🕑 11.30am-11.30pm; metro Kongens Nytorv

An atmospheric café right on the canal, this popular spot has an all-you-can-eat buffet with 10 different kinds of herring, including baked, marinated and rollmops, with condiments to sprinkle on top and boiled potatoes to round out the meal. If you're not a herring-lover, then there's something very wrong with you, but there's also a variety of *smørrebrød* for around 50kr. Dinner, served from 5pm to 11.30pm, betrays French influences, as do many Danish restaurants in this area.

SAHIL Map pp232-4   *Pakistani*
☎ 33 91 46 46; Havnegade 33; mains 59-99kr;
🕑 noon-11pm; metro Kongens Nytorv

Sahil serves authentic Pakistani food with a complete range of both vegetarian-only and chicken and lamb dishes. It's a fun place to dine if you're with a few people sharing orders – but a little subdued as a dining experience if you're on your own.

CHRISTIANSHAVN

Places to eat in Christianshavn include atmospheric canalside spots as well as businesses within the walls of the alternative community of Christiania. In addition to the places that follow, Christiania also has a handful of informal spots that are great for kicking back.

BASTIONEN & LØVEN

Map pp232-4   *Danish*
☎ 32 95 09 40; Lille Mølle, Christianshavns Voldgade 50; mains 105-170kr; 🕑 10am-midnight summer, noon-midnight Mon-Fri & 10am-midnight Sat & Sun winter; metro Christianshavn

The elegant Scandinavian interior of this charming establishment is reason enough to come, but on a sunny day you'll find yourself yearning to sit outside in the tranquil windmill-by-the-water setting. And possibly, the fact that the interior seems riddled with smoke (cigars are popular) might push you out. The whole place feels like a wonderful secret – although the weekend brunch sessions can get mighty packed with local regulars.

CHRISTIANSHAVNS BÅDUDLEJNINGOG CAFÉ

Map pp232-4   *Café*
☎ 32 96 53 53; Overgaden neden Vandet 29; mains 89-188kr; 🕑 10am-midnight May–mid-Sep; metro Christianshavn

If you want to explore Christianshavn's historic canals, this place rents out rowing boats on the canal. If you don't want any part of this outdoor activity, then you can chill out by the water's edge at this sweet little café, where cheap snacks (such as sandwiches) are available, but more substantial dishes are also on offer. For details about boat hire, see p136.

ERA ORA Map pp232-4   *Italian*
☎ 32 54 06 93; www.era-ora.dk; Ovengaden Neden Vandet 33B; menu 620-850kr; 🕑 noon-3pm & 6.30pm-midnight Mon-Sat

Era Ora means 'About Time' in Italian, and you'll want to look lively if you expect to score a table at this most delightful of Copenhagen's restaurants. Run by stalwarts of the Slow Food movement, everything that comes out of the kitchen has been lovingly prepared with the freshest ingredients, and the experience is worth any wait. Utterly romantic to boot too, thanks to the beautiful décor of the newish premises, and the wine list is superb.

OVEN VANDE CAFÉ

Map pp232-4   *French*
☎ 32 95 96 02; Overgade Oven Vandet 44; mains 159-189kr; ✆ 11am-midnight; metro Christianshavn

We loved this place so much we felt like wrapping it up, taking it home and making it the little restaurant on *our* corner. An upmarket, well-run café with a solidly French kitchen, plus the sort of low-key, local feel that sees all types popping in for a coffee or beer in an outdoor setting. We scoffed a baked salmon fillet stuffed with scallops and accompanied by spuds (159kr), washed it down with an excellent glass of wine (available by the glass) and felt utterly satisfied. The brunch here (119kr) is also worth an attempt, but you'll need a big stomach…

RESTAURANT KANALEN

Map pp232-4   *Danish*
☎ 32 95 13 30; Wilders Plads 2; menu 198-450kr; ✆ 11.30am-midnight Mon-Fri; metro Christianshavn

It's hard to imagine a nicer location than this on a sunny day. Everything is daydream perfect – canalside location, charming old building, superb meat and seafood dishes, and attentive service. The thing is though, you won't be doing much daydreaming, as this is a very popular spot for a business lunch, *dansk*-style. So much so, that chef Rasmus Agerliin has even created a special 285kr menu for this very demographic.

SPISELOPPEN

Map pp232-4   *Modern International*
☎ 32 57 95 58; Bådsmandsstræde 43; mains 135-185kr; ✆ 5-10pm Tue-Sun

You might be surprised to find an upmarket evening-only restaurant in the alternative world of Christiania, but Spiseloppen is just that and it draws plenty of city folk from the fancier parts of town. The chefs hail from New Zealand, Ireland, Lebanon and Denmark, and

Christianshavn Top Five

- **Era Ora** (opposite)
- **Restaurant Kanalen** (left)
- **Spiseloppen** (left)
- **Oven Vande Café** (left)
- **Spicy Kitchen** (p116)

the food is creative fusion-style, mixing different cuisines according to the available daily ingredients. The menu changes nightly, but the main dishes always include one vegetarian, one fish and three or four meat options. Spiseloppen is a large, casual hall-like place, but nonetheless gets filled to capacity quite quickly, so reservations are recommended, particularly at weekends.

CHEAP EATS

CAFÉ WILDER Map pp232-4   *Café*
☎ 32 54 71 83; Wildersgade 56; mains 60-85kr; ✆ 9am-2am Mon-Fri, 10am-2am Sat & Sun; metro Christianshavn

Imbued with an inviting shabby-chic ambience, Café Wilder is a perennial favourite with easy-going folks from this neck of the woods. Enjoy a simple lunch dish of juicy roast meat with a choice of wonderful fresh salads, or a rib-sticking brunch with all the trimmings (and a cast of what seems like thousands in this small space) on weekends. At night, the candles come out and it's a cosy neighbourhood bar that seems tailor-made for surreptitious hand-holding.

DAC CAFÉ Map pp232-4   *Café*
☎ 32 57 89 30; Strandgade 27B; mains 75-95kr; ✆ 11am-4pm; metro Christianshavn

Housed in the converted warehouse of the Dansk Arkitektur Center (DAC), this well-run café features simple snacks such as soups and hearty sandwiches, and lots of edgy red-and-white décor and mammoth exposed beams from the building's working-class heyday. There are some great glimpses into the kitchen, but if you nab a balcony you'll have glorious views over the water.

LAGKAGEHUSET Map pp232-4   *Bakery*
☎ 32 57 36 07; Torvegade 45; pastries from 9.25kr, sandwiches 38kr; ✆ 6am-7pm; metro Christianshavn

Copenhagen's sexiest and best-smelling bakery, this great place gets seriously packed on weekends when it seems that everyone simply must have a loaf, a cake and a coffee and *pronto*. Weekday mornings are slightly more sedate, but you'll still want to have a fair idea of what you're ordering by the time you get to the top of the queue, lest you waste too much time and find yourself on the receiving end of an eye-rolling display.

Lagkagehuset (p115)

MORGENSTEDET Map pp232-4 *Vegetarian*
no phone; Langgaden; mains about 45kr; ☺ noon-9pm Tue-Sun; metro Christianshavn

In the centre of Christiania, this is a delightful little place serving only vegetarian dishes, including some vegan and mostly organic. The food is tasty and fresh and prepared homestyle. The menu changes daily, and in winter a wood-burning stove makes the place cosy. Smoking (tobacco or pot) is not allowed.

SPICY KITCHEN Map pp232-4 *Indian*
☎ 32 95 28 29; Torvegade 56; mains 40-70kr; ☺ 2pm-midnight Mon-Fri, noon-midnight Sat & Sun; metro Christianshavn

This place is packed to the gills by 6.30pm, so if you fancy finding a table and some dinner at 8.30pm, you should either cross your fingers, make reservations or be prepared for a short wait. Ultra cheap, ultra moreish lamb curry or chicken tandoori is the speciality, and the house wine is ultra woeful. There's a children's menu, but the cramped space means that it can get very smoky.

NØRREBRO
The Nørrebro area, with its mix of students and immigrants, has a nice variety of eating options. The area around Sankt Hans Torv has developed into one of the city's newest and most youthful café scenes and in summer the square itself is thick with outdoor tables, bicycles and long-limbed locals. Nørrebrogade is definitely the place to go for late-night munchies to soak up the booze or assuage a hash-induced tummy rumble – it's *shawarma* central – and the offerings are, for the most part, perfectly good, thanks to the high turnover of food.

DE GAULLE Map pp236-7 *French*
☎ 35 85 58 66; Kronborggade 3; menu 360kr; ☺ 6-10pm Tue-Sat; bus No 18

De Gaulle is a rare fine-dining experience in grungy Nørrebro, and many locals are glad of it. Smart, understated (yet elegant) and doing fabulous things with fresh seasonal produce, this place represents excellent value for money when compared to restaurants on the 'posh' side of town. Whatever the chef's doing to asparagus, it works, and we know someone who'd happily order their vanilla bavarois for entrée, main and dessert.

KASHMIR Map pp232-4 *Indian*
☎ 35 37 54 71; Nørrebrogade 35; mains 60-110kr; ☺ 11am-11pm; bus Nos 5A, 350S

We were transported straight back to the days of the '70s British sitcom thanks to the décor of this popular Indian restaurant. Think potted plants, flock wallpaper and brassy lighting and have a giggle while you wait for your food. Then you'll forget all about your surrounds – the tandoori dishes are excellent and the fish pakora (85kr) simply delicious. No disputed territory here – grab someone hungry and share as much as you can.

PUSSY GALORE'S FLYING CIRCUS
Map pp236-7 *Café-Bar*
☎ 35 24 53 00; Sankt Hans Torv 30; mains 79-179kr; ☺ 8am-2am Mon-Fri, 9am-2am Sat & Sun; bus Nos 3A, 5A

This breezy place remains one of Nørrebro's most happening digs, with both indoor seating and alfresco tables on the square. Its varied menu includes salads, sandwiches and generous burgers plus a damn fine brunch that will set you up for shopping expeditions in the nearby streets.

SEBASTOPOL Map pp236-7 *Brasserie*

☎ 35 36 30 02; Sankt Hans Torv; mains 98-128kr;
☺ 9am-2am Thu-Sat, 9am-1am Sun-Wed; bus Nos 3A, 5A

In case the name isn't a giveaway, the Sebastopol is a French-style eaterie going for a *belle époque* feel on Nørrebro's most popular square. It offers good light eats and packs in a crowd on Sunday when brunch is often accompanied by live jazz music. In summer, there's outdoor seating.

SELFISH Map pp236-7 *Japanese*

☎ 35 35 96 26; Elmegade 4; sushi menu 70-230kr;
☺ noon-9pm Tue-Sat, 5-9pm Sun; bus Nos 3A, 5A

Great name this, although space is at a premium and there's no alcohol licence. If you don't fancy fighting for one of the five seats on the premises, you can easily order sushi (and Japanese beers) to take away – and it's very good sushi too. Handrolls cost 60kr, but if you're sharing, go for the XX-large platters (230kr) and try to find room inside yourself, let alone here.

CHEAP EATS

ESCOBAR Map pp232-4 *Café*

☎ 35 39 96 06; Blågårdsgade 29A; mains 66-78kr;
☺ 10am-10pm; bus No 5A

Escobar is *hygge* central, with comfy old couches, fairy lights, wooden floorboards, candles on the tables and warm drinks to wrap your hands around. Good meals and brunches are available, although you'll mostly come here for a caffeine hit or a glass of wine.

FLORAS KAFFE BAR

Map pp232-4 *Café*

☎ 35 39 00 18; Blågårdsgade 27; snacks 45-79kr;
☺ 10am-midnight; bus No 5A

Flora's is the sort of place that's perfect for kicking back with a coffee and the paper. Good desserts and reasonably priced soups, sandwiches and salads are also available, and there are usually a couple of hot meal specials for around 65kr. Much of the fare is organic. In summer (or even on a sunny spring day if you're desperate), you can sit outside and soak up the sunshine.

KAFFE PLANTAGEN

Map pp236-7 *Café*

☎ 35 36 22 32; Sankt Hans Torv 3; sandwiches 44-52kr; ☺ 8am-9pm; bus Nos 3A, 5A

Tidy, sweet-smelling and remarkably low-key for its cooler-than-thou location. The KP uses

the chiaroscuro blend to make what we consider the best caffè latte in Copenhagen (with your choice of milk, all organic, some 'quite fat'). Another bonus? It's nonsmoking.

MORGANS Map pp236-7 *Café*

☎ 35 35 26 72; Elmegade 15; brunch 42-95kr;
☺ 11am-midnight Mon-Thu, 11am-2am Fri, 10am-2am Sat, 10am-11pm Sun; bus Nos 3A, 5A

Morgans has a slightly grotty-meets-cool appeal, thanks to the fact that it looks as though they stopped decorating the place about halfway through the job. Neon lights and purple vinyl banquettes will test your hangover, as will some rowdy local youngsters, but it's the 'Grand Slam' brunch that will be the end of you – and your pants. Of course, you could always come here in the evening, *before* you start your hangover…

PICNIC Map pp236-7 *Turkish*

☎ 35 39 09 53; Fælledvej 22; mezze from 28kr;
☺ 11am-10pm Mon-Fri, noon-10pm Sat & Sun; bus Nos 3A, 5A

This delightful little place is a casual, cosy operation with deli-style dishes, including a variety of vegetable and Mediterranean/Middle Eastern salads. Almost everything they serve is organic and it's a charming spot for a Turkish coffee or tea. The décor, a blend of Scandimeets-souk, is another bonus.

Nørrebro Top Five

- De Gaulle (opposite)
- Selfish (left)
- Pussy Galore's Flying Circus (opposite)
- Picnic (above)
- Kashmir (opposite)

SHEIK SHAWARMA

Map pp236-7 *Middle Eastern*

☎ 35 37 40 48; Nørrebrogade 98; shawarma from 15kr; ☺ 11am-1am; bus Nos 5A, 350S

A little hole in the wall with just three café tables, some of the most lurid art that you can possibly stomach on a full bladder of beer (and this is how you'll visit the joint) and the best shawarma in Copenhagen. Something's gotta break up the booze when you're partying in this neck of the woods – not with style, but with savoury meat on a revolving stick.

NØRREPORT & AROUND

The area around Nørreport station has quite a few fast-food options and there are more substantial restaurants near the hotels situated to the west. It's also home to the up-and-coming strip called Nansensgade, where there are a few cafés and restaurants keeping an unfairly attractive crowd fed and watered. The traditional tourist attractions of this area also feature some good cafés for their visitors and the general public.

CAFÉ KLIMT Map pp232-4 *Café*
☎ 33 11 76 70; Frederiksborggade 29; mains 89-99kr; ⏰ 10am-10.30pm; metro & S-train Nørreport

Café Klimt has a bohemian feel, with pale yellow walls, fake palm trees, a relaxed crowd and some interesting international options on its lunch and dinner menu. However, it's best to come here for the brunch, which is big and beautiful (69kr to 85kr) and is served between 10am and 4pm – the standard size will see you wrestling with ham, cheese, chorizo, yogurt, fruit, scrambled eggs, bacon, bread and butter, plus an orange juice to cut through all that sweet cholesterol. More please.

CAFÉ LARS NØRGÅRD
Map pp232-4 *Modern Danish*
☎ 33 74 84 94; Statens Museum for Kunst, Sølvgade 48; mains 74-118kr; ⏰ 10am-5pm Thu-Tue, 10am-8pm Wed; metro & S-train Nørreport

Located in Statens Museum for Kunst, this airy, sunlight-infused space boasts modern Scandinavian décor (in black and white) and a garden view. Every day there's a better-than-decent special that typically includes a salmon dish, salad, bread and a seafood appetiser for about 90kr. We like the veal carpaccio with passion-fruit salsa, rocket, grana cheese and pumpkin seeds. A specific children's menu and wheelchair access are also part of the deal – plus it's nonsmoking.

ROSENBORG SLOT TRAKTØRSTEDET
Map pp232-4 *Café*
☎ 33 15 76 20; Rosenborg Slot, entry Øster Voldgade; mains 59-135kr; ⏰ 11am-4pm; metro & S-train Nørreport

Tucked away by the entrance to this fairy-tale castle is a good little eatery, where the herring

of the day or any other daily special (98kr) gets the thumbs up from the visiting crowds. A good range of wines from as far away as New Zealand and Chile feature on the wine list, and credit cards are accepted. On sunny days, there's outdoor seating with charming castle views.

STICKS 'N' SUSHI Map pp232-4 *Japanese*
☎ 33 11 14 07; Nansensgade 59; menus 265-485kr; ⏰ 6-11pm Mon-Thu, 6pm-midnight Fri & Sat, 6-10pm Sun; metro & S-train Nørreport

This handy Japanese restaurant has added some local twists to its menu to make things more appealing to Danes. Many of the items, such as sushi rolls, are served on sticks popsicle-style, similar to the way grilled items such as yakitori are served in Japan. The range of menus is quite extensive: our favourite (which is happily shared between two people) was the Pay Day Menu (485kr) – we're still salivating at the thought of its melt-in-the-mouth beef tenderloin foie gras. We also loved the Earl Grey sorbet, which served as the best palate cleanser we've come across in ages. Cold Japanese beer and warm sake make ideal accompaniments.

CHEAP EATS

GOVINDAS Map pp232-4 *Indian-Vegetarian*
☎ 33 33 74 44; Nørre Farimagsgade 82; thali 69kr; ⏰ 4.30-9.30pm Mon-Sat; metro & S-train Nørreport

Govindas serves savoury, Indian-style vegetarian food in a pleasant setting with mellow music. Hare Krishna devotees cook up a nine-dish thali meal of basmati rice, soup, salad and a few hot dishes such as eggplant casserole for bargain prices, meaning that the place is very popular with students and travellers. Govindas is run as a business rather than a venue for converting new members, so there's no religious hard-sell, just good, wholesome food.

STICKS 'N' SUSHI TAKEAWAY
Map pp232-4 *Japanese*
☎ 33 16 14 07; Nansensgade 47; sushi menu 64-169kr; ⏰ 2-10pm; metro & S-train Nørreport

This is the fast-food branch of the aforementioned restaurant and it too serves good Japanese fare. Prices are substantially lower here, with a multi-item menu that you can enjoy *in situ* or wherever you fancy. There's a small bar and a handful of tables, plus an excellent selection of local and international glossy mags for lone diners in need of a good read.

and good nosh. The heavenly smell of our neighbour's weever fish, oven-baked with fresh herbs and a fricassee of fennel and red capsicum, started something of a chain reaction amongst the diners here, which is always a good sign.

PASSAGENS SPISEHUS

Map pp232-4   *Danish*
☎ 33 22 47 57; Vesterbrogade 42; mains 170-225kr;
☽ 6-10pm Tue-Thu, 5-10pm Fri, 5-11pm Sat; bus No 6A

You won't be surprised by the solid, masculine feel to the décor of this popular restaurant once you cast your eye over the menu – it features plenty of unusually rustic fare, such as grouse, rooster, veal, fish and game, making it a seemingly lousy choice for vegetarians (although green requests are handled graciously and without fuss), but an excellent choice for those who like their meat imaginatively prepared and beautifully cooked. The grouse with mushrooms, prunes and potato in a port wine sauce is an excellent example.

RESTAURANT TEATERKÆLDEREN

Map pp232-4   *French-Danish*
☎ 33 25 75 00; Gammel Kongevej 29; 2-course menu 258kr, 3-course menu 288kr; ☽ 5pm-midnight; bus No 6A

One of the city's most unusual dining options, as it occupies the converted prop cellar of the century-old Det Ny Teater. The place is thick with character, its red brick walls are adorned with photos of former stage stars and the waiters double as performers. The restaurant caters to theatregoers wanting to wine and dine before or after plays, so non-theatregoers get the place to themselves between 7.30pm and 10pm when shows take place upstairs.

STRASSEN Map pp232-4   *Bar-Café*
☎ 33 22 32 41; Istedgade 128; mains 65-117kr;
☽ kitchen 10am-10pm; S-train Central Station, bus No 10

Strassen is a sexy place to grab a wonderfully warming *osso bucco* (115kr) in a stylish setting – Tom Rossau light fittings, cream leather banquettes and a little less second-hand smoke than at Bang og Jensen next door. The pasta dishes are also worth trying – especially the pasta with parmesan, artichoke, spinach, basil and onion. This place is also a popular **bar** (☽ to about 2am) with locals.

Sticks 'n' Sushi (opposite)

THAI AWAY Map pp232-4   *Thai*
☎ 26 12 21 23; Nansensgade 48; mains 49-78kr;
☽ 5-9.30pm; metro & S-train Nørreport

With limited seating and a reputation for some of the tastiest, easiest eating on this cool strip, you'd do well to get in here early or settle for a takeaway. The *pla lad prick* (72kr), a seafood-and-rice combo, rocks.

VESTERBRO

This district, which encompasses Central Station and extends west, has numerous places to eat, including some good, inexpensive ethnic choices, which are a dime a dozen. We've picked spots for this section with a little more in the way of character.

CAFÉ ANDRÉ CITROËN

Map pp232-4   *Café*
☎ 33 23 62 82; Vesterbrogade 58; mains 98-139kr;
☽ 10am-11pm Sun & Mon, 10am-midnight Tue & Wed, 10am-1am Thu, 10am-2am Fri & Sat; bus No 6A

This well-frequented brasserie, oozing French charm and situated opposite the Bymuseum (p87), features all the requisite Parisian touches: old-fashioned aperitif posters, red-leather banquettes, cane seats for outdoors

CHEAP EATS

BON APPETIT Map pp232-4 *Smørrebrød*
☎ 33 31 17 02; Vesterbrogade 17; smørrebrød from 10kr; ⏱ 7am-4pm Mon-Thu, 7am-1pm Fri; S-train Central Station

A firm favourite of office workers looking for a cheap lunch and commuters who can't bear to face what's on offer inside the main train station. Bon Appetit specialises in good takeaway sandwiches, either smørrebrød-style or on a bulky roll, and there's plenty of choice. Mind you, if you want to eat in, there are only a few chairs, and service doesn't favour any dilly-dallying. If you need help, ask, and ask quickly.

RICCOS Map pp232-4 *Café*
☎ 33 31 04 40; Istedgade 119; snacks 20-50kr; ⏱ 1-11pm Mon-Fri, 10am-11pm Sat & Sun; bus No 10

Shoebox-sized Riccos is such a funky little find that it gets name-checked in the credits for local band Kashmir's CD *Zitilites* (p27). Very good coffees, teas and tiny treats provide a welcome pause on an Istedgade shopping spree, to eat in or have 'out in the world', as the blackboard so cutely says.

OUTLYING DISTRICTS

These areas aren't known for their restaurant scenes as such, but if you're visiting any of the sights in these neighbourhoods, you won't go hungry. Islands Brygge, within spitting distance of the city centre, has some charming restaurants and cafés, and Østerbro has numerous good places to eat.

FREDERIKSBERG

ENCKE & DUERS SMØRREBRØD
DELIKATESSEN Map p238 *Smørrebrød*
☎ 33 22 22 32; Vesterbrogade 204; smørrebrød from 10kr per piece; ⏱ 10am-5pm Mon-Sat; bus No 6A

Two ladies and a talent for tasty Danish lunch treats combine to make this a handy eating spot in this neck of the woods – and speaking

---

Outlying Districts Top Five

- formel b (right)
- Restaurant Viva (opposite)
- Café Alma (opposite)
- Le Saint Jacques (right)
- Peter Lieps Hus (opposite)

---

of which, the smørrebrød travels well as a takeaway snack, so you can happily graze in the nearby park. You can also find delightfully fat sandwiches (35kr to 45kr) and freak-out worthy *frikadeller* (meatballs).

FORMEL B Map p238 *French-Danish*
☎ 33 25 10 66; www.formel-b.dk; Vesterbrogade 182; 5-course menu 550kr; ⏱ 6-10pm Mon-Sat; bus No 6A

One of Copenhagen's most famous restaurants, formel b offers intimate formal dining and a five-course menu of the day accompanied by a five-wine menu (another 550kr). The food is a merge of French and Danish cuisine that utilises seasonally fresh items. Very romantic – especially with such flattering lighting throughout.

MG PETERSENS FAMILIEHAVE
Map p238 *Danish*
☎ 36 16 11 33; Pile Allé 16; mains 70-170kr; ⏱ 11am-11pm; bus No 6A

Southeast of Frederiksberg Have, this restaurant is in tune with the neighbourhood's garden character. A large, casual 140-year-old eatery, it serves Danish family fare at outdoor tables. Specialities include fried pork and boiled potatoes and a platter with herring, boiled shrimp, Danish meatballs, roast pork, pâté, cheese and bread. In the evening there are often musicians playing old-fashioned Danish tunes, plus there's a good menu (24kr to 40kr) for children.

ØSTERBRO

Østerbro seems to specialise in places with a Mediterranean feel, with good food and filled with well-heeled locals choosing to stick close to home.

CIRCUS Map pp236-7 *Spanish-Danish*
☎ 35 55 77 72; Rosenvængets Allé 7; mains 75-189kr; ⏱ 10am-midnight Mon-Wed, 10am-1am Thu-Sat, 10am-6pm Sun; bus Nos 1A, 3A

This is a very popular option that's leading the charge in the trendification of Østerbro. Grab some tapas (a very well-stocked platter will set you back 138kr) and enjoy the convivial, chatty atmosphere that hums most days, but gets to almost-roaring as the weekend approaches.

LE SAINT JACQUES Map pp236-7 *French*
☎ 35 42 77 07; Sankt Jakobs Plads 1; mains 98-195kr; ⏱ noon-10pm; bus Nos 1A, 3A

Smack-bang on a pretty square straight from Paris' right bank, and we loved the care and attention to detail that the staff here lavished on their dishes and their customers. Top off any main course (the lamb is excellent) with a mocha panna cotta (85kr) and you won't need an after-dinner coffee. Lap dogs were an essential fashion accessory when we visited.

THEODORS Map pp236-7 *Café*
☎ 35 26 66 66; Østerbrogade 106; mains 75-198kr; ⏰ 11am-midnight Mon-Wed, 11am-2am Thu, 10am-2am Fri & Sat, 11am-10pm Sun; bus Nos 1A, 3A

Theodors (like so many of its Copenhagen rivals) takes its cue from Paris when it comes to décor, menu and style, although we did notice a juicy little wok creation (75kr) lurking on the menu, and we duly pounced. If you're not hungry, grab a glass of *vin rouge* and watch the world go by with the rest of the *petit bourgeoisie.*

ISLANDS BRYGGE
CAFÉ ALMA Map pp232-4 *Café*
☎ 32 54 32 04; Isafjordsgade 5; mains 75-120kr; ⏰ 11am-midnight Mon-Fri, 10am-midnight Sat & Sun; metro Islands Brygge

Funkiest cab off the rank in this burgeoning artsy 'hood is Café Alma, with excellent coffee and one of the comfiest old sofas we've ever rested our weary bones on. Grab a salad Niçoise (85kr) to keep you going if you're on a mission, or just unwind with a home-made cake. Weekend brunches (including a spiffy vegetarian option) come with all the trimmings, including people-watching opportunities.

IL PANE DI MAURO
Map pp232-4 *Italian Bakery*
☎ 32 96 86 87; Islands Brygge 23; panini from 35kr, pizza from 126kr; ⏰ 11am-7pm Mon-Fri, 11am-3pm Sat; metro Islands Brygge

This stylish bakery has wonderful bread and some fantastic panini (we love the 'etrusco'

Top Five Spots for Brunch
- Café Alma (above)
- Morgans (p117)
- Oven Vande Café (p115)
- Café Klimt (p118)
- Café Wilder (p115)

– with parmesan, mozzarella, rucola, tomato, salad and pesto) that are perfect for takeaway snacks or picnics. The pizzas (which are also available in single serves) are very authentic too – you'll swear you're in Italy.

RESTAURANT VIVA
Map pp232-4 *Seafood*
☎ 27 25 05 05; Langebrogade Kaj 570; menu 325kr; ⏰ 11.30am-3pm & 5.30-10pm Mon-Thu, 11.30am-3pm & 5.30-10.30pm Fri & Sat, 11.30am-4pm & 5.30-9.30pm Sun; metro Islands Brygge

Housed in a revamped boat that sits in the harbour, this is a fabulous place to come for imaginative and beautifully prepared seafood dishes, thanks to chef Paolo Guimaraes. It's run by the same people who own the delightful Aura (p107), which is recommendation enough for many locals – although the fact that there's plenty of caviar on the menu and a wickedly good bar until about 1am always helps.

HELLERUP
STICKS 'N' SUSHI Map p235 *Japanese*
☎ 39 40 15 40; Strandvejen 195; sushi menu from 129kr; ⏰ 11.30am-11pm; S-train Hellerup

This handy branch of the fab Nansensgade fave is midway between Charlottenlund and the Experimentarium in Hellerup. As the name implies, it specialises in Japanese fare and is popular with what seems to be husbands and wives escaping the kids.

KLAMPENBORG
PETER LIEPS HUS Map p230 *Danish*
☎ 39 64 07 86; Dyrehaven 8; mains 96-188kr; ⏰ 11am-9pm Tue-Sun; S-train Klampenborg

A few minutes' walk north of Bakken, this quintessential Danish country restaurant occupies a historic thatch-roofed house and is good for a nice relaxing meal, with *smørrebrød*, venison specialities and other Danish food (including children's portions of *frikadeller* – meatballs – and chips). On sunny days it's a popular place to sit outside and watch the horse and buggy carts go by.

RUNGSTED
There are numerous eating options to be found at Rungsted's large yachting harbour. Among these are kiosks that sell the usual burgers, beer and ice cream, casual

seafood eateries and fancier waterfront restaurants that have varied menus. There are waterfront picnic tables where you can sit and eat while enjoying the view. In addition, a convenient coastal walkway leads between the harbour and the Karen Blixen museum.

CAFÉ RUNGSTEDLUND   Café
☎ 45 57 10 57; Karen Blixen Museum, Rungsted Strandvej 111; mains 60kr; 🕙 10am-5pm Tue-Sun 1 May-30 Sep, 1-4pm Wed-Fri & 11am-4pm Sat & Sun 1 Oct-30 Apr; S-train Rungsted
Situated in the main building of this fine museum, this airy, appealing café has very good light meals and snacks. On sunny days, the outdoor seating is highly sought-after, but worth any wait.

ISHØJ
ARKEN CAFÉ   Café
☎ 43 57 34 21; Arken; mains 69-119kr; 🕙 10am-4.30pm Tue-Sun, 10am-8.30pm Wed; S-train Ishøj
Seemingly suspended off the side of this remarkable building, the café here gets full points for getting right into the swing of things. When we visited, the menu reflected the Spanish flavour of Arken's blockbuster Picasso exhibition with Spanish flavours of its own – from gazpacho to *asado de carne con*

patatas y ensalada (or roast beef with spuds and salad). Children are looked after well, and the brunches are very good.

DRAGØR
This quaint seaside village, south of Copenhagen airport, has a good selection of eating options in keeping with its nautical character.

BEGHUSET   French-Danish
☎ 32 53 01 36; Strandgade 14; mains 148-198kr; 🕙 noon-3pm & 6-9.30pm Tue-Sun; trans 30, 32, 73, 75E, 350S
Beghuset is called Dragør's top restaurant often enough for you to believe it, and features traditional Danish dishes and French-influenced fare (plus the odd gazpacho) in comfortable, bourgeois surrounds, making it a popular choice for wedding receptions and large family celebrations.

DRAGØR IS   Ice Cream
🕙 32 53 27 73; Strandlinien 15; ice cream 25kr; trans 30, 32, 73, 75E, 350S
Opposite the harbour, this place has won the 'golden scoop award' for dishing out the most ice cream in Denmark. And for about 25kr, you can join the crowd and walk out with a couple of scoops of your own.

Entertainment

Entertainment

Copenhagen is Scandinavia's most party-loving city, with locals, sundry Scandi types looking for cheap booze and international visitors all revelling in the wealth of entertainment options on offer. For free daytime entertainment simply stroll along Strøget, especially between Nytorv and Højbro Plads, which in the late afternoon and early evening is a bit like an impromptu three-ring circus with musicians, magicians, jugglers and other street performers. For night-time entertainment pop into any bar in the city centre, before or after a film, play, dance performance or music recital.

Copenhagen has scores of backstreet cafés and clubs with live music, so there's no shortage of places to have a drink or hit the dance floor. Danes tend to be late-nighters when it comes to clubbing, and many places don't really start to get going until 11pm or midnight. Danes also don't mind queuing for a club (or anything else for that matter), and popular places with a 'hot right now' reputation may see you scuffing the sidewalk for a while until you make it past face/fashion control. Some clubs and bars allow you to book a table if your party contains more than a few people – a good idea.

The free entertainment publication *Nat & Dag* lists concerts, club schedules and café events in detail; it can be found at Use It, the tourist office and various clubs and cafés throughout town.

Each summer the Copenhagen area hosts two world-renowned music festivals: the Copenhagen Jazz Festival, which takes place in scores of venues throughout the capital, and the Roskilde Festival, a huge Woodstock-like rock/pop/dance event that takes place in the ancient city of Roskilde, a short train ride from central Copenhagen.

For information on the Copenhagen Jazz Festival, see p20. See the boxed text on Roskilde, p126, for details on that festival.

More-highbrow entertainment is widely attended in the city, with opera and ballet at Det Kongelige Teater reason enough to visit Copenhagen. Other, more-esoteric and experimental art forms such as physical theatre and the like are also found in smaller venues.

While the city isn't a stopover on the international sporting events calendar (no Grand Prix, no Grand Slam etc), there are some sporting events staged throughout the year that will satisfy the armchair sports-lover in most people and there are plenty of physical activities to indulge in if staying fit is your priority.

Tickets & Reservations

If you want to buy tickets on the Internet for various performances, check out www.e-billet.dk.

BILLETNET
☎ 38 48 11 22; www.billetnet.dk
Tickets for most events, including sporting events, can be booked through this service, which is also available at all post offices.

DET KONGELIGE TEATER Map pp239-41
☎ 33 69 69 69; www.kgl-teater.dk; Kongens Nytorv; tickets 60-1000kr
If booking from abroad, you can charge the tickets to a credit card and have them mailed to you. For bookings and information call be-

tween 1pm and 7pm Monday to Saturday, or go online and email your request. Keep in mind that refunds will only be given in case of cancellation of the performance or a change of repertoire. There's also a last-minute deal – whenever there's a performance that hasn't been sold out by 5pm, the box office will begin selling the remaining tickets for that evening's show at a 50% discount. In addition, those aged under 26 or over 67 are entitled to 50% off all standard ticket prices at any time.

TIVOLI BILLETCENTER Map p231
☎ 33 15 10 12; Vesterbrogade 3; ⌚ 10am-8pm Mon-Fri, 11am-5pm Sat & Sun
At the main Tivoli entrance and good for tickets of any kind. Not only does it sell Tivoli performance tickets, but it's also the box of-

fice for ARTE, which handles tickets for plays in Copenhagen, and an agent for BilletNet, which sells tickets for concerts and music festivals nationwide. If you're up for a last-minute theatre experience, it's possible to get half-price tickets for unsold seats in the city's theatres through Tivoli Billet Center, starting at noon for performances taking place that same day.

Performing Arts Venues

Aside from the big venues, there are also a few smaller theatres in Copenhagen that stage performances of popular plays and musicals; programs are published in the daily newspapers, *Copenhagen This Week* and *Teater Kalenderen*.

DET KONGELIGE TEATER Map pp239-41
☎ 33 69 69 69; www.kgl-teater.dk; Kongens Nytorv; tickets 60-1000kr

Den Kongelige Ballet (the Royal Ballet) and Den Kongelige Opera (the Royal Opera) perform at this lavishly beautiful theatre, which is worth coming to for its interior alone. The opera and ballet season runs from mid-August to late May, skipping the main summer months. With the opening of the city's fabulous new Opera House, its repertoires are two-thirds ballet, one-third opera. An English-language brochure with the season schedule for Det Kongelige Teater is available from the tourist office, or write to the Royal Theatre, Box Office, PO Box 2185, 1017 Copenhagen K.

OPERA HOUSE Map pp232-4
www.kgl-teater.dk; Dock Island

Opened in January 2005, the state-of-the-art structure features no fewer than six stages (with 1400 seats in the main auditorium) and a 'floating' roof with a 32m-long cantilever. The Opera House, which takes up its own specially constructed 'island' (a former shipyard) north of Christianshavn, can be seen from many waterside vantage points in the

Gay & Lesbian Copenhagen

Copenhagen has one of the liveliest gay and lesbian scenes in Europe. The city has dozens of gay bars, clubs and cafés, nearly half of them concentrated along Studiestræde in the two blocks between Vester Voldgade and Nørregade. For a complete list pick up a copy of *PAN-bladet*, a monthly newspaper which is available at gay businesses, including the clubs mentioned in this chapter. *PAN-bladet* has information on gay organisations, saunas and other places of interest. Another read worth keeping an eye out for is the newish *Out & About* (free; www.out-and-about.dk), which lists gay venues and events.

Ørstedsparken, a couple of blocks northwest of Studiestræde, is a popular gay cruising site but those visiting the park should be cautious as anti-gay gangs occasionally come through the park as well. The trees at Ørstedsparken have unique 'bird houses', which are lidded boxes stocked with condoms by safe-sex volunteers. The gay clubs and bars also distribute free condoms.

Copenhagen has a handful of gay saunas, video rooms and sex clubs; the aforementioned publications list them.

Some gay and lesbian venues:

Cafe Intime (p130)

Centralhjørnet (p130)

Copenhagen Men's Bar (p131)

Cosy Bar (p133)

Heaven (p133)

Masken (p131)

Pan Disco (p133)

Sebastian (p132)

city. The Opera House hosts performances in the following measures: two-thirds opera, one-third ballet.

TIVOLI KONCERTSAL Map p231
Concert Hall; ☎ 33 15 10 12; www.tivoli.dk; Tietgensgade 30

This is the venue for symphony orchestra, string quartet and other classical music performances by Danish and international musicians. There's a ballet festival each season featuring top international troupes, as well as cabaret performances. They also have modern dance performances by such big names as the Alvin Ailey dance troupe. Tickets are sold at the Tivoli Billetcenter (see opposite).

Vor Free Kirke

Sommerkoncerter I Vor Frue Kirke (Summer Concerts in Vor Frue Kirke) feature free classical music performances throughout the summer months at Vor Frue Kirke, the city's theatre-like cathedral.

Roskilde

The grand Roskilde Festival rocks sleepy Roskilde, a 25-minute train ride west of central Copenhagen, for four consecutive days each summer on the last weekend in June.

Inspired by the Woodstock and Isle of Wight festivals, the first Roskilde Festival was held in 1971, with some 20 bands performing to a gathering of 10,000. Since that time it's mushroomed into northern Europe's largest rock music festival, with more than 150 rock, techno and ethnic bands playing on a number of stages.

Past festival line-ups have included such headliners as Black Sabbath, the Beastie Boys, Bob Dylan, Iggy Pop, Marilyn Manson, Tori Amos, Lou Reed, the Cure, Nine Inch Nails, the Wu Tang Clan, Michael Franti and Spearhead, and Fat Boy Slim. Over the years, the promoters have also been particularly astute at presenting new trends in rock and at booking lesser-known groups that have later gone on to stardom – it's a great place to hear the best and brightest on the music scene and to catch some innovative Scandinavian acts.

The Roskilde Festival is more than just music – it's a huge spirited bash with lots of drinking and partying. The average age of the festival-goers is 24 and about half come from other countries, particularly Germany, Sweden, Finland, the Netherlands, Norway and Belgium. There are stalls selling everything from tattoos to fast food, but you may want to bring some food supplies of your own as prices are high.

Although it's always been a big party scene, the festival organisers have prided themselves on running a safety-conscious event. Nonetheless, tragedy befell the festival in 2000, when nine concertgoers suffocated as they were pressed forward by a crush of fans trying to get closer to a midnight performance by Pearl Jam. The grounds were muddy from rain and the victims, all young men, apparently slipped and fell as the crowd pushed forward.

Since then, the festival has gone from strength to strength and great efforts have been made to ensure that such a tragedy never happens again.

All of the profits from the Roskilde Festival are distributed to charitable causes both at home and abroad. Festival tickets can cost up to 1150kr, including camping at the site, and can be purchased in Denmark through **BilletNet** (☎ 70 15 65 65; www.billetnet.dk).

Tickets can also be obtained by calling ☎ 0870 264 3333 in the UK, ☎ 900 300 1250 in the Netherlands, ☎ 77 170 7070 in Sweden, ☎ 180 537 0000 in Germany or ☎ 0600 10800 in Finland. Advance sales typically start in December. The latest information can be obtained on the festival website at www.roskilde-festival.dk.

Festivals

COPENHAGEN AUTUMN JAZZ
www.jazzfestival.dk

Same management as the monster-sized Copenhagen Jazz Festival, but a little more low-key and mellow. Top jazz musos perform at various city venues over four days in early November.

COPENHAGEN FILM FESTIVAL
www.copenhagenfilmfestival.com

An excellent, well-regarded film festival that showcases both Danish and international cinematic offerings in the second half of September.

COPENHAGEN GAY & LESBIAN FILM FESTIVAL
www.cglff.dk

The city's longest-running film fest highlights the best of gay and lesbian international cinema – it runs for a week from mid-October.

COPENHAGEN INTERNATIONAL BALLET FESTIVAL
www.copenhageninternationalballet.com

Modern choreography is showcased by dancers from the Royal Danish Ballet and visiting performers from foreign ballet corps. Held from the first to the third week in August.

COPENHAGEN JAZZ FESTIVAL
www.jazzfestival.dk

Copenhagen's biggest yearly event runs for 10 days in early July and cements the city's reputation as Jazz Central for this part of the world. Expect big names, both local and international, and all styles of jazz.

NATFILM FESTIVAL
www.natfilm.dk

Say goodbye to the dirty end of winter by getting back out at night and revelling in this excellent film fest, with local and international films both past and present. It takes place over 10 days from late March.

THEATRE

Copenhagen theatres have been suffering in recent years from cuts in government subsidies, dwindling private support and shrinking audiences. In addition, critics have tended to be tough on theatres, taking them to task for producing plays that have been slanted to the mainstream and lacking in artistic innovation, but as theatre companies keep pointing out, it's hard to foster innovative material in an environment where keeping one's head above water is a dominant concern.

That said and done, Copenhagen does have a number of theatres that maintain regular production schedules, so there are always at least a few plays to select from at any one time.

Note that plays are usually produced in Danish – which might be amusing if you've always wondered what *Macbeth* sounds like in a foreign tongue, but it's apt to leave most visitors scratching their heads, particularly if it's a play that they're not already familiar with.

Current productions are listed in the brochure *Teater Kalenderen* and the magazine *Copenhagen This Week*, both produced monthly and available free at the tourist office and many other businesses around town.

For information on getting half-price same-day theatre tickets, see p124.

Theatres at which performances take place:

Betty Nansen (Map p238; ☎ 33 21 14 90; Frederiksberg Allé 57; metro Frederiksberg) In the Frederiksberg area, this smallish theatre shows mostly Danish-language plays.

Café Teatret (Map pp239–41; ☎ 33 12 58 14; Skindergade 3; metro Kongens Nytorv or Nørreport) In the Latin Quarter, this busy little space has a café and a few stages that fairly hum with ideas.

Det Ny Teater (Map pp232–4; ☎ 33 25 50 75; Gammel Kongevej 29; S-train Vesterport) In the Vesterbro area, this gorgeous venue brings mainstream musicals to the masses.

Folke Teatret (Map pp239–41; ☎ 33 12 18 45; Nørregade 39; metro & S-train Nørreport) In the Latin Quarter, this theatre has a strong tradition of showing Danish-language productions but isn't afraid to put on *Annie Get Your Gun* when the time is right.

Kanonhallen (Map pp236–7; ☎ 35 43 20 21; www .kanonhallen.dk; Serridslevvej 2; bus No 150S) Near Fælledparken in Østerbro, and playing host to some excellent physical theatre and performance art.

Puppet on a String

Of special interest for children are the free marionette shows performed during the months of June, July and August at the eastern side of Kongens Have, the public gardens near Rosenborg Slot. These puppet shows last half an hour and begin at 2pm and 3pm daily, except Monday.

Nørrebros Teater (Map pp232–4; ☎ 35 20 90 00; Ravnsborggade 3; bus No 5A) In the Nørrebro area, this medium-sized theatre plays a lot of comedy romps – which won't mean much if you don't speak Danish.

Østre Gasværk Teater (Map pp236–7; ☎ 39 27 71 77; Nyborggade 17; bus No 150S) In the Østerbro area, and a former gas storage warehouse – plays are often mainstream, but prove popular, and the building is a gas – sorry.

TurbineHallerne (Map pp239–41; ☎ 33 69 69 69; www .kgl-teater.dk; Adelgade 10; bus No 350S) This excellent new theatre, housed in the old Turbine Halls, stages plays performed by the Royal Theatre, and is top-notch in every way.

Det Kongelige Teater (p125)

DANCE

Den Kongelige Ballet (the Royal Danish Ballet) performs at Det Kongelige Teater (Map pp239–41; the Royal Theatre) at Kongens Nytorv. The season runs from mid-August to late May, skipping the main summer months. The Royal Danish Ballet performs classic works, such as *Giselle*, *Swan Lake* and August Bournonville's repertoire. It also presents contemporary ballets, some choreographed specifically for the Royal Danish Ballet by such international luminaries of modern dance as Stephen Petronio.

DANSESCENEN Map pp236-7

☎ 35 43 58 58; www.dansescenen.dk; Østerfælled Torv 34; bus No 150S

Near Fælledparken in Østerbro, this rejuvenated warehouse hosts some of the most exciting contemporary dance in Scandinavia, with over 125 performances taking place each year and some excellent youth discounts on offer for the under-30s.

CIRCUS

The circus is a popular form of family entertainment in Denmark, especially during summer, when companies tour the country coaxing laughs from the young and the not-so-young.

Cirkus Arena (☎ 40 30 30 40; 120-200kr)

Cirkus Arli (☎ 21 92 60 10; 65-100kr)

Cirkus Baldoni (☎ 20 80 60 10; 95-125kr)

Cirkus Benneweis (☎ 40 40 20 20; 100-180kr) Gets great reviews and repeat visits from its many fans – if you pick one, this should be it.

Cirkus Charlie (☎ 40 83 44 44; 90-105kr)

Cirkus Dannebrog (☎ 30 26 36 36; 90-180kr)

Cirkus Krone (☎ 75 76 32 00; 60-80kr)

Cirkus Mascot (☎ 20 74 50 52; 75-110kr)

CINEMAS

Danish movie theatres mainly feature the latest in big-name international films, with a heavy dose of Hollywood, but they also mix in some classics, art films and Danish titles – thanks to the fact that the Danish population is, by and large, very cinema-literate and appreciative of interesting tales well told. Movies are shown in their original language with Danish subtitles, making it easy for non-Danish-speaking cinemaphiles to attend any screening they fancy.

At most cinemas, ticket prices vary with the time of day and the day of the week, ranging from around 50kr for weekday matinee shows to about 75kr for movies screened after 6pm at weekends. The increase in prices on weekends reflects the popularity of going to the cinema between Friday and Sunday – and you may want to reserve tickets in advance for special screenings or particularly popular offerings. Like many other pursuits, locals believe that films go better with alcohol – so you can take a glass of wine or a beer into the theatre with you.

The majority of Copenhagen's cinemas are clustered within a few blocks of each other right in the city centre, convenient to both Central Station and the Rådhusplads en bus terminal. Collectively, they have a couple of dozen screens so there's always a wide variety of flicks to choose from.

DAGMAR TEATRET Map pp232-4

☎ 33 14 32 22; www.sandrewmetronome.dk; Jernbanegade 2; 50-70kr; 11.30am-9.45pm; train Central Station, bus Nos 2A, 5A, 6A, 250S, among others

A good central theatre that plays mostly arthouse films, although a few mainstream gems sneak into the mix.

FILMHUSETS CINEMATEK Map pp239-41

☎ 33 74 34 12; www.dfi.dk; Gothersgade 55; 50kr; 10am-10pm Tue-Fri, noon-10pm Sat & Sun; bus No 350S

The Danish Film Institute's wonderful cinema plays classic Danish and foreign films. There's also an excellent book-cum-gift shop and restaurant, Sult (p110), on the swanky premises. It's a great way of supporting the Danish film industry, as Det Danske Filminstitut is the organisation that bankrolls most Danish films.

GRAND TEATRET Map pp239-41

☎ 33 15 16 11; www.grandteatret.dk; Mikkel Bryggersgade 8; 50-70kr; noon-9.40pm; train Central Station, bus Nos 2A, 5A, 6A, 250S, among others

The films shown at this comfortable theatre, just off Strøget, are from the mainstream end of cinema.

IMAX TYCHO BRAHE PLANETARIUM

Map pp232-4

☎ 33 12 12 24; www.tycho.dk; Gammel Kongevej 10; 50-90kr; ◷ 10.30am-8.30pm Fri-Tue, 9.45am-8.30pm Wed & Thu; S-train Vesterport

This flash Imax cinema shows fast-paced nature and adventure films that leap out at you from the giant screen. For more information, see p86.

PALADS Map pp232-4

☎ 70 13 12 11; www.biobooking.dk; Axeltorv 9; 50-75kr; ◷ 11.30am-10pm; S-train Vesterport

You'd have to be colour-blind to miss this garishly painted emporium of film. Blockbuster releases and other mainstream diversions, plus plenty of seating space and a big candy bar.

PALLADIUM Map pp232-4

☎ 70 13 12 11; www.biobooking.dk; Vesterbrogade 1; 50-75kr; ◷ 11.30am-10pm; train Central Station, bus Nos 2A, 5A, 6A, 250S, among others

This cinema shows current-release films in their original language. It's in the Rådhusarkaden Shopping Centre.

PARK BIO Map pp236-7

☎ 35 38 33 62; www.parkbio-kbh.dk; Østerbrogade 72; 55-60kr; ◷ from 10am; bus No 150S

Located in the Østerbro area, the Park screens both contemporary and classic films and has a rather classic appearance thanks to its Art Deco heritage. Special screenings for babies (and parents) take place on a regular basis.

DRINKING

You've come to the right place! Copenhagen is far more affordable and laid-back about drinking than its other Scandinavian neighbours, and the locals love to imbibe. A lot. It's not uncommon to see people walking down the street with a beer. In the morning. Chances are though, you'll find that most people enjoy alcohol as a social lubricant – and that cafés are the preferred location for a beer or a glass of wine (often enjoyed with a snack), rather than pubs. Some cafés/bars add music (live or generally from a DJ) to the mix, particularly at weekends. The 'pubs' that do feature in town are often the sort of theme-park affairs (Irish, English) that feature permanent TV and not much in the way of fun. Alcohol can be bought at supermarkets and convenience stores (like 7-Eleven), but not after 8pm.

Copenhagen's fun-loving attitude means that wherever you find yourself, you'll find a bar of some description, but if you're looking for places with a 'happening at this very instant' feel you'd do well to lurk around the fashionable haunts of the Latin Quarter, Nørrebro, Nørreport and Vesterbro – where bars and clubs (both gay and straight) compete for your affection and crowds shake out the cobwebs until about 5am on the weekends.

Man about Town

Spend enough time hanging around Copenhagen's bar-café-restaurant scene and you may notice that some places have a certain similarity, a shared ambience. It seems that one man single-handedly changed the habits of the city and raised expectations about where to dine and drink, and that man was Torben Olsen. Responsible for such stayers as Dan Turèll (p131), Café Sommersko (p130) and Café Ultimo (p106), Olsen's influence extended to those who worked for him, some of whom have branched out on their own, but stayed true to the Olsen vision of smart décor, updated Danish cuisine and polished service.

BANG OG JENSEN Map pp232-4

☎ 33 25 53 18; Istedgade 130; ◷ 8am-2am Mon-Fri, 10am-2am Sat, 10am-midnight Sun; bus No 10

This reborn pharmacy serves fabulous brunches and treats all day and Danish eye-candy all night, when DJs play and so do the patrons of this very cool spot. Try to grab a sofa in the room at the back if you're aiming for a bit of leg and elbow room.

BANKERÅT Map pp232-4

☎ 33 93 69 88; Ahlefeldtsgade 27; ◷ 10am-midnight Mon-Fri, 11am-midnight Sat & Sun; metro & S-train Nørreport

Our fave bar in all Copenhagen features taxidermied critters in outlandish get-ups in the windows and pickled customers in outlandish get-ups at the tables. Nurse a drink, a hangover, artistic pretensions or your secret crush in lugubrious style.

BAR ROUGE Map pp239-41

☎ 33 45 98 23; www.barrougenights.com; Krystalgade 22; ◷ 3pm-2am Fri & Sat; bus No 6A

Aimed squarely at the cocktail set who like getting gussied up to hear smooth lounge sounds, this bar is a haven from the some-times exuberant but immature drinking dens of the Latin Quarter. It might be a good idea to reserve a table.

Bang og Jensen (p129)

BARSTARTEN Map pp236-7

☎ 25 24 11 00; Kapelvej 1; ☽ noon-midnight Mon, Tue & Sun, noon-2am Wed & Thu, noon-3am Fri & Sat; bus No 5A

Worthy of its own entry in the Eating chapter, but we're including it here because it's the cocktails and the excellent DJ skills that make the patrons smile the most (although the food really is great). Old-skool hip-hop, funk, soul and that '80s electro-boogie sound get things going – so much so that you half expect the residents of Assistens Kirkegård to cross the road and see what the fuss is about.

CAFÉ BOPA Map pp236-7

☎ 35 43 05 66; Løgstørgade 8; ☽ 10.30am-midnight Mon, Tue & Sun, 10.30am-1am Wed, 10.30am-3am Thu, 10.30am-5am Fri & Sat; bus No 150S

The only thing this place could want would be a canalside location – it's that perfect. Hid-den away and offering very good food, it's the kind of easy-going place that puts you in an instantly happy mood – especially when you can nab an outside table. The pace picks up at night though, and DJs turn the space into a very cool nightspot indeed, peopled with the area's best-looking 20-somethings.

CAFÉ EUROPA Map pp239-41

☎ 33 12 04 28; Amagertorv 1; ☽ 9am-midnight Mon-Thu, 9am-1am Fri & Sat, 10am-midnight Sun; metro Kongens Nytorv, bus Nos 1A, 350S

With an unbeatable location, this modern, continental-style café sets up its tables right on Højbro Plads on sunny days, making it a great place for people-watching. Service is a little harried, but understandably so.

CAFE INTIME Map p238

☎ 38 34 19 58; www.cafeintime.dk; Allégade 25; ☽ 5pm-2am Wed-Fri & Sun, 8pm-2am Sat; metro Frederiksberg

In the sedate Frederiksberg area, this is an old-fashioned piano bar owned by a Swedish woman named Monica who leads good-natured, enjoyable sing-alongs. The place attracts a mixed crowd of lesbians and drag queens.

CAFÉ JERNSTANGEN Map pp232-4

☎ 33 31 19 70; Istedgade 61; ☽ noon-1am; bus No 10

Jernstangen means 'the Hitching Post' in Dan-ish, and this place once operated as just such a thing. It's the street's oldest bar (operating since 1891) and is run by a friendly Australian who was in the throes of getting a 3am booze licence when we popped in to sample a very nicely poured draught beer. Laid-back, low-key and slightly louche.

CAFÉ SOMMERSKO Map pp239-41

☎ 33 14 81 89; Kronprinsensgade 6; ☽ 8am-midnight Mon-Wed, 8am-1am Thu, 8am-2am Fri, 9am-2am Sat, 10am-midnight Sun; bus No 350S

This long-time Kronprinsensgade haunt of the bold and the beautiful draws a smartly groomed crowd and serves a wide variety of drinks, including 50 different brands of beer, which never seem to get sprayed on the art that adorns the walls. Service is friendly, and it's very handy for shopping sprees in this most 'zhuzhed' of Latin Quarter streets.

CENTRALHJØRNET Map pp239-41

☎ 33 11 85 49; www.centralhjornet.dk; Kattesundet 18; ☽ noon-2am; train Central Station, bus Nos 2A, 5A, 6A, 250S, among others

Just south of Strøget is Copenhagen's oldest gay bar, dating back over 75 years. Its unflashy, almost kitsch décor, good staff and corner jukebox attracts an older, friendly and easy-going crowd, and it's not a bad spot for a sandwich or coffee.

COPENHAGEN MEN'S BAR Map pp239-41
Teglgårdsstræde 3; ⏰ 3pm-2am; metro & S-train Nørreport
If the name doesn't clue you in, nothing will. This very cruisy man-fest is found in the gay district around the corner from Studiestræde, and it's the place to go for guys into leather, uniform and rough trade in general.

DAN TURÈLL Map pp239-41
☎ 33 14 10 47; Store Regnegade 3; ⏰ 9.30am-midnight Mon-Thu, 9.30am-2am Fri & Sat, 10am-11pm Sun; bus No 350S
Dan Turèll was a Danish writer with a loyal following, and this bar seems to have inspired a similar loyalty among many locals. It has a Parisian feel to it, with lots of mirrors, cane chairs and book jackets on the walls, and a relaxed clientele who give the impression they've just popped in for a quick glass of wine on the way home.

EAT Map pp239-41
☎ 33 33 99 97; Hovedvagtsgade 10; ⏰ 6pm-3am Thu-Sat; bus No 350S
Brand-new and white-hot, Eat is a see-and-be-seen destination for many of the city's media flunkies and their stylishly suited pals. There's a very good **restaurant** (mains 75-155kr; ⏰ 6-10pm Tue-Sat) on the premises as well, but generally it's the sort of spot you head to for fine cocktails, smart décor and a slight fashion crisis.

Top Five Drinking Establishments

- Bankeråt (p129)
- Café Bopa (opposite)
- Ideal Bar (right)
- Zoo Bar (p132)
- Eiffel Bar (below)

EIFFEL BAR Map pp232-4
no phone; Wildersgade 58; ⏰ 9am-2am; metro Christianshavn
In the olden days this place was a brothel, and there's still a crazily seedy air about it (some corners smell of pee...), making it a refreshingly grotty antidote to the city's fashion bars. The fishmonger comes on the first Sunday of the month to sell the catch of the day to bar patrons, payday (Thursday)

is always the best night to come here and get ripped, and generally you can expect a half-shickered nautical type to make filthy jokes about Crown Prince Frederik having to go 'Down Under' to get a wife. Despite this, tables have fresh tulips and great glasses of cheap wine flow freely.

IDEAL BAR Map p238
www.vega.dk; Enghavevej 40; ⏰ 7pm-4am Thu, 7pm-5am Fri & Sat; bus No 3A
Ideal Bar is just that – the ideal place to enjoy a few fabulous cocktails in style. The music is more subdued than at Vega, but the crowd is every bit as cool (in a good way).

KLAPTRÆET Map pp239-41
☎ 33 13 31 48; Kultorvet 11; ⏰ 10am-1am Mon-Thu, 10am-5am Fri & Sat, 11am-midnight Sun; metro & S-train Nørreport
This café overlooking Kultorvet square has a casual, unpretentious atmosphere. Kultorvet itself becomes a popular beer garden in summer, when some of the nearby businesses, including Klaptræet, set up tables in the square and sell beer on tap, meaning you don't have to grapple with any stairs when tipsy.

KRASNAPOLSKY Map pp239-41
☎ 33 32 88 00; Vestergade 10; 10am-2am Mon-Wed, 10am-5am Thu-Sat; train Central Station, bus Nos 2A, 5A, 6A, 250S, among others
Once super 'trendy', Krasnapolsky is now quite OK as a drinking spot and boasts the longest bar in Copenhagen, plus DJs who concentrate on the house end of things musically. The crowd tends to be a little uninteresting by day, but much more fun at night.

MASKEN Map pp239-41
☎ 33 91 09 37; Studiestræde 33; ⏰ 4pm-2am Mon-Thu, 4pm-5am Fri & Sat, 3pm-2am Sun; bus No 6A
Here you'll find a pretty mellow, easy-going atmosphere, with cheap beer and good snacks. It's mainly a hang-out for gay men, but Thursday is Ladies Night. Entertainment options include drag acts, live music and football telecasts.

NYHAVN 17 Map pp232-4
☎ 33 12 54 19; Nyhavn 17; ⏰ 11am-2am; metro Kongens Nytorv
There are plenty of pub-like places along Nyhavn, but we picked this one because it's bright yellow and we can always remember

the address. Like everywhere else on this strip, it excels in cold beer at outdoor tables and hearty Danish food, but you can also enjoy live music most nights of the week. And did we mention the address is easy to remember?

PUSSY GALORE'S FLYING CIRCUS
Map pp236-7

☎ 35 24 53 00; Sankt Hans Torv 30; ⏰ 8am-2am Mon-Fri, 9am-2am Sat & Sun; bus Nos 3A, 5A

Arne Jacobsen chairs, outdoor seating, an excellent cocktail list and some serious queues mean this place has still got some sort of 'it' factor for many locals. A good warm-up bar before you hit the clubs.

RIGA Map pp232-4

☎ 33 25 25 60; Istedgade 79; ⏰ 2pm-1am Tue & Wed, 11am-1am Thu-Sun; bus No 10

Riga bills itself as an Art café, and it does have a slightly self-conscious, too-cool-for-school air about it (obscure films are often shown here), but it's also a perfectly good spot to unwind with a drink while you wait for the DJ to stop faffing about and play some funky electro. The kind of bar that polarises opinion among locals, who all have some kind of story to tell about it (it seems that half of them have worked here).

SEBASTIAN Map pp239-41

☎ 33 32 22 79; Hyskenstræde 10; ⏰ noon-midnight Mon-Wed, noon-2am Thu-Sat; train Central Station, bus Nos 2A, 5A, 6A, 250S, among others

This very pleasant bar/café attracts a mixed gay and lesbian crowd. It's a good spot to visit in the late afternoon, when Happy Hour attracts a relaxed crowd. And we mean crowd – everyone seems to rank this place as one of their faves.

SPUNK BAR Map pp232-4

no phone; cnr Istedgade & Abel Cathrinesgade; ⏰ 11am-2am Mon-Sat, 2pm-2am Sun; train Central Station, bus No 10

We stood outside and wondered: is it a gay bar? A swingers' bar? Full of eye-candy? Reader, it was none of these things – your standard Danish drinkers' bolthole with ciggie burns in the tablecloths and alcohol-related brain damage on display. That said, the name will have you laughing all afternoon and/or night and you can actually buy a T-shirt (150kr) to remind you just how wacky Danes can be.

STEREO BAR Map pp232-4

☎ 33 13 61 13; Linnesgade 16A; ⏰ 8pm-3am Wed-Sat; metro & S-train Nørreport

The effortlessly cool Stereo Bar is the sort of place you grow to think of as yours, as it walks that fine line between being right on the money in terms of DJs, décor and distractions, and having a local, mellow, unpretentious atmosphere. There's a small dance floor with eclectic, catholic music and plenty of flattering lighting.

STUDENTERHUSET Map pp239-41

☎ 35 32 38 60; www.studenterhuset.ku.dk; Købmagergade 52; ⏰ noon-6pm Mon, noon-midnight Tue, noon-2am Wed-Fri; metro & S-train Nørreport

This low-key student hang-out near the Rundetårn features some good light meals to soak up all the cheap beer that's on offer. Not a bad spot to catch some live music either, or the eye of feverish types with Che posters on their bedroom walls.

ZOO BAR Map pp239-41

☎ 33 15 68 69; Kronprinsensgade 7; ⏰ 10am-midnight Mon & Tue, 10am-1am Wed, 10am-2am Thu-Sat; bus No 350S

A smallish bar with a definite 'bright young things' feel to the clientele, who all look gorgeous but don't act like they know it. Music is played on weekends, which always causes a crush, but we prefer it earlier in the week or the evening, when you can enjoy your drink in peace and engage in a little conversation.

Cafe Bopa (p130)

OPERA

Den Kongelige Opera (the Royal Danish Opera) performs at Det Kongelige Teater and at the Opera House (see p125). The Royal Danish Opera not only performs classics by Wagner, Puccini and Verdi, but also stages a couple of innovative new operas each season. See Performing Arts Venues for details of where you'll catch this esteemed company's productions. One alternative opera company devoted to modern works is **Den Anden Opera** (The Other Opera; www.denandenopera.dk) – for more information, see p33.

CLUBBING

Copenhagen's club scene is a pretty late one. Don't expect anything to be happening before 10pm, as things generally don't get into full swing until at least midnight, and then get really interesting from about 2am.

For the latest club schedules, pick up a copy of the free *Musik Kalenderen*, a fold-out monthly brochure found at the tourist office and entertainment venues around the city.

COSY BAR Map pp239-41

☎ 33 12 74 27; Studiestræde 24; 🕙 10pm-6am Sun-Thu, 10pm-8am Fri & Sat; bus No 6A

Only in Denmark would a gay meat-market call itself the Cosy Bar. This is a very popular late-night place for men, with DJs playing Tuesday to Saturday to a packed dance floor and a serious attitude to picking up, and quickly.

HEAVEN Map pp239-41

☎ 33 15 19 00; Kompagnistræde 18; 🕙 noon-2am Sun-Thu, noon-5am Fri & Sat; train Central Station, bus Nos 2A, 5A, 6A, 250S, among others

Does every capital city have a gay bar called Heaven? Anyway, this is more of the same – popular, populist, and filled with the buffed, the bronzed and the beautiful. Maybe the name's not so bad after all.

PAN DISCO Map pp239-41

☎ 33 11 37 84; www.pan-cph.dk; Knabrostræde 3; 🕙 disco 10pm-5am Fri, 10pm-6am Sat; train Central Station, bus Nos 2A, 5A, 6A, 250S, among others

On the southern side of Strøget, this is the city's main mixed gay and lesbian danceteria, with multiple bars and two (frequently packed) dance floors. Typically, one disco spins current house tunes and the other focuses on camp/romantic pop classics that bring out the inner karaoke queen in all of us.

PARK CAFÉ Map pp236-7

☎ 35 42 62 48; www.parkcafe.dk; Østerbrogade 79; admission free-50kr; 🕙 11am-midnight Mon & Sun, 11am-2am Tue & Wed, 11am-5am Thu-Sat; bus No150S

The Østerbro area's main nightspot, the Park has a couple of large dance floors – the upper-level one with live music and the basement floor with a DJ. It's a stylish-looking spot too, with varied but progressive music and a young, spunky crowd – plus plenty of old-fashioned chandeliers, which makes a change in these parts.

RUST Map pp236-7

☎ 35 24 52 00; www.rust.dk; Guldbergsgade 8; admission 50-120kr; 🕙 9pm-5am Wed-Sat; bus Nos 3A, 5A

A thriving, smashing place that attracts one of the largest and coolest club crowds in Copenhagen. There's a choice of spaces here from nightclub to concert hall, and a wide variety of edgy modern music that covers most tastes. Weekends see some earnest queuing. You'll need to be over 21 to enter the nightclub.

STENGADE 30 Map pp232-4

☎ 35 36 09 38; www.stengade30.dk; Stengade 18; admission 30-90kr; bus No 5A

In the Nørrebro area, Stengade 30 has a frequently lively alternative scene with everything from electronica and hip-hop to Berlin-style techno and edgy international DJs like Miss Kittin and Ned Flanders. Big nights last until about 5am or thereabouts.

Festival of Clubbing

Denmark's love of clubbing is so widespread that it even holds a festival devoted to celebrating Copenhagen's clublife. Copenhagen Distortion takes place in early June and involves lots of promoters, performers, punters, bars and clubs getting together and partying for five straight days. For more details go to www.cphdistortion.dk.

Vega (below)

VEGA Map p238
☎ 33 25 70 11; www.vega.dk; Enghavevej 40; admission 50-120kr; 🕑 11pm-5am Fri & Sat; bus No 3A
In the Vesterbro area, this is one of Copenhagen's hippest spots, with big-name rock, pop and jazz bands performing on its main stage (Store Vega) and edgier underground acts on a smaller stage (Lille Vega). It's also home to a cool club that gets packed with seriously good-looking Vesterbro locals. Or you could try the heavenly Ideal Bar (p131).

MUSIC
JAZZ & BLUES
Admission prices in this section vary, depending on a range of things, such as the night of the week and who's performing.

CAFÉ BLÅGÅRDS APOTEK Map pp232-4
☎ 35 37 24 42; Blågårdsgade 20; 🕑 3pm-2am; bus No 5A
This former pharmacy (this seems to be a bit of a trend in Copenhagen) is a smoky, asthma-inducing bar that's a venue for folk, blues and swing music, with rough-round-the-edges locals knocking back plenty of beer and singing along if they damn well feel like it.

COPENHAGEN JAZZ HOUSE Map pp239-41
☎ 33 15 26 00; www.jazzhouse.dk;
Niels Hemmingsensgade 10; 🕑 6pm-midnight Sun-Thu, 6pm-5am Fri & Sat; metro & S-train Nørreport
This is the city's leading jazz spot, featuring top Danish musicians and occasional international performers. The music runs the gamut from bebop to fusion jazz, and there's a large dance floor.

JAZZHUSET VOGNPORTEN Map pp239-41
☎ 33 15 20 02; Rådhusstræde 13; admission free-50kr; 🕑 11am-1am Mon-Sat; train Central Station, bus Nos 2A, 5A, 6A, 250S, among others
Another significant jazz venue in the city centre, this place has lots of Danish performers but also musicians from the USA and UK and a leaning toward the bebop and swing side of things.

LA FONTAINE Map pp239-41
☎ 33 11 60 98; Kompagnistræde 11; admission free-50kr; 🕑 8pm-5am; bus No 350S
Small and secretive-seeming, La Fontaine is a casual late-night venue for swing and mainstream jazz musicians, including visiting artists who sometimes end up jamming together if they can find the elbow room.

MOJO Map pp232-4
☎ 33 11 64 53; www.mojo.dk; Løngangstræde 21; admission 30-60kr; 🕑 8pm-5am; train Central Station
East of Tivoli, a great spot for blues, with live entertainment nightly and draught beer aplenty.

SOFIE KÆLDEREN Map pp232-4

☎ 32 57 27 87; www.sofiekaelderen.dk; Overgaden Oven Vandet 32; admission free-50kr; ✆ from10pm Thu-Sat, from 3pm Sun; metro Christianshavn

This stellar cellar venue in Christianshavn hosts a range of live acts and DJs from Thursday to Sunday – but it's the Jazz Klub, on the last afternoon of the week, that appeals most, when a variety of local and other Scandinavian combos perform Scandi Jazz to an appreciative crowd.

ROCK & SALSA

Most of the Copenhagen clubs that feature live music and dancing have rock bands at least part of the time. The local scene is pretty effervescent at the moment too, with some really good local acts churning out garage rock and fuzzy pop.

If you're up for something with a Latin twist, there are places that offer salsa dancing on Thursday, Friday and Saturday nights. Admission prices vary, depending on what night of the week it is and who's performing.

LOPPEN Map pp232-4

☎ 32 57 84 22; Bådsmandsstræde 43; admission 40-120kr; ✆ Wed-Sat; metro Christianshavn

Housed in an old warehouse in Christiania, this is a popular spot with some of the city's top bands, ranging from funk and soul to punk rock and world music. At weekends, the live concerts are followed by a boisterously fun 'disco' at 2am, usually finishing at 5am.

PUMPEHUSET Map pp232-4

☎ 33 93 14 32; www.pumpehuset.dk; Studiestræde 52; admission 40-120kr; train Central Station, bus No 6A

This 600-seat venue in the city centre features live rock and pop bands, with occasional theme 'tribute' nights highlighting the music of performers such as David Bowie or Tom Jones.

SABOR LATINO Map pp232-4

☎ 33 11 97 66; Vester Voldgade 85; admission free-60kr; ✆ 9pm-3am Thu, 9pm-5am Fri & Sat; train Central Station, bus Nos 2A, 5A, 6A, 250S, among others

This lively space features Cuban-style salsa and merengue, and you can dance sometimes to disco, sometimes to live Latin bands. Neophytes should arrive at 10.15pm for an hour of free dance instruction, which helps alleviate the fear of being an uncoordinated, two-left-feet abomination.

GAMBLING

CASINO COPENHAGEN Map pp232-4

☎ 33 96 59 65; Radisson SAS Scandinavia Hotel, Amager Blvd 70; admission 80kr; ✆ 2pm-4am; metro Islands Brygge

If you want to try your hand with the high rollers, this casino, in the northern part of Amager, has slot machines, stud poker, blackjack tables and both American and French roulette. Admission is restricted to those aged 18 and over, and there's a cover charge to get in.

SPORT, HEALTH & FITNESS
WATCHING SPORT
Football (Soccer)

The national sport is football (soccer) and Denmark's national football team is keenly followed and much-loved by Danes, although they didn't live up to national hopes at Euro 2004. If you're keen to watch an international match, games are played at **Parken** (Map pp236-7; ☎ 35 43 31 31; Øster Allé 50, Østerbro), Denmark's national stadium in Copenhagen, which is at the eastern side of Fælledparken. Parken is also the leading Copenhagen venue for national league games, which occur between late July and early December, and from early March to late May. Local rivals are **Brøndby IF** (☎ 43 63 08 10; www.brondby-if.dk; Brøndby Stadion 30) and **FC København** (☎ 35 43 74 00; www.fck .dk; Parken, Øster Allé 50, Østerbro), but you needn't fear getting caught up in any soccer hooligan-style melees – Danish fans are generally regarded as some of the best-behaved in Europe, and violence is very rare.

Horse Racing

If you're interested in horse races, you can follow the gee-gees at the following places:

Charlottenlund Travbane (Map p230; ☎ 39 96 02 02; www.travbanen.dk; Traverbanevej 10, Charlottenlund; S-train Klampenborg, then bus No 388) A trotting (harness racing) track north of the city and south of Bakken.

Klampenborg Galopbane (Map p230; ☎ 39 06 02 13; www.galopbane.dk; Traverbanevej 10; Charlottenlund; S-train Klampenborg, then bus No 388) A horse-racing track immediately south of Bakken in Klampenborg. Races take place on Saturday.

Ice Hockey

In the dead of winter, ice hockey gets its moment of glory, taking over from football as the main sport. Denmark's team aren't world-beaters, but they are pretty good and local teams often play in the Copenhagen area. Contact the Danish Ice Hockey Association (☎ 43 26 26 26) for more details if you'd like to see a (generally well-behaved) game. If you want to catch what passes for an international grudge match – make it one between Denmark and (of course) Sweden.

KEEPING FIT

Boating

There are a number of possibilities for hiring boats and rowing your way around scenic waterways. Aside from the city's canals, the Lyngby area also has a number of lakes, including Furesø, which is the deepest lake in Denmark.

CHRISTIANSHAVNS BÅDUDLEJNING OG CAFÉ Map pp232-4
☎ 32 96 53 53; Overgaden neden Vandet 29; boats per hr 80kr; ⊙ 10am-sunset May–mid-Sep; metro Christianshavn

If you want to explore Christianshavn's historic canals, this place rents out rowing boats and makes for an experience both more romantic and more authentic than any overpriced gondola in Venice. An added bonus is the sweet little café on the premises (see p114).

FREDERIKSDAL KANO OG BÅDUDLEJNING Map p230
☎ 45 85 67 70; www.frdal.dk; Nybrovej 520; boat hire from 100kr; ⊙ 10am-8pm Tue-Sun; S-train Sorgenfri, bus No 191

Near the locks, Frederiksdal Kano og Bådudlejning hires out canoes and rowing boats for use on the river Mølleåen and the lakes Lyngby Sø, Bagsværd Sø and Furesø, which are interconnected.

HOLTE HAVN Map p230
☎ 45 42 04 49; 22 Vejlesøvej; per hr 80kr; ⊙ 10am-9pm

Hire rowing boats or canoes at this kiosk on the shores of Furesø, and row around either Furesø or the smaller Vejlesø, which are connected by a channel. Holte Havn is near Holte S-train station, two stops north of Sorgenfri.

Cycling

Cycle lanes are found along many city streets and virtually all of Copenhagen can be toured by bicycle, except for pedestrian-only streets such as Strøget. For more information about cycling around the city, see p192.

On Your Bike

The most popular self-guided cycling tour in the Copenhagen area is the 12km ride north to Dyrehaven. There's a cycle path the entire way, much of it skirting the Øresund coast.

To begin, take Østerbrogade north from the city. After passing the S-train station Svanemøllen, the road continues as Strandvejen, passing through the busy suburb of Hellerup, where intersections have blue-marked crossings to indicate cyclist rights of way, and then up through the quiet coastal village of Charlottenlund. Here the cycle lane widens. There's a beach, an old fort and an aquarium for interesting diversions. Once you reach Klampenborg station, a bike path leads into Dyrehaven, a woodland crossed by a network of trails, and a perfect place for a picnic. If you want to continue further north, an off-road cycling path runs parallel to the coastal road to Rungsted. Either way, you have the choice of returning on the same route, taking an alternative route such as the inland road Bernstorffsvej, or putting your bike on the S-train and making it a one-way tour. See Map p230 for the tour route.

DANWHEEL Map pp232-4
☎ 33 21 22 27; Colbjørnsensgade 3; per day/week 40/175kr; ⊙ 9am-5.30pm Mon-Fri, 9am-2pm Sat & Sun; train Central Station

This company hires out really cheap older bikes, so make sure you check their condition before setting off. It's located a couple of blocks northwest of Central Station.

KØBENHAVNS CYKLER Map pp232-4
☎ 33 33 86 13; www.rentabike.dk; Reventlowsgade 11; per day/week from 75/340kr; ⊙ 8am-6pm Mon-Fri, 9am-1pm Sat, summer 10am-1pm Sun; train Central Station

On the Reventlowsgade side of Central Station, this place is one of the most convenient bike-rental options. The bikes are in good working order and children's seats are available for hire.

ØSTERPORT CYKLER Map pp236-7

☎ 33 33 85 13; www.oesterport-cykler.dk; Oslo Plads 9; per day/week from 75/340kr; ⏰ 8am-6pm Mon-Fri, 9am-1pm Sat; S-train Østerport

The sister business to Københavns Cykler and with the same good standards, this place is near track 13 at Østerport S-train station.

Fitness Clubs

If you want to get a good work-out while you're in Copenhagen, there are a handful of fitness clubs where visitors can pay about 75kr to use the weights and fitness machines.

Fitness dk (Map pp239–41; ☎ 33 43 28 00; Adelgade 5; ⏰ 6am-10pm Mon-Thu, 6am-9pm Fri, 8am-6pm Sat, 9am-7pm Sun; bus No 350S) Flashy fitness centre offering a variety of classes, including Pilates, spinning and yoga, plus conventional weight machines.

Radisson SAS Falconer Hotel (Map p238; ☎ 38 10 90 70; Falkoner Allé 9; ⏰ 6am-1pm Mon-Thu, 6am-8pm Fri, 8am-5pm Sat, 8am-8pm Sun; metro Frederiksberg) In the Frederiksberg area, with personal trainers, pump classes and plenty of stationary cycles.

SATS Scala Complex (Map pp232–4; ☎ 33 32 10 02; level 5, Vesterbrogade 2E; ⏰ 6am-10pm Mon-Thu, 6am-9pm Fri, 8am-6pm Sat, 9am-7pm Sun; S-train Vesterport) In the Scala complex in the city centre, and therefore extremely handy. Lots of equipment and classes.

Golf

Denmark is the home of Scandinavian golfing, and Copenhagen has the oldest golf club in Scandinavia, so it's no surprise that the city attracts many keen greens-lovers, especially from mid-March to mid-October. The game is popular with both men and women, young and old, and not as bogged-down in tradition as in some countries.

COPENHAGEN INDOOR GOLF CENTRE Map pp232-4

☎ 32 66 11 00; www.cigc.dk; Refshalevej 177B; 20-min lesson 150kr; bus No 48

It's probably easier to get a game here than at the Golf Klub, but it is indoors. Plenty of finely crafted golfing options await – and year-long membership is a bargain 300/150kr per adult/child. Prices vary according to how long you'll want to play, but you can generally expect to spend at least 150kr for around an hour. Parking is available too.

KØBENHAVNS GOLF KLUB Map p230

☎ 39 63 04 83; www.kgkgolf.dk; Dyrehaven 2; S-train Klampenborg, then bus No 388

This 18-hole golf course at the northern end of Dyrehaven park in Klampenborg is Scandinavia's oldest (1898). Greens fees are 350kr on weekdays, 450kr at weekends, and bookings are paramount.

Ice Skating

Even when the mercury plunges you can raise a sweat in the centre of town. The busy public square Kongens Nytorv, at the head of the Nyhavn canal, is flooded during the winter to form a delightful outdoor ice-skating rink. You can rent skates for 35kr right at Kongens Nytorv during the season, typically from early November to the first weekend in March. Other public ice rinks are constructed in Nørrebro's Blågårds Plads and Østerbro's Trianglen, from about the second half of November, open daily from noon until about 8pm or 10pm. Skate hire is also 35kr.

In addition, during the pre-Christmas season opening of Tivoli, the amusement park's lake becomes a winter playground for ice skaters as well.

Swimming
BEACHES

The greater Copenhagen area has a number of bathing beaches, if brisk water doesn't deter you. Even in July, ocean temperatures average just 17°C, so most beach-goers are Scandinavians and Germans rather than visitors from warmer climes. Those who prefer more tepid waters should choose from one of Copenhagen's indoor swimming pools (p138).

Ocean waters are tested regularly, and if sewage spills or other serious forms of pollution occur the beaches affected are closed and signposted.

Topless bathing is *de rigueur* at all Danish beaches, but nude bathing is typically limited to certain areas; the main rule of thumb is to follow local custom. One place that is popular with nude sunbathers (and gays and lesbians) is the north side of Bellevue beach.

Amager Strandpark (Map p230) A popular beach south of Copenhagen. Playground facilities and shallow water make it ideal for children, while deeper water can be reached by walking out along the jetties. Take the Metro to Lergravsparken.

Bellevue (Map p230) An attractive, popular beach at Klampenborg – this coast is known as the Danish Riviera. The northern end of the beach is popular with gays and lesbians. Take S-train C to Klampenborg.

Charlottenlund (Map p235) An accessible beach north of central Copenhagen. Take S-train C to Charlottenlund.

POOLS

Scattered throughout Copenhagen are a handful of public swimming pools and saunas that are open to the general public and some (if indoors) year-round. Each charges around 26kr for adults, half that for children.

BELLAHØJ FRILUFTSBAD Map pp232-4

☎ 38 60 16 66; Bellahøjvej 1, Brønshøj; adult/child 26/12kr; ⏰ 7.30am-5.30pm Mon-Fri, 10am-5pm Sat & Sun 22 May-15 Aug; bus No 13

At the intersection of Bellahøjvej and Frederikssundsvej (within walking distance of the hostel and camping ground located in this neighbourhood), this is a good Olympic-sized outdoor pool that opens for summer only.

DGI-BYEN Map pp232-4

☎ 33 29 80 00; www.dgibyen.dk; Tietgensgade 65; adult/child 49kr/free; ⏰ 6.30am-9pm Mon-Thu, 6.30am-7pm Fri, 9am-5pm Sat & Sun; train Central Station

An extravagant swim centre with several pools, including a grand ellipse-shaped affair with 100m lanes, a deep 'mountain pool' with a climbing wall, a hot-water pool and a children's pool. If you've forgotten your togs or towels they can be hired for 25kr each. Other features include a wet trampoline and diving platforms. The complex is run by DGI, the Danish Sports and Gymnastic Association.

FREDERIKSBERG SVØMMEHAL Map p238

☎ 38 14 04 04; Helgesvej 29; family/adult/child 75/28/13kr; ⏰ 7am-9pm Mon-Fri, 7am-4pm Sat, 9am-4pm Sun; metro Frederiksberg

This is a spiffy indoor pool with lots of fun amenities, such as a monster slide, salt baths, a solarium, massages and kiddies' pool.

FÆLLEDBADET Map pp236-7

☎ 35 39 08 04; Borgmester Jensens Allé 50, Fælledparken; adult/child 26/12kr; ⏰ 7am-6pm Mon, 7am-8pm Tue, 10am-6pm Wed, 7am-4.30pm Thu, 7am-3pm

Fri, 9am-3pm Sat & Sun 1 Sep-31 May, 7am-5pm Mon & Wed, 7am-8pm Tue, 10am-5pm Thu, 10am-3pm Fri-Sun 1 Jun-31 Aug; bus No 150S

A pool-in-a-bubble but warm enough when you need a swim in winter, and located in leafy Østerbro.

ISLANDS BRYGGE HAVNEBADET

Map pp232-4

☎ 23 71 31 89; Islands Brygge; admission free; ⏰ 7am-7pm 1 Jun-31 Aug; metro Islands Brygge

You'll not have a more authentically local swimming experience than at this natty outdoor pool, which is actually in one of the city's famous canals. Red-and-white striped barriers, interesting architectural shapes and a great mix of locals make for a refreshing and captivating dip. Green flags mean good-quality water, so don't worry about pollution. Grab a panino from Il Pane di Mauro (p121) beforehand and snack by the sea after swimming.

VESTERBRO SVØMMEHAL Map p238

☎ 33 22 05 00; Angelgade 4; adult/child 26/12kr; ⏰ 10am-7pm Mon, 7am-7pm Tue-Thu, 7am-2.30pm Fri, 9am-2pm Sat & Sun; S-train Enghave

This is a handy 25m-long indoor swimming pool (there's also a sports centre on the premises) but it's not as luxurious as the facilities at DGI.

Windsurfing

Denmark's coast attracts more wind than you'll know what to do with, but if you're a keen windsurfer, it will come as a blessing. The beaches at Amager and Ishøj offer decent windsurfing conditions and both have windsurfing operations.

NAUTIC SURF & SKI ISHØJ

☎ 43 54 00 19; Søhesten 6A; S-train Ishøj

At Ishøj, near the Arken museum, this is a long-established operation. Expect to pay about 450kr for a one-day course, use of gear included.

SURF & SNOWBOARD

☎ 32 84 04 57; Amager Strandvej; beginners course 725kr; metro Lergravsparken

This hire outfit is at Amager Beach, a popular family destination that can get a good amount of wind. Beginners courses are run regularly, as are courses for children.

Shopping

Shopping

When it's time for a shopping spree many Danes prefer to go outside their own country to places such as Germany, where things are cheaper (believe it or not), so you shouldn't expect to find many budget-range bargains while shopping in Copenhagen. Simply put, Danes are relatively wealthy and quite stylish, so they tend to be discriminating shoppers who demand high quality, which means that whatever you do choose to spend your money on will be sure to satisfy even the fussiest person. This is not a city where you have to pore over the seams of a suit, test the binding of a book, sniff to see if the perfume's bogus or debate the dodginess of local labour conditions.

Copenhageners enjoy their shopping expeditions, as any stroll down Strøget and its sur-rounding streets will show you – on any day of the week, and whatever the weather. It's an excuse to socialise, acquire and escape, and any excuse seems to do.

Great local goodies to stuff into your suitcase abound, and cover a range of categories. There are wonderful shops stocking Danish porcelain throughout the city, and provided you're careful about shipping and breakage, you should be able to get it home quite easily.

With its clean lines and skilful merging of aesthetics and function, Danish silverwork is prized both in Denmark and abroad. The chief design criteria are that the item be attractive yet simple, as well as easy to use. The father of modern Danish silverwork was sculptor and silversmith Georg Jensen, who artistically incorporated curvilinear designs; his namesake company is still a leader in Danish silverwork today. Goldsmiths are also worth checking out, with some intriguingly modern and elegant designs on sale throughout the city.

Amber is fossilised tree resin that is translucent and brittle. It's polished and made into jewellery, particularly pendants, beaded necklaces, earrings and rings. There are a number of shops selling amber in Copenhagen.

The Danish love of good interior design means that Copenhagen is the mother lode when it comes to homewares – you won't have any trouble finding all manner of knick-knacks and furnishings to make your pad look stylish. The Danish love of keeping your exterior easy on the eye means that Copenhagen has become something of a fashion capital – everywhere you look you'll find clothes shops catering to all shapes, all sizes, all budgets and all tastes. Indeed, shopping for clothes is worth saving for Copenhagen. For more details on Danish labels to keep an eye out for while you're in town, see p15.

Shopping Areas

Along Copenhagen's touristy main shopping street, Strøget, you can find numerous shops selling everything from chain-store clothing to exquisite Danish porcelain, silverware and electronics. Other prime shopping strips include Kronprinsensgade and surrounding streets for designer labels and cutting-edge fashion; streets such as Elmgade, Blågårdsgade and Ravnsborggade in Nørrebro for street wear, edgy fashion, retro Danish homewares and vintage fashion; and Istedgade for crazy kitsch gifts, sex shops and techno fashion. Frederiksborggade is good for outdoorsy accessories, while Værnedamsvej is the place to sniff out gourmet providores. Nansensgade is the sort of up-and-coming, yet still low-key haunt that locals love perusing for interesting clothes. Pisserenden (the old part of town that had a reputation for smelling like urine – hence, Piss Gutters) – the chunk of town in the Latin Quarter that is hemmed in by Strøget, Nørre Voldgade and Nørregade – is good for books (both new and second-hand), music and student-style fashion. For lovers of high-end Danish 20th-century design and antiques, Bredgade is close to heaven. Book collectors will find good browsing in the antique bookshops along Fiolstræde in the block running between Krystalgade and Nørre Voldgade.

Opening Hours

Despite a wealth of wonderful independent shops, Copenhagen doesn't necessarily make it easy for you to get purchasing, thanks to some old-fashioned regulations that mean businesses can open for only a short time on Saturday and (generally) not at all on Sunday. Apparently, shopping hours have been extended to allow shopkeepers to open from 6am to 8pm daily, but finding any shopkeepers keen to do so is another thing. From Monday to Thursday shops usually open from about 9.30am or 10am to 5pm or 6pm. Late-night (or what passes for it) shopping goes to the crazy hour of about 7pm on Friday. Consider yourself warned, or head over the Øresund to Malmö in Sweden (see p188) if you want to shop on Sunday.

Consumer Taxes

On the plus side for tourists, most visitors have an advantage over Danes in that they can get a refund on most of the 25% value-added tax (VAT), as long as they make their purchases (over 300kr) at certain shops. For details on the VAT rebates see Tax & Refunds (p204).

Bargaining

Bargaining is not the norm in Copenhagen, although you may be able to haggle a little in open-air markets. Trying it in fixed-price shops will just get you a blank stare.

RÅDHUSPLADSEN & TIVOLI

This part of town is not known for its shopping as such, but it is a very central location to grab a few souvenirs or a handful of essentials.

DANSK DESIGN CENTER

Map pp232-4 _Danish Design_
☎ 33 69 33 69; www.ddc.dk; HC Andersens Blvd 27; ☺ 10am-5pm Mon, Tue, Thu & Fri, 10am-9pm Wed, 11am-4pm Sat & Sun; train Central Station, bus Nos 2A, 5A, 6A, 250S, among others

The Dansk Design Center has a lobby gift shop selling a variety of items. In addition to books, magazines and posters, it features contemporary objects by leading Danish designers, such as a stainless-steel salad set designed by Arne Jacobsen, a cream pitcher by Ursula Munch-Petersen and glass bowls by Anja Kjær, plus all sorts of natty little items that are suitable for travellers who don't want to compromise their sense of style while on the road.

MATAS

Map pp239-41 _Health & Pharmaceuticals_
☎ 33 33 75 55; Rådhusarkaden, Industriens Hus, Vesterbrogade 1A; ☺ 9am-5.30pm Mon-Thu, 9am-7pm Fri, 10am-5pm Sat; train Central Station, bus Nos 2A, 5A, 6A, 250S, among others

This particular branch of the popular Danish chain of health-care and pharmaceutical supplies is a great place to stock up on necessities such as sunscreen, toiletries and vitamins. Generic brands are available, as well as the excellent Dr Hauschka range from Germany.

NATIONALMUSEET

Map pp232-4 _Gifts & Souvenirs_
☎ 33 13 41 11; Ny Vestergade 10; ☺ 10am-5pm Tue-Sun; bus Nos 1A, 2A 5A, 650S

This well-stocked museum shop carries a great range of jewellery moulded on Viking and Iron Age finds from the museum's collection, Viking-ship models and a fabulous range of posters and books – all with a Danish bent.

Clothing Sizes
Measurements approximate only, try before you buy

Women's Clothing

Aus/UK	8	10	12	14	16	18
Europe	36	38	40	42	44	46
Japan	5	7	9	11	13	15
USA	6	8	10	12	14	16

Women's Shoes

Aus/USA	5	6	7	8	9	10
Europe	35	36	37	38	39	40
France only	35	36	38	39	40	42
Japan	22	23	24	25	26	27
UK	3½	4½	5½	6½	7½	8½

Men's Clothing

Aus	92	96	100	104	108	112
Europe	46	48	50	52	54	56
Japan	S		M	M		L
UK/USA	35	36	37	38	39	40

Men's Shirts (Collar Sizes)

Aus/Japan	38	39	40	41	42	43
Europe	38	39	40	41	42	43
UK/USA	15	15½	16	16½	17	17½

Men's Shoes

Aus/UK	7	8	9	10	11	12
Europe	41	42	43	44½	46	47
Japan	26	27	27½	28	29	30
USA	7½	8½	9½	10½	11½	12½

Top Five Shopping Strips

- **Strøget** The world's longest pedestrian mall is crammed with shops, some of them quite average, but a few heavy-hitters stand out. It's a fun place – many of the shops are in classic period buildings, the streets are abuzz with other shoppers and the squares along the way are enlivened with street musicians and pavement cafés.
- **The Latin Quarter** Caters more to students, intellectuals and the counterculture – dusty second-hand shops abound
- **Kronprinsensgade** Fashion central for those who love labels and hard-to-find accessories from here and abroad
- **Bredgade** Thick with art galleries, top-end antique shops and places specialising in estate sales. If you enjoy browsing for art and quality antiques, this is the street to stroll.
- **Ravnsborggade** Retro second-hand furniture in this resolutely gritty-but-cool part of town. Nearby streets are also good for directional fashion.

NY CARLSBERG GLYPTOTEK

Map pp232-4 *Gifts & Souvenirs*
☎ 33 41 81 41; Tietgensgade 25; ☺ 10am-4pm Tue-Sun; train Central Station, bus Nos 2A, 5A, 6A, 250S, among others

This wonderful museum also holds a wonderful shop, where quality souvenirs can be sourced – from reproductions of well-known works in the collection to luscious silk scarves and games for children.

POLITIKENS BOGHALLEN

Map pp239-41 *Books*
☎ 33 47 25 60; Rådhuspladsen 37; ☺ 10am-7pm Mon-Fri, 10am-4pm Sat; train Central Station, bus Nos 2A, 5A, 6A, 250S, among others

This is a great central bookshop with a large range of travel guides (including plenty of Lonely Planet editions), coffee-table books and novels, plus knowledgeable, helpful staff.

STRØGET & THE LATIN QUARTER

This is Copenhagen's epicentre when it comes to shopping – with Strøget crammed with all sorts of shops that cater to tourists and locals alike, and its surrounding streets dotted with boutique establishments and cosy bars and cafés that provide welcome relief for pooped purchasers. We've included a separate shopping map for the area (Map p143).

AC PERCH Map p143 *Tea*
☎ 33 15 35 62; www.perchs-the.dk; Kronprinsensgade 5; ☺ 9am-5.30pm Mon-Thu, 9am-7pm Fri, 9.30am-2.30pm Sat; bus No 350S

North of Strøget, this fabulously beautiful family-run tea shop (since 1835) is much loved for its blends and quality leaves (the Darjeeling First Flush is justifiably famous). And it's been given the royal seal of approval to boot. Coffee fiends need not apply.

ARNOLD BUSCK Map p143 *Bookshop*
☎ 33 73 35 00; Købmagergade 49; ☺ 10am-6pm Mon, 9.30am-6pm Tue-Thu, 9.30am-7pm Fri, 10am-4pm Sat; metro & S-train Nørreport

General and specialist titles in the Latin Quarter, and with a lot more soul on display than in the many chain bookshops that seem to be taking over the globe.

BANG & OLUFSEN

Map p143 *Audiovisual/Electronics*
☎ 33 15 04 22; www.bang-olufsen.com; Østergade 3; ☺ 10am-5.30pm Mon-Thu, 10am-6pm Fri, 10am-2pm Sat; metro Kongens Nytorv

For sleek, top-priced audio and televisual equipment, it's hard to go past this über-stylish brand. The shop itself is a high-tech marvel that has design nuts drooling.

AC Perch (left)

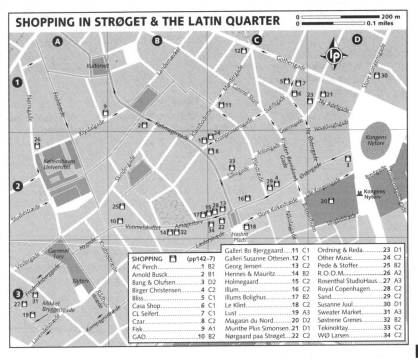

SHOPPING IN STRØGET & THE LATIN QUARTER

0 — 200 m
0 — 0.1 miles

BIRGER CHRISTENSEN

Map p143 *Clothing & Accessories*

☎ 33 11 55 55; Østergade 38; ☻ 10am-6pm Mon-Thu, 10am-7pm Fri, 10am-4pm Sat; metro Kongens Nytorv

This long-running temple of style stocks international heavy-hitters such as Prada, Chanel, YSL and other assorted labels that leave you reeling with fashionitis. Animal-lovers take note: they still sell fur here. And lots of it come winter.

BLISS Map p143 *Beauty & Cosmetics*

☎ 33 93 99 56; Store Regnegade 3; ☻ 11am-6pm Mon-Wed & Fri, 11am-8pm Thu, 11am-3pm Sat; bus No 350S

Bliss is a nifty little beauty spot that can also perform a heavenly facial or manicure. Brands stocked include Nars, Jurlique, Paul & Joe and Annick Goutal.

Top Five Homewares Stores

- Casa Shop (right)
- CPH Square Plus (p149)
- Dansk Design Center (p141)
- Illums Bolighus (p144)
- R.O.O.M (p146)

CASA SHOP Map p143 *Homewares*

☎ 33 2 70 41; www.casagroup.com; Store Regnegade 2; ☻ 11am-5.30pm Mon-Thu, 11am-6pm Fri, 10am-3pm Sat; bus No 350S

Well known for stocking the sort of high-priced luxury modern furnishings that only the childless, wealthy and super-tidy seem to own, Casa is good for 3000kr CD racks and space-age light fittings.

CL SEIFERT Map p143 *Uniforms & Regalia*

☎ 33 12 02 97; www.seifert.dk; Store Regnegade 12; ☻ 9am-5pm Mon-Fri; bus No 350S

Making uniforms and regalia since 1865, this venerable firm helps the royal family out when they need brass buttons, fur hats, military capes and the like. Proud of their traditions, but not so buttoned-up that they won't let you snoop around and play make-believe.

CZAR Map p143 *Cheese*

☎ 33 12 94 03; Købmagergade 32; ☻ 10am-6pm Mon-Thu, 10am-7pm Fri, 10am-3pm Sat; metro & S-train Nørreport

One of the most fabulous *fromageries* we've ever had the privilege to sniff around. A word of warning though: don't come here before a visit to the Museum Erotica (p57) – we're *still* decoding that night's peculiar cheese dreams.

FISK Map p143   *Miscellaneous*
☎ 29 69 91 15; Krystalgade 6; ⏰ 11am-6pm Mon-Thu, 11am-7pm Fri, 11am-3pm Sat; bus No 6A
Specialising in what can best be described as 'odds and sods', this sweet little shop also boasts a wholesome-looking café. Peruse the various shelves and racks for clothes, shoes, books and home furnishings, many of them second-hand.

GAD Map p143   *Bookshop*
☎ 77 66 60 00; Vimmelskaftet 32; ⏰ 10am-7pm Mon-Fri, 10am-5pm Sat; bus No 6A
An excellent range of Danish- and English-language titles, plenty of guidebooks, and what appears to be every single thing HC Andersen ever wrote – and all in a central location.

GALLERI BO BJERGGAARD
Map p143   *Art Gallery*
☎ 33 93 42 21; www.bjerggaard.com; Pilestræde 48; ⏰ noon-6pm Tue-Fri, 11am-3pm Sat; bus No 350S
This established haunt of art-lovers carries the work of leading Danish artists, such as Per Kirkeby, and international contemporary art.

GALLERI SUSANNE OTTESEN
Map p143   *Art Gallery*
☎ 33 15 52 44; Gothersgade 49; ⏰ 10am-1pm & 2-6pm Tue-Fri, 11am-3pm Sat; bus No 350S
This well-regarded gallery is a good place to view and purchase modern Danish art by established contemporary artists.

GEORG JENSEN Map p143   *Silverware*
☎ 33 13 71 81; www.georgjensen.dk; Amagertorv 4; ⏰ 10am-6pm Mon-Thu, 10am-7pm Fri, 10am-5pm Sat; metro Kongens Nytorv
The beautiful new flagship store/museum of this esteemed silversmithing firm features fine cutlery, candleholders, jewellery and designer art pieces. It also has museum-quality displays that are worth a look whether you're a shopper or not. A selection of gold pieces is also available, although it's the silver that stands out.

HENNES & MAURITZ
Map p143   *Clothing & Accessories*
☎ 33 18 88 00; Amagertorv 21-27; ⏰ 10am-6pm Mon-Thu, 10am-7pm Fri, 10am-5pm Sat; metro Kongens Nytorv

The venerable Dutch knock-off emporium H&M specialises in mass-producing fashions by upmarket designers. Low prices, lots of choice and little in the way of originality, although there are sections dedicated to men, women and kids here.

HOLMEGAARD Map p143   *Glassware*
☎ 33 12 44 77; Amagertorv 8; ⏰ 10am-6pm Mon-Thu, 10am-7pm Fri, 10am-5pm Sat; metro Kongens Nytorv
This airy, glass-filled haven resembles some sort of dreamlike igloo at times. Holmegaard, which has been making stunning glass pieces since 1825, is known as Denmark's principal producer of quality glassware and crystal, and is the best place to come and marvel, whilst holding your breath.

ILLUM Map p143   *Department Store*
☎ 33 14 40 02; www.illum.dk; Østergade 52; ⏰ 10am-7pm Mon-Thu, 10am-8pm Fri, 9am-5pm Sat; metro Kongens Nytorv or Nørreport
This large department store, also on Strøget, has a fabulous range of wares arranged around its central glass dome. It has a slightly more upmarket feel than Magasin du Nord.

ILLUMS BOLIGHUS
Map p143   *Department Store*
☎ 33 13 71 81; Amagertorv 10; ⏰ 10am-6pm Mon-Thu, 10am-7pm Fri, 10am-5pm Sat; metro Kongens Nytorv
This fabulous-looking store, by appointment to the Danish queen, stocks wonderful Danish-designed furniture, down comforters, ceramics, silverware and glass, but is also a good place to look for simple gifts such as a quality toy or kitchen utensil. A small but natty selection of clothes and shoes keeps the fashion junkies happy too. Wheelchair accessible.

LE KLINT Map p143   *Lighting*
☎ 33 11 66 63; Store Kirkestræde 1; ⏰ 10am-5.30pm Mon-Thu, 10am-6pm Fri, 10am-2pm Sat; metro Kongens Nytorv
We've come to suspect that Danish citizenship is not granted unless you're in possession of one of Le Klint's lamps. They're that ubiquitous. And that beautiful. And, of course, materials and workmanship are reflected in the price.

LUST Map p143   *Erotica*
☎ 33 33 01 10; www.lust.dk; Mikkel Bryggersgade 3A; ⏰ 11am-7pm Mon-Thu, 11am-9pm Fri, 11am-6pm Sat; train Central Station, bus Nos 2A, 5A, 6A, 250S, among others

If Istedgade's sex shops are a little too red-light for your tastes, then this soothing pink-hued boudoir of a joint will calm your nerves. Run by two women and catering to tastes that are more into, well, lust than hard-core porn, this is the sort of spot where you can find the writings of the Marquis de Sade, blindfolds and leopard-print vibrators.

MAGASIN DU NORD

Map p143   *Department Store*
☎ 33 11 44 33; www.magasin.dk; Kongens Nytorv 13; ✆ 10am-7pm Mon-Thu, 10am-8pm Fri, 10am-5pm Sat; metro Kongens Nytorv

Copenhagen's largest (and oldest) department store covers an entire block on the southwestern side of Kongens Nytorv, and stocks everything from clothing and luggage to books and groceries.

MUNTHE PLUS SIMONSEN

Map p143   *Clothing & Accessories*
☎ 33 32 03 12; Grønnegade 10; ✆ 10am-6pm Mon-Thu, 10am-7pm Fri, 10am-4pm Sat; bus No 350S

Local gals in the know flock to this stunning flagship store of local label Munthe Plus Simonsen. The look they're seeking is part boho-chic, part ethno-dress ups, part luxe detailing, part Stevie Nicks at her most coke-addled.

NORDISK KORTHANDEL

Map pp239-41   *Bookshop*
☎ 33 38 26 38; Studiestræde 26; ✆ 10.30am-5.30pm Mon-Fri, 9.30am-3pm Sat; bus No 6A

Cartophiliacs alert! This shop sells guidebooks as well as an extensive range of cycling and hiking trail maps of Denmark and elsewhere in Europe.

NØRGAARD PAA STRØGET

Map p143   *Clothing & Accessories*
☎ 3312 26 28; Amagertorv 1; ✆ 10am-6pm Mon-Thu, 10am-7pm Fri, 10am-5pm Sat; metro Kongens Nytorv

---

Top Five 'Royal' Shops

Interested in picking up a few goodies that you know have earned the royal seal of approval? Here are five of our faves...
- Le Klint (opposite)
- Illums Bolighus (opposite)
- CL Seifert (p143)
- AC Perch (p142)
- WØ Larsen (p146)

Superstore

The following stores are all connected internally, creating one seamless, elegant retail environment composed of some of Denmark's most revered homeware and design brands. Check individual reviews in the chapter for more details:
George Jensen (opposite)
Holmegaard (opposite)
Royal Copenhagen (p146)
Illums Bolighus (opposite)

This is a popular stop on any shopping expedition for many style-conscious young Danish women. Good international and local labels abound, and there are some pretty cool shoes for sale too. A range of tastes and budgets can be satisfied, from T-shirts to gossamer-fine gowns that cost a small fortune.

ORDNING & REDA   Map p143   *Stationery*
☎ 33 32 30 18; www.ordning-reda.dk; Grønnegade 1B; ✆ 10am-6pm Mon-Thu, 10am-7pm Fri, 10am-4pm Sat; bus No 350S

Even if you're in the grip of the electronic age and spend most of your time communicating via email and text messages, this shop will have you misty-eyed for the days when people put pen to paper to share their thoughts. All the colours of the rainbow can be found in a hundred different types of notebook, notepad or knick-knack, and the pens are excellent.

OTHER MUSIC   Map p143   *Music*
☎ 33 93 14 93; www.theothermusic.com; Kronprinsensgade 7; ✆ 10am-6pm Mon-Thu, 10am-7pm Fri, 10am-5pm Sat; bus No 350S

Buzzing with energy for turntablists and a great spot for those looking to get their hands on Danish electronica. Staff are knowledgeable about not only what they stock, but what's happening in and around Copenhagen.

PEDE & STOFFER

Map p143   *Clothing & Accessories*
☎ 33 33 88 31; Klosterstræde 15-19; ✆ 10.30am-6pm Mon-Thu, 10.30am-7pm Fri, 10.30am-5pm Sat; metro Kongens Nytorv

Side by side sit the two branches of Pede & Stoffer – one for *hommes* and one for *femmes*. Colours are generally prominent, standing out beautifully against the décor details of concrete, wood, wallpaper and plastic. Shoes by Sofie Schnoor are also available.

R.O.O.M Map p143 *Homewares*

☎ 33 41 44 00; Nørregade 12; ☺ 10am-6pm Mon-Thu, 10am-7pm Fri, 10am-4pm Sat; metro & S-train Nørreport, bus No 6A

All sorts of beautiful goodies for your castle can be found here – from striped South American hammocks to the frostiest Scandinavian glassware and all sorts of cute things for children's rooms. It's a spacious, well-designed space too, making it a pleasure to browse through.

ROSENTHAL STUDIOHAUS

Map p143 *Homewares*

☎ 33 14 21 01; www.rosenthal.dk; Frederiksberggade 21; ☺ 10am-6pm Mon-Thu, 10am-7pm Fri, 10am-2pm Sat; train Central Station, bus Nos 2A, 5A, 6A, 250S, among others

Filled with brightly coloured glassware, this is a popular stop on the gift-buying circuit, with famous Scandinavian brands such as iittala, Målerås, Orrefors, Kosta Boda and Rosendahl on offer. Not all of it is as tasteful as you may have been led to believe.

ROYAL COPENHAGEN

Map p143 *Porcelain*

☎ 33 13 71 81; www.royalshopping.com; Amagertorv 6; ☺ 10am-6pm Mon-Thu, 10am-7pm Fri, 10am-5pm Sat; metro Kongens Nytorv

Makers of the most expensive porcelain setting in the world (Flora Danica) and of the immensely popular Blue Fluted range, Royal Copenhagen is the place to come for eminently breakable beauties that silently taunt you to make like a bull in the proverbial china shop.

SAND Map p143 *Clothing & Accessories*

☎ 33 14 21 21; www.sand-europe.com; Østergade 40; ☺ 10am-7pm Mon-Thu, 10am-8pm Fri, 10am-5pm Sat; metro Kongens Nytorv

Posh Sand sells Danish-designed men's and women's clothing with lots of subtle neutral tones punctuated by just-so bursts of next-season's hippest colours. Not exactly budget-priced, but beautifully made and built to last.

To Market, To Market...

Copenhagen's main produce market is at Israels Plads, a few minutes' walk west of Nørreport station. Stalls are set up until 5pm Monday to Friday and until 2pm on Saturday, when it doubles as a flea market.

SUSANNE JUUL Map p143 *Millinery*

☎ 33 32 25 22; Store Kongensgade 14; ☺ 11am-5.30pm Tue-Fri, 10am-2pm Sat; metro Kongens Nytorv

Going strong for over 13 years, Susanne Juul's delightful boutique is the best place we can think of to come for creative yet wearable millinery. Pieces range from beautiful beanies to more elaborate affairs that are perfect for formal occasions.

SWEATER MARKET

Map p143 *Clothing & Accessories*

☎ 33 15 27 73; www.sweatermarket.dk; Frederiksberggade 15; ☺ 10am-6pm Mon-Thu, 10am-7pm Fri, 10am-5pm Sat; train Central Station, bus Nos 2A, 5A, 6A, 250S, among others

Scandinavian sweaters are typically made of heavy wool, in rich blue or black colours accented with white and sporting snowflake-like designs. They are very distinctive, and ideally suited for warding off the chill in cold climates. A wide variety, including popular Norwegian styles, can be found at the Sweater Market, plus a range of other winter woollies.

SØSTRENE GRENES

Map p143 *Miscellaneous*

no phone; Amagertorv 29; ☺ 10.30am-6pm Mon-Thu, 10.30am-7pm Fri, 10am-4pm Sat; metro Kongens Nytorv

This one-way maze of a shop is packed to the rafters with all sorts of knock-down stuff you never knew you needed. It's the Danish version of a 'pound' or 'two dollar' shop, with crockery, cutlery, glassware, gifts and unclassifiables competing for your attention while you compete with the hordes to find space. Worth a visit just to see the Danish get pushy and cheap.

TEKINOKTAY

Map p143 *Clothing & Accessories*

☎ 33 91 60 11; Silkegade 13; ☺ 11am-6pm Mon-Thu, 11am-7pm Fri, 10am-4pm Sat; bus No 350S

The hippest scanties in Copenhagen come from this delightful little store. Grown women who love lollipop-hued, fairyfloss-fine knickers and bras will feel like kids in candy stores (although basic black and very, very bad are also available). Be warned: you'll get little change from 600kr for a bra, and knickers start at about 400kr.

WØ LARSEN Map p143 *Smoking Requisites*

☎ 33 12 20 50; Amagertorv 9; ☺ 10am-6pm Mon-Thu, 10am-7pm Fri, 10am-5pm Sat; metro Kongens Nytorv

Flower stall, Israels Plads

With one-third of Danes determined to keep puffin' no matter what the pink-lung brigade says, this shop-cum-museum is something of a rite of passage – and word has it that the Queen, an avid smoker, gets her fags here.

NYHAVN TO KASTELLET

This respectable, tony part of town features some of the most important shopping prospects that lovers of Danish design and art are likely to come across. Bredgade, in particular, is lined with quality auction houses and art dealers just waiting to show you something special once you ring the doorbell.

GALERIE ASBÆK Map pp232-4 *Art Gallery*
☎ 33 15 40 04; www.asbaek.dk; Bredgade 20; 11am-6pm Mon-Fri, 11am-4pm Sat; bus No 1A
This is among the city's leading private galleries, and sells and shows both Danish and international art. Don't expect only paintings and sculpture either – some intriguing installations and performances take place too.

GALLERI CHRISTIAN DAM
Map pp232-4 *Art Gallery*
☎ 33 15 78 78; www.gcd.dk; Bredgade 23; noon-5pm Mon-Fri, noon-3pm Sat; bus No 1A
With a deadly serious atmosphere, this is the place to get equally serious about collecting Scandinavian art, including plenty from emerging painters, sculptors and photographers.

HOUSE OF AMBER Map pp232-4 *Amber*
☎ 33 11 04 44; Kongens Nytorv 2; 10am-6pm Mon-Sat; metro Kongens Nytorv
This rather touristy but extremely central establishment also houses a small amber museum (p66) in its 17th-century quarters. Service and standards are high, and staff are multilingual.

JØRGEN L DALGAARD
Map pp232-4 *Danish Decorative Arts*
☎ 33 14 09 05; www.jdalgaard.dk; Bredgade 28; 10am-6pm Mon-Fri, noon-3pm Sat; bus No 1A
Ring the bell here to enter a world of stunning 20th-century decorative arts, all in tip-top condition. A fine collection of Jensen silver and other lovelies will have you making comparisons with Kunstindustrimuseet up the street.

KLASSIK MODERNE MØBELKUNST
Map pp232-4 *Danish Design*
☎ 33 33 90 60; www.klassik.dk; Bredgade 3; 11am-6pm Mon-Fri, 10am-3pm Sat; bus No 1A
If you're a fan of Danish chair design, then you'll really need to sit down once you spy this place. Packed with design classics and catering to budgets from 100kr (for a poster of famous Danish chairs) to 'you wish' (for Hans Wegner and Arne Jacobsen originals) on this most famous of streets for Danish furniture.

CHRISTIANSHAVN

Not known for its shopping, Christianshavn is nevertheless a good spot to search for out-of-the-ordinary, distinctive souvenirs from your time in Copenhagen, whether it be Greenlandic goods (the island has a large Greenlandic community) or avowedly local bicycles from the car-free Christiania.

AURUM Map pp232-4 — Jewellery

☎ 32 96 34 22; Wildersgade 26; ☺ 11am-6pm Mon-Fri, 11am-2pm Sat; metro Christianshavn

Aurum stocks a charming range of modern gold and silver jewellery, but it's the more whimsical, humorous pieces that had us smiling – bracelets fashioned from toy cars and the like. The prices, less ferocious than some of the other jewellers in town, were another reason to smile.

CHRISTIANIA BIKES

Map pp232-4 — Bicycles

☎ 32 54 87 48; www.christianiabikes.dk; Christiania Smedie, Refshalevej 2; ☺ 9am-5pm Mon-Fri; metro Christianshavn

Spend any time in Copenhagen and you'll soon notice the large wheelbarrow-meets-bicycle products of this famous local company. Generally they'll be transporting anything from groceries to pets to kids to office equipment – and all in comfort and style. Special orders are catered to.

GAMMEL DOK BOGHANDEL

Map pp232-4 — Bookshop

☎ 32 54 04 54; Gammel Dok; ☺ 10am-5pm Mon-Sat; metro Christianshavn

Housed in the redeveloped Gammel Dok building, this is an excellent bookshop for perusing (and purchasing) architecture and design tomes that concentrate on matters Scandinavian.

GINNUNGAGAB Map pp232-4 — Souvenirs

☎ 32 54 22 11; Overgaden oven Vandet 4A;
☺ 11am-6pm Tue-Fri, 11am-3pm Sat; metro Christianshavn

The word 'souvenirs' doesn't quite cut it when describing the goodies found in this shop, which is unlike any other we found in Copenhagen. You'll find various animal skins and woollen garments, Greenlandic footwear and frost-beating headwear, plus an equally warming welcome. Don't even attempt to pronounce the name though.

KVINDESMEDIEN Map pp232-4 — Metalwork

☎ 32 57 76 58; Bådsmandsstraede 43; ☺ 9am-5pm Mon-Fri, 11am-3pm Sat; metro Christianshavn

The good blacksmithing ladies of Kvindesmedien conjure up some extraordinary shapes from metal, fashioning candelabra, platters and other useful objects from tough beginnings. Worth popping into just to see what a Christiania cottage industry (other than bong-making) looks like.

NØRREBRO

While it's not Copenhagen's premier shopping district, Nørrebro is gaining a reputation as a groovy spot to discover up-and-coming local designers (of both clothes and jewellery) and trawl for fashionable second-hand clothing. Good streets to spend time on include Elmegade and Blågårdsgade, and smart cafés allow you to either reflect on purchases or debate an article's merit with ease.

CAPPALIS Map pp236-7 — Clothing & Accessories

☎ 35 39 00 06; Elmegade 30; ☺ 11am-5.30pm Mon, 11am-6pm Tue-Thu, 11am-7pm Fri, 11am-3pm Sat; bus Nos 3A, 5A

So tiny that if you blinked you might miss it. And that would be a real shame, as this cute shop stocks some delightful modern jewellery (silver and gold), cool accessories (think felt hats and bags with naïf motifs) and a few garments that are begging to be taken home. Service is friendly, and if they don't have your size you can generally get them to make something for you, time permitting.

FREDERIKSEN

Map pp236-7 — Clothing & Accessories

☎ 35 35 05 66; Ravnsborggade 15; ☺ 11am-6pm Mon-Fri, 11am-3pm Sat; bus No 5A

Filled with funky stuff from Scandinavia and Italy, this small shop caters to young, whippet-thin, media-savvy lasses about town. Great accessories with a twist keep things from veering too far into uniform territory, and some of the jewellery is both eye-catching and affordable.

KK VINTAGE Map pp232-4 — Vintage

☎ 33 33 85 70; Blågårdsgade 31C; ☺ noon-6pm Tue-Fri, 11am-3pm Sat; bus No 5A

The crazy folk at KK offer more than standard vintage wear – they actually play around with the stock, resewing, re-creating and restyling it, making for some very individual-looking garments. Retro with a twist.

KLÆDEBO Map pp232-4 *Clothing & Accessories*

☎ 35 36 05 27; Blågårdsgade 3; ⏰ 11am-6pm Mon-Fri, 10.30am-2pm Sat; bus No 5A

Down a small flight of stairs, this tiled basement shop stocks funky garments for women and children from a quartet of young Danish designers, including Karen Pers and Marina Lundquist. The children's wear is particularly appealing, making this a good spot for spoiling the littlest fashion victims in your life.

NIOBIUM Map pp232-4 *Jewellery*

☎ 35 37 77 99; www.niobium.dk; Guldbergsgade 7B; ⏰ 11am-5.30pm Tue-Fri, 11am-2pm Sat; bus No 3A, 5A

Close to Sankt Hans Torv, this is a great little shop for sourcing one-off jewellery pieces such as earrings, arm rings and cufflinks. The creativity and quality is first-rate, meaning you'll have a souvenir that doubles as a conversation piece.

VESTERBRO

Funky Vesterbro, with Istedgade's mix of sex shops, cutting-edge fashion boutiques and kooky shoe-box-sized dens of kitsch, will appeal to the younger end of the retail therapy scene. A bonus? The good bars and cafés that line this rejuvenated strip. The other main drag here is Vesterbrogade, which at times has an English high-street feel, but isn't much use in the way of good shopping.

CPH SQUARE PLUS

Map pp232-4 *Homewares*

☎ 33 31 21 10; Istedgade 97; ⏰ 10am-5.30pm Mon-Thu, 10am-6pm Fri, 10am-3pm Sat; bus No 10

This well-designed retail space can't quite make up its mind as to what it sells, so you'll find a good range of children's clothes and articles, cookbooks, homewares, gourmet foodstuffs and nifty kitchen utensils. Grab the attention of one of the staff (they're a social lot and might need a bit of prompting) and make plans to refurbish your living space and your life.

GIRLY HURLY Map pp232-4 *Kitsch*

☎ 33 24 22 41; Istedgade 99; ⏰ 11am-5.30pm Mon-Thu, 11am-6.30pm Fri, 10am-3pm Sat; bus No 10

Ludicrous novelties that never fail to raise a smile and provide the antidote to Copenhagen's good taste epidemic. Although a few classy pieces do make it into the mix, you can rest assured that Frederik and Mary commemorative wedding candles can be tracked down.

LABORATORIUM

Map pp232-4 *Miscellaneous*

☎ 33 22 22 20; www.pluslaboratorium.com; Istedgade 92; ⏰ noon-7pm Tue-Fri, 11am-1pm Sat; bus No 10

The sort of place that can handle your art, fashion, architecture 'and stuff like that' needs, this cool little spot is quaint and a little kooky. Temporary exhibits are worth checking out.

PLAN E Map pp232-4 *Erotica*

☎ 33 21 99 30; Istedgade 30; ⏰ 11am-6pm Mon-Thu & Sat, 11am-7pm Fri; train Central Station, bus No 10

This is a well-lit, well-stocked, one-stop erotic supershop on red-lit Istedgade. Fairly easy-going in its tone, women need not feel intimidated by their run-of-the-mill fellow browsers sussing out the usual array of phallic objects and the sort of stuff that makes you wonder 'Where is *that* supposed to go?'. Black plastic bags keep your purchases anonymous once you step back onto the increasingly gentrified street.

TOM ROSSAU Map pp232-4 *Lighting*

☎ 33 79 47 17; www.tomrossau.dk; Istedgade 59; ⏰ 11.30am-5.30pm Mon-Thu, 11.30am-6pm Fri, 11am-3pm Sat; bus No 10

We crossed the road to take a closer look at Tom's shop, which has a few lighting ideas so cool that we had to come back and buy some, certain that one day we would be able to boast to dinner party guests that we had spotted Tom's talent in the early days and snapped up a space-age plastic light fitting before anyone else outside Copenhagen. They can be easily boxed up and transported. T-shirts available too.

Gammel Dok Boghandel (p148)

OUTLYING DISTRICTS

Copenhagen's outlying districts aren't particularly known for their shopping strips and opportunities, but that doesn't mean you won't find a few places that stock some interesting or specialised products – particularly in Islands Brygge, which is showing all the hallmarks of developing quite an alternative scene to the city centre.

FREDERIKSBERG

BERTONI Map p238-   *Clothing & Accessories*
☎ 38 10 37 70; www.bertoni.dk; Frederiksberg Centret, Falkoner Allé 21; ☽ 10am-7pm Mon-Fri, 10am-4pm Sat; metro Frederiksberg
Smart suiting and even more stylish casual wear is on offer at this popular men's store, which can show non-Danish men just how attractive a blazer, scarf and beard combo can be when it's done right. And it's always done right by the sales assistants here.

ISLANDS BRYGGE

RETROGRAD Map pp232-4   *Retro Homewares*
☎ 22 42 46 57; Gunløgsgade 7; ☽ noon-7pm Tue-Fri, noon-5pm Sat; metro Islands Brygge
When it comes to retro, no-one beats Retrograd. Every piece is sourced by the friendly owners (and all via public transport!) and they can tell you a story for each and every one – its providence, the designer, its place on the table. Great egg cups, ashtrays, candleholders and assorted sundries that have just that

little bit more character than the modern stuff. A firm fave.

STORM MORTENSEN

Map pp232-4   *Clothing & Accessories*
☎ 32 57 37 35; Islands Brygge 7; ☽ noon-6pm Mon-Fri, noon-4pm Sat & Sun; metro Islands Brygge
With a small selection of 10 directional young Danish designers and a tiny café on the premises, this collective-style boutique is a good example of the changes taking place in this neighbourhood. Prices are reasonable.

TIGER Map pp232-4   *General Store*

no phone; cnr Njalsgade & Thorshavnsgade;
☽ 10am-5.30pm Mon-Wed, 10am-6pm Thu & Fri, 10am-2pm Sat; metro Islands Brygge
Who knows what sort of trash or treasure you'll find in this Danish version of the five-and-dime (or two dollar or pound, depending on where you're from). It's part of a chain, and everything costs either 10kr or 20kr – expect to have more fun than you thought possible trawling through discount Danish flags, toiletries, homewares, underwear and confectionary.

X Map pp232-4   *Homewares/Clothing/Art*

☎ 25 75 80 55; Isafjordsgade 6; ☽ 3-6pm Tue-Fri, 11am-2pm Sat; metro Islands Brygge
X marks the spot to find fantastic *Arabian Nights*-style footwear for adults and children plus out-of-the-ordinary jewellery and intriguing, locally produced modern art. Opening hours are *very* limited, but the welcome once you find this little troglodyte warren is not.

Sleeping

Sleeping

Copenhagen offers good solid accommodation options in every price range and you don't always have to pay a premium to be in the city centre.

The main hotel quarter (and, incidentally, home to the city's red-light district) is along the western side of Central Station, where rows of six-storey, 19th-century buildings house one hotel after the other. Despite the neighbourhood's porn shops and occasional street-walkers, the area is neither unpleasant nor notably dangerous, at least not by the standards of large cities elsewhere in Europe. Still, if you prefer a better neighbourhood, there are numerous options that are also central, as well as others that offer a quieter suburban set-ting, such as tony Frederiksberg, which is expensive to live in but well supplied with budget sleeping options for visitors.

Copenhagen is a popular convention city and if you happen to arrive without reserva-tions when one is taking place, finding a room can be a challenge. These conventions, referred to in Denmark as congresses, can occur at any time of the year and the largest ones can book out virtually every hotel in the city. There are some new hotel projects that were constructed in the new millennium and aimed at increasing the city's room capacity, but they still don't always provide relief from the convention crunches, and some pundits reckon they just attract more and larger conventions! If you don't like to take chances, your best bet is to book well in advance.

Some hotels consistently apply their listed rates, but with many hotels the rates are upped when they expect to be very busy and lowered when things slacken off. As a general rule, you can expect the best deals in the off season and the highest rates during sum-mer. The hotel rates given in this section include service charge, the 25% value-added tax (VAT) and, except where noted, a complimentary buffet-style breakfast. Remember that weekends are often the time to nab some serious discounts on mid-range and top-end accommodation, as the congresses head home and the hotel staff start hankering to fill the rooms again. Internet bookings can also offer substantial reductions from the 'rack rate' (which is what we've quoted throughout this chapter). The rack rate is the standard walk-in-off-the-street price that hotels quote, and it can often be circumvented by book-ing via the Internet or a travel agent. So use this guide as a rough estimate, and feel free to ask the hotel you've got your eye on if they have a special price for your visit. Generally, when we've given the nonsmoking symbol it means that nonsmoking rooms are available, not that the hotel is entirely smoke-free.

Green Dreams

Ecology-minded Denmark has instituted a system known as Den Grønne Nøgle, or the Green Key, to acknowledge environmentally friendly hotels and hostels.

Numerous criteria must be fulfilled for a place to be awarded the Green Key. These include limiting water consumption by using water-saving shower heads, using low-energy light bulbs and ecology-friendly detergents, recycling wastes, having smoke-free rooms and serving at least two organic products at breakfast.

Places that qualify for the Green Key display a special logo that looks like a smiling green-coloured key standing on end.

Those of you who expect stunning Scandinavian interior design to be part and parcel of a hotel stay may be a little disappointed. Many hotels (particularly if they're part of a chain) have succumbed to the could-be-anywhere design ethos and have little in the way of originality or aesthetic experimentation. Or good taste. We were surprised to see so many chintzy bedspreads and dreary patterned carpets during our time here. That said, when we did find a place with stand-out design and décor, we've let you know about it in indi-vidual reviews. See also the Top Five Design Hotels boxed text on p157. One thing you won't have to worry about in Copenhagen is cleanliness – Scandinavians do not take kindly to grot, filth or grime – and they ex-tend that fastidious concern to their guests.

Hotel rooms are uniformly spick and span, and facilities, communal or otherwise, well maintained and repaired.

The hotels and hostels that comprise the Cheap Sleeps sections offer accommodation (sometimes a double with bathroom) for under 1000kr per night. The hotels that comprise the mid-range section have standard rates for double rooms with bathroom priced between 1001kr and 1600kr. Top-end sleeps are anything over 1601kr for a double room with bathroom.

Curling up in Copenhagen

Here are some words you'll come across on hotel and hostel brochures:

adgang til køkken access to kitchen

bad og toilet på gangen shower and toilet in the hallway

dobbeltværelse double room

eget bad og toilet with shower and toilet

enkeltværelse single room

køjsenge bunk beds

lejlighed flat, apartment

med opredning with extra bed

morgenmad inkl i prisen breakfast included in the price

senge beds

vaskemaskine og tørretumbler washing machine and tumble dryer

værelse room

Booking Services

COPENHAGEN RIGHT NOW Map pp232-4
☎ 70 22 24 42; www.woco.dk; Vesterbrogade 4A; ⌚ 9am-6pm Mon-Sat May & Jun, 9am-8pm Mon-Sat, 10am-6pm Sun Jul & Aug, 9am-4pm Mon-Fri, 9am-2pm Sat Sep-Apr

The city tourist office can help you find accommodation (for free if you book via the phone or Internet). Rooms in private homes around the city cost from around 300kr for singles and 400kr for doubles. This office also books unfilled hotel rooms, typically at discounted rates that vary from around 100kr off for budget hotels to as much as 50% off for top-end hotels. These discounts are based on supply and demand and are not always available during busy periods. There's a 75kr to 100kr fee per booking.

DANSK BED & BREAKFAST
☎ 39 61 04 05; www.bbdk.dk; Bernstorffsvej 71A, 2900 Hellerup

This well-regarded service handles 365 homes throughout Denmark (97 in the Copenhagen area), offering private rooms from around 250/350kr for singles/doubles. It will make the bookings for you or you can order a brochure listing the homes and book them directly yourself.

TOURIST INFORMATION COPENHAGEN AIRPORT
⌚ 6am-midnight

Just outside customs, this place also books unfilled Copenhagen hotel rooms at similarly discounted rates for a 60kr booking fee. If you're flying in and looking for a hotel, this is definitely the way to go.

USE IT Map pp239-41
☎ 33 73 06 20; www.useit.dk; Rådhusstræde 13; free; ⌚ 9am-7pm 15 Jun-15 Sep, 11am-4pm Mon-Wed, 11am-6pm Thu, 11am-2pm Fri 16 Sep-14 Jun)

Books rooms in private homes, which cost from around 200kr for singles and 250kr for doubles. There's no booking fee for the service. Use It also keeps tabs on which hostel beds are available and is a good source of information on subletting student housing and other long-term accommodation.

Hostelling International

Copenhagen's HI hostels are clean, welcoming and well managed, with some of them providing stiff competition to certain mid-range hotels in terms of standards, facilities, and, of course, price. We've included the pick of the bunch in our Cheap Sleeps sections.

Two hostels *(vandrerhjem)* in the Copenhagen suburbs and two more just outside the city are members of the Hostelling International (HI) organisation, known in Denmark as **Danhostel** (Map pp232-4; ☎ 33 31 36 12; www.danhostel.dk; Vesterbrogade 39). To join HI before you leave home, ask at your nearest hostel or contact your national hostelling association.

Travellers who don't have an international hostel card can buy one once they arrive in Denmark for 160kr (annual fee) or pay 30kr extra for each night's stay. If you're not sure whether you'll be staying at hostels often enough to make it worth buying an annual card, ask for a sticker each time you pay the 30kr per-night fee; if you accumulate six stickers you'll have yourself an annual hostel card.

Most of Denmark's HI hostels have private rooms in addition to dormitory rooms, which makes them a good-value alternative to hotels. Danish hostels appeal to a wide range of guests in all age categories and are oriented as much towards families and groups as they are to backpackers, students and other budget travellers. Facilities in hostels vary, but most newer hostels have two-bed and four-bed rooms and thus are well suited for use by couples or small groups of friends travelling together.

HI hostels are categorised by a star system, from one to five stars. One-star hostels meet the basic requirements, whereas two-star hostels add on luggage-storage facilities and a small shop. Three-star hostels also have a TV lounge. Four-star and five-star hostels fancy up the facilities and a minimum of 75% of their rooms have private shower and toilet.

All Danish hostels provide an all-you-can-eat breakfast for 40kr and many also provide dinner (65kr maximum). Most hostels also have guest kitchens with pots and pans where you can cook your own food.

Blankets and pillows are provided at all hostels, but if you don't bring your own sheets you'll have to hire them for around 40kr per stay. Sleeping bags are not allowed. A handy, lightweight pouch-style sleeping sheet with an attached pillow cover can be purchased at many hostels worldwide and will save you a bundle on sheet-rental charges.

You can pick up the handy *Danhostel Danmarks Vandrerhjem* guide free from hostels or tourist offices; it gives information on individual hostels, including each hostel's facilities and a simple sketch map showing its location. In the summer and other holiday periods, hostels often book out entirely, so it's always a good idea to make advance reservations.

Longer-Term Rentals

Flats (or apartments) can be a good deal, especially for those who want to prepare their own meals rather than frequenting restaurants. They can be anything from a one-room studio with a small kitchenette to a commodious flat with a fully equipped kitchen, a living room with stereo and cable TV, and a cosy bedroom or two.

In the last 10 years or so a couple of Copenhagen businesses have surfaced that specialise in arranging apartment rentals for visitors. Some of these rentals are places that have been set aside permanently for this purpose, but many others are people's private flats that they put up for hire while they're away on travels of their own or visiting their summer house up the coast. Such businesses generally have more units available in summer, as that's the peak time for Danes to be away on holiday. Generally, flats are offered on the basis of a three-night minimum stay.

FINDING A FLAT

The housing market in Copenhagen is a tight one and landing a long-term flat rental at a reasonable price can be a challenge. Prices vary according to the condition of the flat, the neighbourhood and its proximity to the city centre, but generally begin at around 5000kr a month for a small flat with a kitchen, bath and separate bedroom.

Good places to look for listings are in the classified sections of Copenhagen's main newspapers, *Politiken* and *Berlingske Tidende*; in both papers, the greatest number of listings appear in the Sunday editions. These papers are in Danish only. You can also look in the classified section of the *Copenhagen Post*, which is in English and published on Friday, but the apartment listings are usually quite meagre.

APARTMENT HOTEL VALBERG

Map pp232-4

☎ 33 25 25 19; www.valberg.dk; Sønder Blvd 53; s/d apt 700/750kr; 💻 ; S-train Dybbølsbro

As neat and shiny as a new pin, these 15 gorgeous apartments take pride of place on the top floor of a handsome early-20th-century building. They're well suited to long-term stays, with well-equipped kitchens and a cleaning service. And only one stop from Central Station.

CITILET APARTMENTS Map pp239-41

☎ 33 25 21 29; www.citilet.dk; Fortunstræde 4; apt per day/week from 950/6000kr; metro Kongens Nytorv

Citilet specialises in top-end places that are clustered in a couple of buildings right in the city centre. It's a fixed group of 21 apartments and functions like a hotel in some ways, with daily cleaning service and breakfast included in the rates. There can be long waiting lists for these apartments, so you must book in advance.

HAY 4 YOU Map pp239-41

☎ 33 33 08 05; www.hay4you.dk; Vimmelskaftet 49; apt per day/week/month from 450/2200/7500kr; metro Kongens Nytorv

This sterling, very helpful company has a pool of over 100 apartments and some of the best prices in town, which include sheets, towels and utilities. Apartments are fully furnished, very cosy and available in a variety of locations throughout the city. If you're a tenant, you can access the Internet at the company's HQ on Strøget gratis.

Copenhagen Marriott (right)

RÅDHUSPLADSEN & TIVOLI

The area around Rådhuspladsen, the central city square, is a convenient place to be based, as it's near the head of Strøget and within a short walk of some of the city's leading sights, as well as Central Station. That said, parking is problematic – even if your hotel has a designated parking station, you'll often have to fork out for it.

COPENHAGEN MARRIOTT

Map pp232-4   *Hotel*

☎ 88 33 99 00; www.marriott.com/property/propertyPAGE/CPHDK; Kalvebod Brygge 5; s/d from 2000kr; P ✕ ✕ 🖳 ; train Central Station

The monster-sized Mariott dominates Kalvebod Brygge in a flashy, modern, glass-and-steel creation that scrapes Copenhagen's skies (11 storeys in all). Everything here is five-star plush and efficient, making it an excellent choice for business travellers – it's got good restaurants, solid sports facilities and commercial connections. Facilities for the disabled and those travelling with children are also top-notch.

HOTEL ALEXANDRA Map pp239-41   *Hotel*

☎ 33 74 44 44; www.hotel-alexandra.dk; HC Andersens Blvd 8; s/d from 1325/1525kr; ✕ ; train Central Station, bus Nos 2A, 5A, 6A, 250S, among others

This wonderful hotel is a highlight of a visit to Copenhagen, particularly if you're a fan of Danish design classics. Many rooms feature the designs of such masters as Wegner, Juhl and Jacobsen, and the hotel is a favourite of people who appreciate luxury but don't like the anonymity of large chain hotels. Try to nab a 'Design Classic' room (1925kr) if you want to guarantee aesthetic rapture.

HOTEL ASCOT Map pp232-4   *Hotel*

☎ 33 12 60 00; www.ascothotel.dk; Studiestræde 61; s/d from 900/1200kr; P 🖳 ; train Central Station, bus Nos 2A, 5A, 6A, 250S, among others

The friendly Ascot occupies a former bathhouse erected 100 years ago by the same architect (Martin Nyrop) who designed Copenhagen's city hall. The lobby boasts some interesting bas-reliefs depicting scenes from the bathhouse days. Most of the 155 rooms are large and decorated in a hotchpotch of styles, although each has a deep soaking tub in the bathroom, and some have a kitchen and Internet access. Not good for wheelchair access though.

Sleeping – Rådhuspladsen & Tivoli

HOTEL ASTORIA Map pp232-4 *Hotel*

☎ 33 42 99 00; www.astoriahotelcopenhagen.dk; Banegårdspladsen 4; s/d from 990/1290kr; train Central Station

Housed in a Funkis-style building that's loaded with character but showing its age a tad, the Astoria is a handy three-star choice for those into architecture and design that hasn't been tampered with too radically. Rooms have good amenities and are comfortable, although the hotel's location is *very* close to the main train station.

HOTEL DANMARK Map pp232-4 *Hotel*

☎ 33 11 48 06; www.hotel-danmark.dk; Vester Voldgade 89; s/d from 1025/1200kr, ste 1800kr; P ⊠ ; train Central Station, bus Nos 2A, 5A, 6A, 250S, among others

A stone's throw from Rådhuspladsen, the Danmark is a very well run establishment with appealingly decorated rooms. Everything is in good condition, but the beds deserve a special mention – the hotel bills them as being 'comfortable', but that's just modesty. They were fantastic. Check the website for weekend offers or low-season deals that make this place closer to budget range.

HOTEL IMPERIAL Map pp232-4 *Hotel*

☎ 33 12 80 00; www.imperialhotel.dk; Vester Farimagsgade 9; s/d from 1495/2450kr; P ⊠ ⊠ 💻 ; S-train Vesterport

Despite its rather nondescript (ie grotty and rather ugly) façade, opposite an S-train station, the Imperial has one of the best reputations for service among Copenhagen's top-end establishments. Each of the 164 rooms has good-looking modern décor (with some very nice Danish furnishings) and a deep Japanese-style bathtub. Definitely worth booking for a weekend of escapism and quality bath-time.

HOTEL KONG FREDERIK

Map pp239-41 *Hotel*

☎ 33 12 59 02; www.remmen.dk; Vester Voldgade 25; s/d from 1040/1240kr; P ⊠ 💻 ; train Central Station, bus Nos 2A, 5A, 6A, 250S, among others

This is a classic English-style hotel with four stars on its door and a solidly historic character including dark woods, antique furnishings and paintings of Danish royalty. Its 110 rooms are poshly comfortable and each has a TV, phone, minibar, hairdryer and Internet connection, plus there's complimentary access to the spa/fitness centre at the Hotel d'Angleterre.

MERCURE COPENHAGEN

Map pp232-4 *Hotel*

☎ 33 12 57 11; www.mercure.com; Vester Farimsgade 33; s/d 800-1400kr; P ⊠ ⊠ ; S-train Vesterport

Smack-bang in the thick of this busy district, the Mercure offers a warm welcome and sparingly attractive rooms at very decent rates, allowing you to get down to business on a sensible budget. Try to get an attic-style room – they have just that little bit more soul. About one-quarter of the rooms here are designated nonsmoking.

MERMAID HOTEL Map pp239-41 *Hotel*

☎ 33 12 65 70; www.mermaid-hotel.dk; Løngangstræde 27; s/d from 1199/1399kr; P ; train Central Station, bus Nos 2A, 5A, 6A, 250S, among others

You'll find the little three-star Mermaid tucked behind the Rådhuspladsen area and you certainly won't be disappointed. Nicely renovated rooms are functional and stylish, and there's a very attractive rooftop area where you can unwind when the sun's shining. It's the sister hotel to the nearby four-star Palace, but we think this is a better option for those wanting to stay in this neck of the woods.

PALACE HOTEL Map pp239-41 *Hotel*

☎ 33 14 40 50; www.palace-hotel.dk; Rådhuspladsen 57; s/d 1825/2025kr; ⊠ ; train Central Station, bus Nos 2A, 5A, 6A, 250S, among others

In a picturesque period building overlooking Rådhuspladsen, the 162 rooms at the Palace are spacious and well equipped. The décor is old fashioned, with upholstered chairs, heavy curtains and brass lamps in what's considered the 'English style'. It's incredibly handy to the centre of town, without the somewhat grubby surrounds of Vesterbro's hotel district just across the square. Service is whip-smart and incredibly helpful.

RADISSON SAS ROYAL HOTEL

Map pp232-4 *Hotel*

☎ 33 42 60 00; www.radisson.com/copenhagendk_royal; Hammerichsgade 1; s/d from 1595/1895kr; P ⊠ ⊠ 💻 ; S-train Vesterport

Centrally located and famous as all get out (Arne Jacobsen designed it and Room 606 – a tidy 3940kr per night – has been left intact), this 265-room, multistorey hotel is popular with well-to-do business travellers and visiting dignitaries. And, dare we say it, it has been resting on its laurels for some time. While rooms are in good order and some of the views breathtaking, service seems a little slack and many communal areas are just plain bland. That said, the hotel has computer work stations with Internet access, a very respected restaurant (p105) and a fitness centre, and we couldn't fault the 23,000kr per night Royal Panorama Suite.

SCANDIC HOTEL COPENHAGEN

Map pp232-4   *Hotel*

☎ 33 14 35 35; www.scandic-hotels.com/copenhagen; Vester Søgade 6; s/d from 1520/2020kr; Ⓟ ☒ ☒ ☐ ; S-train Vesterport, bus Nos 2A, 250S

Near the Imax Tycho Brahe Planetarium and with over 450 rooms, this is a well-regarded chain hotel with all the expected facilities, including a health club, concierge and top-notch secretarial services. Cheaper promotional deals are common and represent good value, especially at weekends.

SCANDIC HOTEL WEBERS

Map pp232-4   *Hotel*

☎ 33 31 14 32; www.scandic-hotels.com/webers; Vesterbrogade 11B; s/d from 1345/1445kr; ☒ ; train Central Station

With some very good deals available, this can be a good choice for families wanting to stay close to transport and Tivoli – although ask to see your room first. They're all clean and well equipped, but some are on the dull side, while others are very attractive indeed. There's also a sauna on the premises.

SOFITEL PLAZA COPENHAGEN

Map pp232-4   *Hotel*

☎ 33 14 92 62; sofitel@accorhotel.dk; Bernstorffs-gade 4; s/d from 1799/1999kr; ☒ ☐ ; train Central Station

One of the things we most liked about this top-end hotel was the fact that some character had been allowed to shine through (via the odd frayed carpet detail, a scratch or a chip here and there) in the communal areas, allowing this well-located and well-run place to rise above the sterile attack of the same-olds that afflicts so many big chain places. Great bathrooms too.

SQUARE Map pp232-4   *Hotel*

☎ 33 38 12 00; www.thesquare.dk; Rådhuspladsen 14; s/d from 1260/1560kr; ☒ ☐ ; train Central Station, bus Nos 2A, 5A, 6A, 250S, among others

Ultramodern and so hip it almost hurts (Jacobsen chairs, cowhide fabric, red leather), the

Square is an excellent three-star hotel with design touches and amenities generally associated with greater expense and more stiffness. Rooms are beautifully equipped, and some have sterling views of the main square – plus all the city's main sights are in walking distance.

CHEAP SLEEPS
CIRCUIT Q AT CARSTEN'S

Map pp232-4   *B&B*

☎ 33 14 91 07; www.circuitq.dk; Christians Brygge 28, Level 5; dm 150kr, s/d/tr/q 420/520/620/720kr, studio from 750kr, apt from 850kr; ☐ ; train Central Station

Heartily recommended by many gay travellers, this charming B&B attracts repeat business and a friendly clientele. Facilities in this welcoming, light and airy apartment are homely and attractive, and the location is incredibly handy. You'll get all sorts of tips about enjoying the city too, with the lowdown on gay nightlife, drinking and dining – if you can tear yourself away from the rooftop terrace.

STRØGET & THE LATIN QUARTER

Not as flush with accommodation options as you might expect. Still, what is here is very good, whether intimate and closer to the 'boutique' end of things or as grand as a wedding cake and stuffed with chandeliers and king-size beds. Don't expect anything in the way of budget sleeping though – space is at a premium here, and landlords and hoteliers alike know it.

HOTEL CHRISTIAN IV Map pp232-4 *Hotel*
☎ 33 32 10 44; www.hotelchristianIV.dk; Dronningens Tværgade 45; s/d from 1090/1390kr; ⊠ 🖵 ; bus Nos 1A, 26, 350S

This intimate 42-room hotel (established in the 1950s) has the air of a well-kept secret, with its charming location near Kongens Have, cosy, low-key rooms and welcoming service. Weekend rates are excellent.

HOTEL D'ANGLETERRE Map pp239-41 *Hotel*
☎ 33 12 00 95; www.dangleterre.dk; Kongens Nytorv 34; s/d from 2170/2470kr; Ⓟ ⊠ 🖵 ; metro Kongens Nytorv

Visiting high-profile celebrities often opt for the exclusive, reassuringly five-star d'Angleterre, which has enough chandeliers, marble floors and history (dating back to the 18th century) to give you a gilt complex. It also has some of Copenhagen's highest rates, hitting the heights of 14,870kr for the royal suite. Breakfast is an extra 135kr per person. Despite its lengthy history, the hotel no longer enjoys the solidly pre-eminent reputation it once had among Copenhagen's top hotels, and service, while perfectly pleasant, is not quite up to the bow-

and-scrape standards we've come to expect when we pop our scruffy heads into these sorts of places. That said, the gym and spa are top class, and business facilities are excellent.

HOTEL SANKT PETRI Map pp239-41 *Hotel*
☎ 33 45 91 00; www.hotelsanktpetri.com; Krystalgade 22; s/d from 2095/2395kr; Ⓟ ✗ ⊠ 🖵 ; metro & S-train Nørreport, bus No 6A

Swanky is as swanky does, and this place is so hot right now that you'll get burnt walking past it. Fabulous rooms (many with charming views over the Latin Quarter's rooftops) in classic Scandinavian 21st-century style and amenities you didn't know you needed (anti-allergy quilts and the like). Plus there's a fantastic bar on the premises (Bar Rouge – see p129).

PARK HOTEL Map pp232-4 *Hotel*
☎ 33 13 30 00; www.copenhagenparkhotel.dk; Jarmers Plads 3; s/d from 925/1100kr; 🖵 ; bus Nos 2A, 5A, 6A, 250S, among others

Family-owned and cosy as all get out, this smallish (61 rooms) hotel is in a very good location for those intent on Latin Quarter sightseeing. Rooms are attractive enough, but to get the most out of them, try to nab one with a dormer-style window – they're much more atmospheric. Free Internet access is available in the lobby.

Hotel Sankt Petri (above)

NYHAVN TO KASTELLET

The Nyhavn canal area is a fun (albeit heavily touristed) part of the city to be in, particularly in summer when it's lined with pavement cafés, colourful sailing boats and a mass of humanity. The hotels in this part of the world are respectable and well appointed, often combining imaginative refurbishments of waterside warehouses, when such things used to be anything but salubrious places to doss down. The residents of the upmarket section around Amalienborg include the royal family and many of high society's stalwarts.

71 NYHAVN HOTEL Map pp232-4 *Hotel*
☎ 33 43 62 00; www71nyhavnhotelcopenhagen.dk; Nyhavn 71; s/d from 1390/1650kr, weekends s/d 990/1290kr; 🖳 ; metro Kongens Nytorv

Well, you certainly won't forget your address if you stay here, and you won't forget the experience either. Slicker than grease and housed in a fabulous 200-year-old canalside renovated warehouse, this wonderful hotel has incorporated some of the building's period features and great views of both the harbour and Nyhavn canal. Everything runs like clockwork, and the location is unbeatable. Popular with business travellers, and therefore a real bargain on weekends.

COPENHAGEN ADMIRAL HOTEL
Map pp232-4 *Hotel*
☎ 33 74 14 16; www.admiral-hotel.dk; Toldbodgade 24-28; s/d from 1225/1470kr; Ⓟ 🖳 ; metro Kongens Nytorv

For nautical atmosphere, it's hard to beat the waterfront Admiral between Nyhavn and Amalienborg Slot. Hell, it's hard to beat this hotel period. It occupies a wonderfully renovated 18th-century granary and is replete with brick archways and sturdy old beams of Pomeranian pine. Each of the 366 rooms has a nice blend of period charm and modern conveniences, and no two rooms are the same. The hotel has everything you could want, plus a very good restaurant and a popular bar for networking.

COPENHAGEN STRAND
Map pp232-4 *Hotel*
☎ 33 48 99 00; www.copenhagenstrand.dk; Havnegade 37; s/d from 1260/1560kr; ✕ 🖳 ; metro Kongens Nytorv

The Strand is an excellent mid-range hotel overlooking Copenhagen Harbour. Its 174 rooms, which have a suitably maritime décor, are equipped with cable TV, minibar and phone. There's an on-site business centre and a lobby bar, making this a good choice for business travellers. Parking shouldn't be a hassle in the street, although it is metered.

HOTEL CITY Map pp232-4 *Hotel*
☎ 33 13 06 66; www.hotelcity.dk; Peder Skrams Gade 24; s/d from 995/1250kr; ✕ ; metro Kongens Nytorv

This relatively small hotel has 81 pleasant (and green-keyed) rooms, each with cable TV, phone and trouser press. Most contain two single beds, placed side by side. The lobby has Jacobsen chairs and a water feature that would have him turning in his grave, but we give the place thumbs up for friendliness and patience with children.

HOTEL ESPLANADEN Map pp232-4 *Hotel*
☎ 33 48 10 00; info.esplanaden@comfort.choicehotels.dk; Bredgade 78; s/d from 900/1100kr; ✕ 🖳 ; bus No 1A

This 117-room Choice Hotels affiliate is a sister hotel to the top-end Neptun Hotel. Located opposite Churchillparken, Hotel Esplanaden is a nice choice for those who want to be near green space but still close to central sights such as Marmorkirken. The hotel is a pleasant, older place offering modernised rooms with beautifully high ceilings and all the mod cons, plus helpful management.

HOTEL MARITIME Map pp232-4 *Hotel*
☎ 33 13 48 82; www.hotel-maritime.dk; Peder Skrams Gade 19; s/d from 950/1250kr; Ⓟ ; metro Kongens Nytorv

The three-star Maritime goes for a 1980s nautical-but-nice vibe with its furnishings and has 64 rooms that are a little on the small side, but otherwise perfectly adequate, with TV and phone, plus a solid city location. Book via a tourist service and you may get a very sweet discount.

HOTEL OPERA Map pp232-4 *Hotel*
☎ 33 47 83 00; www.operahotelcopenhagen.dk; Tordenskjoldsgade 15; s/d from 1160/1490kr; ✕ ; metro Kongens Nytorv

Just south of Det Kongelige Teater (hence the name), this hotel has an inviting English-style character that is reminiscent of a gents' club and befits its theatre-district location. Although it's not strictly as fancy as other top-end period hotels, the 91 three-star rooms are very pleasant, each with phone and TV. Weekend rates drop substantially.

NEPTUN HOTEL Map pp232-4 *Hotel*
☎ 33 96 20 00; info.neptun@clarion.choicehotels.dk; Sankt Annæ Plads 18; s/d from 1375/1775kr; P X X 🖳 ; metro Kongens Nytorv

The Neptun is a well-regarded and secure four-star hotel a block north of Nyhavn (without the noise). Each of the 122 rooms and 12 suites has TV, phone, an electronic room safe, a minibar and a trouser press, and almost half are non-smoking. The Neptun is an affiliate of Choice Hotels, meaning that you can find good deals for Internet bookings and weekend stays.

PHOENIX Map pp232-4 *Hotel*
☎ 33 95 95 00; www.phoenixcopenhagen.dk; Bredgade 37; s/d from 1490/2190kr; 🖳 ; bus No 1A

Located a block north of Nyhavn, the Phoenix is one of the city's more fastidious deluxe hotels and fairly hums with efficient (yet discreet) service. The 200-plus plush rooms have heavy carpets, upholstered chairs, chandeliers and the like, all in keeping with a Louis XIV feel. Business facilities are excellent, as is its proximity to Copenhagen's financial district. Weekend prices plummet by at least 30%.

SOPHIE AMALIE HOTEL Map pp232-4 *Hotel*
☎ 33 13 34 00; booking.has@remmen.dk; Sankt Annæ Plads 21; s/d from 875/1075kr; P X 🖳 ; metro Kongens Nytorv

Popular with business travellers and the sort of person who has decided that the two-star joint they're staying at near the red-light district just ain't worth it. The 134 modern rooms each have the standard amenities plus sauna and solarium. What really sets this place apart is the service, which is charming and incredibly helpful. Go for a 6th-floor split-level suite with harbour views; each has a living room with a sofa bed on the lower level and a loft bedroom above (2075kr).

CHEAP SLEEPS
SØMANDSHJEMMET BETHEL
Map pp232-4 *Hotel*
☎ 33 13 03 70; fax 33 15 85 70; Nyhavn 22; s/d 795/895kr; metro Kongens Nytorv

The well-managed Bethel was once the city's seamen's hotel but is now open to all. This simple but effective little place has a nice location, a lift to all floors, and two dozen good-sized

rooms with serviceable, tidy furnishings. All rooms have TV and a phone. Many also have unbeatable views of Nyhavn – for the best view, ask for a corner room. For a good night's sleep in summer, ask for a room at the back (about 100kr to 200kr less).

Top Five Hotel Views

- **Hotel Sankt Petri** (p158) The best Latin Quarter views from the best Latin Quarter hotel.
- **Mermaid Hotel** (p156) A nice little rooftop garden open to all guests.
- **Radisson SAS Royal Hotel** (p156) The original skyscraper views over all Copenhagen.
- **Sophie Amalie Hotel** (left) Charming harbour views courtesy of its 6th-floor suites.
- **71 Nyhavn Hotel** (p159) The Nyhavn canal or the harbour? Take your pick.

NØRREBRO

Nørrebro is the main accommodation area for travellers looking for a less-expensive, hostel-style sleep away from Vesterbro. There are no mid-range or top-end options here, in keeping with the area's previous working-class flavour.

CHEAP SLEEPS
HOTEL NORA Map pp232-4 *Hotel*
☎ 35 37 20 21; www.hotelnora.dk; Nørrebrogade 18B; s/d incl breakfast 850/975kr; P 🖳 ; bus No 5A

An excellent low-cost addition to Copenhagen's hotel scene is the Nora, which is squeaky clean and situated in Nørrebrogade. While it's not as flash and focused on design as many of the city's places to stay, it's very comfortable and service is considerate and reliable.

SLEEP-IN GREEN Map pp236-7 *Hostel*
☎ 35 37 77 77; www.sleep-in-green.dk; Ravnsborggade 18; dm 100kr, breakfast 40kr; 🕑 24hr late May-late Oct; 🖳 ; bus Nos 5A, 350S

In the Nørrebro area, and on one of its funkiest shopping streets, this environmentally friendly hostel has 66 dorm beds. The place takes its name from its ecological orientation, and guests are welcome to help themselves to a healthy breakfast of organic fare. Handy to good restaurants and nightlife, it's also very easy to walk into town from here.

SLEEP-IN HEAVEN Map pp232-4 *Hostel*

☎ 35 35 46 48; www.sleepinheaven.com; Struenseegade 7; dm 125kr, bridal ste 445kr, breakfast 40kr, sheets 30kr; ☼ year-round; ▯; bus No 3A

This privately run hostel, in the Nørrebro area, has 76 beds in a basement dorm. There's no group kitchen but there are a number of cheap eating places within walking distance. It even has 'bridal suites' for couples. All bathrooms are shared.

NØRREPORT & AROUND

The Nørreport area, which extends westward from Nørreport station, is a bit of an alternative community (but nothing like Christiania), with the city's main flea market, some gay-oriented hotels and some good little shops and eateries on groovy Nansensgade. The hotels that follow are about a five-minute walk west of Nørreport station in a quiet neighbourhood, close to the city lakes, which is itself a very pleasant area for walking.

HOTEL KONG ARTHUR Map pp232-4 *Hotel*

☎ 33 11 12 12; www.kongarthur.dk; Nørre Søgade 11; s/d from 1145/1400kr; Ⓟ; metro & S-train Nørreport

The Kong Arthur is a 107-room establishment in an attractive 19th-century building that fronts the lake Peblinge Sø. Throughout the building you'll find such period details as suits of armour, Persian rugs and antique furniture. Room amenities include TV, minibar, trouser press and an inviting bathroom. The hotel has an attractive inner courtyard, and there's also a lovely glassed-in atrium for breakfast in inclement weather. Ask about possible discounts for internet bookings or slow periods.

IBSENS HOTEL Map pp232-4 *Hotel*

☎ 33 13 19 13; www.ibsenshotel.dk; Vendersgade 23; s/d from 925/1025kr; metro & S-train Nørreport

Ibsens has 118 rooms spread across four floors of a renovated period building. The place has the character of a 'boutique hotel' with creative décor and no two rooms looking exactly the same – décor styles vary between modern (with contemporary Scandinavian design features), romantic and traditional (right down to the antiques and plush fabric details) – all boast a comfortable bed, telephone and TV. There are also suites with kitchenettes for 2100kr.

Situated right near happening Nansensgade, this is a great location for those who are in Copenhagen to experience more than the tourist sights.

CHEAP SLEEPS

HOTEL JØRGENSEN Map pp232-4 *Hotel*

☎ 33 13 81 86; www.hoteljoergensen.dk; Rømersgade 11; dm incl breakfast 130kr, s/d incl breakfast 575/700kr; metro & S-train Nørreport

Popular with gay travellers but open to all. Simple, sometimes quaintly (and cutely) decorated rooms are comfortable, clean and functional, although some can seem very dark at all hours of the day or night. The hotel also has dorm rooms. There are lockers for dorm guests and a coin laundry is just metres away.

HOTEL WINDSOR Map pp232-4 *Hotel*

☎ 33 11 08 30; www.hotelwindsor.dk; Frederiksborggade 30; s/d/tr 600/650/700kr; metro & S-train Nørreport

An exclusively gay hotel in an older building opposite Israels Plads. The Windsor's two dozen rooms are straightforward and a bit worn but all have TV and some have VCRs and refrigerators. Communal areas are a tad shabby, but this actually adds to the appeal, providing a welcome antidote to the Scandi obsession with the neat and stylish. Also a good place to get information about the gay scene in Copenhagen.

VESTERBRO

The hotels listed are all within walking distance of Central Station and the entertainment, eating and shopping options in this ethnically diverse neighbourhood. The area at the western side of Central Station has the most convenient central location and most of the city's mid-range accommodation, which is also closest to the city's redlight district.

ABSALON HOTEL Map pp232-4 *Hotel*

☎ 33 24 22 11; www.absalon-hotel.dk; Helgolandsgade 15; s/d/tr 550/725/925kr, s/d/tr with bathroom 1005/1235/1435kr; ▯; train Central Station

At the three-star, 165-room Absalon you'll find chintz-laden rooms with good amenities, including cable TV and office facilities available to guests. Cheaper rooms with shared bathroom facilities are good value if you're pinching pennies, but not nearly as attractive as the other rooms in the main wing. If you want a little more luxury, there are rooms on the top floor for a few hundred *kroner* more. Parking is available nearby.

DGI-BYEN HOTEL Map pp232-4 *Hotel*
☎ 33 29 80 50; www.dgi-byen.dk; Tietgensgade 65; s/d from 1295/1495kr, weekends s/d from 825/925kr; P 🖳 🖳 ; train Central Station

Part of a late-millennium sports complex development 200m south of Central Station, in the old cattle market district (the smell has long gone), this hotel consists of 104 rooms on three storeys of the complex. The rooms have modern Scandinavian décor with blond hardwood floors and sleek, modest furnishings. Rates drop by a very decent amount on weekends, making this a very good choice for a minibreak. For 100kr more you can opt for a superior room, which is slightly larger and has a bathtub rather than a shower.

FIRST HOTEL VESTERBRO
COPENHAGEN Map pp232-4 *Hotel*
☎ 33 78 80 00; reception/copenhagen@firsthotels .dk; Vesterbrogade 23; s/d from 1799/2049kr; P ⊠ 🖳 🖳 ; bus No 6A

This newish 403-room hotel caters to high-end travellers and has a smart Scandinavian décor that's elegant yet low-key. The rooms are allergen free, with wood floors instead of carpeting, and half of them are set aside for nonsmokers. All are equipped with the latest amenities including voice mail, an ISDN outlet and Internet access via the TV; they also have minibars, room safes, air-con and trouser presses. There's also a bar, restaurant and business centre. The hotel is geared for business, so weekend rates are worth checking out at www.firsthotels.com.

GRAND HOTEL Map pp232-4 *Hotel*
☎ 33 27 69 00; www.grandhotelcopenhagen.dk; Vesterbrogade 9; s/d from 1290/1590kr; ⊠ 🖳 🖳 ; train Central Station, bus No 6A

Conveniently located just north of Central Station is this pleasant 100-year-old hotel with about 160 rooms. Nonsmoking rooms are available and various discount schemes mean you can sometimes get a steeply reduced last-minute price through the tourist office's room-booking counter, the hotel's website or the fact that it's a weekend. Not much soul in the décor, but plenty of polish.

Top Five Copenhagen Sleeps

- **Best Waterside Hotel** Copenhagen Admiral Hotel (p159)
- **Coolest Boutique Hotel** Hotel Guldsmeden (opposite)
- **Getting Down to Business** Copenhagen Marriott (p155)
- **Nicest Newcomer** The Square (p157)
- **Hippest Hotspot** Hotel Sankt Petri (p158)

HOTEL ANSGAR Map pp232-4 *Hotel*
☎ 33 21 21 96; www.ansgar-hotel.dk; Colbjørnsensgade 29; s/d 975/1200kr; train Central Station

The Ansgar, named after a local saint, is a very decent option in this price range, and offers free parking for motorcyclists. The rooms don't exactly set the design world on fire in terms of innovation, but you'll have no complaints about cleanliness or standards. Expect cable TV, phone and marble bathrooms for every customer, plus a pleasant courtyard in the warmer months.

HOTEL CENTRUM Map pp232-4 *Hotel*
☎ 33 31 31 11; www.hotelcentrum.dk; Helgolandsgade 14; s/d 975/1175kr; train Central Station

The rooms here are in very good condition, with a new-looking fit-out that makes the most of room sizes and shapes. Even though the hotel doesn't have a pool as such, a stay here gives you access to the DGI-byen Hotel's pool (see left), and (for a fee) its parking lot. The Centrum is popular with conventions, so book ahead, or ask about a discount on weekends and during the slower months.

HOTEL DU NORD Map pp232-4 *Hotel*
☎ 33 22 44 33; www.hoteldunord.dk; Colbjørnsensgade 14; s/d from 1080/1350kr; P ⊠ 🖳 🖳 ; train Central Station

A truly comfortable option in this area, and while it doesn't go all out in terms of originality in décor, it does keep the standards high. A whole floor is reserved for nonsmokers, every room has three telephones and a bathtub, and children and business travellers alike are well-looked after.

HOTEL EXCELSIOR Map pp232-4 *Hotel*
☎ 33 24 50 85; info.excelsior@comfort.choicehotels. dk; Colbjørnsensgade 6; s/d from 950/1250kr; ⊠ 🖳 ; train Central Station

A smallish (99 rooms) choice in this hotel district, but excellent weekend savings and Internet deals are available. Rooms are serviceable, as you'd expect from a chain operation, but clean and quiet. Large windows allow the street-side rooms to be filled with light, making them the more attractive option.

HOTEL GULDSMEDEN Map pp232-4 *Hotel*
☎ 33 22 15 00; www.hotelguldsmeden.dk; Vesterbrogade 66; s/d 995/1295kr; bus No 6A

This wonderful 64-room, three-star hotel deserves more stars and repeat stays. It's got an arty, Montmartre feel about it, and oozes intimacy and style. Many of the rooms feature a four-poster bed, some feature claw-footed bathtubs and all have original (and pretty damn good) art on the walls. Charming touches such as Persian rugs, clubby leather chairs and sisal matting only add to its rare appeal. A bargain.

HOTEL MAYFAIR Map pp232-4 *Hotel*
☎ 33 31 48 01; mayfair@comfort.choicehotels.dk; Helgolandsgade 3; s/d from 1195/1295kr, ste 1795kr; ☒ ☒ ☐ ; train Central Station

There's something cool about a hotel that adds plenty of Chinese flourishes to its walls, floors and ceilings without any reason, but after

more Scandinavian 'design fetish' blond wood, white walls and classy light fittings than you can poke a stick at, there's something about mother of pearl, rosewood and patterned silk that seems revolutionary. Good service and proximity to tourist attractions too.

MISSIONSHOTELLET NEBO
Map pp232-4 *Hotel*
☎ 33 21 12 17; www.nebo.dk; Istedgade 6; s/d/tr/q 760/860/1100/1250kr; ☐ ; train Central Station

The good old Nebo is very convenient, a mere stone's throw from Central Station, and has been tarted up to within an inch of its mid-range life. A real bargain in this category and friendly to boot – mind you, it's not in the most salubrious of surrounds, situated in the thick of the sex shops. There's free Internet access in the hotel's lobby, and all rooms have bathroom, TV and a desk.

SAVOY HOTEL Map pp232-4 *Hotel*
☎ 33 26 75 00; www.savoyhotel.dk; Vesterbrogade 34; s/d & tw 975/1275kr, f 1795kr; bus No 6A

The lovely Savoy is a century-old hotel that was renovated a few years ago but still retains some of its period character and Art Nouveau décor. Although the hotel fronts a busy road, all of its 66 rooms face a winningly

Hotel Guldsmeden (above)

quiet courtyard, and each room has cable TV, a minibar and coffee maker. Plus, the service is some of the sweetest and most efficient we came across – no mean feat in a town used to hosting conventions.

TIFFANY Map pp232-4 *Hotel*
☎ 33 21 80 50; www.hoteltiffany.dk; Colbjørnsensgade 28; s/d/tr/q 895/1095/1295/1495kr; ⊠ ⊠ ▱; train Central Station

The Tiffany, which proudly bills itself as a 'Sweet Hotel', is a pleasant little place filled with character and warmth. The 29 rooms each have a TV, phone, trouser press, private bathroom and kitchenette with refrigerator and microwave oven. A buffet breakfast is not included, but coffee, tea and fresh pastries are available each morning and you can help yourself to fruit in the lobby. Service is kind and considerate, making this little jewel excellent value for money in this price range.

CHEAP SLEEPS

BERTRAMS HOTEL Map p238 *Hotel*
☎ 33 25 04 05; bertramshotel@mail.dk; Vesterbrogade 107; s/d 575/785kr, s/d with bathroom 785/995kr; bus No 6A

We were transported back to the heady early 1990s when we walked in here – it was like one of those heroin shoots from *The Face* – all heroin chic, ciggie smoke, kitsch-meets-grunge décor and louche types lounging round the lobby. A lot of atmosphere but less in the way of fancy amenities. Well suited to rock 'n' rollers on a budget, as there are some cheaper rooms without bathrooms.

CAB INN CITY Map pp232-4 *Hotel*
☎ 35 39 84 00; city@cabinn.dk; Mitchellsgade 14; s/d/tr/q 510/630/750/870kr; ℗ ⊠ ▱; train Central Station

Behold the budget-priced behemoth! With a whopping 350 rooms, a no-smoking policy and 24-hour reception, this is one of the best cheapies in town. You won't get any sense of intimacy or that famous Danish cosiness, but you will sleep soundly and cheaply and be close to all the action. Wheelchair access is very good.

COPENHAGEN TRITON HOTEL
Map pp232-4 *Hotel*
☎ 33 31 32 66; triton@accorhotel.dk; Helgolandsgade 7-11; s/d 525kr; ⊠ ▱; train Central Station

The business-on-a-budget Triton (part of the Ibis chain) has 123 clean, characterless rooms with functional Scandinavian (ie Ikea) décor. That said, all rooms have cable TV, phone, minibar, desk and tidy bathrooms. One plus – the rear rooms face a courtyard and are quieter than most in this generally bustling neighbourhood. The hotel is scheduled for an overdue renovation that never seems to happen (hence the rock-bottom year-round rates). We don't sound so keen, but truth be told, this is a very good deal for the price and level of service available.

HOTEL HEBRON Map pp232-4 *Hotel*
☎ 33 31 69 06; www.hebron.dk; Helgolandsgade 4; s/d & tw from 750/975kr, ste from 1125kr; ⊠ ⊠; train Central Station

The Hebron is a quiet hotel in an attractive early-20th-century building with about 100 cosy, renovated rooms, each with desk, TV and phone. Despite its proximity to both the main train station and the red-light district, you should sleep soundly, thanks to the miracle of double-glazing. Staff are a good source of sightseeing tips and transport information. The hotel shuts down for Christmas between 22 December and 3 January.

SAGA HOTEL Map pp232-4 *Hotel*
☎ 33 24 49 44; booking@sagahotel.dk; Colbjørnsensgade 18; s/d from 550/650kr; train Central Station

With 76 rooms, most of which look ship-shape thanks to a navy-and-white paint job, this is a handy little spot close to the main train station (and some of the sex shops). There's no lift and it's multistorey, so you may have to climb some stairs, but the minimalist approach to luxuries helps keep the rates relatively low. The rooms have phone and TV (singles are quite small though), and the service is friendly and personal.

SELANDIA HOTEL Map pp232-4 *Hotel*
☎ 33 31 46 10; www.hotel-selandia.dk; Helgolandsgade 12; s/d 525/650kr, s/d with bathroom from 795/975kr; train Central Station

The recently renovated Selandia has 84 spiffy rooms, each with a desk, sink and TV. Cheapest are the two dozen or so rooms with shared bathroom. Service is quintessentially helpful, and it's worth perusing the website for special deals that make this place quite a bargain. When the lobby gets a facelift, there'll be no stopping the Selandia.

SLEEP-IN FACT Map pp232-4 *Hostel*
☎ 33 79 67 79; www.sleep-in-fact.dk; Valdemarsgade 14; dm 120kr; ☷ 7am-noon & 3pm-3am 28 Jun-31 Aug; 🖳 ; bus No 6A

Housed in a renovated factory and doing service as a summer hostel, this is a nifty central spot to treat as a crash-pad. There are 80 dorm beds in two large rooms, but it's the flower-bedecked rooftop terrace that's the real star. Facilities are spick and span, and the staff eager to help visitors get the most out of the city.

OUTLYING DISTRICTS
FREDERIKSBERG

Frederiksberg is generally more residential than central Copenhagen but it does have the following well-priced hotels. This sizable area begins at the western side of the city lake Sankt Jørgens Sø and extends several kilometres west, bordering gritty Vesterbro.

RADISSON SAS FALCONER HOTEL
Map p238 *Hotel*
☎ 38 15 80 01; http://sas.radisson.com; Falkoner Allé 9; s/d from 1500kr; metro Frederiksberg

Situated west of Copenhagen's centre, this hotel, which is a *very* popular convention spot, has a large banquet hall, a health club, a restaurant and a bar. Some rooms have been specially adapted for disabled people and all have modern luxury amenities. Non-smoking rooms are available. If you're part of grey power, ask about the excellent discounts for seniors (available year-round) and a similarly discounted summer family rate. Weekends attract big discounts too, as do Internet bookings.

Cheap Sleeps
AVENUE HOTEL Map pp232-4 *Hotel*
☎ 35 37 31 11; www.avenuehotel.dk; Åboulevard 29; s/d/tr/q 775/975/1075/1075kr; metro Forum

The warm and welcoming Avenue has 68 tidy rooms kitted out in another era (we're guessing the early 1980s…). Close to both sedate Frederiksberg and so-funky-it-hurts Vesterbro, this is a good choice if you want to be close to town but not in the thick of it. Good rates can be negotiated for longer stays.

CAB INN COPENHAGEN EXPRESS
Map pp232-4 *Hotel*
☎ 33 21 04 00; express@cabinn.dk; Danasvej 32; s/d/tr/q 510/630/750/870kr; 🅿 🖳 ; metro Forum

A few blocks to the southwest of the Cab Inn Scandinavia, this sister operation has the same type of rooms and rates, although it has less than 100 rooms, making it a little more intimate than the Scandinavia. Reception is open 24 hours and standards are solid. Two rooms here are accessible to people in wheelchairs.

CAB INN SCANDINAVIA
Map pp232-4 *Hotel*
☎ 35 36 11 11; scandinavia@cabinn.dk; Vodroffsvej 57; s/d/tr/q 510/630/750/870kr; 🅿 🖳 ; metro Forum

Modern, well managed and wheelchair accessible, the Scandinavia has 201 sleekly compact rooms that resemble cabins in a cruise ship, complete with upper and lower bunks, but no seasickness. Although small, the rooms are very comfortable and have cable TV, phone, complimentary tea and bathroom. Reception is open 24 hours and the neighbourhood is quiet and safe – making this place ideal for budget-conscious families.

Handy for the Airport

Hilton Copenhagen Airport (Map p230; ☎ 32 50 15 01; www.hilton.dk; Ellehammersvej 20, Kastrup; s/d from 1400/1900kr; 🅿 ✗ ♨ 🖳 ; S-train Kastrup) This newish hotel, right at the airport, has around 375 very large rooms with full amenities, including top-end touches such as Bang & Olufsen TVs. There's a fitness centre, a swimming pool and conference facilities. As airport hotels go, it's an excellent one, and service is impeccable. Children are also welcome, with babysitting services provided for a fee.

Transfer Hotel (Map p230; ☎ 32 31 24 55; transfer@cph.dk; Copenhagen Airport; s/d for 2 hrs from 200/250kr; S-train Kastrup) In the basement of the airport's international terminal, this handy facility has simple rooms with private amenities geared for those in transit. The hotel has showers and solariums for those simply wanting to freshen up (90kr) or top up their tan.

Cab Inn Scandinavia, (p165)

HOTEL EUROGLOBE Map pp232-4   *Hotel*
☎ 33 79 79 54; www.hoteleuroglobe.dk; Niels
Ebbesens Vej 20; s/d/tr/q with shared bathroom
450/550/650/800kr; metro Forum
The Euroglobe has 28 budget rooms in an old
building that's been splashed with a fresh coat
of paint and is in reasonable (if minimalist)
condition. Rooms are pretty basic but sparsely
stylish, with beds, an end table, chairs and
washbasin; bathrooms are shared. You can
also take bus No 3 or 29 to get here, with
stops a few blocks away.

HOTEL JOSTY Map p238   *Hotel*
☎ 38 86 90 90; www.josty.dk; Pile Allé 14A; s/d/ste
700/900/1400kr; P ; bus No 26
With only seven rooms, the early-19th-century
Josty is a small delight in this classy part of
town, so you're advised to book ahead. Quiet,
old-fashioned charm keeps this place ticking
along nicely – and proximity to the park means
that we can say the grounds are excellent.

HOTEL SANKT THOMAS
Map pp232-4
    Hotel
☎ 33 21 64 64; www.sctthomas.com; Frederiksberg
Allé 7; s/d 595/795kr; P 💻 ; bus No 6A

The groovy little Sankt Thomas lies tucked
away off busy Vesterbrogade in a 19th-century
building that just scored a well-earned facelift.
It's close to the area's new bars, restaurants
and theatres, and it's charmingly run. There are
some cheaper rooms (without toilet) for s/d
495/595kr (even less in the low season).

ØSTERBRO

The leafy Østerbro district comes alive when
large sporting events and pop concerts are
staged in Parken and Fælledparken. Other
than that, it's a middle-class borough of
well-ordered normalcy, with some good
budget accommodation. Despite its middle-
class demographic, Østerbro's accommodation is suited more to those looking for
budget-conscious sleeps.

Cheap Sleeps
HOTEL 9 SMÅ HJEM

Map pp236-7   *Apartments*
☎ 35 26 16 47; www.9smaahjem.dk; Classengade
38; s per day/week 485/2940kr; d 625/3815kr; S-train
Østerport

Not exactly a hotel, but a very good option for those after a longer-term accommodation option. Frills and extras are not in evidence, but it's perfectly comfortable and well maintained. Apartments (that can sleep up to four people) are better value than rooms, as they cost the same price but feature kitchens (rooms have shared kitchen facilities).

SLEEP-IN Map pp236-7 *Hostel*
☎ 35 26 50 59; www.sleep-in.dk; Blegdamsvej 132A; dm 99kr; ☾ Jul & Aug; ▣ ; bus Nos 1, 15

This seasonal budget place, a few kilometres north of the city centre in the Østerbro district, is Copenhagen's largest summer hostel, with some 280-plus beds occupying a sports hall that's curtained off into 'rooms' with four to six beds; there are no doors, but curtains offer a little privacy. There are free lockers, a guest kitchen and a café. You can use your own sleeping bag or rent bed linen (30kr). From the city centre take bus No 1 or 15, get off at Trianglen and walk 300m southwest on Blegdamsvej. Bakeries, shops and restaurants are within easy walking distance.

ISLANDS BRYGGE
RADISSON SAS SCANDINAVIA
HOTEL Map pp232-4 *Hotel*
☎ 33 96 50 00; www.radissonsas.com; Amager Blvd 70; s/d from 1695/1895kr; ⓟ ✗ ▨ ▣ ; metro Islands Brygge, bus Nos 5A, 250S

In an unmissable high-rise building in the northern part of Amager, the Scandinavia offers all the luxury-hotel amenities and goodies that any business traveller could want, as well as Copenhagen's only casino. Its 542 rooms offer generous weekend reductions and plenty of comfort, but we got the distinct feeling that service was a 'by numbers' deal and cosiness (that most Danish of qualities) was distinctly lacking.

Cheap Sleeps
DANHOSTEL COPENHAGEN AMAGER
Map p230 *Hostel*
☎ 32 52 29 08; copenhagen@danhostel.dk; Vejlands Allé 200; dm/d 95/300kr; ☾ 2 Jan-15 Dec; metro Bella Center

In an isolated part of Amager just off the E20, about 5km from the city centre, this place ranks as one of Europe's largest hostels, with 528 beds in a series of low-rise wings containing cells of two-bed and five-bed rooms. There's a laundry room, disabled access and a cafeteria.

LYNGBY
DANHOSTEL LYNGBY-TÅRBÆK
VANDRERHJEM Map p230 *Hostel*
☎ 45 80 30 74; www.danhostel.dk/lyngby; Rådvad 1; dm 115kr, r 360-690kr; ☾ 1 Apr-25 Oct; ⓟ ; S-train Lyngby

Nestled in a small hamlet on the northern side of Dyrehaven, this older, one-star hostel occupies a manor-like whitewashed house that can accommodate over 90 people, mostly in rooms with four to six beds. The area is quite pretty, with swan-filled ponds, and it's within walking distance of the house where silversmith Georg Jensen was born in 1866; however, it's not a terribly practical place to make a base if your main focus is

Sleeping – Outlying Districts

Worth the Detour

Belægningen Avedørelejren (Map p230; ☎ 36 77 90 84; www.belaegningen.dk; Avedøre Tværvej 10, Hvidovre; dm 110kr, s/d with bathroom 360/460kr, breakfast 55kr; ☾ year-round; ⓟ ▣; bus No 650S) About 7km southwest of the city centre, this hostel in the well-renovated barracks of a former military camp has friendly staff, high standards and quite cosy rooms with only four beds in the dorm rooms. The hostel also offers cheap bicycle rentals and a good group kitchen. As an added perk you might spot some of Denmark's hottest screen stars, as the camp's rear buildings have been turned into a Danish 'Hollywood' housing the country's main movie companies, including Lars von Trier's Zentropa production company.

Danhostel Copenhagen Bellahøj (Map p230; ☎ 38 28 97 15; bellahoej@danhostel.dk; Herbergvejen 8, Brønshøj; dm/d/tr 95/300/390kr; ☾1 Feb-2 Jan; ▣; bus No 2A) The most easily accessible HI-hostel, this place is in the quiet suburban neighbourhood known as Bellahøj, 4km northwest of the city centre. Although it has 250 beds, it's quite cosy for its size. Facilities include a laundry room, cafeteria, TV room and table tennis, plus reception is open 24 hours.

exploring central Copenhagen. Bus No 187 runs from the Lyngby S-train station to the hostel, but it's an infrequent weekday-only bus, so check the schedule in advance. Otherwise it's a 2km walk between the hostel and the nearest regularly serviced bus stop in Hjortekær.

ISHØJ

ISHØJ STRAND VANDRERHJEM *Hostel*
☎ 43 53 50 15; www.danhostel.dk/ishoj; Ishøj Strandvej 13; dm 115kr, r 450-690kr; ☯ 1 Jan-21 Dec; Ⓟ ⌨ ; S-train Ishøj
This is a relatively new five-star hostel in the seaside community of Ishøj, 15km southwest of central Copenhagen. It has 229 beds in 40 rooms; each room has its own toilet and bath and all are housed in a mammoth red barn-like structure that's reminiscent of a Swedish holiday home. The hostel has a restaurant that offers three square meals a day, bicycle rental and wheelchair-accessible facilities. There's a beach with swimming and windsurfing possibilities just 1km away. Restaurants and a grocery store are within easy walking distance. The hostel is 800m east of Ishøj station (well signed); the travel time from Copenhagen's Central Station is just 15 minutes if you take the E line.

Excursions

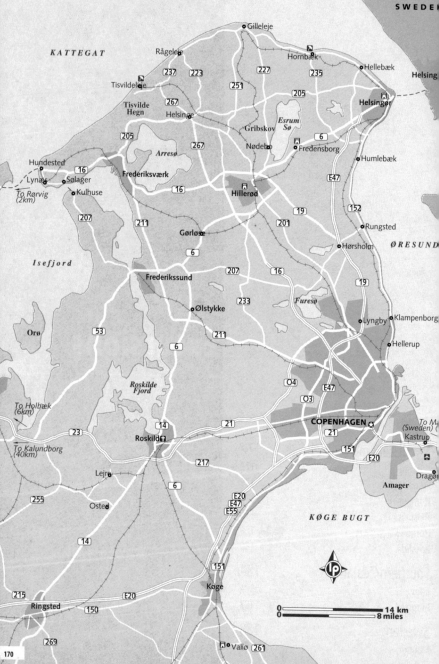

SWEDEN

KATTEGAT

Gilleleje

Rågeleje

Hornbæk

Hellebæk

Helsing

Tisvildeleje

237 223

227

235

Helsingør

251

Tisvilde
Hegn

267

205

Helsinge

Gribskov

Esrum
Sø

6

205

267

Arresø

Nødebo

Fredensborg

Humlebæk

Hundested

16

Frederiksværk

16

Hillerød

E47

Lynæs   Sølager

To Rørvig
(2km)

Kulhuse

207

211

Gørløse

19

201

152

Rungsted

Hørsholm

ØRESUND

6

Isefjord

207

16

Frederikssund

19

Ølstykke

233

Furesø

Orø

53

211

Lyngby   Klampenborg

6

Hellerup

Roskilde
Fjord

O4

E47

To Holbæk
(6km)

23

14

O3

COPENHAGEN

To M
(Sweden) (

Roskilde

21

21

Kastrup

To Kalundborg
(40km)

217

151

E20

Lejre

6

E20
E47
E55

Dragø

255

Osted

Amager

KØGE BUGT

14

151

LP

215

Køge

0 ——————— 14 km

Ringsted

150

0 ——————— 8 miles

269

Vallø   261

170

Excursions

The island of Zealand is compact and well covered by public transport, meaning that you could visit any place on it as an easy day trip. Copenhagen is within easy reach of a number of interesting options for those who wish to escape the city – and you can even venture 'overseas' (especially to nearby Sweden) with little fuss.

The northern half of Zealand offers a wonderful variety of excursion options, with most destinations less than an hour from Copenhagen. Considering its proximity to the capital, North Zealand is surprisingly rural, with small farms, wheat fields and beech woodlands. It also boasts fine beaches and some notable historic sights.

Steeped in history, southern Zealand has played an important role since the Viking era. In medieval times it was a stomping ground for Copenhagen's founder Bishop Absalon and in the 17th century the area was the stage for many of the battles in the lengthy wars between Denmark and Sweden. The most pivotal loss in Danish history was played out here in 1658 when Swedish King Gustav marched across southern Zealand en route to Copenhagen and forced a treaty that nearly cost Denmark its sovereignty.

Today the region contains a mix of peaceful towns, rural villages and patchwork farmland, and it has a strong sense of Viking heritage.

For most of the excursions in this chapter, you're better off buying a 24-hour train ticket for 100kr if you intend returning to Copenhagen on the same day or within 24 hours of commencing your journey.

Art

One of the country's best art museums can be found at the world-famous **Louisiana** (p175) in Humlebæk, an architectural gem with fabulous views of the sea and plenty of masterpieces both inside and scattered throughout the grounds. It's reason enough to come to Denmark to marvel at such a sterling collection presented in a simple, elegant building that's often flooded with Nordic light. Less well-known but also worth popping into are Roskilde's **Museet for Samtidskunst** (Museum of Contemporary Art; p183) and Køge's **Skitsesamling** (Art and Sketch Collection; p185).

Castles

Denmark's well-maintained castles attract admiring hordes each year, and frequently host exhibitions on various royal or historic themes. Denmark being the egalitarian country that it is, you can even pop into the summer home of the royal family, **Fredensborg Slot** (p173), during the month of July – and the grounds are free to all year-round. Still, the castle that most visitors gravitate to is the extraordinary **Kronborg Slot** (p176), otherwise known as Hamlet's Castle, and home both to summer performances of the famous Shakespeare play and to the Danish Maritime Museum. For a sight that will have the words 'fairy tale' playing over and over in your head, you simply must catch sight of **Frederiksborg Slot** (p172), a glorious Dutch Renaissance confection of red brick, moats, copper roofing and fantasy-land interiors; it also has a fascinating portrait gallery. **Vallø Slot** (p186), the former 'spinster's home' for noble ladies, is another centuries-old attraction, on a slightly less grand scale. Over in Sweden, **Malmöhus** (p189) contains a number of attractions, such as an art museum and aquarium.

Coast

Denmark's Kattegat coast is comprised of small fishing villages such as endearing Hornbæk. Beaches around the area are safe havens with white sands and simple charms that are enormously popular with Danish families come summertime. In the best Danish tradition, even though this area is popular with wealthy Copenhagen locals, the area has avoided the ritzy seaside atmosphere that has ruined similar villages in Italy and France. The trip up to the north, by train or car, will generally hug the Zealand coastline – an attraction in itself.

History

If you've come to Denmark to learn a little about the Vikings, then Roskilde is a must, with its **Viking Ship Museum** (p182), the collection of re-created Viking boats being constructed on the fjord and its magnificent, imposing **cathedral** (p181), where Denmark's kings and queens are buried. **Køge** (p184) is a very well-preserved medieval town with some architectural points of interest in the town centre and **Sankt Nicolai Kirke** (p184).

NORTH ZEALAND

HILLERØD

Hillerød is a small town centred on a grand lakeside castle, Frederiksborg Slot.

An administrative centre and transport hub for North Zealand, Hillerød isn't notably quaint in itself but the castle and the surrounding gardens are absolutely lovely. You can enjoy picturesque views of the castle by following the path that skirts the castle's lake. If you feel like taking a longer stroll, paths run through Slotshaven, an expansive baroque-style privet garden immediately north of the castle and lake. The paths leading through Slotshaven connect with trails in the adjacent woodlands of Lille Dyrehave and Indelukket which, taken together, could easily make a pleasant one- or two-hour outing.

The impressive Dutch Renaissance castle **Frederiksborg Slot** spreads across three islets on the eastern side of the castle lake, Slotsø. The oldest part of Frederiksborg Slot dates from the reign of Frederik II, after whom the castle is named, but most of the present structure was built in the early 17th century by Frederik II's more extravagant son, Christian IV.

As you enter the main gate you'll pass old stable buildings dating from the 1560s and then cross over a moat to the second islet, where you'll enter an expansive central courtyard with a grandly ornate Neptune fountain. The relatively modest wings that flank the fountain once served as residences for court officers and government officials. A second bridge crosses to the northernmost islet, the site of the main body of the castle, which served as the home of Danish royalty for more than a century.

Frederiksborg Slot was ravaged by fire in 1859. Unable to undertake the costly repairs, the royal family decided to give up the property. Carlsberg beer baron JC Jacobsen then stepped onto the scene and spearheaded a drive to restore the castle as a national museum, a function it still serves today.

The sprawling castle has a magnificent interior boasting gilded ceilings, wall-sized tapestries, period paintings and antique furnishings, with exhibits occupying 70 of its rooms. The richly embellished Riddersalen (Knights Hall) and Slotskirken (Coronation Chapel), where Danish monarchs were crowned from 1671 to 1840, are alone worth the admission fee. The chapel, incidentally, was spared serious fire damage and retains the original interior commissioned by Christian IV, including a lavish hand-carved altar and pulpit created by Mores of Hamburg in 1606 and a priceless Compenius organ built in 1610. The organ is played each Thursday between 1.30pm and 2pm.

At the end of your tour of the castle you'll reach the **20th-century portraits section**, with some noteworthy depictions of notable Danes, including Henrik Saxgren's 2002 photograph of Lars von Trier and Per Kirkeby, von Trier's enigmatic 1975 self-portrait, Andy Warhol's 1986 portrait of Queen Margrethe (from his Reigning Queens series) and Kay Christensen's 1956 portrait of Karen Blixen.

Sights & Information

Frederiksborg Slot (☎ 48 26 04 39; adult/child 60/15kr; ☯ 10am-5pm Apr-Oct, 11am-3pm Nov-Mar) Outside opening hours visitors are still free to stroll around the grounds and enter the castle courtyard.

Hillerød Turistbureau (☎ 48 24 26 26; www.hillerod turist.dk; Slangerupgade 2; ☯ 10am-5pm Mon-Fri, 10am-1pm Sat) Fifty metres south of the castle entrance.

Eating

El Castillo (☎ 48 26 19 11; Slotsgade 61; mains 43-115kr; ☯ 5-10pm) If you're staying overnight here you could do worse than eat at this cheery Mexican joint that seems popular with the town's residents.

Spisestedet Leonora (☎ 48 26 75 16; Frederiksborg Slot; mains 70-135kr; ☯ 10am-5pm Mon-Fri) With its moatside setting and palace location, this is the pick of the bunch when it comes to dining in Hillerød. Try the guinea fowl with potatoes (125kr).

Sleeping

Hotel Hillerød (☎ 48 24 08 00; www.hotelhillerod.dk; Milnersvej 41; s/d 965/1080kr) About 2km south of the castle, this good hotel has an atrium filled with flowering plants and 74 modern, light-filled rooms with bath, TV and kitchenette. Bicycles are available too.

Star Gazing

As in many palaces of Europe, even the ceilings are flash at Frederiksborg Slot – and our favourite would have to be the zodiac ceiling in Room 30. Don't forget to look up and take it all in.

FREDENSBORG

Fredensborg is a quiet town with a royal palace, a lakeside location and some good walking tracks. Slotsgade, the road that terminates at the palace gate, has a number of historic buildings, including the classic inn **Hotel Store Kro** at No 6; **Villa Bournonville**, the former home of the 19th-century ballet master Auguste Bournonville, at Slotsgade 9; **Havremagasinet**, Slotsgade 11, which once served as horse stables; and **Kunstnergården**, an art and crafts gallery a bit further south at Slotsgade 17, originally an inn built in 1722.

Fredensborg Slot, the royal family's summer residence, was built in 1720 by Frederik IV. It was named Fredensborg, which means Peace Palace, to commemorate the peace that Denmark had recently achieved with its Scandinavian neighbours. The palace certainly reflects the more tranquil mood of that era and is largely in the style of a country manor house, in contrast to the moat-encircled fortresses of Kronborg and Frederiksborg that preceded it.

The main mansion was designed by the leading Danish architect of the day, JC Krieger, and is in Italian baroque style with marble floors and a large central cupola. It's fronted by a large octagonal courtyard framed by two-storey buildings.

Partly because of its spread-out design, the palace is not as impressive as other Danish royal palaces in North Zealand. Fredensborg's interior can only be visited during July, when the royal family holidays elsewhere; guided tours of the palace and the gardens take place every 15 minutes or so.

The palace is backed by 120 hectares of **wooded parkland**, crisscrossed by trails and open to the public year-round. Take a stroll through **Nordmandsdalen**, west of the palace, to a circular amphitheatre with 70 life-sized sandstone statues of Norwegian folk characters – fisherfolk, farmers and so on – in traditional dress. The statues depict 60 Norwegian and 10 Faroese peasants, an unusual subject for the time (the 1760s) and one suggested by King Frederik V – although his reasons are not clear. If you continue walking a few minutes' west from there you'll reach Esrum Sø, a lake skirted by another trail.

Transport

Distance from Copenhagen 50km

Direction Northwest

Travel time Up to 1½ hours

Train Fredensborg is midway on the railway line between Hillerød (17kr, 12 minutes) and Helsingør (42.50kr, 20 minutes). Trains run twice hourly from early morning to around midnight. To get to Fredensborg Slot from the train station, turn left onto Stationsvej and then turn right onto Jernbanegade, which merges with Slotsgade near the palace gate; the whole walk takes about 10 minutes.

Bus Bus Nos 336 and 339 run hourly between Fredensborg train station and Hillerød (17kr, 20 minutes), stopping en route near Fredensborg Slot.

Fredensborg Slot (p173).

The southeastern shore of **Esrum Sø**, Denmark's second-largest lake, borders Fredensborg and offers opportunities for swimming, boating and fishing. Along the shore you can sometimes spot ospreys and cormorants, and the surrounding woods are the habitat of roe deer.

It's a 10-minute walk west from the palace gate along Skipperallé to **Skipperhuset**, a lakeside restaurant where there's a summer ferry service and rowing boats for hire. The main beach is nearby. The ferry can take you to **Gribskov**, a forested area with trails and picnic grounds that borders the western side of Esrum Sø.

Sights & Information

Fredensborg Slot (☎ 33 40 10 10; www.slotte.dk; Palace & Chapel adult/child 40/15kr, Reserved Gardens, Orangery & Herb Garden adult/child 40/15kr, joint ticket adult/child 60/25kr; Palace & Chapel ☺ 1-4.30pm July, Reserved Gardens ☺ 9am-5pm July)

Fredensborg Turistinformation (☎ 48 48 21 00; Slotsgade 2; ☺ 10am-6pm late Jun-Aug, 10am-4pm Mon-Fri & 11am-3pm Sun Sep-Jun) Just outside the palace.

Eating & Sleeping

Danhostel Fredensborg Vandrerhjem (☎ 48 48 03 15; www.fredensborghostel.dk; Østrupvej 3; dm 100kr, r with handbasin 185-500kr, r with toilet 219-404kr, r with bathroom 459-599kr) Has a prime location just 300m south of the palace and it's open year-round. Most of the 80-plus beds are in double rooms; some have toilets (showers are off the hall) and the new rooms all have bathrooms. There's a TV room, a guest kitchen and a great terrace for warmer weather. To get there turn west off Slotsgade at Hotel Store Kro and continue for about 50m.

Hotel Store Kro (☎ 48 40 01 11; www.storekro.dk; Slotsgade 6; s 1100kr, d 1500-1700kr) Just outside the palace

gate is this lavish place, the earliest sections of which were built by Frederik IV in 1723 to accommodate palace guests. No two rooms are alike but all have very traditional décor as well as a bathroom, TV, phone and minibar, and the communal areas are palatial, of course. A very good, rather fancy restaurant is also on the premises.

Pension Bondehuset (☎ 48 48 01 12; Sørupvej 14, Box 6; s/d 790/1350kr) For an upmarket rural getaway, try this place, which also dates from the early 18th century. By the lake on the western outskirts of Fredensborg, it has classic manor-house furnishings and provides rowing boats for guests to use. Half-board catering is available and comes highly recommended.

Skipperhuset (☎ 48 48 01 07; Skipperallé 6; menu 188-268kr) Traditional Danish dishes served in a lovely lakeside setting – perfect on a sunny day.

Home Sweet Home

Wondering which part of Fredensborg Slot Crown Prince Frederik and Crown Princess Mary call home? It's the Chancellery, which was renovated for them as their first home. Before that it served as the home of Queen Margrethe's mother, Queen Ingrid.

HUMLEBÆK

The coastal town of Humlebæk has a couple of harbours and bathing beaches and some wooded areas, but the main focus for visitors is the modern art museum Louisiana.

Louisiana, Denmark's most renowned modern art museum, is on a seaside knoll in a strikingly modernistic complex featuring sculpture-laden grounds.

The sculptures on the lawns, which include works by Henry Moore, Alexander Calder and Max Ernst, create an engaging interplay between art, architecture and landscape. Louisiana is a fascinating place to visit even for those not passionate about modern art.

Items from the museum's permanent collection of paintings and graphic art from the postwar era are creatively displayed and grouped. There are sections on constructivism, Cobra-movement (COpenhagen-BRussels-Amsterdam) artists, some abstract expressionism, minimal art, pop art and staged photography. Works on display include those by international luminaries Pablo Picasso, Francis Bacon and Alberto Giacometti. Prominent Danish artists represented are Asger Jorn, Carl-Henning Pedersen, Robert Jacobsen and Richard Mortensen.

The museum also has top-notch temporary exhibitions, which over the years have included such diverse themes as Toulouse-Lautrec & Paris, the works of Juan Muñoz, the world of Andy Warhol and the architectural achievements of Jørn Utzon.

If you're travelling with kids this is one museum that can be lots of fun. It has an entire children's wing where kids can explore their artistic talents using an interactive computer and various hands-on media; ask about the free Friday-afternoon workshops that attract lots of international youngsters.

The museum also presents concerts and films and has a substantial shop selling art books and quality gift items ranging from children's toys to homewares and glossy coffee-table tomes. Disabled facilities at Louisiana are very good.

> ## Transport
>
> **Distance from Copenhagen** 30km
>
> **Direction** North
>
> **Travel time** 45 minutes
>
> **Train** DSB trains leave Copenhagen a few times each hour for Humlebæk (51kr). Louisiana is 1km from Humlebæk train station, a 10-minute signposted walk along Gammel Strandvej.

> ## Driving an Art Bargain
>
> DSB offers a Louisiana excursion ticket for an easy-peasy 128kr that includes the museum admission price and the return train fare from Copenhagen. Buy the ticket at the main train station in Copenhagen.

Sights

Lousiana Museum of Modern Art (☎ 49 19 07 91; www.louisiana.dk; Gammel Strandvej 13; adult/concession/child 74/67/20kr; ☾ 10am-5pm Thu-Tue, 10am-10pm Wed)

Eating

Solarium Café (Lousiana Museum, Gammel Strandvej 13; buffets 52-99kr; ☾ 10am-4.30pm Tue-Thu, 10am-9.30pm Wed) A picturesque setting with some delightful sea views, good hearty brunches and buffets.

HELSINGØR

Helsingør (known in English as Elsinore), at the narrowest point of the Øresund, has long been a busy port town. While the new Øresund Bridge in Amager has relieved some of the traffic, this is still Scandinavia's busiest shipping channel, with ferries shuttling to/from Sweden throughout the day.

Although Swedish shoppers hopping over on day trips comprise many of Helsingør's visitors (which accounts for the plethora of liquor shops near the harbour), the town offers enough sightseeing possibilities to fill an enjoyable half-day of touring.

Helsingør has maintained some of its historic quarters, including a block of old homes and warehouses known as Sundtoldkarreen (Sound Dues Square) at the northeastern end of Strandgade. Helsingør's top sight, perched across the harbour on the northern side of town, is the imposing Kronborg Slot, made famous as Elsinore Castle in Shakespeare's *Hamlet*.

Despite the attention **Kronborg Slot** has received as the setting of Shakespeare's *Hamlet*, the castle's primary function was not as a royal residence but rather as a grandiose tollhouse, wresting taxes from ships passing through the narrow Øresund. The castle's history dates from the 1420s, when the Danish king Erik of Pomerania introduced the 'sound dues' and built a small fortress, called Krogen, on a promontory at the narrowest part of the sound.

Financed by the generous revenue from shipping tolls, the original medieval fortress was rebuilt and enlarged by Frederik II between 1574 and 1585 to form the present Kronborg Slot. Much of Kronborg was ravaged by fire in 1629, but Christian IV rebuilt it, preserving the castle's earlier Renaissance style. In 1658, during the war with Sweden, the Swedes occupied Kronborg and removed practically everything of value, leaving the interior in shambles. After that, Danish royalty rarely visited the castle, although the sound dues were collected for another 200 years. In 1785 Kronborg was converted into barracks and that remained its chief function until 1922. Since then the castle has been thoroughly restored and is now open to the public as a museum.

Transport

Distance from Copenhagen 47km

Direction North

Travel time 45 minutes

Car From Copenhagen, head north on the E47/E55. There's free parking throughout the city, including car parks northeast of the tourist office, to the west of the Kvickly supermarket and outside Kronborg Slot. See also 'Detour', p178.

Train Helsingør train station has two adjacent terminals: the main DSB terminal for national trains and the Helsingør–Hornbæk–Gilleleje Banen (HHGB) terminal for the private railway that runs along the north coast. DSB trains to and from Copenhagen run about three times hourly from early morning to around midnight (59.50kr, 55 minutes). DSB trains to and from Hillerød (42.50kr, 30 minutes) run at least once hourly until around midnight. The HHGB train from Helsingør to Gilleleje via Hornbæk runs an average of twice hourly (45kr, 40 minutes), with the last train pulling out of Helsingør at 10.54pm.

Boat For information on the frequent ferries to Helsingborg in Sweden (one way/return 15/30kr, 20 minutes), see p194.

Some of the castle's more interesting quarters include the king's and queen's chambers, which have marble fireplaces and detailed ceiling paintings; the small chamber, which boasts royal tapestries; and the great hall, one of the longest Renaissance halls in Scandinavia. The chapel is one of the best-preserved parts of the castle and has some choice woodcarvings, while the gloomy dungeons make for more unusual touring.

In the dungeon you'll pass the resting statue of the legendary Viking chief Holger Danske (Ogier the Dane), who is said to watch over Denmark, ever-ready to come to her aid should the hour of need arise. The low-ceilinged dungeon includes areas that once served as soldiers' quarters and storerooms for salted fish, which these days are homes for nesting bats! If you're easily spooked, this part of the castle can be quite intimidating.

To Be or Not to Be...

When Shakespeare penned his tragedy *Hamlet* in 1602, he used Kronborg Slot (calling it Elsinore) as its setting. There is no evidence that Shakespeare ever visited Helsingør, but when the stately Kronborg Slot was completed in 1585, word of it was heralded far and wide and it apparently struck Shakespeare as a fitting setting. Although the play was fiction, Shakespeare did include two actual Danish nobles in his plot – Frederik Rosenkrantz and Knud Gyldenstierne (Guildenstern), both of whom had visited the English court in the 1590s.

The fact that Hamlet, the Prince of Denmark, was a fictional character has not deterred legions of sightseers from visiting 'Hamlet's Castle'. Indeed, due to the fame bestowed on it by Shakespeare, Kronborg is the most widely known castle in all of Scandinavia.

During the past few decades, Kronborg Slot has been used many times as the setting for staged performances of *Hamlet*, featuring such prominent actors as Sir Laurence Olivier, Richard Burton, Michael Redgrave, Kenneth Branagh and Simon Russel Beale.

Excursions – Helsingør

Also housed in the castle is **Handels- og Søfartsmuseet** (Danish Maritime Museum), a collection of model ships, paintings, nautical instruments and sea charts illustrating the history of Danish shipping and trade. Model ship enthusiasts will find it very interesting, and even those who aren't of a nautical disposition will soon get the idea that shipping is a very important part of Øresund life. The remains of the original Krogen fortress can be seen in the masonry of the museum's showrooms No 21 and 22.

Kronborg is 1km from the Helsingør train station (see the Helsingør Walking Tour for a suggested route) but you can also take the Hornbæk-bound train to Grønnehave station and walk east for a few minutes to the castle.

About 1.5km northwest of the town centre is **Marienlyst Slot**, a three-storey manor house. It was built in 1763 in the Louis XV neoclassical style by French architect NH Jardin and encompasses parts of an early summerhouse constructed by Frederik II. The interior exhibits include local paintings and silverwork. Hornbæk-bound trains stop at Marienlyst station, just north of the manor house.

If you'd like to examine technological inventions from the late 19th and early 20th centuries, the **Danmarks Tekniske Museum**, opposite the hostel, displays early gramophones, radios, motor vehicles and a 1906 Danish-built aeroplane that lays claim to being the first plane ever flown in Europe (it stayed airborne for a sizzling 11 seconds!). It's a short walk east from Højstrup train station, or you can take bus No 805.

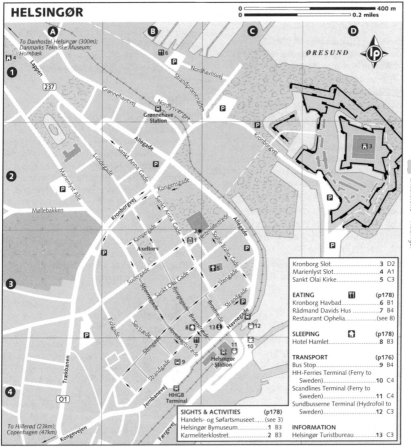

HELSINGØR

| | 400 m |
| | 0.2 miles |

ØRESUND

Kronborg Slot	3 D2
Marienlyst Slot	4 A1
Sankt Olai Kirke	5 C3
EATING 🍴	(p178)
Kronborg Havbad	6 B1
Rådmand Davids Hus	7 B4
Restaurant Ophelia	(see 8)
SLEEPING 🏠	(p178)
Hotel Hamlet	8 B3
TRANSPORT	(p176)
Bus Stop	9 B4
HH-Ferries Terminal (Ferry to Sweden)	10 C4
Scandlines Terminal (Ferry to Sweden)	11 C4
Sundbusserne Terminal (Hydrofoil to Sweden)	12 C3
SIGHTS & ACTIVITIES	(p178)
Handels- og Søfartsmuseet	(see 3)
Helsingør Bymuseum	1 B3
Karmeliterklostret	2 B3
INFORMATION	
Helsingør Turistbureau	13 C3

Helsingør Walking Tour

This little walk through the oldest parts of Helsingør takes a scenic, and virtually direct, route to Kronborg Slot. Begin the walk at the northern side of the tourist office; stroll up Brostræde, a pedestrian alley, and then continue north along Sankt Anna Gade.

You'll soon come to the 15th-century Gothic cathedral **Sankt Olai Kirke**, which occupies the block between Stengade and Sankt Olai Gade. The cathedral has an ornate altar and baptistry.

A block further north is **Helsingør Bymuseum**, Sankt Anna Gade 36, built by the monks of the adjacent monastery in 1516 to serve as a sailors' hospital. It did stints as a poorhouse and a town library before being converted to a history museum in 1973. The hotchpotch of exhibits includes antique dolls and a model of Helsingør as it was in 1801. **Karmeliterklostret** (Carmelite monastery), comprising the red-brick buildings north of the Bymuseum, is one of Scandinavia's best-preserved medieval monasteries. Christian II's mistress, Dyveke, is thought to have been buried at the monastery when she died in 1517. To continue on to Kronborg Slot, follow Sankt Anna Gade to Kronborgvej, turn right and follow that road to the castle, about a 15-minute walk away. En route, at the intersection with Allégade, is a little public garden where flowers attract colourful butterflies.

Sights & Information

Danmarks Tekniske Museum (☎ 49 22 26 11; www .tekniskmuseum.dk; Fabriksvej 25; adult/child 50/25kr; ✆ 10am-5pm Tue-Sun)

Handels- og Søfartsmuseet (☎ 49 21 06 85; www .maritime-museum.dk; Kronborg Slot; adult/child 30/10kr, combined ticket adult/child 75/25kr; ✆ 10.30am-5pm May-Sep, 11am-4pm Tue-Sun Apr & Oct, 11am-3pm Tue-Sun Nov-Mar)

Helsingør Bymuseum (☎ 49 28 18 00; www.helsingor .dk/museum; Sankt Anna Gade 36; adult/child 10kr/free; ✆ noon-4pm)

Helsingør Turistbureau (☎ 49 21 13 33; www.visit helsingor.dk; Havnepladsen 3; ✆ 9am-6pm Mon-Fri, 9am-4pm Sat Jun-Aug, 9am-4pm Mon-Fri, 10am-1pm Sat Sep-May) Opposite the train station and offering a wide range of services, including selling phonecards.

Kronborg Slot (☎ 49 21 30 78; www.kronborgslot.dk; adult/child 50/15kr; combined ticket adult/child 75/25kr; ✆ 10.30am-5pm May-Sep, 11am-4pm Tue-Sun Apr & Oct, 11am-3pm Tue-Sun Nov-Mar)

Marienlyst Slot (☎ 49 28 18 30; www.helsingor .dk/museum; Marienlyst Allé 32; adult/child 20kr/free; ✆ noon-4pm)

Eating

Kronborg Havbad (☎ 49 20 13 30; Strandpromenaden 6; mains 78-138kr; ✆ 11.30am-11pm, closed Mon-Wed Oct-Mar) This is a breezy, cheery spot for lunch on a sunny day, and it has wheelchair access and children's menus. Try to get your hands on some Wiibroe pilsener – it's Helsingør's own brew.

Restaurant Ophelia (☎ 49 21 05 91; www.hotelhamlet.dk; Bramstræde 5; mains 132-195kr; ✆ 9am-11pm) Attached to (what else?) Hotel Hamlet, the lovely Restaurant Ophelia

provides hearty Danish fare to guests and visitors in pleasant surrounds. There's not much for vegetarians though.

Rådmand Davids Hus (Strandgade 70; mains 98-178kr; ✆ 10am-10pm Mon-Sat) This popular café is housed in a 300-year-old half-timbered building. The special is the 'shopping lunch' (68kr), a generous plate of traditional Danish foods, typically salmon pâté, salad and slices of pork, cheese and bread, served 10am to 4pm Monday to Saturday.

Sleeping

Danhostel Helsingør (☎ 49 21 16 40; www.helsingorhostel .dk; Strandvej 24; dm 110kr, r 350-650kr) Two kilometres northwest of the town centre in a renovated coastal manor house with its own beach access. This 180-bed hostel is open year-round except during December and January. Most of the rooms have baths and just two to six beds, and many are equipped for disabled visitors. From Helsingør train station catch bus No 340 or take the train to Højstrup Trinbræt.

Hotel Hamlet (☎ 49 21 05 91; www.hotelhamlet.dk; Bramstræde 5; s/d from 695/925kr) The sweetly run Hamlet has 36 rooms with private bath, phone and TV, and some have great traditional touches such as low, beamed ceilings. Ask about Scan+ and other discount schemes that can sometimes lower the rate.

Detour

If you're driving up the coast to Helsingør, ignore the motorway and take the coastal road, Strandvej (Route 152), which is far more scenic. The Øresund coast, which extends north from Copenhagen to the Helsingør area, is largely a succession of small seaside suburbs and yachting harbours. On clear days you can look across the Øresund (Sound), which separates Denmark from Sweden, and see southern Sweden on the opposite shore.

HORNBÆK

The north coast of Zealand, also known as the Kattegat coast, is a charming mix of dunes, heathlands and coastal woodlands. Development is limited to a handful of small fishing towns that date back to the 1500s, their backstreets bordered by half-timbered thatch-roofed houses with tidy flower gardens. Although the towns have only a few thousand residents in winter, the population swells with throngs of beachgoers in summer.

Hornbæk has the best beach on the north coast, a vast expanse of soft white sand that runs the entire length of the town. It's backed by sand dunes with beach grass and thickets of *Rosa rugosa*, a wild pink seaside rose that blooms all summer. Even though it borders the town the beach is pleasantly undeveloped, with all of the commercial facilities on the inland side of the dunes.

Danish poet Holger Drachmann, who died in Hornbæk in 1908, is memorialised by a harbourside monument. These days the salty fisherfolk, about whom Drachmann often wrote, share their harbour with scores of sailing boats and yachts.

From the train station it's a five-minute walk directly north along Havnevej to the harbour. Climb the dunes to the left and you're on the beach.

The **beach** is Hornbæk's main attraction and offers good swimming conditions and plenty of space for sunbathing.

If you're interested in windsurfing, contact Hornbæk Surfudlejning og Surfskole, which provides gear rental and lessons. To charter a boat to go fishing, contact the tourist office or the

Transport

Distance from Copenhagen 63km

Direction North

Travel time Between Helsingør and Hornbæk it's 25 minutes by train.

Car Take the Strandvej all the way up the north coast or inland route 19 (E47/E55).

Train Trains between Helsingør and Hornbæk (25.50kr, 25 minutes) run about twice hourly on weekdays, once hourly at weekends.

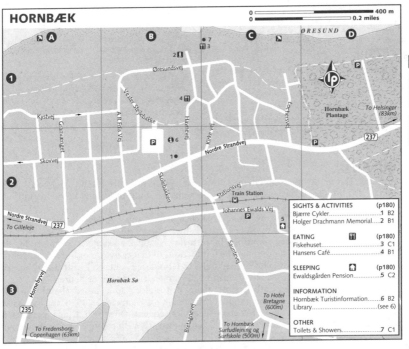

HORNBÆK

ØRESUND

To Helsingør (83km)

Hornbæk Plantage

Øresundsvej

Nordre Strandvej

To Gilleleje

Train Station

Johannes Ewalds Vej

Hornbæk Sø

To Hotel Bretagne (600m)

To Fredensborg; Copenhagen (63km)

To Hornbæk Surfudlejning og Surfskole (500m)

SIGHTS & ACTIVITIES	(p180)
Bjærre Cykler	1 B2
Holger Drachmann Memorial	2 B1

EATING	(p180)
Fiskehuset	3 C1
Hansens Café	4 B1

SLEEPING	(p180)
Ewaldsgården Pension	5 C2

INFORMATION	
Hornbæk Turistinformation	6 B2
Library	(see 6)

OTHER	
Toilets & Showers	7 C1

harbourmaster's office at the southern side of the harbour; expect to pay from 450kr to 850kr depending upon boat size. You can rent bicycles at Bjærre Cykler on Nordre Strandvej.

If you're up for an enjoyable nature stroll, **Hornbæk Plantage**, a public woodland that extends 3.5km along the coast east from Hornbæk, has numerous interconnecting trails branching out either side of route 237. There are wild roses along the coast and pine trees and flowering Scotch broom inland. One trail follows the coast from Lochersvej in Hornbæk to the eastern end of the *plantage*. Other trails go inland, including one path that leads to Hornbæk Camping. There are several areas along Nordre Strandvej (route 237) where you can park a car and start your wanderings. A free forestry map, *Vandreture i Statsskovene, Hornbæk Plantage*, shows all the trails and is available from the tourist office.

Bravery & Brawn for Brauwn

In 1774, Hornbæk fishermen came to the rescue of British captain Thomas Brauwn, whose ship was being battered by a raging storm. These unhesitant Danes, braving treacherous seas, so inspired their country folk that a popular play, *Fiskerne*, was written about them by the lyricist poet Johannes Ewald. A song taken from the play became Denmark's national anthem. The rescue was also immortalised by the artist CW Eckersberg, who used it as a theme in a number of his paintings.

Sights & Information

Bjærre Cykler (☎ 49 70 32 82; Nordre Strandvej 338; bicycle hire per day from 75kr)

Hornbæk Surfudlejning og Surfskole (☎ 49 70 33 75; Drejervej 19; windsurf hire per day from 300kr, lessons from 550kr)

Hornbæk Turistinformation (☎ 49 70 47 47; www .hornbaek.dk; Vester Stejlebakke 2A; ☻ 1-7pm Mon, 1-5pm Tue, 10am-5pm Wed, 1-5pm Thu, 10am-5pm Fri, 10am-2pm Sat) Inside the library – to get there take the walkway at the side of Den Danske Bank.

Eating

Fiskehuset (☎ 4970 04 37; Havnevej 32; ☻ Mon-Sun Apr-Sep, Sat & Sun Oct-Mar) One of a number of eating opportunities down at the harbour, Fiskehuset sells peel-and-eat shrimp by weight.

Hansens Café (☎ 49 70 04 79; Havnevej 19; smørrebrød from 32kr; ☻ from 4pm Mon-Sat, from noon Sun) A great,

casual eatery in the town's oldest house – a sod-roofed and half-timbered building with a pleasant pub-like atmosphere. The handwritten menu changes daily but you can expect to find good Danish food at moderate prices.

Sleeping

Ewaldsgården Pension (☎ 49 70 00 82; www.ewalds gaarden.dk; Johannes Ewalds Vej 5; s/d 450/675kr, f 900kr) Southeast of the train station and about a 10-minute walk from the harbour, this beautiful place occupies an early-18th-century country house. The interior is light and airy with a cosy mix of antiques and cottage-style furnishings. All 12 rooms have a washbasin; shared showers and toilets are off the hall.

Hotel Bretagne (☎ 49 70 16 66; www.hotelbretagne .dk; Sauntevej 18; s/d from 650/1150kr) The Bretagne stands sentinel-like on top of a hill and is the last word in Scandinavian restraint. Rooms are well equipped though and there are some good views to be had from some of the 29 rooms.

ROSKILDE

Roskilde, Denmark's first capital, was a thriving trade centre throughout the Middle Ages. It was also the site of Zealand's first Christian church, built by Viking king Harald Bluetooth in AD 980.

In 1026 Canute I, in a rage over a chess match, had his brother-in-law Ulf Jarl assassinated in that church. Ulf's widow, Canute's sister Estrid, insisted that the wooden stave church in which her husband was ambushed be torn down, and then donated property for the construction of a new stone church. The foundations of that early stone church are beneath the floor of the present-day Roskilde Domkirke (Roskilde Cathedral). Estrid and her son Svend Estridsen are among many Danish royals now buried in the cathedral.

As the centre of Danish Catholicism, medieval Roskilde had a cathedral and nearly 20 churches and monasteries. After the Reformation swept Denmark in 1536, the monasteries and most of the churches were demolished. Consequently the town, which had been in decline since the capital moved to Copenhagen in the early 15th century, saw its population shrink radically.

Transport

Distance from Copenhagen 35km

Direction West

Travel time 25 minutes

Car From Copenhagen, Route 21, then exit onto Route 156, which leads into Roskilde's centre. Car park at the Viking Ship Museum.

Train Trains from Copenhagen to Roskilde are frequent (51kr)

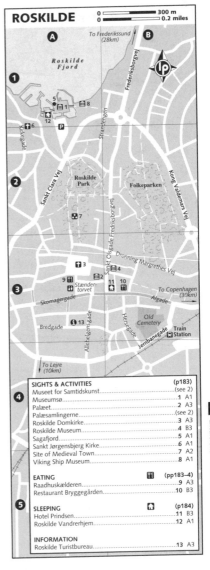

Today, Roskilde is a likeable, low-profile town with about 52,000 inhabitants, on Denmark's main east–west train route. Each summer it hosts a huge international music festival which attracts thousands of people from Denmark and around the world. For more information on the Roskilde Festival, see p126.

Although most of Roskilde's medieval buildings have vanished in fires over the centuries, **Roskilde Domkirke** still dominates the city centre. Begun in 1170 by Bishop Absalon, the cathedral has been rebuilt and added to so many times that it represents a millennium of Danish architectural styles.

Roskilde Domkirke is a Unesco World Heritage Site. It boasts tall spires, a splendid interior and the crypts of 37 Danish kings and queens. Some of the crypts are spectacularly embellished and guarded by marble statues of knights and women in mourning, while others are simple stone coffins. There's something quite awesome about being able to stand next to the bones of so many of Scandinavia's most powerful historical figures.

Of particular interest is the chapel of King Christian IV, off the northern side of the cathedral. It contains the coffin of Christian flanked by his young son, Prince Christian, and his wife, Anne Cathrine, as well as the brass coffins of his successor, Frederik III, and his wife, Queen Sofie Amalie. The bronze statue of Christian IV beside the entranceway is the work of Bertel Thorvaldsen, while the huge wall-sized paintings, encased in trompe l'oeil frames, were created by Wilhelm Marstrand and include a classic scene depicting Christian IV rallying the troops aboard the warship *Trinity* during the 1644 battle of Kolbergerheide.

Some of the cathedral's finest pieces were installed by Christian IV, including the intricately detailed pulpit made of marble, alabaster and sandstone in 1610 by Copenhagen sculptor Hans Brokman.

The enormous gilt 'cupboard-style' altarpiece, made in 1560 in Antwerp, is adorned with 21 plates depicting the life of Christ. The story of how it came to Roskilde is as interesting as the piece. Apparently, when the altarpiece was being sent to its intended destination of Gdansk, its shipper attempted to cheat on the sound dues in Helsingør by

181

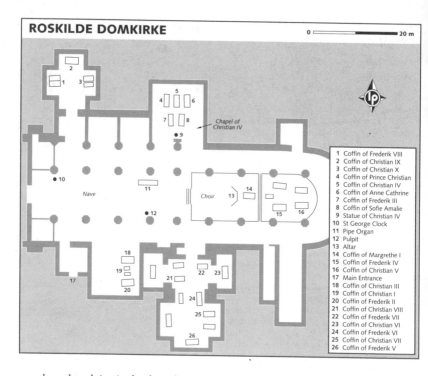

ROSKILDE DOMKIRKE

0 — 20 m

Chapel of Christian IV

Nave

Choir

1 Coffin of Frederik VIII
2 Coffin of Christian IX
3 Coffin of Christian X
4 Coffin of Prince Christian
5 Coffin of Christian IV
6 Coffin of Anne Cathrine
7 Coffin of Frederik III
8 Coffin of Sofie Amalie
9 Statue of Christian IV
10 St George Clock
11 Pipe Organ
12 Pulpit
13 Altar
14 Coffin of Margrethe I
15 Coffin of Frederik IV
16 Coffin of Christian V
17 Main Entrance
18 Coffin of Christian III
19 Coffin of Christian I
20 Coffin of Frederik II
21 Coffin of Christian VIII
22 Coffin of Frederik VII
23 Coffin of Christian VI
24 Coffin of Frederik VI
25 Coffin of Christian VII
26 Coffin of Frederik V

grossly undervaluing it; the shrewd customs officer, asserting his right to acquire items at their valuation price, snapped up the altarpiece.

An unusually light-hearted item is the cathedral's early-16th-century clock, poised above the entrance, on which a tiny St George on horseback marks the hour by slaying a yelping dragon.

It's not unusual for the cathedral to be closed on Saturdays for weddings and occasionally on other days for funerals. You can check in advance whether it's open by calling the tourist office, or by checking the notice board at the church's entrance.

Free concerts given on the splendid 16th-century baroque pipe organ are held at 8pm every Thursday in June, July and August.

The intriguing **Viking Ship Museum** displays five reconstructed Viking ships (c AD 1000) which were excavated from the bottom of Roskilde Fjord in 1962. The wooden ship fragments are reassembled on new skeleton frames that provide a very good idea of the shape, size and structural elements of these fine vessels. As some of the wood was lost over the centuries, none of the ships are complete but all have been reconstructed enough that with some good descriptive text as support (in English) you should have no hassle re-creating a sense of what it was like to go to sea in Viking times.

The ships include an 18m warship of the type used to raid England and a 16.5m trader that may once have carried cargo between Greenland and Denmark. Appropriately, the museum is at the eastern side of the harbour overlooking Roskilde Fjord, which provides a scenic backdrop for the displays.

The latest addition to this seaside attraction is **Museumsø** (Museum Island), a relatively new harbourfront facility adjacent to the main museum. At this pier-like island, craftspeople painstakingly employ Viking-era techniques and tools to build replicas of Viking ships. Three substantial replicas, *Helge Ask, Kraka Fyr* and *Roar Ege,* are moored in the harbour and numerous other reconstructions are in the works. Museumsø also holds an archaeological workshop where recent excavations are being preserved and analysed by researchers from the National Museum.

Summer is a fun time to visit as there are seasonal workshops where children can try their hand at sail making and other maritime crafts, and possibilities for taking short sailing trips on the fjord.

After visiting the Viking Ship Museum, a five-minute walk west along the harbour will bring you to the **Sankt Jørgensbjerg quarter**, where the cobbled Kirkegade leads through a neighbourhood of old thatch-roofed houses and into the courtyard of the hill-top **Sankt Jørgensbjerg Kirke**. This church – with a nave dating from the 11th century – is one of the oldest in Denmark.

The well-presented and organised **Roskilde Museum** covers Roskilde's history in displays ranging from the Stone Age up to the contemporary 'rock age' of the Roskilde Festival. And naturally there's coverage of Roskilde's glory days as the former capital of Denmark.

Palæet (the Palace), an attractive 18th-century baroque building fronting Torvet, is a former bishops' residence that now houses **Museet for Samtidskunst** (Museum of Contemporary Art), a small museum with changing exhibits that covers the bases from out-there digital art to soundscapes, and the **Palæsamlingerne** (Palace Collections), which contains 18th- and 19th-century paintings and various objects that once belonged to wealthy Roskilde merchants.

Seafaring types can take a turn on the water with the MS **Sagafjord**, which sails from Roskilde Harbour around the fjord.

Sights & Information

Museet for Samtidskunst (☎ 46 31 65 70; Stændertorvet 3D; adult/concession/child 20/10kr/free; ⏲ 11am-5pm Tue-Fri, noon-4pm Sat & Sun)

Museumsø (☎ 46 30 03 00; www.vikingeskibsmuseet .dk; Vindeboder 12; adult/concession/child 75/55/25kr May-Sep, adult/concession/child 45/35/25kr Oct-Apr; ⏲ 10am-5pm)

Palæsamlingerne (☎ 46 35 78 80; Stændertorvet 3E; adult/concession/child 25/15kr/free; ⏲ 11am-4pm 15 May-14 Sep, noon-4pm Sat 18 Sep-14 May)

Roskilde Domkirke (☎ 46 31 65 65; www.roskilde domkirke.dk; Domkirkepladsen; adult/child 25/15kr; ⏲ 9am-4.45pm Mon-Fri, 9am-noon Sat, 12.30-4.45pm Sun Apr-Sep, 10am-3.45pm Tue-Sat, 12.30-3.45pm Sun Oct-Mar, guided tours in English 11am & 2pm Mon-Fri, 11am Sat, 2pm Sun 20 Jun-15 Aug)

Roskilde Museum (Sankt Olsgade 18; adult/concession/ child 25/15kr/free; ⏲ 11am-4pm)

Roskilde Turistbureau (☎ 46 35 27 00; Gullandsstræde 15; ⏲ 9am-5pm Mon-Fri, 10am-1pm Sat) Good town maps and plenty of information about Roskilde and surrounds.

Sagafjord (☎ 46 75 64 60; www.sagafjord.dk; adult/child 85/35kr; sailings Apr-Oct)

Viking Ship Museum (☎ 46 30 03 00; www.vikingeskibs museet.dk; Vindeboder 12; adult/concession/child 75/55/25kr May-Sep, adult/concession/child 45/35/25kr Oct-Apr; ⏲ 10am-5pm)

Eating

Market at Stændertorvet (Stændertorvet; ⏲ mornings Wed & Sat) Fresh fruit and vegetables as well as handicrafts and flowers.

Raadhuskælderen (☎ 46 36 01 00; www.raadhusk.dk; Fondens Bro 1; mains 148-218kr; ⏲ 11am-11pm Mon-Sat) In the cellar of the old town hall (c 1430), and not short on atmosphere – or lava-rock BBQ dishes for the

Digging up the Past

Towards the end of the Viking era, the narrower necks of Roskilde Fjord were purposely blocked to prevent raids by Norwegian fleets. The five Viking ships that are now displayed at Roskilde's Viking Ship Museum were thought to have been deliberately sunk in one such channel and then piled with rocks to make a reinforced barrier similar to an underwater stone wall. Although people had long suspected that there was a ship beneath the ridge of stones, folklore had led them to believe it was a single ship sunk by Queen Margrethe in the 15th century.

It wasn't until researchers from the National Museum made a series of exploratory dives in the late 1950s that it was discovered that there were several ships at the site and that they dated from the Viking period. Excavations began in 1962, when a cofferdam was built around the ships in the middle of the fjord and pumps were used to drain seawater from the site. Within just four months archaeologists were able to unpile the mound of stones and excavate the ships, whose wooden hulks were now in thousands of pieces. The ship fragments were then reassembled within a purpose-built museum that opened on the harbourfront in 1969.

In the mid-1990s, during the deepening of the harbour and the construction of an artificial island west of the museum, workers were stunned to discover nine more ships, seven dating from the Middle Ages and two from the Viking period. The largest is a 36m-long Viking ship thought to have been built in 1030. In response to these new finds, the National Museum established an archaeological workshop right on the site where the recovered ship fragments are cleaned, preserved and documented.

happy carnivore. Not a bad spot if you don't mind being away from the main action.

Restaurant Bryggegården (☎ 46 35 01 03; Algade 15; mains 98-158kr; ☺ 11am-11pm Mon-Sat, noon-10pm Sun) This cheery pub does a mean weekend brunch (98kr) and has surprisingly flash toilets.

Sleeping

Hotel Prindsen (☎ 46 30 91 00; www.prindsen.dk; Algade 13; s/d from 1175/1275kr) Denmark's oldest continuously operating hotel (since 1695) and its guest list reads like a who's who of great Danes, from King Frederik VII to Hans Christian Andersen. As befits an old hotel, the rooms are different sizes and have varied décor, but all are sumptuous and pretty damn sexy.

Roskilde Vandrerhjem (☎ 46 35 21 84; Vindeboder 7; dm 110kr, d per person 175-200kr; ☺ year-round) Adjacent to the Viking Ship Museum with 152 beds in 40 rooms (some with water views, each has its own bathroom). With TV lounge, guest kitchen and laundry. An excellent-value hostel.

SOUTHERN ZEALAND

Southern Zealand lacks many of the obvious charms of the north, but that may well be part of its appeal. Instead of a wealth of palaces, galleries and glamorous coastal strips, you'll find regular Danish life lived at an enjoyably relaxed pace – and a few historical diversions that will capture your interest.

If you're travelling across the region with your own transport, the rural route 150 makes a fine alternative to zipping along on the E20 motorway. Not only is it a slower, greener route but it will take you right into some interesting towns and villages.

KØGE

Køge has a rich history that dates from 1288, when it was granted its municipal charter by King Erik VI. With its large natural harbour, Køge quickly developed into a thriving fishing and trade centre.

In 1677 one of the most important naval engagements of the Danish–Swedish wars was fought in the waters off Køge. Known as the Battle of Køge Bay, it made a legend of Danish admiral Niels Juel, who resoundingly defeated the attacking Swedish navy and thwarted their attempted invasion.

Today the harbour still plays an important role in Køge's economy, having been developed into a modern commercial facility.

While parts of the city have been industrialised, Køge has done a superb job of retaining the period character of its central historic quarter. The narrow streets that radiate from Torvet, the town square, are lined with old buildings, some that survived a sweeping fire in 1633 and many others that were built in the construction boom spawned by that blaze.

Sankt Nicolai Kirke, on Kirkestræde, two blocks north of Torvet, is named after St Nicholas, the patron saint of mariners. At the upper eastern end of the church tower there's a little brick projection called the Lygten, which for centuries was used to hang a burning lantern as a guide for sailors returning to the harbour. It was from atop the church tower that Christian IV kept watch on his naval fleet as it successfully defended the town from Swedish invaders during the Battle of Køge Bay.

The church dates from 1324, but was largely rebuilt in the 15th century. Most of the ornately carved works that adorn the interior were added later, including the 17th-century altar and pulpit. In midsummer you can climb the tower between 10am and 1.30pm.

Køge Museum occupies a lovely building dating from 1619 that was once a wealthy merchant's home and store. It now holds a few dozen exhibit rooms illustrating the

Transport

Distance from Copenhagen 42km
Direction Southwest
Travel time 40 minutes
Car Take the E47/55 from Copenhagen and then pick up Route 151 south into the centre of Køge. Free parking on Torvet (one-hour limit during business hours); less-restricted parking off Havnen, north of the harbour.
Train Køge is at the end of the E (and A+) lines, the southernmost point of greater Copenhagen's S-train network. Trains from Copenhagen run three to six times an hour (51kr).

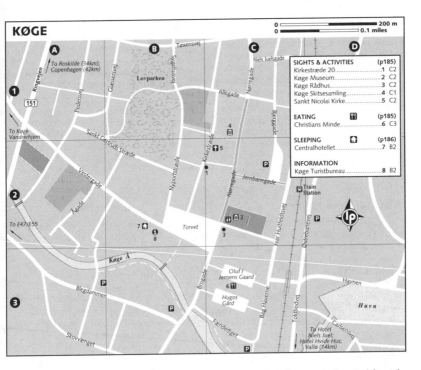

KØGE

SIGHTS & ACTIVITIES	(p185)
Kirkestræde 20	1 C2
Køge Museum	2 C2
Køge Rådhus	3 C2
Køge Skitsesamling	4 C1
Sankt Nicolai Kirke	5 C2

EATING	(p185)
Christians Minde	6 C3

SLEEPING	(p186)
Centralhotellet	7 B2

INFORMATION	
Køge Turistbureau	8 B2

cultural history of the town and surrounding region. As well as the expected period furnishings and artefacts, there's an interestinghotchpotch of displays ranging from a Mesolithic-era grave to recently discovered silver coins, part of a huge stash thought to have been hidden during the Swedish wars of the late 17th century. The museum also has a desk used by Danish philosopher NFS Grundtvig, who lived on the outskirts of Køge, and a windowpane onto which Hans Christian Andersen, during an apparently stressed-out stay at a nearby inn, scratched the words 'Oh God, Oh God in Kjøge'.

The **Køge Skitsesamling** (Art and Sketch Collection), Nørregade 29, is a unique art museum that specialises in outlining the creative process from an artist's earliest concept to the finished work. The displays include original drawings, clay models and mock-ups by several 20th-century Danish artists. The admission fee also covers the aforementioned Køge Museum.

Sights & Information

Køge Museum (☎ 56 63 42 42; Nørregade 4; adult/child 25/20kr; 🕙 11am-5pm Jun-Aug, 1-5pm Tue-Fri & Sun, 11am-3pm Sat Sep-May)

Køge Skitsesamling (☎ 56 67 60 20; Nørregade 29; adult/child 30kr/free; 🕙 11am-5pm Tue-Sun)

Køge Turistbureau (☎ 56 67 60 01; www.koegeturist.dk; Vestergade 1; 🕙 9am-5pm Mon-Fri year-round, 9am-3pm Sat Jun-Aug, 10am-1pm Sat Sep-May) Near Torvet, and distributes a free booklet, with English and German translations, describing the town's sights.

Sankt Nicolai Kirke (☎ 56 65 13 59; Kirkestræde 20; admission free; 🕙 10am-4pm Mon-Fri, 10am-noon Sat mid-Jun–31 Aug, 10am-noon Sat & Sun Sep–mid-Jun)

Eating

Billeder Restaurant (☎ 56 65 36 90; www.hotelhvide hus.dk; Strandvejen 111) The restaurant inside Hotel Hvide Hus. There's not much on offer for vegetarians, but there are plenty of excellent dishes for carnivores or 'vegaquarians', including the salmon tartar.

Christians Minde (☎ 56 63 68 56; Brogade 7; mains 138-198kr; 🕙 11.30am-10pm) The town's affordable fine-dining option.

Quintus (☎ 56 63 18 00; www.hotelnielsjuel.dk; Toldbodvej 20; mains from 145kr) Inside Hotel Niels Juel and serving some very fine fish and meat dishes. A good selection of wine is also available.

Sleeping

Centralhotellet (☎ 56 65 06 96; fax 56 66 02 07; Vestergade 3; s/d incl breakfast 450/630kr) Fittingly named, and adjacent to the tourist office, this place has a dozen rooms above a small bar and in a separate wing out back. The rooms, which are straightforward but adequate, have bathrooms.

Hotel Hvide Hus (☎ 56 65 36 90; www.hotelhvidehus .dk; Strandvejen 111; s/d from 775/1175kr), near the beach at the less-developed southern end of town. It has 126 modern, comfortable rooms that are often reduced in price on summer weekends. Some lovely views of the harbour and the beach are available.

Hotel Niels Juel (☎ 56 63 18 00; www.hotelnielsjuel.dk; Toldbodvej 20; s/d 965/1195kr) Near the inner harbour, a couple of blocks south of the train station, is a modern 50-room hotel with some very pleasant water views from most rooms – and plenty of comfy amenities. Summer weekend prices drop to a very decent 875kr for a single or double.

Køge Vandrerhjem (☎ 56 65 14 74; www.danhostel.dk; Vamdrupvej 1; dm 100kr, r 440-500kr) This 72-bed hostel is in a quiet neighbourhood 2km northwest of the town centre. The hostel is open from 1 March to 1 December. To get there from the Køge train station, take bus No 210, get off at Agerskovvej and follow the signs to the hostel, 400m away.

Detour from Køge

Vallø is a charming hamlet with cobblestone streets, a dozen mustard-yellow houses and an attractive moat-encircled Renaissance castle, Vallø Slot. Situated in the countryside about 7km south of Køge, Vallø makes an enjoyable excursion for those looking to get off the beaten path. If old-world character and mildly eccentric surroundings appeal, it could also be a fun place to spend the evening.

The red-brick **Vallø Slot** dates from 1586 and retains most of its original style, even though much of it was rebuilt following a fire in 1893.

The castle has a rather unusual history. On her birthday in 1737, Queen Sophie Magdalene, who owned the estate, established a foundation that turned Vallø Slot into a home for 'spinsters of noble birth'. Until a few decades ago, unmarried daughters of Danish royalty who hadn't the means to live in their own castles or manor houses were allowed to take up residence at Vallø, supported by the foundation and government social programs.

In the 1970s, bowing to changing sentiments that had previously spared this anachronistic niche of the Zealand countryside, the foundation amended its charter to gradually make the estate more accessible to the general public. For now, the castle remains home solely to a handful of ageing blue-blooded women who had taken up residence prior to 1976.

Vallø Slot is surrounded by 2800 hectares of woods and ponds and 1300 hectares of fields and arable land reaching down to the coast. Although the main castle buildings are not yet open to the public, visitors can walk in the gardens and adjacent woods.

Hestestalden, the stables at Vallø Slot, has an exhibition on the history of the castle. Entry free if you have a same-day Køge Museum ticket.

Information

Vallø Slot (☽ 11am-4pm)
Hestestalden (adult/child 20/10kr; ☽ 11am-4pm mid-May–Aug)

Sleeping & Eating

Vallø Slotskro (☎ 56 26 70 20; Slotsgade 1; s/d 745/925kr) This 200-year-old inn sits just outside the castle gate. The 11 pleasantly decorated rooms feature lots of floral fabric and much drapery. All rooms have TV and a phone, and a few rooms with shared bathrooms are cheaper. The inn's restaurant serves moderately priced Danish country cuisine with a changing menu.

Transport

Distance from Copenhagen 49km
Direction Southwest
Travel time 55 minutes
Car By car, take route 209 south from Køge, turn right onto Billesborgvej and then left onto Valløvej, which leads to Slotsgade.
Train Take the train to Vallø station, two stops south of Køge, and from there it's a pleasant 1.25km stroll east down a tree-lined country road to the castle.

RINGSTED

Situated at a crossroads in central Zealand, Ringsted was an important market town during the Middle Ages and also served as the site of the *landsting*, a regional governing assembly. The town grew up around the Sankt Bendts Kirke, which was built during the reign of Valdemar I (1157–82). This historic church still marks the town centre and is Ringsted's most interesting sight.

Immediately east of the church is Torvet, the central square, which has a statue of Valdemar I sculpted by Johannes Bjerg in the 1930s, as well as three sitting stones that were used centuries ago by the *landsting* members.

The imposing **Sankt Bendts Kirke**, erected in 1170, is a monument to the political intrigue and power struggles of its day. Valdemar I built it partly to serve as a burial sanctuary for his murdered father, Knud Lavard, who had just been canonised by the Pope, and partly as a calculated move to shore up the rule of the Valdemar dynasty and intertwine the influences of the Crown and the Catholic Church.

Although Sankt Bendts Kirke was substantially restored in the 1900s, it retains much of its original medieval style and still incorporates travertine blocks from an 11th-century abbey church that had earlier occupied the same site.

The nave is adorned with magnificent frescoes, including a series depicting Erik IV (known as Erik Ploughpenny, for the despised tax he levied on ploughs), which were painted in about 1300 in a failed campaign to get the assassinated king canonised. These frescoes show Queen Agnes, seated on a throne; on her left is a scene of Ploughpenny's murderers stabbing the king with a spear, while the right-hand scene depicts the king's corpse being retrieved from the sea by fishermen.

Sankt Bendts Kirke was a burial place for the royal family for 150 years. In the aisle floor beneath the nave (in order from the font) are flat stones marking the tombs of Valdemar III and his queen, Eleonora; Valdemar II, flanked by his queens Dagmar and Bengærd; Knud VI; Valdemar I, flanked by his queen, Sofia, and his son Christoffer; and Knud Lavard. Also buried in the church is Erik VI (Menved) and Queen Ingeborg, whose remains lie in an ornate tomb in the chancel, and King Birger of Sweden and his queen Margarete, who occupy the former tomb of Erik Ploughpenny. Some of the tombs, including the empty one that once held Queen Dagmar, have been disturbed over the centuries to make room for later burials. A few of the grave relics removed from these tombs can be found in the museum chapel.

The church also has some interesting carved works, including pews from 1591 (note the dragons on the seats near the altar), an elaborate altarpiece from 1699 and a pulpit from 1609. The oldest item in the church is the 12th-century baptismal font, which, despite its historical significance, once served a stint as a flower bowl in a local garden.

Note that the church is closed whenever there are weddings, a particularly common occurrence on Saturdays in spring. There are free concerts on the first Saturday of the month at 12.30pm.

Ringsted Museum, a small repository of local cultural history, includes a restored 1814 Dutch windmill, and is on the eastern side of town, within walking distance of Torvet and the train station.

Built Like a Brick Church

Shortly after the end of the Viking era, two things happened that had a significant and lasting impact on church architecture in Denmark. First, King Sweyn II (1047–74) found himself deep in a power struggle with the Archbishop of Bremen, the leader of the Danish Church. To weaken the influence of the archbishop, the king divided Denmark into eight separate diocese, which set the stage for a flurry of new church and cathedral building.

Then, in the 12th century, the art of brick-making was introduced to Denmark from northern Italy and Germany. Before that, most churches were constructed of wood or calcareous tufa and rough stone. The use of bricks allowed for construction on a much larger scale and within a few decades grand churches were being built all around Denmark. A couple of the churches from that era still stand today, including Sankt Bendts Kirke in Ringsted and the Roskilde Domkirke.

Sights & Information

Ringsted Museum (☎ 57 62 69 02; http://museum
.ringsted.dk; Køgevej 41; adult/child 25/10kr;
🕐 11am-4pm Tue-Thu, Sat & Sun)

Ringsted Turistbureau (☎ 57 61 34 00; www.met-2000.
dk; Sankt Bendtsgade 6; 🕐 10am-5pm Mon-Fri year-round,
9am-2pm Sat 15 Jun-31 Aug, 10am-1pm Sat 1 Sep-14 Jun) A
friendly info point at the northern side of Sankt Bendts Kirke.
Staff can book rooms in private homes for 200kr to 280kr per
person, including breakfast, plus a small booking fee.

Sankt Bendts Kirke (☎ 57 61 40 19; Sankt Bendtsgade;
admission free; 🕐 10am-noon & 1-5pm 1 May-15 Sep,
1-3pm 16 Sep-30 Apr)

Eating & Sleeping

Raadhuskroen (☎ 57 61 68 97; Sankt Bendtsgade 8;
mains 118-175kr; 🕐 11am-8.45pm Mon-Wed, 11am-
9.45pm Thu-Sat, 4-8.45pm Sun) Next to the tourist office,
this is a pub-style restaurant that specialises in steaks and
traditional Danish fare, with good smørrebrød (from 35kr
per piece) and a popular herring buffet (45kr).

Ringsted Vandrerhjem (☎ 57 61 15 26; ringsted@
danhostel.dk; Sankt Bendtsgade 18; dm 115kr, r 290-
690kr) This 78-bed hostel is in an ideal location opposite
Sankt Bendts Kirke, and each room has its own bathroom.
The hostel is closed 15 December to 5 January.

SWEDEN

MALMÖ

If you're starting to tire of Denmark's charms (unlikely, but keep reading) you can always go to another country – Sweden. Connected by the Øresund bridge (Europe's longest – at 7.8km) and tunnel, Malmö and Copenhagen are less than an hour away from each other and easy to get to. So easy, in fact, that many Danes commute from Sweden to their jobs in Copenhagen, as Malmö is a cheaper residential base than Denmark's capital. Danes also love coming to Malmö on Sunday, as many shops remain open for business, unlike at home.

Malmö, the most 'continental' of Sweden's cities, is a lively and vibrant place, perhaps due to the influence of Copenhagen across the Øresund; the relatively large proportion of immigrants in the city adds a multicultural element.

In the 13th century Malmö consisted of little more than a few streets centred around Adelgatan, then on the shore of Øresund. With the arrival of the Hanseatic traders in the following century, grand houses were built for the wealthy merchants and large churches were constructed. The first castle was built in 1434 and housed the Danish royal mint. The greatest medieval expansion of Malmö occurred under the auspices of Jörgen Kock, who became mayor in 1524. The town square, Stortorget, was laid out and many of the buildings from this period are still extant.

After the city capitulated to the Swedes in 1658, Malmö rose further in importance as a commercial centre and the castle was strengthened to protect trade. In the 20th century, the city developed as a centre for heavy industry, including car and aircraft manufacture, and shipbuilding. The huge Kockums submarine and shipyard was opened in 1909 and dominated shipbuilding worldwide for many years. However, as elsewhere in Europe, the heavy industries have disappeared and have been replaced by smaller companies, particularly in the service, financial and IT sectors. There has also been an upsurge in the number of students living in Malmö with the opening of a new university campus here in the late 1990s.

Gamla Staden (the old town) is the city centre, and is encircled by a canal. There are three principal squares here: Stortorget, Lilla Torg and Gustav Adolfs Torg. **Stortorget** holds the large equestrian statue of King Karl X Gustav. The square is fringed by majestic buildings from different eras, including the 16th-century **Rådhuset** (town hall). However, our favourite is **Apoteket Lejonet**, a pharmacy that's been operating since 1571, with a deliriously beautiful 1897 Art Nouveau interior.

Transport

Distance from Copenhagen 30km
Direction West
Travel time 35 minutes
Car If you're travelling solo, you're better off catching the train. Bridge tolls for Øresund Broen are one way/ return 230/460kr (Skr280/560). The Øresund bridge is about 8km west of the city centre, served by a motorway which passes south and east of the city.
Train An integrated Øresundregionen transport system is operational, with trains from Helsingborg via Malmö and Copenhagen to Helsingør. Copenhagen to Malmö (75kr or Skr85) trains leave every 20 minutes from around 5am to midnight (and hourly in the wee hours).

Lilla Torg is the postcard-perfect encapsulation of Nordic charm, with half-timbered period buildings, bustling outdoor cafés and the city's best dining options. Just off Lilla Torg you'll find **Saluhallen**, a covered market that's excellent for picnic provisions.

The main museums of Malmö are based in and around the castle called **Malmöhus**, which, in its park setting, guards the western end of Gamla Staden. You can walk through the royal apartments with their interiors and portrait collections and see the **Stadsmuseum** with its Malmö collection, and the art of **Konstmuseum**. Especially interesting are the **aquarium** and the **Naturmuseum**. The old **Kommendanthuset** arsenal is opposite the castle and **Teknikens och Sjöfartens Hus** is a short way to the west. The latter is a well-presented technology and maritime museum displaying

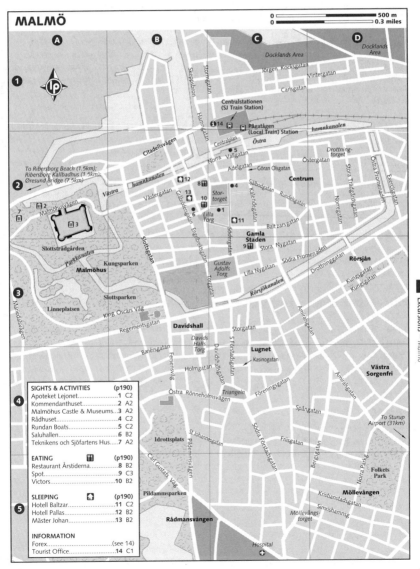

MALMÖ

0 ⸻ 500 m
0 ⸻ 0.3 miles

SIGHTS & ACTIVITIES	(p190)
Apoteket Lejonet	1 C2
Kommendanthuset	2 A2
Malmöhus Castle & Museums	3 A2
Rådhuset	4 C2
Rundan Boats	5 C2
Saluhallen	6 B2
Teknikens och Sjöfartens Hus	7 A2

EATING	(p190)
Restaurant Årstiderna	8 B2
Spot	9 C3
Victors	10 B2

SLEEPING	(p190)
Hotell Baltzar	11 C2
Hotell Pallas	12 B2
Mäster Johan	13 B2

INFORMATION	
Forex	(see 14)
Tourist Office	14 C1

aircraft, motor vehicles, steam engines and a submarine.

Boat tours of the town's canals run regularly from late April through September from the kiosk of **Rundan**, by the canal, opposite Centralstationen.

Ribersborg is a long sandy beach backed by parkland and recreational areas about 2km west of the town centre. Out in Öresund, and reached by a 200m-long pier, is the naturist **Ribersborgs Kallbadhus**, dating from 1898. There's a cold, open-air saltwater pool and wood-fired sauna, and separate sections for men and women. Take bus No 20 or 22 to get there.

What's That Sound?

In Denmark it's Øresund – and in Sweden it's Öresund – the sound (as in body of water) that separates these two traditional rivals. We'll stick with Øresund for this section of the book.

Sights & Information

Apoteket Lejonet (Stortorget 8)

Malmöhus (☎ 344437; Malmöhusvägen; combined ticket adult/child Skr40/free; ☉ 10am-4pm Jun-Aug, noon-4pm Sep-May)

Ribersborgs Kallbadhus (☎ 260366; www.ribban.com; adult/child Skr45/30; ☉ noon-7pm Mon-Fri, 9am-4pm Sat & Sun)

Rundan Boat Tours (☎ 6117488; tours adult/child Skr75/40)

Saluhallen (☉ 10am-6pm Mon-Fri, 10am-4pm Sat)

Tourist Office (☎ 341200; www.malmo.se; Centralstationen; ☉ 9am-7pm Mon-Fri, 10am-5pm Sat & Sun Jun-Aug, 9am-6pm Mon-Fri, 10am-3pm Sat & Sun May & Sep, 9am-5pm Mon-Fri, 10am-2pm Sat Oct-Apr) Inside the train station. Pick up the free official booklet *Malmö This Month*, which lists tourist information and a guide to events.

Telephone Codes & Currency

The international telephone code for Sweden is ☎ 46, while Malmö's telephone code is ☎ (0) 40. If you're calling Malmö from Copenhagen, dial ☎ 00 46 40 and then the rest of the number. Generally, one Danish *krone* equals 1.25 Swedish *kronor* (Skr).

Eating

Restaurant Årstiderna (☎ 230910; www.arstiderna.se; Stortorget; mains Skr195-355; ☉ 11.3am-midnight Mon-Fri, 5pm-midnight Sat) You'll find this excellent Swedish restaurant in a historic building dating from the 16th century, which features vaulted ceilings and interesting set menus. The Swedish menu (Skr525) includes whitebait roe, fillet of reindeer and cloudberry dessert. Dinner reservations advised.

Spot (☎ 120203; Stora Nygatan 33; dishes Skr49-75; ☉ 9am-5pm Mon-Sat) For delicious Italian sandwiches, salads and coffee, visit stylish Spot. There's also great gelati available, and an Italian deli for gourmet picnic or self-catering supplies.

Victors (☎ 127670; Lilla Torg 1; mains Skr165-185; ☉ 11.30am-1am Mon, Tue & Sun, 11.30am-3am Wed-Sat) One of the best options in town – and packed with stylish folk. By night it's a fantastic bar with excellent cocktails, but for lunch plump for the grilled lamb with pear and goat-milk cheese and tapenade gravy.

Sleeping

Hotel Pallas (☎ 611 5077; http://home.swipnet.se/Hotell_Pallas/; Norra Vallgatan 74; s Skr395, d Skr455-535) An affordable pension-style hotel close to the train station, with shared bathrooms and breakfast for an additional Skr30. Opt for a 'large' double room, as these are huge.

Hotell Baltzar (☎ 665 5710; www.baltzarhotel.se; Södergatan 20; s/d from Skr980/1300) Pretty Hotell Baltzar turns on the turn-of-the-century charm in spades, with chandeliers, luxe fabrics, parquet floors and burnished wood. Reservations are a good idea, as this place gets very popular.

Mäster Johan (☎ 664 6400; www.masterjohan.se; Mäster Johansgatan 13; s/d from Skr1595/2045) Weekend deals at this super-stylish inn (that's packed with business travellers from Monday to Friday) see prices plummet to Skr1050/1300 – a real bargain for a hotel of this quality.

Directory

Directory

TRANSPORT

AIR

You can fly into Copenhagen on scheduled flights from points all over Europe (including all the major capitals) and from the US (Seattle, Chicago, Washington and New York), South America (Rio de Janeiro and Sao Paolo), North Africa (Tunis and Cairo), the Middle East (Beirut, Tehran, Islamabad, Pakistan and Karachi) and Asia (Bangkok, Singapore, Beijing, Tokyo and Shanghai). Charter flights cover many 'sunny' destinations such as the Canary Islands, where Danes flock to escape winter.

Airlines

Most airline offices are north of Central Station, within a block or two of the intersection of Vester Farimagsgade and Vesterbrogade. Airline offices in Copenhagen can be found under *Luftfartsselskaber* in the Yellow Pages. Several airlines share the same address, while others don't have street addresses and can only be contacted by phone at the appropriate airport desk. Following are the office locations and reservation numbers of major airlines serving Copenhagen:

Aer Lingus (Map pp239–41; ☎ 33 12 60 55; aerlingus@target-marketing.dk; Jernbanegade 4)

Air China (Map pp232–4; ☎ 33 14 92 22; www.airchina .dk; Rådhuspladsen 16)

Alitalia (Map pp232–4; ☎ 70 27 02 90; www.alitalia.dk; Vesterbrogade 6D)

British Airways (Map pp232–4; ☎ 80 20 80 22; www .britishairways.dk; Rådhuspladsen 16)

Finnair (Map pp232–4; ☎ 33 36 45 45; www.finnair .com; Nyropsgade 47)

Iberia (Map pp239–41; ☎ 33 12 22 22; Jernbanegade 4)

Icelandair (Map pp239–41; ☎ 33 70 22 00; www .icelandair.net; Frederiksberggade 23)

KLM-Royal Dutch Airlines (☎ 70 10 07 47; www.klm .com; Copenhagen Airport)

Lufthansa Airlines (Map pp232–4; ☎ 70 10 20 00; www .lufthansa.dk; Hammerichsgade 1)

Maersk Air (Map pp232–4; ☎ 33 14 60 00; www .maersk-air.dk; Rådhuspladsen 16)

Scandinavian Airlines (Map pp232–4; SAS; ☎ 70 10 20 00; www.scandinavian.net; Hammerichsgade 1)

Swissair (☎ 70 10 50 64; www.swissair.com; Copenhagen Airport)

Airport

The modern international airport is in Kastrup, 9km southeast of Copenhagen's city centre, and sees about 18.2 million passengers each year. It has good eating, retail and information facilities, plus left-luggage and banking options. Note that this is a 'silent' airport and there are no boarding calls, although there are numerous monitor screens throughout the terminal.

If you judge a city by how easy it is to get to and from the airport, Copenhagen takes top marks. The rail system speedily (and cheaply) links the airport arrival terminal directly with Copenhagen's Central Station. The trains run every 20 minutes until midnight from 4.55am on weekdays, 5.35am on Saturday and 6.35am on Sunday. The trip takes just 12 minutes and costs 25.50kr.

By taxi, it takes about 15 minutes to travel from the airport to the city centre, as long as traffic isn't too heavy. The cost is about 170kr.

BICYCLE

Three out of four Danes own bicycles, and half use them on a regular basis. Postal workers are more likely to deliver mail by bicycle than by motor vehicle, and it's not uncommon to see well-heeled executives beating the rush hour by cycling through city traffic.

Copenhagen is a great city for getting around by bicycle. There are separate cycle lanes along many of the main roads and bicycle racks can be found at museums and other public places. One caveat – if you're travelling with a bicycle, be careful, as expensive bikes are hot targets for thieves on Copenhagen streets.

Except during weekday rush hours, it's possible to carry bikes on S-trains (buy the

10kr ticket from the red machine). You can load your bicycle in any carriage that has a cycle symbol and you must stay with the bike at all times.

When touring the city, cyclists should be cautious of bus passengers who commonly step off the bus into the cycle lanes, and of pedestrians (particularly tourists) who sometimes absent-mindedly step off the kerb and into the path of oncoming cyclists. This is particularly a problem on roads such as Nørregade, where cyclists are allowed to ride against the one-way traffic. Surprisingly, Denmark – a country that seems to have sensible behaviour implanted in its citizens – is a land of devil-may-care types when it comes to the use of helmets when cycling.

Cycling maps, including a 1:50,000-scale map of the greater Copenhagen area called *Københavns Amt*, are produced by the Danish cycling federation, **Dansk Cyklist Forbund** (Map pp232–4; www.dcf.dk), and can be readily purchased at bookshops. For information on bicycle hire, see right.

If you're flying into Copenhagen you should be able to take your bicycle along with you on the plane relatively easily. You can dismantle the bicycle and put the pieces in a bike bag or box, but it's easier to simply wheel your bike to the check-in desk, where it should be treated as a piece of baggage. You may have to remove the pedals and turn the handlebars sideways so that your bike takes up less space in the aircraft's hold. Check all this with the airline well in advance, preferably before you pay for your ticket.

Free Copenhagen Bikes

The city of Copenhagen has a generous scheme called **Bycykler** (City Bikes; ☎ 35 43 01 10; www.bycyklen.dk), in which anyone can borrow a bicycle for free. In all there are over 1000 bikes available from 1 May to 15 December.

Although these bicycles are not stream-lined and are certainly not practical for long-distance cycling, that's part of the plan – use of the cycles is limited to the city centre. To deter theft and minimise maintenance, the bicycles have a distinctive design that includes solid spokeless wheels with puncture-resistant tyres. The bikes can be found at 125 widely scattered street stands in public places, including S-train stations.

The way it works is that if you're able to find a free bicycle, you deposit a 20kr coin in the stand to release the bike. When you're done using the bicycle, you can return it to any stand and get your 20kr coin back.

Cycling Regulations

Cycling is taken seriously in Denmark, and Danish cyclists steadfastly follow prescribed cycle regulations. Before setting out you should become familiar with the following:

- All traffic in Denmark, both bicycle and motor vehicle, is on the right-hand side of the road.
- Cyclists are obliged to obey traffic lights, pedestrian right-of-ways and most other road rules that apply to motor vehicles.
- When making a left turn at crossings, a large left turn is mandatory; that is, you must cycle straight across the intersecting road, staying on the right, before turning left into the right-hand lane of the new road. Do not cross diagonally.
- Use hand signals to indicate turns: a left arm outstretched for a left-hand turn, and a right arm outstretched for a right-hand turn.
- When entering a roundabout (traffic circle), yield to vehicles already on the roundabout.
- If you're transporting children, the bicycle must have two independent brakes. A maximum of two children under the age of six can be carried on the bicycle or in an attached trailer.

Hire

If you didn't bring a bike with you, you can readily hire one in Copenhagen. In addition to the rental rates, expect to pay a refundable deposit of around 500kr for a regular bike, 1000kr for a mountain bike or tandem.

Danwheel (Map pp232–4; ☎ 33 21 22 27; Colbjørnsensgade 3; per day/week 40/175kr; 9am-5.30pm Mon-Fri, 9am-2pm Sat & Sun) A couple of blocks northwest of Central Station, Danwheel hires out bargain-basement older bikes.

Københavns Cykler (Map pp232–4; ☎ 33 33 86 13; www.rentabike.dk; Reventlowsgade 11; per day/week from 75/340kr; 8am-6pm Mon-Fri, 9am-1pm Sat, summer 10am-1pm Sun) One of the most convenient rental options is at the Reventlowsgade side of Central Station. The bicycles are in good working order and children's seats are available for hire.

Østerport Cykler (Map pp236–7; ☎ 33 33 85 13; www.oesterport-cykler.dk; Oslo Plads 9; per day/week from 75/340kr; 8am-6pm Mon-Fri, 9am-1pm Sat) At Østerport S-train station near track 13, this is a sister business to Københavns Cykler and has the same good standards.

BOAT

Taking a boat to Denmark can be a pleasant way to travel as they are generally of a high standard. The long-distance boats usually have duty-free shops, lounges, nightclubs and both cafeterias and formal restaurants. Many of the boats between Denmark and other Scandinavian countries have floating casinos and small grocery shops on board as well.

Remember that the same ferry company can have a whole host of different prices for the same route, depending upon the day of the week you travel and the season. Car fares inch up as the vehicle increases in size, and fares for camper vans are higher still.

You should always make reservations well in advance, particularly if you're bringing along a vehicle – this is doubly true in summer and at weekends. During busy periods you'll also get the best cabin selection by booking in advance.

There are daily sailings between Oslo and Copenhagen and Bornholm and Copenhagen, which leave from Kvæsthusbroen, north of Nyhavn. The companies DFDS Seaways (☎ 33 42 30 00; www.dfdsseaways .com) and Bornholm Ferries (☎ 33 13 18 66; www.bornholmferries.dk) are reliable and regular. Polferries (www.polferries.com.pl) boats to Swinoujscie in Poland leave from Nordre Toldbod, east of Kastellet, five times a week (10 hours). Around 200 cruise ships use Langelinie harbour, just north of the Little Mermaid, in the busy mid-May to mid-September cruise season.

The cheapest ferry route between Denmark and Sweden is the 'booze boat' shuttle between Helsingborg and Helsingør, which takes 20 minutes and costs just 15/30kr one way/return and gives you the chance to see just how leglessly drunk Swedes can get (Danish licensing laws are temptingly lax compared to Sweden's). Ferries depart every 20 minutes during the day and once an hour through the night. The fare for a car with up to five passengers is 240kr. There are various car discounts, and you can often get a return ticket for around the same price as a one-way ticket. Both HH-Ferries (in Helsingør ☎ 49 26 01 55, in Helsingborg ☎ +46 42 19 80 00; www.hh -ferries.dk) and Scandlines (in Helsingør ☎ 33 15 15 15, in Helsingborg ☎ 42 18 61 00; www.scandlines.dk) ply this route.

There's also a frequent passenger-only hydrofoil service offered by Sundbusserne (☎ 49 21 35 45; www.sundbusserne.dk) that shaves a few minutes off the travel time and costs 19/34kr one way/return.

Travel agencies, particularly those specialising in cruises, can detail all the possibilities and pile you high with brochures. They can also give you the lowdown on special promotions and discounts, such as those for early booking, which can cut as much as 25% to 40% off the standard fares.

Canal boats can be a fine traffic-free way of getting to some of Copenhagen's famous waterfront sites. Public transit company HUR (☎ 36 13 14 15; www.hur.dk; ☼ 7am- 9.30pm) runs the 901 and 902 ferry service (Havnebus) along Copenhagen's canals. The boats operate every 20 minutes from early morning until about 7pm year-round, weather permitting. Stops include Nyhavn, the southeastern side of Churchillparken, the Royal Library and a couple of locales in Christianshavn. One-hour tickets cost adult/child 30/15kr and can be purchased on the boat.

In addition, DFDS Canal Tours (Map pp232–4; ☎ 33 42 33 20; www.canal-tours.dk) operates a summertime water bus that runs along a route similar to its guided tours (see p49) but has no commentary. These boats leave Nyhavn every 30 minutes daily from 10.15am to 4.45pm between early May and early September (to 5.45pm from mid-June to mid-August), and make a number of stops, including Slotsholmen, Christianshavn and the Little Mermaid. A day pass (adult/child 45/20kr) allows you to get on and off as often as you like, while a two-day pass allows you to access all routes (75/35kr). You can also ride from just one stop to another (30/20kr).

CAR & MOTORCYCLE

Except for the weekday-morning rush hour, when traffic can bottleneck coming into the city (and vice versa around 5pm), traffic in Copenhagen is generally manageable. Getting around by car is not problematic, apart from the usual challenge of finding an empty parking space in the most popular places.

To explore sights in the centre of the city, you're best off on foot or using public transport, but a car is convenient for getting to the suburban sights.

Driving

Bring your home driving licence, as Denmark accepts many foreign driving licences without restriction, including those issued in the USA, Canada, the UK and other EU countries.

If you don't hold a European driving licence and plan to drive outside Denmark, it's a good idea to obtain an International Driving Permit (IDP) from your local automobile association before you leave home. You'll need a passport photo and a valid licence. IDPs are usually inexpensive and are valid for one year.

Hire

The following car hire companies have booths at the airport in the international terminal. Each also has an office in central Copenhagen:

Avis (Map pp232–4; ☎ 33 73 40 99; www.avis.dk; Kampmannsgade 1)

Budget (Map pp232–4; ☎ 33 55 05 00; www.budget.dk; Helgolandsgade 2)

Europcar (Map pp232–4; ☎ 33 55 99 00; www.europcar.dk; Gammel Kongevej 13)

Hertz (Map pp232–4; ☎ 33 17 90 21; www.hertzdk.dk; Ved Vesterport 3)

Parking

To park on the street in Copenhagen centre, you have to buy a ticket from a kerbside machine, labelled *billetautomat*. Put in enough money to advance the read-out to the time you desire and then push the button to eject the ticket from the machine. Place the ticket, which shows the exact time you must leave, face up inside the car windscreen.

The *billetautomat* only charges for hours when a ticket is required. Copenhagen parking is zoned so that the spaces most in demand, such as those in the central commercial area, are the most costly. Your best bet is to search out a blue zone where parking costs just 7kr per hour. If you can't find an empty blue space then opt for a green zone where the fee is 12kr per hour. Avoid red zones where it's a steep 20kr per hour. Parking fees must be paid on weekdays from 8am to 6pm (to 8pm in red zones), and also on Saturday from 8am to 2pm in red and green zones.

If you cannot find street parking, there are multistorey car parks at the main de-partment stores, at the Radisson SAS Royal Hotel and on Jernbanegade east of Axeltorv, among other places. Car parks charge around 12kr per hour.

In the suburbs and in smaller towns, most locations are delightfully free of coin-hungry *billetautomats* and street parking is free within the time limits posted. These parking spaces will be marked by a blue sign with the letter 'P'; beneath it will be the time limit for free parking (*1 time* is one hour, *2 timer* is two hours).

You will need a windscreen parking disk. This is a flat plastic card with a clock face and a movable hour hand, which must be set to show the time you parked the car. Parking disks can be picked up for a nominal fee from tourist offices and petrol stations, or for free from **Parkering** (☎ 70 80 80 90; www.parkering.dk). This company can also give you information about weekly and monthly parking cards.

Parkering forbudt means 'no parking' and is generally accompanied by a round sign with a red diagonal slash. You can, however, stop for up to three minutes to unload bags and passengers. A round sign with a red 'X', or a sign saying *Stopforbud,* means that no stopping at all is allowed. Parking tickets will set you back a cool 510kr.

PUBLIC TRANSPORT
Bus

Copenhagen has a vast bus system called HUR (Hovedstadsens Udviklingsråd); the main terminus is at Rådhuspladsen.

Buses and trains use a common fare system based on the number of zones you pass through. The basic fare of 17kr for up to two zones covers most city runs and allows transfers between buses and trains on a single ticket as long as they're made within an hour.

On buses, you board at the front and pay the fare to the driver (or stamp your clip card in the yellow machine next to the driver). Buses generally run from about 5am (6am on Sunday) to around 12.30am, and some continue to run through the night (charging double the usual fare) on a few main routes.

The free Copenhagen city maps that are distributed by the tourist office show bus routes (with numbers) and are very useful for finding your way around the city. If you plan to use buses extensively, you might want to buy HUR's hefty timetable book *Busser og tog* (40kr), which comes with a colour-coded bus route map (covering the entire HUR route throughout North Zealand), or get just the map for 5kr. Both are sold at **HUR's information office** (Map pp232–4) on Rådhuspladsen.

Throughout this book the numbers of some of the more frequent buses to individual destinations are listed, but since there can be as many as a dozen buses passing any particular place (eg Rådhuspladsen), our listing is often only a partial one.

Metro

The brand-new **metro** (☎ 70 15 16 15; www.m.dk) system, which is driverless and still under construction, connects the east and west of Copenhagen via the city centre. There are two metro lines – M1 (green) and M2 (yellow). At the time of writing M1 connects Vanløse to Vestamager, and M2 connects Vanløse with Lergravsparken. The metro runs from 5am to 1am and all night on weekends. Metro stations that will be of most interest/use to visitors to Copenhagen are Kongens Nytorv, Nørreport and Christianshavn. By the end of 2005, the metro system will connect with the city's airport and by 2007 two new metro lines will connect Central Station to the metro system, which will make an enormous difference to getting around the city. Tickets for the metro (which must be validated in the yellow boxes posted near the stations' entrances) cost from 17kr for one hour and are integrated with the city's other public transport options. Bicycles and dogs are allowed on the metro, and disabled access is very good.

Tickets

Basic ticket prices for the integrated (ie bus, train and metro) public transport system start with two-zone tickets at 17kr. Two- and three-zone tickets are valid for one hour. Four- to six-zone tickets are valid for 1½ hours and all-zone tickets are valid for two hours. Instead of buying a single destination ticket, you can buy a *klippekort* (clip card) that is valid for 10 rides in two zones (105kr) or three zones (145kr), or you

can get a 24-hour ticket valid for unlimited travel in all zones (100kr). Ordinary tickets are purchased from vending machines, ticket offices and on buses, and are stamped with information such as date, time and the zones you are travelling in (from two zones to the maximum of seven). Each 'clip' in the yellow box allows travel for a certain distance – extra clips allow for longer travel. Passengers who are stopped and found to be without a stamped ticket are liable for a fine of 500kr.

For schedules and other information try: **HUR** (☎ 36 13 14 15; www.hur.dk; 7am-9.30pm); **DSB S-tog** (☎ 33 14 17 01; www.dsb.dk/s-tog; 6.30am-10pm); **DSB trains** (☎ 70 13 14 15; www.dsb.dk; 7am-10pm); or **Metro** (☎ 70 15 16 15; www.m.dk; 9am-4pm Mon-Fri).

Train

Copenhagen's S-train network has 11 lines passing through Central Station (København H).

Buses, S-trains and the metro use a common fare system based on the number of zones you pass through. The basic fare of 17kr for up to two zones covers most city runs and allows transfers between buses and trains on a single ticket as long as they're made within an hour. Third and subsequent zones cost 8.50kr more, with a maximum fare of 59.50kr for travel throughout North Zealand. DSB, the national railway, also includes its lines in the common fare system as far north as Helsingør (p175), west to Roskilde (p180) and south to Køge (p184).

On S-trains, tickets are purchased at the station and then punched in the yellow time clock on the platform before boarding the train. Trains run from about 5am (6am on Sunday) to around 12.30am.

TAXI

Taxis with signs saying *fri* (available) can be flagged down or you can call **Københavns Taxa** (☎ 35 35 35 35) or **Taxa Motor** (☎ 38 10 10 10). The cost is 23kr at flag fall, plus about 10kr per kilometre (13kr at night and at weekends). Most taxis accept credit cards. A service charge is included in the fare, so tips are not expected.

PRACTICALITIES

ACCOMMODATION

Our listings for the Sleeping chapter are arranged by neighbourhood and ordered alphabetically, with mid-range and top-end listings first. Budget accommodation is listed at the end of each neighbourhood under the heading Cheap Sleeps.

Peak tourist season in Copenhagen is summer, and, as the city is a popular business convention destination, rates are higher from Monday to Friday. We have quoted high-season, weekday prices throughout this guide. Check-in and check-out times are standard – in at noon, out by 10am or 11am. Visit hotel websites for better deals than off-the-street rack rates. The city has about 14,000 beds in its hotels.

Booking Services

The city tourist office, Copenhagen Right Now (Map pp239–41; ☎ 70 22 24 42; www.woco .dk; Vesterbrogade 4A; ☯ 9am-4pm Mon-Fri & 9am-2pm Sat Sep-Apr, 9am-6pm Mon-Sat May & Jun, 9am-8pm Mon-Sat & 10am-6pm Sun Jul & Aug) can help you find accommodation (for free if you book via the phone or Internet). Rooms in private homes around the city cost from around 300kr for singles and 400kr for doubles. This office also books unfilled hotel rooms, typically at discounted rates. There's a 75kr to 100kr fee per booking.

For more information about these services, see p153 in the Sleeping chapter.

CHILDREN

Travelling in Copenhagen with children is no sweat – many businesses accommodate the enormous prams that Danes wield through the streets, children's portions are not unheard of in many restaurants and babysitting services can be arranged at many hotels. Neighbourhood play areas are well maintained, certain attractions are geared specifically for kids and children are regarded with fond respect.

Some of Copenhagen's leading museums have special features of interest just for kids. Statens Museum for Kunst (p84), the state art museum, added a new children's gallery when it was renovated in the late 1990s. The stalwart Nationalmuseet (p53) has, in addition to stuffy mummies and millennium-old archaeological finds, a fun hands-on section just for kids, as well as an antique toy collection. Louisiana (p175), the splendid modern art museum in Humlebæk, boasts a special children's section where budding young artists can let the paint hit the canvas.

Younger children will enjoy the free marionette theatre performed on summer afternoons in Kongens Have (p83), the city's oldest public park; and as long as you're there the kids might want to cross the swan-filled moat and visit Rosenborg Slot (p84), where kings and queens once lived. If flowers entertain, the adjacent botanical gardens (p82) have an abundance of them, including a huge greenhouse with brilliant tropicals.

And of course there are the more conventional sites. Copenhagen's substantial zoo, Zoologisk Have (p88), has elephants, lions and other awesome beasts as well as a children's zoo with more approachable creatures.

Keep in mind that successful travel with young children requires planning and effort. When you plot out your day, try not to overdo things. Include children in the planning progress; if they've helped to work out where you're going, they'll be much more interested when they get there. A good book to pick up is Lonely Planet's *Travel with Children* by Cathy Lanigan; it's loaded with tips and information.

Copenhagen's infrastructure in general is very child-friendly. For example, on public transport children under the age of 12 can travel free when accompanied by an adult. Children between 12 and 15 years of age are eligible for a child's ticket (half the adult fare) and two children under 16 years of age are allowed to travel on one adult ticket or one clip of an adult *klippekort*.

Many public toilets have nappy-changing facilities, such as the toilet in the basement at Central Station. Breastfeeding in public is rare (especially in the colder months), but would never cause offence.

In Copenhagen, there are several public parks with play areas for kids. Hotels and other accommodation options often have 'family rooms' which accommodate up to two adults and two to four children for little more than the price of a regular double.

Car rental firms hire out children's safety seats at a nominal cost, but it's essential that you book them in advance. Highchairs and cots (cribs) are standard in many restaurants and hotels. Danish supermarkets offer a relatively wide choice of baby food, infant formulas, soy and cow's milk, disposable nappies (diapers) etc.

The only major hassle is the amount of cigarette smoke that fills many of the city's restaurants and cafés. Don't be surprised either by the sight of a well-covered pram left out on the street in cold weather, complete with baby! Danes are relaxed about such things – and assume no-one will kidnap their (very well-rugged-up) child while they duck indoors for a coffee.

Baby-sitting

HH Babysitting (☎ 70 20 81 51; www.hh-baby .dk; Bårsevej 26) will provide baby-sitting and child-minding services from 40kr (booking fee) plus 40kr per hour (minimum three hours) and transport costs.

CLIMATE

In the coldest winter months of January and February, the average daily temperature hovers around freezing point – and while that may be cold, it's nearly 10°C above average for this latitude. Winter, however, also has the highest relative humidity (90%) and the cloudiest weather (with greater than 80% cloud cover on an average of 17 days a month), both of which can make it feel much colder than the actual mercury reading.

Expect to see rain and grey skies: measurable rain falls on average from 11 days in June to 18 days in November, with the greatest amount of precipitation from July to December – although, when all's said and done, rain is fairly evenly spread over the year.

You can get a five-day weather forecast in English from the Danish Meteorological Office at its website at www.dmi.dk or by calling ☎ 1854.

COURSES
Folk High Schools

Scandinavia's unique *folkehøjskole,* literally 'folk high school' (the 'high' denoting an institute of higher learning), provides a liberal education within a communal living environment. Folk high schools got their start in Denmark, inspired by philosopher Nikolai Grundtvig's concept of 'enlightenment for life'. The curriculum includes such things as drama, peace studies and organic farming.

Those 17½ and older can enrol; there are no entrance exams and no degrees. Tuition, including room and board, averages €110 a week (about 820kr). There are courses in (among other things) philosophy, music, sports and history, lasting between one week and 10 months. For more information, including a catalogue of the nearly 100 schools, contact Højskolernes Sekretariat (Map pp239–41; ☎ 33 13 98 22; www.folkeho jskoler.dk; Nytorv 7, 1450 Copenhagen K).

While most folk high schools teach in Danish, the International People's College (☎ 49 21 33 61; www.ipc.dk; Montebello Allé 1, 3000 Helsingør), has students and teachers from around the world, and most instruction is given in English.

Foreigners are welcome to enrol in short-term courses, typically lasting two to eight weeks. In summer these include an intensive Danish language and culture program.

Language

Contact the Danish Cultural Institute (Map pp239–41; Det Danske Kulturinstitut; ☎ 33 13 54 48; www.dankultur.dk; Kultorvet 2, 1175 Copenhagen K) for information on Danish-language courses that might be offered in your home country. The government-sponsored Danish Cultural Institute also arranges cultural events and exchanges, sponsors Danish-language classes in Denmark and abroad, and distributes information on various aspects of Danish culture.

In Denmark, there are a number of schools that teach Danish to foreigners, but most focus on teaching immigrants or other long-term residents. Expect to pay around 80kr per hour for language instruction.

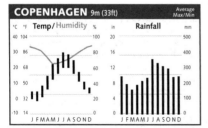

COPENHAGEN 9m (33ft)   Average Max/Min

°C °F   Temp/Humidity %   in   Rainfall   mm

J F M A M J J A S O N D   J F M A M J J A S O N D

Following are four of the schools that offer Danish-language courses to foreigners:

AOF (☎ 39 16 82 00; Lersø Park Allé 44, 2100 Copenhagen Ø)

HOF (Map pp239–41; ☎ 33 11 88 33; Købmagergade 26, 1150 Copenhagen K)

KISS (Map pp232–4; ☎ 35 36 25 25; www.kiss.dk; Nørrebrogade 32, 2200 Copenhagen N)

Studieskolen (☎ 33 14 43 22; www.studieskolen.dk; Antonigade 6, 1106 Copenhagen K)

CUSTOMS

One litre of spirits and 200 cigarettes can be brought into Denmark duty free if you're coming from outside the EU. Those coming from an EU country are allowed to bring in 300 cigarettes and 1.5L of spirits.

When you arrive in Denmark, there will be two customs channels. You must use the red channel if you're bringing in more than the usual allowance of duty-free goods or any restricted items (guns, drugs etc). Use the green channel – which is generally a quick exit – if you have nothing to declare.

DISABLED TRAVELLERS

Copenhagen tries to be a handicapped-friendly city, but facilities do vary greatly. The main hotel district has a lot of older hotels that were not erected with wheelchair patrons in mind, and many of these are not accessible. Newer hotels are the best bets for up-to-date handicapped facilities.

Most Danish tourist literature (the Danish Tourist Board's hotel guide, the camping association listings and the hostel booklet) indicate which places have rooms and facilities accessible to people in wheelchairs.

Dansk Handicap Forbund, the national association for the handicapped, publishes a free booklet called *København og Frederiksberg... uden besvær?* (Copenhagen & Frederiksberg... without difficulty?) listing hotels, restaurants, museums, churches and entertainment venues that are handicapped-accessible in the greater Copenhagen area.

The booklet is in Danish, but is fairly straightforward to use as it employs international symbols to indicate facilities such as handicapped parking, elevators and accessible toilets. It can be picked up free at the Copenhagen tourist office.

Once in Copenhagen, disabled travellers with specific questions can contact

Dansk Handicap Forbund (☎ 39 29 35 55; Kollektivhuset, Hans Knudsens Plads 1A, 2100 Copenhagen Ø).

DISCOUNT CARDS
Copenhagen Card

The Copenhagen Card is a tourist pass that allows unlimited travel on buses and trains in Copenhagen and throughout North Zealand, as well as free admission to about 60 of the region's museums and attractions.

An adult card costs 199/399kr for 24/72hrs; a child card costs 129/229kr for the same period. Cards can be purchased at Central Station, at tourist offices and in some hotels. Days are calculated on a 24-hour basis; for example, if you begin a one-day card on Saturday at 6pm, it's valid until Sunday at 5:59pm.

If you want to run through a lot of sightseeing in a few days, the Copenhagen Card can be a real bargain. However, for a more leisurely exploration of select places it may work out cheaper to pay individual admission charges and use one of the transport passes.

ELECTRICITY

Denmark, like most of Europe, runs on 220V (volts), 50Hz (cycles) AC.

Check the voltage and cycle (usually 50Hz) used in your home country. Most appliances that are set up for 240V (such as those used in the UK) will handle 220V without modifications and vice versa. It's always preferable to adjust your appliance to the exact voltage if you can – a few items, such as some electric razors and radios, will do this automatically. If your appliance doesn't have a built-in transformer, don't plug a 110/125V appliance (the kind used in the USA and Canada) into a Danish outlet without using a separate transformer.

Denmark uses the 'europlug' with two round pins. Many europlugs and some sockets don't have provision for earth wiring because most local home appliances are double-insulated; when provided, earth usually consists of two contact points along the edge.

If your plugs are of a different design, you'll need an adapter. These are usually available in shops specialising in travel needs. Make sure to get one before you leave, because most adapters available in Copenhagen are intended for Danes travelling to a country that doesn't use the europlug.

EMBASSIES

It's important to realise what your own embassy can and can't do.

Generally, it won't be much help in emergencies if the trouble you're in is your own fault. Remember you are bound by the laws of the country you are visiting. In most cases, your embassy is not likely to be terribly sympathetic if you are jailed after committing a crime locally, even if such actions are legal in your own country. Some embassies do send representatives to visit citizens arrested abroad, so don't hesitate to contact them.

In genuine emergencies you might be given assistance, but only if other channels have been exhausted. If you need to get home urgently, a free ticket home is exceedingly unlikely as the embassy would expect you to have insurance. If you have all your money and documents stolen, its assistance will likely be limited to issuing you a new passport.

Most of the following embassies can be reached by bus Nos 1A or 15.

Australia (Map pp236–7; ☎ 70 26 36 76; www.denmark .embassy.gov.au; Dampfærgevej 26, Copenhagen)

Canada (Map pp239–41; ☎ 33 48 32 00; www.dfait -maeci.gc.ca/canadaeuropa/denmark/; Kristen Bernikows Gade 1, Copenhagen)

Finland (Map pp232–4; ☎ 33 13 42 14; www.finamb.dk; Sankt Annæ Plads 24, Copenhagen)

France (Map pp239–41; ☎ 33 67 10 00; www.amba-france.dk; Kongens Nytorv 4, Copenhagen)

Germany (Map pp236–7; ☎ 35 45 99 00; Stockholmsgade 57, Copenhagen)

Iceland (Map pp232–4; ☎ 33 18 10 50; www.iceland .org/dk; Dantes Plads 3, Copenhagen)

Ireland (Map pp236–7; ☎ 35 42 32 33; Østbanegade 21, Copenhagen)

Netherlands (Map pp232–4; ☎ 33 70 72 00; www .nlembassy.dk; Toldbodgade 33, Copenhagen)

Norway (Map pp232–4; ☎ 33 14 01 24; www.norsk.dk; Amaliegade 39, Copenhagen)

Poland (Map pp235; ☎ 39 62 72 45; www.ambpol.dk; Richelieus Allé 12, Hellerup)

Russia (Map pp236–7; ☎ 35 42 55 85; Kristianiagade 5, Copenhagen)

Sweden (Map pp232–4; ☎ 33 36 03 70; www.sverigesa mbassad.dk; Sankt Annæ Plads 15A, Copenhagen)

UK (Map pp236–7; ☎ 35 44 52 00; www.britishembassy .dk; Kastelsvej 40, Copenhagen)

USA (Map pp236–7; ☎ 35 55 31 44; www.usembassy.dk; Dag Hammarskjölds Allé 24, Copenhagen)

EMERGENCY

In the event of an emergency, call ☎ 112 and request ambulance, police or fire services. Calls from public telephones to this number are free and do not require any coins. English is spoken by operators.

Police station (☎ 33 15 38 01; Central Station; ⏱ 7am-midnight)

Police station (Map pp232–4; ☎ 33 25 14 48; Halmtorvet 20)

Politigården (Map pp232–4; ☎ 33 14 14 48; Polititorvet; ⏱ 24hr) Police headquarters

GAY & LESBIAN TRAVELLERS

Copenhagen is a popular destination for gay and lesbian travellers. It has an active gay community and lots of nightlife options. The main gay and lesbian festival of the year is the Mermaid Pride parade, a big Mardi Gras-like bash that occurs on a Saturday in early August.

There's also the Copenhagen Gay & Lesbian Film Festival, held each year in October. For more information on activities and nightlife, see p124.

Danes have a high degree of tolerance for 'alternative' lifestyles of all sorts, and gays are as free as anyone to express themselves. The LBL (see below) was established back in 1948, and in 1989 Denmark became the first country in Europe to legalise same-sex marriages and to offer gay partners most of the same legal rights as heterosexual couples. Adoption laws are liberal compared to other Western countries and public displays of affection between people of the same sex are unlikely to provoke ire. Lesbians wishing to have access to artificial insemination do not provoke the sort of scandals that can occur in other societies.

Landsforeningen for Bøsser og Lesbiske (Map pp239–41; LBL; ☎ 33 13 19 48; www.lbl .dk; Teglgårdsstræde 13), the national organisation for gay men and lesbians has a library, bookshop, café, various gay and lesbian support groups, religious services and counselling. There's also a telephone information line (☎ 33 36 00 86; ❂8-11pm Mon, Thu & Sat).

LBL also publishes the main gay magazine in Denmark, *PAN bladet,* which covers gay-related issues, upcoming events and entertainment. There's an annual English-language version published each June.

A network of gay and gay-friendly businesses in the city is **Copenhagen Gay Life** (www .copenhagen-gay-life.dk). The website includes useful tourist information and listings in English, as well as links to LBL and other gay organisations. Another good website that's worth visiting is www.gay guide.dk.

A fun general book if you're looking for something to read before coming to Denmark is *Are You Two... Together? A Gay and Lesbian Travel Guide to Europe,* by Lindsy Van Gelder and Pamela Robin Brandt, which has a particularly enjoyable chapter on Copenhagen.

For information on gay-friendly hotels, see the listings for Circuit Q at Carsten's (p157), Hotel Jørgensen (p161) and Hotel Windsor (p161) in the Sleeping chapter.

HOLIDAYS

Summer holidays for school children begin around 20 June and end around 10 August. Schools also break for a week in mid-October and during the Christmas and New Year period. Many Danes take their main work holiday during the first three weeks of July.

Banks and most businesses are closed on public holidays, and transport schedules are commonly reduced as well. For more information on holidays in Copenhagen, see p8. Country-wide public holidays include:

New Year's Day (Nytårsdag) – 1 January

Maundy Thursday (Skærtorsdag) – the Thursday before Easter

Good Friday (Langfredag) – the Friday before Easter Day

Easter Day (Påskedag) – a Sunday in March or April

Easter Monday (2.påskedag) – the day after Easter Day

Common Prayer Day (Stor Bededag) – the fourth Friday after Easter

Ascension Day (Kristi Himmelfartsdag) – the sixth Thursday after Easter

Whitsunday (Pinsedag) – the seventh Sunday after Easter

Whitmonday (2.pinsedag) – the eighth Monday after Easter

Constitution Day (Grundlovsdag) – 5 June

Christmas Eve – 24 December (from noon)

Christmas Day (Juledag) – 25 December

Boxing Day (2.juledag) – 26 December

INTERNET ACCESS

A growing number of hotels in Denmark are adding modem hookups in guest rooms, so if you intend to use your own computer, you should inquire when making reservations. Many hostels will also have facilities for guests to check their email accounts.

Public libraries in the Copenhagen area have computers with Internet access, though access policies vary and you may need to book in advance.

As most families in Denmark have their own computers, cybercafés are not terribly abundant and tend to be short-lived.

Hovedbiblioteket (Map pp239–41; ☎ 33 73 60 60; Krystalgade 15) The main public library – computers can be used free for up to 30 minutes, but queuing can take an hour.

Det Kongelige Bibliotek (Map pp239–41; ☎ 33 47 47 47; www.kb.dk; Søren Kierkegaards Plads) Library on the southern side of Slotsholmen, computers can make a quick online run as long as no-one else is waiting.

Boomtown (Map pp239–41; ☎ 33 32 10 32; Axeltorv 1; per 30 min from 20kr; ❂ 24hr) Large, modern and the most convenient cybercafé by a long shot.

Use It (Map pp239–41; ☎ 33 73 06 20; www.useit .dk; Rådhusstræde 13; free; ❂ 11am-4pm Mon-Wed, 11am-6pm Thu & 11am-2pm Fri 16 Sep-14 Jun, 9am-7pm Mon-Fri 15 Jun-15 Sep) Budget travel information centre offering free Internet access on four computers for 20 minutes at a time. Bookings advised.

LEFT LUGGAGE

Luggage lockers at Central Station (small/large per 24hr, maximum 72hr, 25/35kr)

Left luggage office at Central Station (☎ 33 69 21 15; suitcase, bag, parcel per piece 30kr, rucksack, pram, bike per piece per 24hr, maximum 10 days, 40kr; ❂ 5.30am-1am Mon-Sat, 6am-1am Sun)

Luggage Lockers at Copenhagen Airport (per piece per 24hr from 20kr)

Left-luggage Room at Copenhagen Airport (☎ 32 47 47 32; per piece per 24hr 30kr; ❂ 6am-10pm) Near the airport's post office.

Use It (Map pp239–41; ☎ 33 73 06 20; www.useit.dk; Rådhusstræde 13; luggage lockers free; ☺ 11am-4pm Mon-Wed, 11am-6pm Thu & 11am-2pm Fri 16 Sep-14 Jun, 9am-7pm 15 Jun-15 Sep)

LEGAL MATTERS

The drinking age in Denmark is 18 years of age. It's illegal to drive with a blood-alcohol concentration of 0.05% or greater. Drivers under the influence of alcohol are liable to receive stiff penalties and a possible prison sentence.

Always treat drugs with a great deal of caution. There is a fair bit of marijuana and hashish available in the region, sometimes quite openly, but note that in Denmark (unlike in the Netherlands) all forms of cannabis are officially illegal.

MAPS

The tourist office produces a free colour map of Copenhagen with a street index and keys for hotels and major attractions. It covers the entire greater Copenhagen area and includes a detailed blow-up of the city centre. You can pick one up at the airport information desk, at the tourist office and at the front desk of many hotels.

Although there's not much that the free tourist map doesn't show, you can also buy commercial maps and street directories at bookshops. These maps are larger and have more complete indexes; one of the best is the street directory *Kraks Kort over København og Omegn,* which costs 229kr.

MEDICAL SERVICES

Denmark is a healthy place and travellers shouldn't need to take any unusual health precautions. Sanitation standards are high and tap water is safe to drink (but makes vile tea, due to the high lime content).

Visitors whose countries have reciprocal agreements with Denmark are covered by the Danish national health-insurance program. For citizens of EU countries, in most cases you'll need to present EU form E-111; inquire at your national health service or travel agent before leaving home. In some situations you may have to pay pharmacies and doctors directly, then obtain a refund from the nearest health insurance office. Travel insurance may still be advisable because of the flexibility it offers, as well as covering expenses for an emergency flight home.

All visitors, regardless of where they are from, receive free hospital treatment in the event of an accident or a sudden illness, provided the patient has not come to Denmark for the purpose of obtaining treatment.

Controlled medicine is only available from a pharmacy with a prescription that is issued by a Danish or other Scandinavian doctor.

Clinics

Private doctor visits usually cost from around 500kr. Dentists' fees must be paid in cash (and start at about 500kr).

City General Practice & Travel Medicine (Map pp239–41; ☎ 70 27 57 57; Ny Østergade) Behind the Hotel d'Angleterre, English spoken.

Tandlægevagten (Map pp236–7; ☎ 35 38 02 51; Oslo Plads 14) Emergency dental service.

Emergency Rooms

The following hospitals have 24-hour emergency wards:

Amager Hospital (Map p230; ☎ 32 34 32 34; Italiensvej 1)

Bispebjerg Hospital (Map pp236–7; ☎ 35 31 35 31; Bispebjerg Bakke 23)

Frederiksberg Hospital (Map p238; ☎ 38 16 38 16; Nordre Fasanvej 57)

METRIC SYSTEM

Denmark uses the metric system. Petrol and beverages are sold by the litre, meats and vegetables are weighed in kilograms, distance is measured either in kilometres or in metres and speed limits are posted in kilometres per hour (km/h).

Fruit is often sold by the piece *(stykke,* abbreviated *stk).* Decimals are indicated by commas and thousands by points.

MONEY

The Danish krone is most often written DKK in international money markets, Dkr in northern Europe and kr within Denmark.

The krone is divided into 100 øre. There are 25-øre, 50-øre, one-krone, two-kroner, five-kroner, 10-kroner and 20-kroner coins. Notes come in 50-, 100-, 200-, 500- and 1000-kroner denominations.

Banks & ATMs

Banks can be found on nearly every second corner in central Copenhagen. Most are open from 10am to 4pm weekdays (to 6pm on Thursday). The best place to go for longer hours is Central Station, which has a branch of Den Danske Bank that's open from 8am to 8pm daily, although higher commissions are charged outside normal banking hours. Most banks in Copenhagen have ATMs, many of them accessible 24 hours a day and in a multitude of languages.

Changing Money

The following Forex branches are convenient and reliable. The Danske Bank branch at the airport will change currency and give advances on credit cards. If you're on an international ferry to Denmark, you'll typically be able to exchange US dollars and local currencies to Danish kroner on board. The US dollar is generally the handiest foreign currency to bring. However, Danish banks will convert a wide range of other currencies as well, including the euro, Australian dollar, British pound, Canadian dollar, Japanese yen, kroner from Norway and Sweden, and the Swiss franc. Foreign coins are seldom accepted by banks, so try to unload those before arriving in Denmark.

Danske Bank at Airport (Arrival & Transit Halls; ☾ 6am-10pm)

Forex Central Station (☎ 33 11 21 13; Central Station; ☾ 7am-9pm)

Forex Nørreport (Map pp232–4; ☎ 33 32 81 00; Nørre Voldgade 90; ☾ 9am-7pm Mon-Fri, 9am-4pm Sat)

Forex Vesterbrogade (Map pp232–4; ☎ 33 93 77 70; Vesterbrogade 2B; ☾ 9am-7pm Mon-Fri, 9am-4pm Sat)

Credit Cards

Credit cards such as Visa and MasterCard (also known as Access or Eurocard) are generally widely accepted in Denmark, although you will get a surprise in many shops and supermarkets, where only local credit cards (such as DanKort) are accepted. Charge cards like AmEx and Diners Club are also accepted, but not as often. On the plus side, charge cards have a reputation for quick replacement, often within 24 hours of reporting the card lost.

If a card is lost or stolen, inform the issuing company as soon as possible. Here are Copenhagen numbers for cancelling your cards:

AmEx (☎ 70 20 70 97)

Diners Club (☎ 36 73 73 73)

MasterCard, Access, Eurocard (☎ 80 01 60 98)

Visa (☎ 80 01 85 88)

You can also call ☎ 44 89 25 00, which handles lost Danish-issued credit cards, for 24-hour advice if you're unable to get through on any of the credit card reporting numbers listed above.

NEWSPAPERS & MAGAZINES

Copenhagen's leading daily newspaper is *Politiken*. There are scores of smaller papers too. All of the dailies are in Danish only.

English readers can pick up the *Copenhagen Post,* a weekly newspaper that publishes an interesting mix of Danish news, events and entertainment information every Thursday. You can also read this English-language paper online at www.cphpost.dk.

Copenhagen This Week – despite its name, a monthly publication – is a pocket-sized English-language magazine loaded with tourist-related information, from event and entertainment schedules to listings of restaurants and escort services. It's free at the tourist office and many hotels.

English-language magazines and newspapers are readily available at the Interkiosk newsstand in Central Station, at the newspaper kiosk on Rådhuspladsen and in the lobbies of larger hotels. The 7-Eleven convenience stores also sell international papers, but may not have as wide a selection.

Among more common English-language newspapers sold in Copenhagen are the *International Herald Tribune, USA Today, Wall Street Journal,* the *European* and the *Guardian*. In addition, numerous British and US magazines on various topics can be found at Interkiosk in Central Station and at bookshops throughout Copenhagen.

PHARMACIES

There are numerous pharmacies around the city; look for the sign *apotek*. Most have the same opening hours as other shops, but there are some 24-hour pharmacies.

Steno Apotek (Map pp232–4; ☎ 33 14 82 66; Vesterbro-gade 6; ⏰ 24hr) is located opposite Central Station and very handy – although you will pay extra for a late-night purchase.

POST

Standard letters weighing up to 50g sent within Denmark cost 4.50kr. To Europe, such letters cost 6kr and to the rest of the world it's 7kr. International mail sent from Copenhagen is generally out of the country within 24 hours.

Main Post Office (Map pp232–4; 33 41 56 00; Fisketorvet; ⏰ 11am-6pm Mon-Fri, 10am-1pm Sat) If you're having poste restante mail sent to Copenhagen, it can be picked up here. Have letters addressed to: addressee, Poste Restante, Main Post Office, Fisketorvet, 1500 Copenhagen V.

Post Office (Map pp239–41; ☎ 33 89 90 00; Købmager-gade 33; ⏰ 10am-5.30pm Mon-Fri, 10am-2pm Sat) A handy post office just near Strøget and in the Latin Quarter.

Post office in Central Station (☎ 33 41 56 00; ⏰ 8am-9pm Mon-Fri, 9am-4pm Sat, 10am-4pm Sun)

RADIO

There is a a five-minute news brief in English at 10.30am, 5.05pm and 10pm weekdays on Radio Danmark International at 1062MHz. The BBC World Service is broadcast on short wave at 6195kHz and 9410kHz.

SAFETY

Denmark is by and large an incredibly safe country and travelling presents no unusual dangers, even in the capital city. Travellers should nevertheless be careful with their belongings, particularly in busy places such as Copenhagen's Central Station.

You'll need to quickly become accustomed to the busy cycle lanes that run beside roads between the vehicle lanes and the pedestrian pavement, as these cycle lanes (and fast-moving cyclists) are easy to veer into accidentally.

TAX & REFUNDS

Visitors from countries outside the EU who buy goods in Denmark can get a refund of the 25% VAT, less a handling fee, if they spend at least 300kr at any retail outlet that participates in the 'Tax Free Shopping Global Refund' plan. This includes most shops catering to tourists. The 300kr can be spent on a single item or several items, as long as they're purchased from the same shop.

Be sure to obtain the 'Global Refund cheque' from the store when you make the purchase; it should include the date, both the buyer's and seller's name and address, the number and type of goods, the selling price and the VAT amount.

Contact the Global Refund office at your point of departure from Denmark to get the refund, and allow extra time in case there's a queue at the booth. At Copenhagen airport, you'll find a booth in the international departure hall; if you depart by ship, inquire at the port as you board. If you have any questions about these VAT refunds call ☎ 32 52 55 66, visit the website at www.globalrefund.com or pick up a brochure on the program from participating shops.

TELEPHONE

Denmark has an efficient phone system and pay phones abound in busy public places such as train stations and shopping areas.

You have a choice of using either card-phones or coin phones. Coin phones take all Danish coins in denominations of 1kr to 20kr, but they won't return change from larger coins, so it's generally best to use the smaller denominations.

Domestic Calls

All telephone numbers in Denmark have eight numbers. There are no area codes and all eight numbers must be dialled, even when making calls within the same city.

Local calls are timed and you get twice as much calling time for your money on domestic calls made between 7.30pm and 8am. For directory inquiries, call ☎ 118. For overseas inquiries, call ☎ 113.

International Calls

To call Denmark from another country, dial the international access code for the country you're in, followed by ☎ 45 and the local eight-digit number.

To make direct international calls from Denmark dial ☎ 00 followed by the country code for the country you're calling, the area code, then the local number.

Mobile Phones

Denmark uses the worldwide GSM network, so you shouldn't have any difficulties getting your own phone to work while in Copenhagen. As befits a techno-savvy Scandinavian country, many locals carry a mobile phone – but they also know how to use them politely, and judiciously. Service providers include:

Orange (☎ 80 40 40 40)

Sonofon (☎ 80 29 29 29)

TDC-mobil (☎ 80 80 80 20)

Telia (☎ 80 10 10 80)

Phonecards

Phonecards that can be used in the city's public telephones come in denominations of 30kr, 50kr and 100kr and can be purchased at kiosks (especially at train stations) and post offices throughout Copenhagen. They beat messing around with coins, and work out slightly cheaper than coin phones because you pay for the exact amount of time you speak; an LCD screen keeps you posted on how much time is left on the card.

You can replace an expiring card with a new card without breaking the call. Cardphones are posted with information in English detailing their use as well as the location of the nearest place that sells phonecards.

Phone Books

Denmark's *Yellow Pages* are also on the Internet at www.degulesider.dk. You can use the website to search for business, government and residential details – although it is in Danish. Note that the letters æ, ø and å are placed at the end of the Danish alphabet, and so come after z in the hard copy of telephone directories.

TELEVISION

British and US network programs are common on Danish TV and are often presented in English with Danish subtitles. Many hotels have live CNN news, BBC World Service and other English-language cable and satellite TV programing. And yes, hard-core porn is broadcast late at night on free-to-air TV, but you'll have to find the channel yourself.

TIME

Time in Denmark is normally one hour ahead of GMT/UTC, the same as in neighbouring European countries. When it's noon in Copenhagen, it's 11am in London, 6am in New York and Toronto, 3am in San Francisco, 9pm in Sydney and 11pm in Auckland.

Clocks are moved forward one hour for daylight-saving time from the last Sunday in March to the last Sunday in October. Denmark uses the 24-hour clock system, and all timetables and business hours are posted accordingly. *Klokken*, which means o'clock, is abbreviated kl (kl 19.30 is 7.30pm).

Dates are written with the day followed by the month, thus 3/6 means 3 June and 6/3 means 6 March.

TIPPING

Restaurant bills and taxi fares include service charges in the quoted prices. Further tipping is unnecessary, although rounding up the bill is not uncommon when the service has been particularly good.

TOURIST INFORMATION

Copenhagen Right Now (Map pp232–4; ☎ 70 22 24 4; www.woco.dk; Vesterbrogade 4A; ⊙ 9am-4pm Mon-Fri & 9am-2pm Sat Sep-Apr, 9am-6pm Mon-Sat May & Jun, 9am-8pm Mon-Sat & 10am-6pm Sun Jul & Aug) Brand-new information office with a café, free Internet access, gift shop and multilingual staff. The best source of information in town – free maps, booking services and hotel reservation available for a fee.

Use It (Map pp239–41; ☎ 33 73 06 20; www.useit.dk; Rådhusstræde 13; ⊙ 11am-4pm Mon-Wed, 11am-6pm Thu & 11am-2pm Fri 16 Sep-14 Jun, 9am-7pm 15 Jun-15 Sep) A terrific alternative information centre catering to young budget travellers but open to all. Books accommodation, stores luggage, holds mail, provides information on everything, all free of charge.

VISAS

Citizens of the USA, Canada, Australia and New Zealand need a valid passport to enter Denmark, but they don't need a visa for tourist stays of less than three months. No entry visa is needed by citizens of EU and Scandinavian countries.

Citizens of many African, South American, Asian and former Soviet bloc countries do require a visa. The Danish Immigration Service publishes a list of countries whose citizens require a visa on www.udlst.dk/english/Visa/who_needs_visa.htm.

If you're in Copenhagen and have questions on visa extensions or visas in general, contact the Danish Immigration Service: **Udlændingestyrelsen** (Map pp236–7; ☎ 35 36 66 00; www.udlst.dk; Ryesgade 53; ☾ 8.30am-noon Mon-Fri, 3.30-5.30pm Thu).

WOMEN TRAVELLERS

Sexual equality is a high priority in Denmark. Women travellers should encounter little or no discrimination in Copenhagen, and sexual harassment is rare compared to other Western countries. Although women travellers are less likely to encounter problems in Copenhagen than in most other capital cities, the usual common-sense precautions apply when it comes to potentially dangerous situations such as hitchhiking and walking alone at night.

KVINFO, Center for Information om Kvinde og Kønsforskning (Danish Centre for Information on Women and Gender; ☎ 33 13 50 88; www.kvinfo.dk; Christians Brygge 3, Copenhagen), is a good place to get involved in local feminist issues. It houses Kvindehuset – a help centre and meeting place for women.

If you think you might be pregnant, pregnancy tests are available at pharmacies – you'll need a prescription to purchase birth control pills though. **Foreningen Sex og Samfund** (the Danish Family Planning Association; ☎ 33 13 19 13; www.sexogsamfund.dk; Rosenørns Allé 12; clinic ☾ 4-7pm Mon, Tue & Thu, phoneline ☾ 3-4pm Mon, Tue & Thu) can provide information on the morning-after pill and other pregnancy-related issues.

Dial ☎ 112 for rape crisis assistance or in other emergencies.

Recommended reading for first-time women travellers is the *Handbook for Women Travellers,* by Maggie and Gemma Moss, published by Piatkus Books but now out of print.

There are several good websites for women travellers, including those at www.passionfruit.com and www.journeywoman.com, and the women travellers page on the Lonely Planet website's Thorn Tree travel forum (http://thorntree.lonelyplanet.com).

WORK

Denmark has a significant level of unemployment and the job situation is not particularly promising for those who are not Danes, doubly so for those who don't speak Danish.

In terms of qualifying to work in Denmark, foreigners are generally divided into three categories: Scandinavian citizens, citizens of EU countries and other foreigners. Essentially, Scandinavian citizens have the easiest go of it, as they can generally reside and work in Denmark without restrictions. Visit the very informative website www.workindenmark.dk for more information about legalities.

Doing Business

Copenhagen is the commercial and financial centre of Denmark and home to the country's main transportation and shipping facilities. Scandinavia's busiest commercial airport, which serves as a hub for much of the region, is just a 10-minute train ride from central Copenhagen.

Many international companies have their regional headquarters based in Copenhagen and the city is a major host of international conferences.

Several 1st-class hotels provide business facilities ranging from secretarial services to conference rooms. In addition, top-end hotels equip guestrooms with business-friendly amenities such as voicemail and Internet access.

Work Visas

Citizens of EU countries are allowed to stay in Denmark for up to three months searching for a job and it's generally straightforward to get a residency permit if work is found. The main stipulation is that the job provides enough income to adequately cover living expenses.

Citizens of other countries are required to get a work permit before entering Denmark. This means securing a job offer, then applying for a work and residency permit from a Danish embassy or consulate while still in your home country. You can enter Denmark only after the permit has been granted and they are usually limited to people with specialised skills in high demand.

Language

Language

It's true – anyone can speak another language. Don't worry if you haven't studied languages before or that you studied a language at school for years and can't remember any of it. It doesn't even matter if you failed English grammar. After all, that's never affected your ability to speak English! And this is the key to picking up a language in another country. You just need to start speaking.

Learn a few key phrases before you go. Write them on pieces of paper and stick them on the fridge, by the bed or on the computer – anywhere that you'll see them often.

You'll find that locals appreciate travellers trying their language, no matter how muddled you may think you sound. So don't just stand there, say something! If you want to learn more Danish than we've included here, pick up a copy of Lonely Planet's comprehensive but user-friendly *Scandinavian Phrasebook*.

SOCIAL
Meeting People

Hello.
  Hej/Goddag.
Goodbye.
  Farvel.
Please.
  Vær så venlig …

The expression *vær så venlig* means literally 'be so kind' (to which a verb introducing your request is added). Another simple way of expressing 'please' is to add the word *tak* (thanks) to the end of your request.

Thank you (very much).
  (Mange) Tak.
Yes.
  Ja.
No.
  Nej.
Do you speak English?
  Taler du/De engelsk? (inf/pol)
Do you understand (me)?
  Forstår du/De mig? (inf/pol)
Yes, I understand.
  Ja, jeg forstår.
No, I don't understand.
  Nej, jeg forstår ikke.

Could you please …?
Kunne De …?

repeat that	gentage det
speak more slowly	tale langsommere
write it down	skrive det ned

Going Out

What's on …?
Hvad sker der …?

locally	lokalt
this weekend	i weekenden
today	i dag
tonight	i aften

Where are the …?
Hvor ligger der …?

clubs	natklubber
gay venues	steder at gå ud for homoseksuelle
places to eat	spisesteder
pubs	barer

Is there a local entertainment guide?
Er der en lokal underholdningsguide?

PRACTICAL
Question Words

Who?	Hvem?
What?	Hvad
When?	Hvornår?
Where?	Hvor?
How?	Hvordan?

Numbers & Amounts

1	en
2	to
3	tre
4	fire
5	fem

6	seks
7	syv
8	otte
9	ni
10	ti
11	elve
12	tolv
13	tretten
14	fjorten
15	femten
16	seksten
17	sytten
18	atten
19	nitten
20	tyve
21	enogtyve
22	toogtyve
30	tredive
40	fyrre
50	halvtreds
60	tres
70	halvfjerds
80	firs
90	halvfems
100	hundrede
1000	tusind
2000	totusind

Days

Monday	mandag
Tuesday	tirsdag
Wednesday	onsdag
Thursday	torsdag
Friday	fredag
Saturday	lørdag
Sunday	søndag

Banking

I'd like to …
Jeg vil gerne …

cash a cheque	indløse en check
change money	veksle penge
change some travellers cheques	veksle nogle rejsechecks

Where's the nearest …?
Hvor er ….?

automatic teller machine	den nærmeste hæveautomat
foreign exchange office	det nærmeste vekslekontor

Post

Where is the post office?
Hvor er postkontoret?

I want to send …
Jeg vil gerne sende …

a fax	en fax
a letter	et brev
a parcel	en pakke
a postcard	et postkort

I want to buy …
Jeg vil gerne købe …

an aerogram	et aerogram
an envelope	en konvolut
a stamp	et frimærke

Phones & Mobiles

I want to buy a phone card.
Jeg vil gerne købe et telefonkort.

I want to make …
Jeg vil gerne …

a call (to …)	ringe (til …)
reverse-charge/ collect call	have at modtageren betaler

Where can I find a/an …?
Hvor kan jeg finde …?
I'd like a/an …
Jeg vil gerne have …

adaptor plug	et adaptor stik
charger for my phone	en oplader til min telefon
mobile/cell phone for hire	en mobiltelefon til leje
prepaid mobile/ cell phone	en forudbetalt mobiltelefon
SIM card for your network	et SIM kort til jeres netværk

Internet

Where's the local Internet café?
Hvor er den lokale Internet cafe?

I'd like to …
Jeg vil gerne …

check my emails	checke mine emails
get online	online

Transport

What time does the … arrive/leave?
Hvornår ankommer/går …?

bus	bussen
ferry	færgen
plane	flyet
train	toget

What time's the first/next/last bus?
Hvornår går den første/næste/sidste bus?

Are you free? (taxi)
Er du fri?
How much is it to …?
Hvor meget koster det at køre til …?
Please take me to …
Vær så venlig at køre mig til …
 this address
 denne adresse

FOOD

breakfast	morgenmad
lunch	frokost
dinner	middag/aftensmad
snack	mellemmåltid
eat	spise
drink	drikke

Can you recommend a …
Kan du/De anbefale en …? (inf/pol)

bar/pub	bar
café	cafe
restaurant	restaurant

For more detailed information on food and dining out, see the 'Eating' chapter (pp103-22).

EMERGENCIES

It's an emergency!
Det er en nødsituation!

Could you please help me/us?
Kan du/De hjælpe mig/os? (inf/pol)
Call the police/a doctor/an ambulance!
Ring efter politiet/en læge/en ambulance!
Where's the police station?
Hvor er politistationen?

HEALTH

Where's the nearest …?
Hvor er …?

chemist (night)	det nærmeste (nat)apotek
dentist	den nærmeste tandlæge
doctor	den nærmeste læge
hospital	det nærmeste hospital

I need a doctor (who speaks English).
Jeg har brug for en læge (der taler engelsk).

Symptoms

I have …
Jeg har …

diarrhoea	diarré
fever	feber
headache	hovedpine
pain	smerter

Glossary

Note that the Danish letters æ, ø and å fall at the end of the alphabet.

allé – avenue
apotek – pharmacy, chemist

bageri – bakery
bibliotek – library
billetautomat – automated parking-ticket dispenser
bro – bridge
bugt – bay
by – town
børnemenu – childrens menu

dagens ret – special meal of the day
Danmark – Denmark
Dansk – Danish
domkirke – cathedral
DSB – Danske Statsbaner (Danish State Railroad), Denmark's national railway

folketing – ferry harbour
frikadeller – Danish meatballs
færgehavn – ferry harbour

gade – street

gammel – old

have – garden
havn – harbour
hygge – cosy

IC – intercity train
ICLyn – business-class train
IR – inter-regional train

jernbane – railway

kirke – church
kirkegård – churchyard, cemetery
klippekort – type of multiple-use transport ticket
kloster – monastery
konditori – bakery with café tables
kro – inn
København – Copenhagen
køreplan – timetable

lur – Bronze Age horn

museet – museum
møntvask – coin laundry

nord – north

plantage – plantation, tree farm, woods

privat vej – private road

røgeri – fish smokehouse
rådhus – town hall, city hall

samling – collection, usually of art
Sjælland – the island of Zealand
skov – forest, woods
slagter – butcher
slot – castle or palace
smørrebrød – open sandwich
S-tog – S-train; metropolitan train service
strand – beach, shoreline
stykke – piece
sund – sound

syd – south
sø – lake

torv, torvet – square, marketplace
tårn – tower

vandrerhjem – youth and family hostel
vej – street, road
vest – west

ø – island, usually attached as a suffix to the proper name
øl – beer
øst – east

å – river

Behind the Scenes

THE LONELY PLANET STORY

The story begins with a classic travel adventure: Tony and Maureen Wheeler's 1972 journey across Europe and Asia to Australia. There was no useful information about the overland trail then, so Tony and Maureen published the first Lonely Planet guidebook to meet a growing need.

From a kitchen table, Lonely Planet has grown to become the largest independent travel publisher in the world, with offices in Melbourne (Australia), Oakland (USA) and London (UK). Today Lonely Planet guidebooks cover the globe. There is an ever-growing list of books and information in a variety of media. Some things haven't changed. The main aim is still to make it possible for adventurous travellers to get out there — to explore and better understand the world.

At Lonely Planet we believe travellers can make a positive contribution to the countries they visit — if they respect their host communities and spend their money wisely. Every year 5% of company profit is donated to charities around the world.

THIS BOOK

This edition of *Copenhagen* was written and updated by Sally O'Brien, based on the first edition, which was written by Ned Friary and Glenda Bendure. The guide was commissioned in Lonely Planet's London office, and produced by:

Commissioning Editor Judith Bamber
Coordinating Editor Emma Koch
Coordinating Cartographer Emma McNicol
Coordinating Layout Designer Brendan Dempsey
Editor Janet Austin
Cover Designer Wendy Wright
Managing Cartographers Mark Griffiths, Alison Lyall
Project Manager Charles Rawlings-Way
Language Editor Quentin Frayne

Thanks to Darren O'Connell, Louise McGregor, Nicholas Stebbing, Glenn Beanland, Ryan Evans, Wayne Murphy

Cover photographs Det Gamle Hus (The Old House), Nyhavn, Damien Simonis/Lonely Planet Images (top); Nyhavn at dusk, Jon Davison/Lonely Planet Images (bottom); Tivoli poster, Martin Lladó/Lonely Planet Images (back)

Internal photographs Martin Lladó/Lonely Planet Images except for the following: p74 (#1, 3) Anders Blomqvist; p74 (#2) Jon Davison; p74 (#4) Lee Foster; p174 Christina Dameyer. All images are the copyright of the photographers unless otherwise indicated. Many of the images in this guide are available for licensing from Lonely Planet Images: www.lonelyplanetimages.com.

ACKNOWLEDGMENTS

Many thanks to DSB for the Copenhagen S-Train and metro map. © DSB 2004.

THANKS

SALLY O'BRIEN

Tusund tak to my colleague and good friend Carolyn Bain, who provided more laughs in Copenhagen, Stockholm and Malmö than seems decent for work. It simply would not have been half as much fun without you there in many of those bakeries, bars, restaurants, shops and squares, and yes, this city really is full of *kunst*. Thanks also to Judith Bamber, Mark Griffiths, Emma Koch, Emma McNicol and everyone at Lonely Planet who toiled on this book, plus Ned Friary and Glenda Bendure for their work on the first edition. Many thanks to Sita Linddahl for all her help with accommodation scouting, weather inquiries and email access, and Susanne Juul and Karen Tjur for my fabulous living quarters in Nørrebro and Christianshavn. Thanks to Karin Eklind for savvy predeparture tips and Bridget Lloyd Jones for looking after my apartment in Melbourne. And to my parents, for just being there, wherever I am, and for their love of Scandinavian design.

OUR READERS

Many thanks to the travellers who used the last edition and wrote to us with helpful hints, useful advice and interesting anecdotes. Your names follow:

Lisa Altieri-Leca, Ben Arthur, Michael Barr, Ann Best, Lotte Borg, Christian Borgesen, Thessa Brongers, Narelle Castles, Sutapa Choudhury, Trevor Dartford, Michael T Donnellan, Katie Elder, Gary Gregerson, Arthur Hay, Emma Horton, Kevin Kilburn, Melanie Kilburn, Gitte Kongstad, Olivier Laborde, Queenie Lau, Anne Marimuthu, Sheila Mennell, Judith Miller, Geraldine Moran, Evan Nass, Tracy Powis, Cor Schreuders, Danielle Schreuders, Alan Sirulnikoff, Peter K Sorensen, Tom Steffens, Karl Trell, Carolyn Urquhart-Barham, Ann Wallace, Celina Wang, Julia Werner.

SEND US YOUR FEEDBACK

We love to hear from travellers – your comments keep us on our toes and help make our books better. Our well-travelled team reads every word on what you loved or loathed about this book. Although we cannot reply individually to postal submissions, we always guarantee that your feedback goes straight to the appropriate authors, in time for the next edition. Each person who sends us information is thanked in the next edition – and the most useful submissions are rewarded with a free book.

To send us your updates – and find out about Lonely Planet events, newsletters and travel news – visit our award-winning website: www.lonelyplanet.com/feedback

Note: We may edit, reproduce and incorporate your comments in Lonely Planet products such as guidebooks, websites and digital products, so let us know if you don't want your comments reproduced or your name acknowledged. For a copy of our privacy policy visit www.lonelyplanet.com/privacy.

Index

See also separate indexes for Eating (p227), Drinking (p227), Shopping (p228) and Sleeping (p228).

000 map pages
000 photographs

Index

227

MAP LEGEND

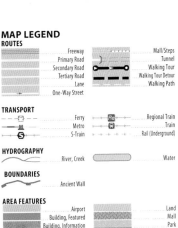

ROUTES
- Freeway
- Primary Road
- Secondary Road
- Tertiary Road
- Lane
- One-Way Street
- Mall/Steps
- Tunnel
- Walking Tour
- Walking Tour Detour
- Walking Path

TRANSPORT
- Ferry
- Metro
- S-Train
- Regional Train
- Train
- Rail (Underground)

HYDROGRAPHY
- River, Creek
- Water

BOUNDARIES
- Ancient Wall

AREA FEATURES
- Airport
- Building, Featured
- Building, Information
- Building, Other
- Building, Transport
- Cemetery, Christian
- Land
- Mall
- Park
- Sports
- Urban

POPULATION
- ☉ **CAPITAL (NATIONAL)**
- ● Small City
- ⊙ Medium City

SYMBOLS

Sights/Activities
- Beach
- Castle, Fortress
- Christian
- Jewish
- Monument
- Museum, Gallery
- Ruin
- Swimming Pool
- Zoo, Bird Sanctuary

Eating
- Eating

Drinking
- Drinking
- Café

Entertainment
- Entertainment
- Jazz

Shopping
- Shopping

Sleeping
- Sleeping
- Camping

Transport
- Airport, Airfield
- Bus Station
- Cycling, Bicycle Path
- Parking Area
- Petrol Station

Other
- Other Site

Information
- Bank, ATM
- Embassy/Consulate
- Hospital, Medical
- Information
- Internet Facilities
- Police Station
- Post Office, GPO
- Toilets

Map Section

GREATER COPENHAGEN

0   5 km
0   3 miles

SIGHTS & ACTIVITIES	(pp87–94)
Amager Strandpark	1 D
Bakken	2 C
Bellahøj Friluftsbad	3 B
Bellevue Beach	4 C
Dragør Museum	5 D
Eremitagen	6 C
Frilandsmuseet	7 B
Holte Havn	8 A
Ordrupgaard	9 C

EATING	(pp120–2)
Peter Lieps Hus	10 C

ENTERTAINMENT	(pp124–38)
Bella Center	11 C
Charlottenlund Travbane	(see 13)
Frederiksdal Kano og	
Bådudlejning	12 A
Klampenborg Galopbane	13 C
Københavns Golf Klub	14 C

SLEEPING	(pp165–8)
Belægningen Avedørelejren	15 A
Danhostel Copenhagen	
Amager	16 C
Danhostel Copenhagen	
Bellahøj	17 B4
Danhostel Lyngby-Tårbæk	
Vandrerhjem	18 C
Hilton Copenhagen Airport	19 D
Transfer Hotel	20 D

TRANSPORT	(pp192–6)
Airport Terminal	21 D

INFORMATION	
Amager Hospital	22 C4

TIVOLI

0 ━━━━━━━━━━ 200 m
0 ━━━━━━━━━━ 0.1 miles

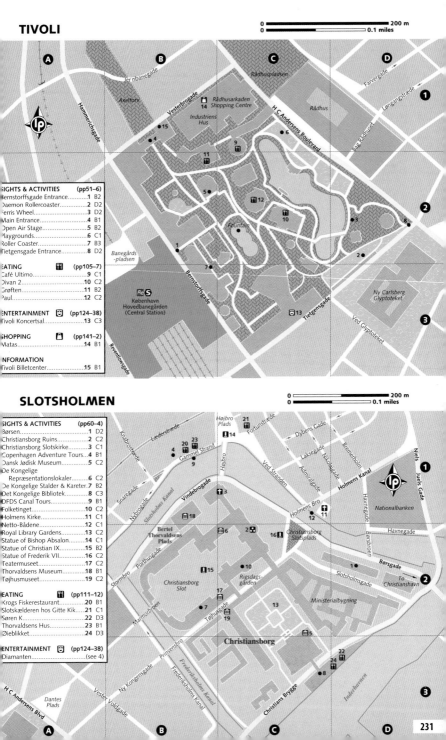

SIGHTS & ACTIVITIES	(pp51–6)
Bernstorffsgade Entrance	1 B2
Daemon Rollercoaster	2 D2
Ferris Wheel	3 D2
Main Entrance	4 B1
Open Air Stage	5 B2
Playgrounds	6 C1
Roller Coaster	7 B3
Tietgensgade Entrance	8 D2

EATING	(pp105–7)
Café Ultimo	9 C1
Divan 2	10 C2
Grøften	11 B2
Paul	12 C2

ENTERTAINMENT	(pp124–38)
Tivoli Koncertsal	13 C3

SHOPPING	(pp141–2)
Matas	14 B1

INFORMATION	
Tivoli Billetcenter	15 B1

SLOTSHOLMEN

0 ━━━━━━━━━━ 200 m
0 ━━━━━━━━━━ 0.1 miles

SIGHTS & ACTIVITIES	(pp60–4)
Børsen	1 D2
Christiansborg Ruins	2 C2
Christiansborg Slotskirke	3 C1
Copenhagen Adventure Tours	4 B1
Dansk Jødisk Museum	5 C2
De Kongelige Repræsentationslokaler	6 C2
De Kongelige Stalder & Kareter	7 B2
Det Kongelige Bibliotek	8 C3
DFDS Canal Tours	9 B1
Folketinget	10 C2
Holmens Kirke	11 C2
Netto-Bådene	12 C2
Royal Library Gardens	13 C2
Statue of Bishop Absalon	14 C1
Statue of Christian IX	15 B2
Statue of Frederik VII	16 C2
Teatermuseet	17 C2
Thorvaldsens Museum	18 B1
Tøjhusmuseet	19 C2

EATING	(pp111–12)
Krogs Fiskerestaurant	20 B1
Slotskælderen hos Gitte Kik	21 C1
Søren K	22 D3
Thorvaldsens Hus	23 B1
Øieblikket	24 D3

ENTERTAINMENT	(pp124–38)
Diamanten	(see 4)

231

CENTRAL COPENHAGEN

Churchill-
parken

Gernersgade

Skt Pauls Gade

Esplanaden

To Copenhagen
Indoor Golf
Center

Rigensgade

Kronprinsessegade

Klerkegade

Borgergade

Adelgade

Sølvgade

195

56

34

24

13

141

194

20

Amaliegade

Toldbodgade

9

Larsens Plads

Store Kongensgade

Frederiksgade

23
1

Frederiks-
Gade

12

Bredgade

52
62

137

8

72

38

Dronningens

Tværgade

Amaliegaden

Kronbiørnsgraven

Olfert
Fischers
Vej

29

Holmen

Danneskiold-Samsøes Allé

Kanonbådsvej

Refshalevej

Gothersgade

159

101

28
104

100

193

125

171

201

179

Sankt Anne Plads

106

16

58
78

183

157

188

45

Store Strandstræde

Toldbodgade

Kvæsthusgade

Grønnegade

Kongens
Nytorv

177

47

117

Nyhavn

Østergade

Kongens
Nytorv

170

Bernt Trolles Gade

Larslejsstræde

Niels Juels Gade

Holmens
Kanal

151

Peder Skrams Gade

149

Tordenskjoldsgade

127

138

66

Havnegade

Bergsgade

Nyhavnsbro

Christiansborg

Christians Brygge

14

61

Halvtolv

Christianshavn

Knippelsbro

Strandgade

Torvegade

Wildersgade

Overgaden neden Vandet

Overgaden oven Vandet

Dronningensgade

77
44

48
46

96

4

6

Prinsessegade

Refshalevej

97

30

108

11
68

57

Christiania

Bådsmandsstræde

59

Klavermarksvej

Stadsgraven

37

93

198

55

102

Christianshavn

Prinsessegade

Christianshavns Voldgade

39

67

Christmas
Møllers
Plads

Vermlandsgade

Langebrogade

Stadsgraven

Amager Blvd

161

Amager Blvd

Uplandsgade

Dahlandsgade

Prags Blvd

Amagerfælledvej

Amagerbrogade

Holmbladsgade

Arildsvej

Islands
Brygge

Njalsgade

203

Ørestads Blvd

Sundholmsvej

Hallandsgade

Hollænderdybet

Frelsers
Kirkegård

Amagerbro

Amager
Centret

Alsbacke

Amagerbrogade

Frankrigshusene

Bryggergade

Strøget & the Latin
Quarter pp240–1

CENTRAL COPENHAGEN (pp232–3)

CHARLOTTENLUND & HELLERUP

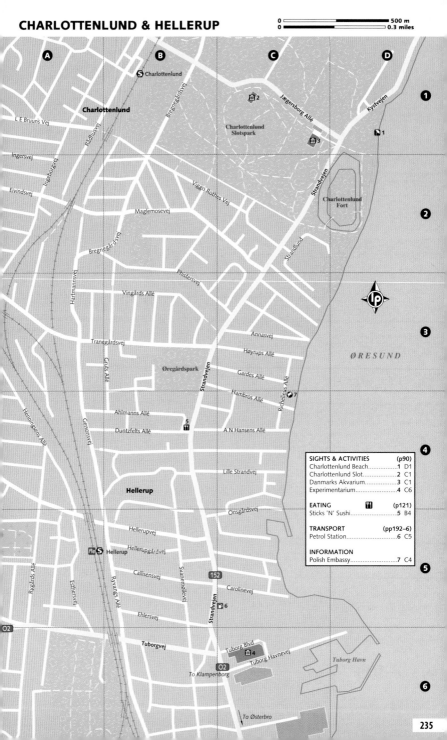

0 — 500 m
0 — 0.3 miles

A · B · C · D

S Charlottenlund

Charlottenlund

L E Bruuns Vej

Radhusvej

Ingeborgsvej

Ingersvej

Eivindsvej

Bregnegårdsvej

Jægersborg Allé

Kystvejen

🏛 2

**Charlottenlund
Slotspark**

🏛 3

Viggo Rothes Vej

Maglemosevej

Bregnegårdsvej

Hartmannsvej

Phistersvej

Vingårds Allé

Strandlund

Strandvejen

**Charlottenlund
Fort**

Tranegårdsvej

Gruts Allé

Annasvej

Høyrups Allé

Øregårdspark

Strandvejen

Gardes Allé

Hambros Allé

Richelieus Allé

🏢 7

Ahlmanns Allé

Duntzfelts Allé

5 🍴

A N Hansens Allé

Henningsens Allé

Gersonsvej

Lille Strandvej

Hellerup

Onsgårdsvej

Hellerupvej

Hellerupgårdvej

Fe S Hellerup

Callisensvej

Strandmøllevej

Carolinevej

152

Ryvangs Allé

Rygårds Allé

Ethelsvej

Ehlersvej

Strandvejen

🅿 6

O2

Tuborgvej

Tuborg Blvd

🏛 4

Tuborg Havnevej

O2

To Klampenborg

Tuborg Havn

To Østerbro

🏴 1

ØRESUND

SIGHTS & ACTIVITIES (p90)
Charlottenlund Beach	1 D1
Charlottenlund Slot	2 C1
Danmarks Akvarium	3 C1
Experimentarium	4 C6

EATING 🍴 (p121)
Sticks 'N' Sushi	5 B4

TRANSPORT (pp192–6)
Petrol Station	6 C5

INFORMATION
Polish Embassy	7 C4

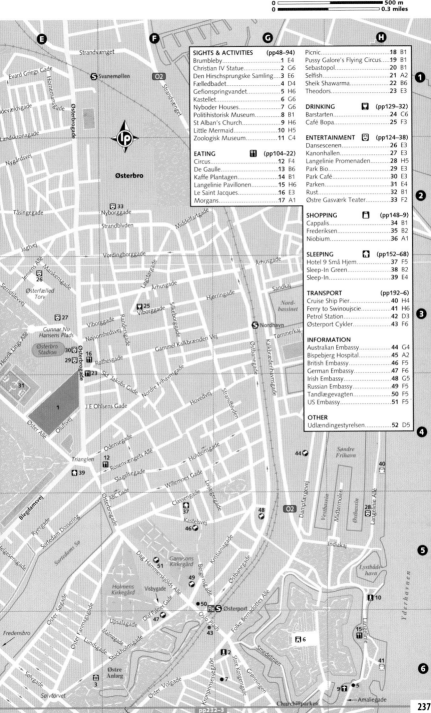

SIGHTS & ACTIVITIES (pp48–94)
Brumbleby..............................**1** E4
Christian IV Statue..................**2** G6
Den Hirschsprungske Samling...**3** E6
Fælledbadet............................**4** D4
Gefionspringvandet.................**5** H6
Kastellet.................................**6** G6
Nyboder Houses.......................**7** G6
Politihistorisk Museum.............**8** B1
St Alban's Church....................**9** H6
Little Mermaid........................**10** H5
Zoologisk Museum..................**11** C4

EATING 🍴 (pp104–22)
Circus....................................**12** F4
De Gaulle...............................**13** B6
Kaffe Plantagen......................**14** B1
Langelinie Pavillonen..............**15** H6
Le Saint Jacques.....................**16** E3
Morgans.................................**17** A1

Picnic....................................**18** B1
Pussy Galore's Flying Circus....**19** B1
Sebastopol..............................**20** B1
Selfish....................................**21** A2
Sheik Shawarma......................**22** B6
Theodors................................**23** E3

DRINKING 🍷 (pp129–32)
Barstarten..............................**24** C6
Café Bopa..............................**25** F3

ENTERTAINMENT 🎭 (pp124–38)
Dansescenen...........................**26** E3
Kanonhallen...........................**27** E3
Langelinie Promenaden...........**28** H5
Park Bio..................................**29** E3
Park Café................................**30** E3
Parken....................................**31** E4
Rust.......................................**32** B1
Østre Gasværk Teater.............**33** F2

SHOPPING 🛍 (pp148–9)
Cappalis.................................**34** B1
Frederiksen............................**35** B2
Niobium..................................**36** A1

SLEEPING 🛏 (pp152–68)
Hotel 9 Små Hjem...................**37** F5
Sleep-In Green........................**38** B2
Sleep-In..................................**39** E4

TRANSPORT (pp192–6)
Cruise Ship Pier......................**40** H4
Ferry to Swinoujscie................**41** H6
Petrol Station..........................**42** D3
Østerport Cykler.....................**43** F6

INFORMATION
Australian Embassy..................**44** G4
Bispebjerg Hospital.................**45** A2
British Embassy.......................**46** F5
German Embassy......................**47** F6
Irish Embassy..........................**48** G5
Russian Embassy.....................**49** F5
Tandlægevagten......................**50** F5
US Embassy.............................**51** F5

OTHER
Udlændingestyrelsen...............**52** D5

FREEDERIKSBERG

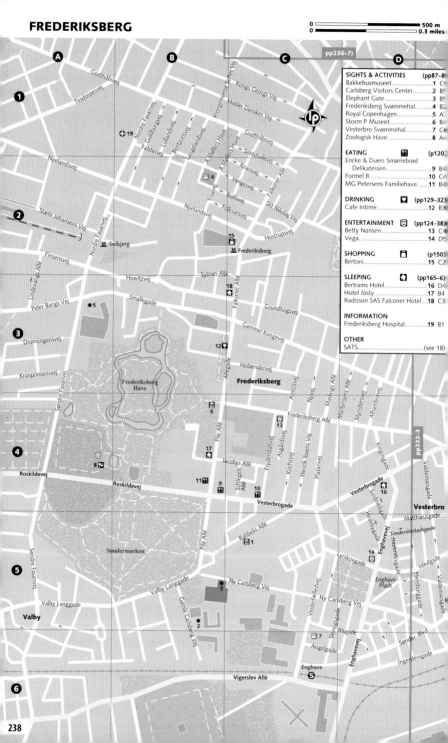

0 ————— 500 m
0 ————— 0.3 miles

SIGHTS & ACTIVITIES	(pp87–8
Bakkehusmuseet.....................1	C
Carlsberg Visitors Center.........2	B
Elephant Gate........................3	B
Frederiksberg Svømmehal........4	B2
Royal Copenhagen..................5	A
Storm P Museet.....................6	B4
Vesterbro Svømmehal.............7	C
Zoologisk Have......................8	A

EATING	(p120)
Encke & Duers Smørrebrød	
Delikatessen...........................9	B4
Formel B..............................10	C4
MG Petersens Familiehave......11	B4

DRINKING	(pp129–32)
Cafe Intime.........................12	B3

ENTERTAINMENT	(pp124–38)
Betty Nansen.......................13	C4
Vega..................................14	D5

SHOPPING	(p150)
Bertoni...............................15	C2

SLEEPING	(pp165–6)
Bertrams Hotel....................16	D4
Hotel Josty.........................17	B4
Radisson SAS Falconer Hotel...18	C3

INFORMATION	
Frederiksberg Hospital...........19	B1

OTHER	
SATS...................................(see 18)

A
B
C
D

1
2
3
4
5
6

Rømersgade
Israels Plads
Linnésgade
Vendersgade
Nørre Voldgade
M Re S Nørreport
Frederiksborggade
Rosenborggade
Åbenrå
45
Hausergade
Hauser Plads
Kultorvet
99
Pustervig
Rosengården 56
Peder Hvitfeldts Stræde
Landemærket 11
Købmagergade
60
71
Nørregade
Fiolstræde
21
16 95
Krystalgade
Kannikestræde
63
Skindergade
85
28
Københavns Universitet
17
Gråbrødretorv
12
40
77 Vor Frue Plads
32
39
19
42
Klosterstræde
Valkendorfs
96
Tullinsgade
Sankt Peders Stræde
Studiestræde
Vimmelskaftet
67
81
Sankt Pederstræde
Larsbjørnstræde
36
Nygade
Badstuestræde
Hyskenstræde
22
59
Landemærket
52
Gammeltorv
75
26
78
37
1
Købmagergade
Studiestræde
58
57
31
73
Nørre Voldgade
Vestergade
69
24
74
Vester Voldgade
82
Nytorv
55
84
3
44
Rådhusstræde
Kattesundet
23
Kompagnistræde
49
79
98
Magstræde
Frederiksberggade
91
Hestemøllestræde
Nyhavnsgade
Mikkel Bryggers Gade
65
89
72
Læderstræde
90
88
18
10
87
15
Rådhuspladsen
Tivoli p231
20
38
Vester Voldgade
Farvergade
86
14
6
Vesterbrogade
Rådhus
H C Andersens Blvd
Langangstræde
Frederiksholms Kanal
Stormbro
Stormgade

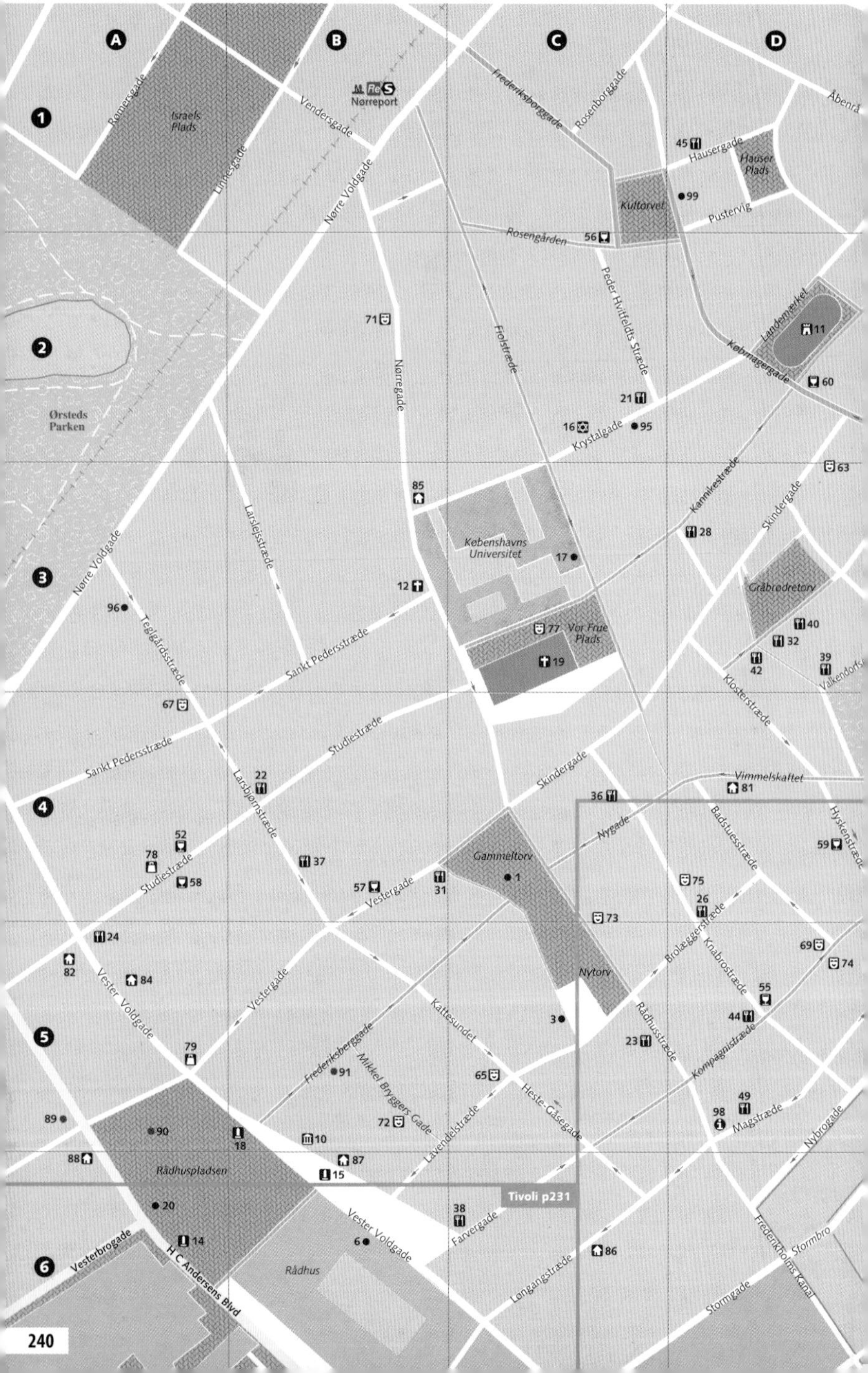

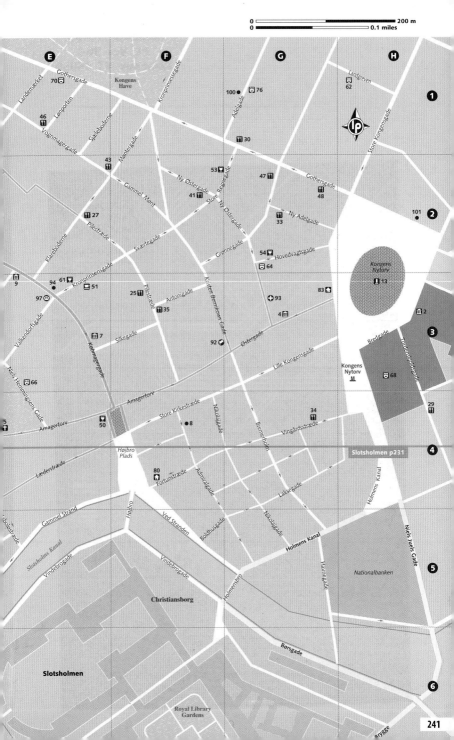

E   F   G   H

1

Landemærket
70 Gothersgade
Kongens Have
Kronprinsessegade
Landgreven
62

Lønporten
46
Vognmagergade
Sjæleboderne
Møntergade
100
76
Adelgade

2

43
Gammel Mønt
30
Ny Østergade
53
Store Regnegade
47
Gothersgade
48

27
Pilestræde
41
Ny Østergade
33
Ny Adelgade
101

9
Klareboderne
Sværtegade
Grønnegade
54
Hovedvagtsgade
Kongens Nytorv
13

94 61
Kronprinsensgade
51
Pilestræde
64

97
25
Antonigade
93
83
2

7
Silkegade
35
Kirsten Bernikows Gade
4

Kejsergade
92
Østergade

66
Niels Hemmingsens Gade
Lille Kongensgade
Kongens Nytorv
M
Bredgade
68

Amagertorv
Store Kirkestræde
Nikolajgade
Bremerholm
Vingårdsstræde
34
Tordenskjoldsgade
29

5
Amagertorv
50
8
Slotsholmen p231

Højbro Plads
80
Fortunstræde
Admiralgade
Laksegade

Læderstræde
Gammel Strand
Højbro
Ved Stranden
Boldhusgade
Nikolajgade
Holmens Kanal
Niels Juels Gade

Slotsholms Kanal
Vindebrogade
Vindebrogade
Holmensbro
Havnegade
Nationalbanken

5

Christiansborg

Slotsholmen
Børsgade

6

Royal Library Gardens
Brygge
241

S-train & Metro Map

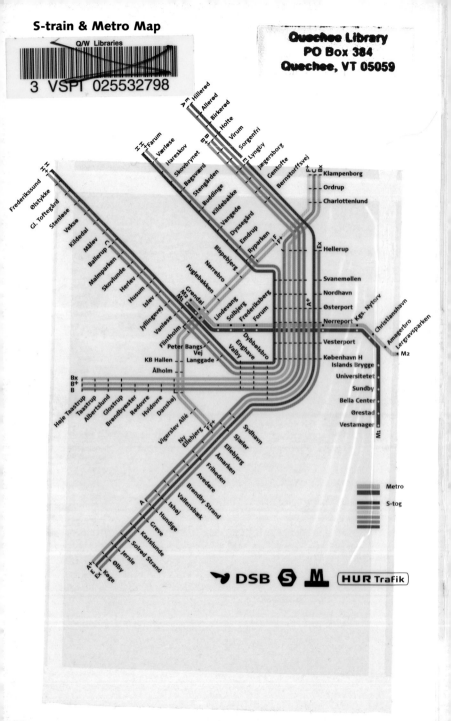

Metro
S-tog

DSB · S · M · HUR Trafik